BEST CANADIAN SCREENPLAYS

BEST CANADIAN SCREENPLAYS

edited by
Douglas Bowie and Tom Shoebridge

Quarry Press

Copyright © for the Authors, 1992.
All rights reserved.

The publisher gratefully acknowledges the assistance of The Canada Council and the Ontario Arts Council.

The editors would like to thank Clarke Mackey, Department of Film Studies, Queen's University; D. John Turner, National Film Archives; and the staff of Cinématheque Ontario.

Photographic stills from *Goin' Down the Road* and *The Grey Fox* were kindly provided by The Film Reference Library, Cinématheque Ontario; from *Mon oncle Antoine* by the National Film Board of Canada; from *My American Cousin* by Peter O'Brian; and from *Jésus de Montréal* by Max Films.

Canadian Cataloguing in Publication Data

ISBN 1-55082-045-1

1. Canadian drama (English) --20th century --
2. Canadian drama (French) --20th century --
Translations into English. 3. Motion picture plays
I. Bowie, Douglas   II. Shoebridge, Tom.
1942-

PN1997.A1B48 1992   C812'.5408   C92-090446-7

Typeset by Susan Hannah.
Printed and bound in Canada by Best Gagné, Toronto, Ontario.

Published by **Quarry Press**, Inc., P.O. Box 1061, Kingston, Ontario K7L 4Y5.

CONTENTS

- 6   **Preface** by Tom Shoebridge
- 8   **Introduction** by Douglas Bowie

- 15   **GOIN' DOWN THE ROAD** by William Fruet
- 83   **MON ONCLE ANTOINE** by Clément Perron
- 147   **THE GREY FOX** by John Hunter
- 251   **MY AMERICAN COUSIN** by Sandy Wilson
- 339   **JESUS DE MONTREAL** by Denys Arcand

- 430   Notes on Contributors

PREFACE

This book is the first anthology of Canadian screenplays ever published. After hosting over one hundred screenwriting workshops at the Summer Institute of Film and Television at Algonquin College in Ottawa and after teaching screenwriting myself for fifteen years, I was frustrated by the lack of published Canadian screenplays for my own reading pleasure and for use in the classroom. To satisfy this need and to commemorate the tenth anniversary of the Summer Institute in 1991, screenwriter Douglas Bowie and I decided to initiate this publication.

A further powerful motivation was a desire to place the achievement of Canadian screenwriters beside the achievements of their American and British counterparts. The publication of American film and television screenplays has proliferated in recent years. As well, growing numbers of British screenplays have been finding their way into our bookstores. Although studying screenplays from other countries is essential for Canadian screenwriters to continue improving their craft, we do need to celebrate and perpetuate the achievement of our own screenwriters with their distinctive storytelling styles and myths, with their unique cultural and philosophical resonances.

Faith (or the lack thereof) in homegrown stories and storytellers has an analogous precedent in Canadian literature. In the 1950s when I was attending university, there was almost no Canadian content on my curriculum. According to the prevalent thinking of the day, the real stuff of literature was the prose, poetry, and plays of the United States and the British Isles. Today, of course, we enjoy an impressive array of Canadian Literature courses, featuring internationally respected authors like Margaret Laurence, Margaret Atwood, Morley Callaghan, Alice Munro, Robertson Davies, Mordecai Richler, and W.P. Kinsella, among others. The work of these writers forms a distinctive Canadian literary culture.

At present, there is also a growing group of film and television screenwriters whose dramas form the basis of a distinctive, popular, and entertaining screen culture. This nucleus of talented screen storytellers has touched enthusiastic audiences in Canada and abroad. (Even my own teenage children watch

Canadian films and television programs and admit to having enjoyed them!) Yet due to the fragile nature of all national dramas in a world increasingly filled with all-pervasive satellite delivery systems, Canadians must work hard at building on what has been achieved to date.

The five screenplays included in this anthology are all original stories and display the basic elements of effective screen storytelling — interesting characters whose dilemmas and development the audience cares about, and whose actions, encounters, and conflicts draw readers deep into their fascinating worlds. Well aware of the changes that inevitably take place during the collaborative process of filmmaking, we determined that these screenplays would be the screenwriters' version of their stories. What you are about to read is the draft that each screenwriter believes is closest to his or her original conception — before "Lights! Camera! Action!"

When exploring any aspect of the Canadian screen industry, one should be mindful that it is still in its infancy compared to most of its international counterparts. The first Canadian feature-length film, *Evangeline*, was made in 1913 (with American directors and two imported American "stars". Some things never change!) The real birth of our private feature film industry, however, did not occur until the late 1960s with the creation of the Canadian Film Development Corporation, and it was not until 1981 that we had 1,000 films in the can. Compare this to the Hollywood studio factories which used to churn out 1,000 films every two or three years, and which still annually produce over 20 times as many screen dramas as Canada.

This volume of production is important in the evolution of the quality of film and television productions. It is even more so in the development of excellent screenwriting. Practice makes perfect, and in the difficult area of creating stories on paper that will work magic on the screen, screenwriters need to see their scripts produced. As one experienced scriptwriter recently noted, "I learn nothing about improving my craft from writing a screenplay that does not get produced."

The five scripts in this volume did get produced, and by comparing them to the final films, students of cinema will learn a lot about the creative process of filmmaking. (Heaven forbid, there may even be a few theses in documenting the reasons for the differences between script and film.) Most general readers will be seeing Canadian screenplays for the first time and will be able to compare them to their favorite Canadian prose story or stage play. Novice and veteran screenwriters will savor fine examples of what some successful novelists and playwrights admit is the most difficult kind of writing of all. After reading these screenplays, I hope that most readers will want to experience the films which sprang from them — whether for the first time or through new eyes.

Tom Shoebridge

INTRODUCTION

Screenwriters. Ignored. Belittled. Maligned. Forgotten (but not gone). Starved for recognition, respect, approbation. Yearning for hyphenation — writer-producer, writer-director.

Prophets without honor in their own countries, their own industry. Unmentioned in reviews of films they've labored over for months. Or years. "Schmucks with Underwoods," Jack Warner called them. (Nowadays, presumably he'd say "schmucks with Mac PowerBooks".) The butt of jokes. (Did you hear the one about the starlet who was so stupid that when she wanted to get ahead in Hollywood she slept with the screenwriter?)

Awash in self-deprecation, discontent, powerlessness, frustration, anhedonia. All simmering beneath a sardonic layer of cynicism, and punctuated by the Screenwriter's Lament — "It's not the film I wrote."

Conventional wisdom seems to have it that screenwriting is somehow not "real writing", but is, at best, a kind of secondary craft — scarcely more elevated than painting on velvet or designing lawn ornaments; that screenplays are the product, not of inspiration, but of formulas and file cards and expensive computers.

And it gets worse. The perception of the screenwriter as sellout, hack, whore has found a permanent niche in American literary mythology. The tale of The Talented Writer who is lured to Hollywood, forced to do work which is beneath him, and is driven to drink, self-loathing and ruination, has been told so often (reiterated yet again in *Barton Fink*) that it's achieved archetypal status. Who cares if it's actually true?

Indeed, there's a certain allure, a dramatic poignancy to the notion of the ruined artist, and screenwriters, shame on them, have done their part to contribute to it, taking perverse pleasure in fostering this tarnished, tarty image. To wit:—

"Wanting to be a screenwriter is like wanting to be a co-pilot." "Screenwriting is shitwork." "Millions are to be grabbed, and your only competition is idiots." "The screenwriter is the highest paid secretary in the world." "Filmmaking is a collaborative business. Bend over." (Facts of movie life as explained to a screenwriter.)

INTRODUCTION

As many will recognize, these quotes originate, not with critics or Jack Warner, but with screenwriters all, and rich and successful ones at that. (Dunne, Goldman, Mankiewicz, the other Mankiewicz, Mamet)

Is it any wonder that others have picked up on it? In fact, a screenwriter doesn't have to look far to find slights, sometimes in unlikely places — such as a Morningside segment on screenwriting a couple of years ago. Normally Peter Gzowski is a conscientious supporter of Canadian writers and writing — but this piece treated screenwriting, not as a difficult (let alone honorable) craft, but rather as a *racket* — something to get in on, akin to a foolproof system at the track or blackjack table. Peter allowed that he'd be more than happy to pick up a package of file cards and get in on the game himself, if any producers listening would give him a call.

He also dwelt on the idea that screenplays must be a snap to do because they're *short*! — evidently having forgotten what every writer knows — that it's easier to write long than short. (And would he talk to Alice Munro like this? "Short stories are really *short*, aren't they, Alice? Here's one that's only 12 pages. It must have been a breeze.") Granted, the tone of the Morningside segment was jocular, not mean-spirited — but the message, heard by thousands, was clear: screenwriting is something of a lark, a source of easy money, a game that anyone can play, a subject for banter rather than serious discussion.

Recently, of course, screenwriting has acquired a certain cachet. A few scripts, written "on spec", have made news by selling for huge sums. Screenwriter wannabes flock to hear self-proclaimed gurus who travel the land dispensing magic formulas, and secret buzzwords — "plot point", "deep characterization", "arena", "three act structure", "paradigm". While raising the profile of screenwriting, one wonders if all this doesn't also reinforce the idea that screenwriting isn't a real art, or even real work — that anyone with a weekend and $375 U.S. to spare can learn a few simple tricks and then dash off a screenplay (that sells.) This weekend — screenwriting. Next weekend — beating drums and howling in the woods.

The truth is that it's not a game or a bag of tricks, but *writing* — and a difficult, demanding, and notoriously thankless form of it at that. (If it's so easy, why did it defeat so many of those Great Writers who trekked to Hollywood to try it?)

A little test cooked up by screenwriter Ernest Lehman (*North by Northwest*) is illustrative. A writer has an idea. He takes it to a producer who responds with interest. The writer locks himself up in his study for six months (or more) with a ream of paper and a typewriter and writes a first draft. The producer loves it. A director comes on board. Rewrites are done. Stars are hired. And, to cut to the chase, the script is produced and is a smash hit. Question. What are we talking about here? Answer: A movie, obviously. Wrong. A play. The point is, of course, that the creative process involved in writing a screenplay or a play is virtually identical. Yet playwrights are respected, lionized, Pulitzered, even Nobeled. While screenwriters are ignored, belittled, etc., etc. See above. A comparable selection of disparaging quotes by and about playwrights would be unimaginable.

If one accepts that film is an art form — indeed *the* art form of our age — then surely no less than a playwright, a composer, an architect — a fine screenwriter provides a blueprint for a work of art. No less than our playwrights, our poets, our novelists, our screenwriters tell our stories.

Obviously, the purpose of this book is to highlight and celebrate the Canadian screenwriter — and high time too. But surely it is possible to do so without denigrating the role of the director. (And two of our five scripts were directed by their authors.) William Goldman has said that there's a natural adversarial relationship between directors and writers. Directors, unable to write themselves and yet determined to be *auteurs*, can't resist downgrading the role of the writer. But does it need to be so? George Cukor said "give me a good script and I become a hundred times better as a director." And isn't it as simple as that? It's a truism, and certainly no slur on the director, to say that a good screenplay is an essential prerequisite to a good film. Period. And yet it seems to be forgotten as often as not.

Goin' Down the Road provides an interesting case in point. Long and justly celebrated for its nitty gritty, improvisational style, we now see that it was, in fact, scripted by William Fruet in painstaking detail. At the same time a comparison of script and finished film leaves no doubt as to Don Shebib's crucial role in honing, shaping, giving life to the material. And the final result is an inspired collaboration of writer, director, and actors resulting in an enduring work of film art.

One other example. The famous scene in *Mon oncle Antoine* in which the mine owner rides through town dispensing trinkets to the children is described virtually shot by shot in Clémont Perron's script. But it still takes Claude Jutra's sensitive realization of it to make it come fully alive, to linger in the memory. It's just a little scene really, but one which is at once political, pointed, humorous, sad, and ultimately almost farcical — all in two minutes. That's screenwriting. That's filmmaking. By true collaborators, not adversaries.

As if screenwriters don't have problems enough — (and we haven't even mentioned aching backs, unproduced scripts, — and scripts which are produced, but rendered unrecognizable, distorted, ruined through carelessness, arrogance, incompetence) — Canadian screenwriters, as compared to Americans at least, face an additional hurdle.

Any American script which goes into production will be gussied up, buffed up (and, yes, sometimes tarted up) — given a patina of cinematic magic that only $27 million U.S. (or $37 million, or $47 million) plus promotion can

INTRODUCTION

buy. The script's deficiencies will be hidden behind a glossy veneer of cinematographic power, star power, Hollywood "production values". (Of course — a script's *virtues* may occasionally be distorted by overblown production values as well. And some might argue that *no* amount of money or cinematic magic can hide the cracks in a script which is truly flawed. And that is one of the problems with Hollywood films today; production values have become God, at the expense of great stories, great characters. But that's another discussion.)

A Canadian screenplay will receive no such cinematic cosseting, but will go comparatively naked into the world. With a lot less production value between the script and the audience — the cracks, if cracks there be, are sure to show.

This is a problem faced by the Canadian film industry as a whole, of course — (the "But it looks *Canadian!*" problem) — but it's faced first and arguably most crucially, by the screenwriter. The playing field is only level at the first step, when the writer confronts the blank page, the blank screen. Like a strategist before a battle, he knows when zero hour (production) comes, he's going to be outmanned, outfinanced, outstarred, outgunned. The paying audience won't know or care — nor should it — about production limitations, or lack of funds. From the audience's standpoint, all films are equal when the lights go down. And *Terminator III* will be playing right next door. So the pressure is directly on our writers to come up with something more ingenious, more original, more heartfelt, more "bullet proof" — and so cleverly conceived and executed that it won't suffer by having to be shot on a (relative) shoestring. Each of these five scripts meets that test in its own way.

Another myth, widely held even among people who should know better, is that screenwriters are basically dialogue writers — that everything else, all the cinematic elements of a film, are provided by the director.

As each of these scripts shows, however, good screenwriters don't merely write dialogue — they write movies. Read any of these scripts and find dialogue, of course, but also character, emotion, action, conflict, and above all a structured story. And one need only look at the first three or four pages of *The Grey Fox*, for example, to see that the writer also provides subtler textures and nuances — mood, feel, style, sounds.

These scripts also reveal that ideas, themes, even images, normally, perhaps lazily, attributed to directors are — lo and behold — right there on the written page. Screenwriter Robert Riskin once made this point better than anyone. A trifle fed up, so the story goes, with Frank Capra getting *all* the credit for films like *It Happened One Night* and *Mr. Deeds Goes to Town*, he handed him a blank sheaf of pages and challenged him to "Give *that* the Capra Touch." (And if that's not true, it should be.)

No less a personage than David Lean cropped up on TV recently reiterating the old saw that films are a visual medium, rather than a medium of words, a writerly medium. He offered as proof of this the test — "How many great lines of dialogue can one remember from films?"

(The test, a silly one, fails even on its own terms, because any self-respecting film buff can rhyme off dozens of lines — "Frankly, my dear . . .". "Go ahead. Make my day". "I made him an offer he couldn't refuse". "E.T. phone home". "Too many notes". "I love the smell of napalm in the morning . . ." "Come up sometime, and see me". "Yonda lies the castle of my fadduh". A handful from Casablanca alone. And some day, if we have a second or third edition of this book, let's hope we'll be able to include some Canadian examples.)

When you think about it, how many catchy lines from great novels pop to mind either?—as if this is a valid test of a writer's contribution. It trivializes screenwriters to suggest that their job is to write catchy or memorable lines, or simply to write dialogue. Their job, their mission, their elusive goal is to write memorable movies — movies of the mind — which is what the best of them do.

Here's looking at five of them. Five of our very best.

Our primary selection criterion was simply excellence. We picked what we considered to be outstanding scripts. (And, working independently, we came to immediate agreement on four of the five.) As it turns out, these scripts are also "important" in the sense that they were all made into significant films — each a landmark on the tortuous road that is Canadian film history.

Our other working rules were few and simple. No writer would be represented more than once (although several had more than one script on the short list) and, for this first volume at least, we would include only original screenplays, not adaptations, however distinguished, and no scripts written specifically for television — although there are many fine examples of these as well.

Although we didn't consciously plan it, our scripts turn out to be representative culturally and geographically of both the country and the industry. The stories are both contemporary (*Jésus de Montréal*) and period (*The Grey Fox, Mon oncle Antoine, My American Cousin*) and include a contemporary story which, with the passage of time, has taken on the feel of a period piece (*Goin' Down the Road*).

In style they range from the last word in urban intellectual sophistication of Arcand, to the evocative backwoods of Perron's imagination and memory — (treated with no less sophistication) — to Fruet's quintessential quest through Salvation Army hostels and bottling factories for the Canadian dream. They include two very different exercises in Western mythmaking by Hunter and Wilson, both of whom cleverly take American archetypes — the wily old gun-toting train robber, and the kid with a tight T-shirt, tighter jeans, a James Dean aura, and a big red Cadillac convertible — and make them their own, our own.

While the five scripts could hardly be more different, they have one thing

INTRODUCTION

in common — a sense of integrity, of being true to themselves, their vision and, yes, let's say it — their country. Snapshots on the bulletin board of our collective memory, they're universal, and yet rooted in place, strangely, surprisingly Canadian. In the Quebec bush, a boy's first brush with death; in the Okanagan Valley, a girl's first kiss; on the road from Nova Scotia, two guys in a battered heap, heading for the city of their dreams — Toronto. No one could read this collection and mistake these for five American scripts.

Tom Shoebridge reminds us in his preface that our film industry is still in its infancy. Certainly one could easily compile fat volumes of great American screenplays from the 1930s, the 40s, the 50s — while our earliest script, *Goin' Down the Road*, dates from 1969. Relative youth not withstanding, there was much of quality to sift through. We could equally well have chosen from among *Bye Bye Blues*, *Les Bons débarras*, *I've Heard the Mermaids Singing*, *The Decline of the American Empire*, *Pouvoir intime*, *The Rowdyman*, *Un zoo la nuit*, *Wedding in White*, *Réjeanne Padovani*, *The Adjuster*, *Les Ordres*, and many others. All worth reading, worth saving.

If some readers disagree with our choices, it only underscores the point. There is a literature of Canadian film, a growing body of work — to choose from, to enjoy, to study, to argue about.

To those who suggest that our choices are mainstream, rather than experimental, we say, absolutely — for the simple reason that this is the first book of its kind. It would be difficult to justify the inclusion of *Highway 61*, say, when its cultural forebear, *Goin' Down the Road*, is not only generally unavailable, but, in fact, almost impossible to locate. Trying to track down a complete copy of the script turned into a major undertaking, and it's equally difficult to obtain a copy of the film itself, arguably the seminal film in our history. This situation is ridiculous, laughable, scandalous, typically Canadian — take your pick.

Like our country, our film industry has not done particularly well in celebrating, or even preserving its past. This book is a small attempt to counter that — a finger in the dike of Canadian diffidence, Canadian forgetfulness.

Perhaps it makes no sense for Canada to have a "film industry" at all. Logic, economics, the elephantine entertainment machine immediately to the South all mitigate against it. But in spite of all this we do have one — uneven, sporadic — but one which, frequently, we can be proud of. And one of the main reasons is right here between these covers. Scripts like these. Writers like these — with the persistence, the foolhardiness, the talent — to defy the odds and create memorable stories, uniquely ours, uniquely suited to the screen — to build the cornerstone of an industry.

Long denied a place in the sun — at least now they have a place on the shelf.

Douglas Bowie

GOIN' DOWN THE ROAD

BY WILLIAM FRUET

It was during the late 1960s while working on a road script about two drifters that I met Don Shebib. He was planning a dramatic documentary for the CBC based upon Maritimers migrating to Toronto in search of work. I was impressed with the style and energy in Don's films and we were soon exchanging ideas about the "Maritimer." We spent a lot of evenings drinking and talking with real Maritimers who were going through such an experience. Most were stories of disillusionment and disappointment but none of self-pity. These were tough people accustomed to hardship, yet somehow maintaining a warmth and sincerity equalled only by their lust for living. I also drew upon my own experiences as a Westerner who had confronted the same indifferent Toronto years earlier — cheap rooming houses, hundreds of applicants for every low paying job.

We worked very closely, Don never wanting to lose sight of the story, while my fascination was with the characters themselves. There were often differences and heated debates, but this is the basis of any good working relationship. The project would also go through several transitions before the final outcome. Starting as a dramatic documentary for the Public Affairs Department of the CBC, the script met favorable reaction and was promoted to the Drama Department for further development. Unfortunately, just as I finished the first draft, a new head of drama was appointed, and all projects under development suddenly ended in the archives. At the time there were few outlets for aspiring writers and film-makers in Canada, except the CBC and it looked like the project was terminated. A few months later the Canadian Film Development Corporation came to the rescue, awarding Don a grant for nineteen thousand dollars to pursue the project.

Shebib never looked back and daringly set out to shoot it as a low-budget feature. When this money ran out, he sold his car and scraped together whatever he could but was soon broke and little better off than the people in the story we were trying to tell. Then an entrepreneur named Bennett Fode saw the half-finished product and together with the Canadian Film Development Corporation financed the completion of the movie. It never would have happened without this kind of support: people like the late Ross McLean who initiated and pushed the project forward; Michael Spencer, a friend of film-makers and Canadian films, and many others who believed and gave their support but are too numerous to mention. And lastly, of course, Don himself, whose determination and fortitude made it happen.

In retrospect, even with all the difficulties, it was an exciting time for both of us. A time before big business and institutions like the Securities Commission felt they must protect the investor from the likes of film-makers in favor of a more trustworthy group such as lawyers and accountants.

Goin' Down the Road was shot on 16m/m reversal and blown up to a 35m/m negative at a total cost of eighty-three thousand dollars.

William Fruet

GOIN' DOWN THE ROAD

ACT I

TEASER:

1. Houses — Nova Scotia.

An old two storey frame house sitting in the first light of dawn. On a dirt driveway nearby, is an old 1958 Plymouth: a rusted out heap with big fins, shiny useless auto accessories, mud flaps, etc. The early morning mist blends everything into a haze of soft pastels. It is very quiet.

The screen door opens and Joey Mills comes down the steps of the veranda, loaded down with a duffel bag, and a suitcase held shut with a piece of cord. (Joey is a thin, pale looking kid, with a greasy cowlick hanging down his forehead and tattoos adorning both arms. He is easy going, carefree, and a ball of nervous energy.)

He throws the luggage into the back of car and pauses to exchange a look with his mother, an elderly dried up woman who peers out at him through the screen door. He waves . . . she simply turns and shuffles back to the sanctuary of her old house. He shrugs, hops into the car, and roars off down the dusty street, shattering the quiet solitude with the rumble of his rusted out mufflers.

CUT TO *the setting of another old frame house where a small picket fence sags around a yard littered with junk. An old car sits up on blocks beside the house. Joey drives up. He hits the horn a couple of times. Peter Robinson comes out of the front door, carrying a duffle bag, an old battered guitar case, and some bags of sandwiches. He yells some last goodbyes back into the house . . .*

(Peter is a husky moody looking guy. He does everything in a flippant cock-sure way, which tends to rub most people the wrong way. In a limited way he is a rebel. He has a tendency to daydream and dominate Joey). Throwing his things into the back seat, he hops in, and the two break into wide grins, not saying a word. The car roars off down the street.

2. Nova Scotia.

TRAVELING SHOT *moving through a shabby old mining town in Nova Scotia: unhappy streets of broken-fenced, weed-infested yards and unpainted wooden shacks. Silent sober faces watch us pass . . .*

We pass an old deserted mine. The buildings rundown and crumbling.

A vacant field where a rusted old jalopy sits overgrown with weeds.

An old shack with a line full of faded old clothes, dogs barking, etc.

The car pulls up at the side of the road and the two of them stare back at the town behind them . . .

3. Car.

> JOEY: (*Mock sadness*) . . . So long Springhurst . . . (*Swinging around front ways again*) . . . Helloo Toronto!!

They both break out in loud yells and cheers as the car takes off with screeching tires and spewing gravel.

Loud twangy western music comes up from the car radio.

CUT TO *the license plate — "Nova Scotia 1969."*

CUT TO *baby boots swinging from the rearview mirror of the car. The image of the town disappearing in a cloud of dust behind us.*

From the moving car, SEVERAL SHOTS *of the gloom and depression spread across the Maritimes: miles of uncut pine trees with tar paper shacks along the highway, the countless towns all alike with their rundown buildings and listless people . . .*

4. Flat Tire.

CUT TO A TIGHT SHOT *of a flat tire. Pull back establishing Joey changing the tire on the shoulder of the highway. Peter sits in the shade of the car picking absently at the guitar and handing Joey the tools . . .*

> JOEY: (*Having trouble with the wrench. Second thoughts*) . . . Boy I hope we're doing the right thing. I heard they were

taking on guys at the cannery next week. Just when we leave . . .

PETER: (*Exasperated*) The cannery! Come on Joey, I'm not working in any more cannerys! That's why we're leaving. You'd be working for a $1.25 an hour the rest of your life!

JOEY: . . . I dunno. I just keep thinking of Carry, Merts and Freddy, they sure didn't do so hot. They were back in three months.

PETER: Three dummies. (*Shaking his head*) I don't get you? When we were leaving, you couldn't get out of the place fast enough. Now you go on about some job in the cannery . . . (*Picking at the guitar, and continuing in a quiet dreamy tone*) Oh listen Joey, it's gonna be so different. There you can get all kinds of jobs. Not just sweat and dirt all the time . . . (*Excited*) And the places to go: we're gonna hit some night spots, have us some good times! No sitting in some restaurant all night or cruising up and down main street, looking for something you know damn well isn't there . . . Joey there's going to be so much there, we won't know where to begin.

JOEY: (*Enthusiastic now*) When we start making the money, we'll get us a place in one of them fancy apartment buildings, with a swimming pool and broads everywhere, eh?!

PETER: (*Chuckles*).

5. *Highways.*

CUT TO A SHOT *as the car screams by, passing everything on the highway.*

Music up.

CUT TO *the front seat. Joey drives while Peter sits slouched back draining the last of a bottle of beer. He chucks the bottle away.*

CUT TO *the bottle as it bounces down the embankment and smashes in the ditch. Sign on the edge of the road reads, "You Are Entering Ontario, etc. etc." The countryside is green and lush, and the farms prosperous.*

6. Freeway.

CUT TO Gardiner Expressway with LONG LENS: *cars packed together bumper to bumper in the evening rush hour.*

CUT TO *interior of car. Joey stands up in the front seat jumping about with uncontrolled excitement and pointing at the skyline. Peter drives.*

7. Toronto.

Carry Joey's cry echoing through the dark railroad underpass until we come out into the open again, and onto Bay Street. Music comes up as the towering buildings of Toronto unfold all around us.

CUT TO A SEQUENCE OF SHOTS *of Toronto's downtown, contrasted by the twangy country music blaring away on the radio.* INTERCUT *the happy and cocky faces of Peter and Joey as they excitedly take in this whirling push of the city all around them: the big billboards advertising the good life, easy credit, no down payments, etc. Fast, exciting.*

8. Avenue Road.

CUT TO LONG SHOT *coming over the Avenue Road dip. The Plymouth appears followed by a police car with flashing light. They are pulled over to the curb.*

Music ends.

CUT TO MEDIUM SHOT *as the cops get out and come around each side of the car. Joey and Peter sit with big smirks on their faces trying to play it real cool . . .*

> **JOEY:** (*Chipper*) How are you officers? What seems to be the trouble?
>
> **COP 1:** (*To Peter*) Okay Nova Scotia . . . Let's see your driver's license.
>
> **PETER:** (*Smart Alec*) Certainly . . . certainly . . . now let me see what'd I do with it? (*Goes through a great act, shuffling through his pockets, etc. Opens glove compartment. Laughs*) Joey you didn't use my driver's license for anything did you?

JOEY: (*Giggling*) You can use mine if you want.

COP I: Okay, both of you, out of the car.

COP II: You heard him — out.

Joey and Peter slowly get out, realizing they had probably pushed it too far already. Cop I examines Peter's license.

COP I: You Peter Robinson?

PETER: (*Still cocky but a little worried*) Yeah, that's right.

COP II: Where you guys going?

PETER: (*Shrugs*) Nowhere . . . (*Cop gives him a look*) . . . Well we were going to Toronto. So we're here now . . . and we're not going anywhere. Right?

COP I: Okay Robinson, get in the car . . . (*Peter climbs back into the car*) Not that one wise guy! The patrol car! (*He and Peter walk over to the patrol car while Cop II begins to rummage through their luggage and things*).

JOEY: (*Getting more nervous*) Hey, what'd we do anyway?

CUT TO squad car where Cop I is having a routine check done by radio. Peter is more annoyed now than anything.

COP I: License 31764. (*Hangs up the radio mike*).

CUT TO AN EXTERIOR SHOT. Joey has wandered over to the squad car. He pokes around, finally springing the hood.

COP II: (*Marching over like an angry bear*) What the hell are you doing?

JOEY: Nothing, Nothing, I just wanted to see what you had inside here . . . Wow, a three eighty two, huh?

COP II: (*Grabbing him by the arm and taking him back*) Get in your car and sit down!

JOEY: (*Moving quickly over and hopping in the car*) Yes sir, yes sir!

CUT BACK TO interior of squad car.

COP I: Alright, where will you be staying?

PETER: With my aunt and uncle.

COP I: . . . Job?

PETER: Yeah a friend has a job waiting for us . . . Listen what is this anyway?

COP I: (*Cop keeps writing his report for a few seconds before answering*) Okay Robinson, here are some of the hard facts of life in this city. We've got a lot of you boys coming here. No money, no jobs, no nothing. Most of you can't seem to stay out of trouble either. This is just a routine check with a little good advice thrown in — keep your nose clean . . . or else. Follow me?

PETER: Yeah, I follow you.

CUT BACK *to Joey and the other Cop who is just closing the trunk. A small group of people have gathered to watch.*

Doug McGrath (Peter), Paul Bradley (Joey), and director Don Shebib consult the script on location in a Yonge Street bar.

9. Car.

Peter and Joey get in the Plymouth and drive away.

>**JOEY:** (*Whistle*) Wow, they sure don't like us here! You see that guy's face when he saw our license plate.

>**PETER:** The Creep. Big man, thinks he's a General or something.

>**JOEY:** What we going to do first? Call Hanson about the job — go see this aunt and uncle of yours, or what?

>**PETER:** We'll call Hanson later. Right now we better go see my aunt and uncle . . .

10. Scarborough.

CUT TO *a spotless little house with a meticulously manicured lawn and all the trimmings. A small white picket fence discourages dogs and small children. Fred and Hazel are a couple in their late forties, who both have full time jobs and have never wanted children. They are the kind of people who slave away a whole weekend on the upkeep of a house they little more than sleep in during the week. They are petty self-indulgent bores.*

CUT TO *the car which has pulled up at the curb.*

11. Scarborough House.

CUT TO *Fred and Hazel hiding in the semi-darkness of their livingroom. They peek through a small opening in the drapes. There is a long pause.*

>**HAZEL:** (*Timidly*) . . . Are they still there?

Burst of loud knocking. Both jump with a start.

>**FRED:** Damnation! Why in the blazes won't they go away?

>**HAZEL:** Anyone with any sense would have given up long ago. They've been knocking for five minutes now.

There is a long silence. Fred tiptoes across the room. He peers from the darkness of an archway trying to get a glimpse of them through the window of the front door. Hazel peeks through the curtains again.

> **HAZEL:** Tch . . . just look at that dreadful car. I can imagine what the neighbors are thinking . . .
>
> **FRED:** . . . They must have left. I can't see them . . .

Burst of loud knocking from the back door. Both jump nervously around.

> **FRED:** (*Moaning*) . . . Of all the confounded luck!
>
> **HAZEL:** I don't think they're going to go away Fred. Do you think I should have them in for tea at least?
>
> **FRED:** No No No. Don't let them in the house or we'll never get rid of them . . . (*Groans*) Just give me a few minutes to think of something.

12. Car.

It is evening and the sun just setting.

CUT TO A LONG SHOT *of a silhouette of the car moving slowly back toward the city.*

> **JOEY:** (*Mimicking Fred*) "What a shame Hazel and I are going on holidays tomorrow . . ."
>
> **PETER:** (*Mimicking Hazel*) "And the painters will be coming in to paint the whole house . . ."
>
> **JOEY:** (*Mimicking Fred*) "Now let's see what's in the newspapers — here's a good one — Driftwood on the Park: one bedroom: $250.00 per month: that's not bad you know."
>
> **PETER:** (*Mimicking Hazel*) "That is expensive, but it's such a nice district."

13. Telephone Booth.

CUT TO A LOW ANGLE SHOT LOOKING UP *at an expensive highrise around Jarvis and Bloor.* CAMERA PANS DOWN *to street level where Peter is in a phone booth and Joey sits waiting in the car. It is a warm night and the* street is filled with traffic and people. Several patrol cars pass, eyeing Joey suspiciously. Peter bangs on the glass to Joey giving him the "Roger Sign."

CUT TO *interior of booth.*

> PETER: Hi Hanson?! . . . How are ya, it's Pete . . . Pete Robinson . . . (*Laughing*) Yeah yeah, that's right. Me an Joey got in today! . . . (*Uncomfortable*) Ah, I don't know . . . for a while I guess. Hey how ya doing anyway? Long time no see! . . . (*The smile slowly leaving his face*) . . . Yeah?

CUT TO *the outside where Joey is getting edgy as another patrol car passes. He knocks on the glass signaling Peter to speed it up. Peter nods. A few seconds pass and then Peter comes out. He wears a big phony smile and avoids Joey's questions.*

> JOEY: Well, what'd he say? Can he put us up?
>
> PETER: Naw, naw, he's only got this small room. He says we should go to the Salvation Army for the night . . .
>
> JOEY: (*Distaste*) What, a flophouse?
>
> PETER: No no, it's a nice place.
>
> JOEY: (*Getting suspicious*) . . . What about the jobs?
>
> PETER: (*Deep sigh*) Oh yeah . . . well he says I should call him back in a few days.
>
> JOEY: (*Angry*) In a few days?!
>
> PETER: (*Lamely*) He's out of work himself. Things ain't so good right now. He might even go back. Says we picked a bad time to come . . .
>
> JOEY: We picked??! You told me everything was set! There was going to be a job waiting and everything!
>
> PETER: (*Losing his temper*) Relax will ya! Couple of things go wrong and you start running around like a chicken with its head cut off!
>
> JOEY: Listen we're fifteen hundred miles from home! We got $30 bucks between us. How long you think that's going to last?
>
> PETER: Ahh, go sit in the car and shut up! I can't think with you flapping all over the place.

JOEY: (*Muttering as he obediently goes to the car*) Lousy aunt and uncle . . . now no job . . . This town's crawling with cops.

Peter paces back and forth, grumbling to himself. Joey sits in the car sulking.

14. Flophouse.

CUT TO *sign of flophouse: "Bed's 75 Cents per Nite"*

CUT TO *Joey and Peter as they are led up a dimly lit hallway by a toothless old man in slippers and undershirt. They enter a dormitory crowded with rows of double bunks. There is the heavy odor of dirty feet and the sound of snoring everywhere. Peter pays the old man for two towels.*

Peter motions to Joey.

They put their gear down and slowly look over the setting. Several men are asleep while others lie reading "True Detective" magazines, etc. Several others are washing up, in a large washroom at the end of the hall.

Peter struggles to open the window. Joey sits on the bunk very depressed.

JOEY: (*Scared*) Maybe we should head back huh?

PETER: We've got $26 left. That isn't even gasoline to get us half way.

JOEY: Whew! Does this place stink!

PETER: It ain't going to kill you for one night Joey . . . (*Sits down on the bottom bunk and opens one of the newspapers they have bought*) . . . We just got to figure things out better that's all. No more hangups like today.

JOEY: The place gives me the creeps.

PETER: (*He stops and stares at the paper bewildered*) . . . What is this? There's hundreds of jobs in here! (*Excited*) Look, look here, three pages of them.

JOEY: (*Grabbing the other paper*) Let me see, let me see!

PETER: Listen to this . . . Reservation Agents — Textile Salesman, Assistant Manager, Sales Trainees — We offer excellent promotional opportunities for the right man. Or listen to this: "Management Trainer: Large Advertising Co. has opening for young man interested in the advertising business." (*Flops back on the bed, ecstatic with excitement*) Now this is more like it!! It's right here, all you gotta do is go out and get it! What's wrong with that Hanson?

JOEY: Hey listen to this: "68 Plymouth Fury 2, auto, buckets, sharp! $1699.00." (*Whistles*) Jeeze, that's about $400 less than you'd pay at home!

PETER: (*Cocky, confident*) Joey, I got it all figured! We'll check out a bunch of these jobs see! Take a look at things, take our pick. Yeahhhh . . .(*Lies back, lapsing into his own world of daydreams*).

CAMERA PANS OFF *them* AND ACROSS *this strange selection of men who have taken shelter in a place like this for the night: men without roots, drifters and misfits.*

JOEY'S VOICE: . . . Hey you can even phone someone if you're lonely. Says right here: "Lonely? Telephone 923-1116." Wow! Wow! Wow!

CAMERA PANS *to the dirty window and the sleeping city outside.*

PETER'S VOICE: (*Dreamy*) You know, I wouldn't mind having a job in an office.

JOEY'S VOICE: What for? You'd have to get dressed up all the time.

CUT TO *the streets outside. Peter's words drifting over the big towering buildings sitting silent and amused.*

PETER'S VOICE: Some chick for a secretary . . . company car . . . the whole bit. Why not?

DISSOLVE OUT.

15. Montage: Jobs.

Music comes up full and street comes alive with cars and activity of the morning rush hour, as everyone hurries to their place, their thing. CUT TO

Peter moving in the heavy crowded downtown streets. He wears a white shirt and tie and his hockey club windbreaker. CUT TO *Joey wandering along taking in the sights of the city. He comes upon a traffic jam.* CUT TO A SEQUENCE *of Peter having several refusals in various offices. Music fades.*

16. Advertising Agency.

CUT TO *the frowning face of a personnel man who examines Peter's application form. His bewildered eyes keep coming up to Peter then darting back to the form. Finally he sits back and treats the situation with honesty and frankness.*

>   **MAN:** . . . What ever possessed you to come here for a job? I mean looking at this I can't see anything in your background to even suggest an interest in advertising?

17. Bus Depot.

DISSOLVE TO *Peter slumped asleep in the bus depot. Several bums doze nearby. Joey enters.*

>   **JOEY:** (*Nudging Peter*) Psst, hey Buddy boy!

Peter wakes with a start.

>   **JOEY:** (*Laughing*) Thought it was a cop hey?

>   **PETER:** Real funny. Where the hell you been, it's one in the morning?

>   **JOEY:** Looking the town over. Hey I got a job!

>   **PETER:** (*Leaping up*) You did? That's great! Great! (*Punches him*) Joey you son-of-a-gun! Where? What kind of job?

>   **JOEY:** Load, unload boxcars. Eighty bucks a week. I already worked half a day. Great bunch of guys! Lot of em from down home.

>   **PETER:** (*Sigh of relief*) Now we can at least go get a hot meal. I don't think I could look at another doughnut.

>   **JOEY:** How did you do?

PETER: *(Hedging)* Naww, I didn't see anything I liked.

JOEY: No sweat. You can get on there with me. They're gonna hire more guys tomorrow!

PETER: *(Shrugs)* Sure, for now I guess it's be okay.

18. Warehouse.

CUT TO *a large grey warehouse where piles of produce stand high to the ceiling for as far as the eye can see. A husky foreman walks back and forth barking orders here and there. He has a heavy French Canadian accent and the mannerisms of a Southern Redneck. Joey and Peter stand waiting to talk to him.*

FRENCHY: All right what is dis, ehhh? Come on come on you guys pull out the rag ehh! *(To Joey)* What's the matter Mills, you working here or not? Get your can moving, it's already 8:05. You wanna get docked?!

JOEY: Hey boss, this is my friend Pete. They just hired him.

FRENCHY: *(Not looking at him)* What're they doing to me??! I gotta enough of Easterners already! Bastards are always just up and leaving one day or else they do too much boozing!

PETER: I don't drink.

FRENCHY: *(Loud mocking laugh)* Ha Haaaaa! Show me an Easterner who don't drink, I show you a liar.

PETER: *(Challenging)* I'm used to hard work. I can keep up to anyone here.

FRENCHY: *(Scoffing)* Ha, that ain't good enough! I got lots of Pisanos here. Stinking people but they work like hell! You can't keep up to them! Okay, show him his locker, then get your butt back here on the double. We see how good you are Newfie!

CUT TO *Peter and Joey working side by side. It is hard work and they are sweating, but happy. The noon whistle goes. They put down the crates they* were holding, grab their shirts, and join Vince, another worker. CAMERA DOLLIES with them as they move past a maze of machinery toward the lunch room.

JOEY: (*Eager*) Well, what'd ya think? Not bad huh?

PETER: (*Disappointed*) What are you so excited about? (*Shrugs*) It's a factory . . . it's okay. It'll do til we can find something better.

19. Lunchroom.

CUT TO *a large lunchroom: it is split into various factions starting with executives at one end and working down next to office staff, general workers, and a large group of Italian women at the back. Vince, Peter, and Joey enter and are guided over to a corner where several tables have been pushed together and the boys are eating, playing cards, and just gabbing.*

VINCE: Hey you guys this is Joey and he's Peter. (*Winks to the group*) They just came in from Springhurst, N.B. yesterday.

EDDY: (*Holding his nose*) I knew there was a strong stink of fish this morning! Any of you guys notice it?

MIKE AND HAROLD: Yeah it was everywhere! Is that what it was? Etc.

Peter and Joey stand silent saying nothing.

VINCE: That's Eddy, he's from P.E.I. (*Eddy breaks into a wide grin*). Harold's from Truro and Mike's from Cape Breton.

PETER: Bunch of lousy Newfies!!

Peter and Joey break into laughter and start shaking hands. Everyone starts questioning them when Freddy, a fourth, comes over.

FREDDY: Quiet, quiet!! Are you guys ready? Well getta load of this!

He swings around and whips up his T-shirt displaying several fingernail scratches on his back. They all break into cheers, whistles, and catcalls.

EVERYONE: Woooooeeee!! Freddy the tiger — Here Pussie Pussie! Meoowwww Meowww!!

EDDY: Ah, that's nothing! (*Whipping up his T-shirt and displaying scratches and bruises*) Take a look at these Freddy!

EVERYONE: Wow! Holy cow, who was she!? Yeah can we have her telephone number Eddy?

Vince winks to Peter.

EDDY: (*Smirking*) What'd ya talking about, I was drunk and fell out of the car the other night!

Laughter and boos from all.

VINCE: Heyyy quiet! Knock it off you guys, here she comes!

They all swing around, eyes on the doorway. Complete silence falls over the group.

SERIES OF QUICK CUTS *to the other groups. Executives take quick side looks, trying not to be seen. The office workers smile sheepishly to one another. (The office girls pay no attention). The Italian women at the back give long burning looks.*

CUT TO *Stella, enormous breasts, and really built. Her clothing is tight and taut, looking as though she was poured into it.*

CUT TO A TIGHT SHOT *of her breasts heaving with every breath she takes.*

CUT TO *a tight shot of Vince wearing a blissful smile.*

VINCE: This is the one I was telling you about . . .

PAN TO *Peter.*

PETER: What a pair of knockers . . .

CUT TO C.U. *of her behind as she reaches for a sandwich.*

CUT BACK TO A C.U. *of the table. All heads bending forward in unison with her. No one takes his eyes from her when speaking.*

JOEY: You ever been out with her?

EDDY: Nawww . . . she's not my type.

CUT TO C.U. *of her leg, outstretched as she bends.* CUT TO C.U. *of Harold.*

HAROLD: She don't even talk to us guys in the plant . . . (*Sighs*) . . . She's French.

PETER: (*Blissful smile*) Is she ever!

VINCE: Ah, wait till you see the broads on Yonge Street.

Joey, Peter and the boys cope with a distraction (Nicole Morin) at the factory. "She don't even talk to us guys in the plant."

20. Montage: Yonge St.

QUICK CUT TO *the crowded setting of Yonge Street strip, ablaze with neon, noise and excitement. The five of them move quickly along through the crowds, clowning and making a pass at anything wearing a skirt. They are continually rebuffed, but take it in their stride — laughing it off.*

21. A. & A. Record Store.

CUT TO *the crowded setting of the A.& A. Record Store. The five of them are clowning around below the stairway, looking up girls' skirts as they go up the stairs. Peter is suddenly taken by one of the girls. He leaves the group and quickly goes up the stairs after her.*

CUT TO *the second floor. Peter stands at a distance watching her. She is a very soft, gentle, and beautiful looking girl. To Peter she represents everything a girl should be and look like. She stands by a turntable listening to a record of Satie. Peter shyly edges his way over. He pretends to be concentrating on the music.*

She purchases the record. Peter watches her as she goes down the stairs and onto the street. He walks over to the fag clerk.

    PETER: Hey, what's the name of that?

    CLERK: "Trois Gymnopedies" by Eric Satie. Beautiful isn't it?

    PETER: Yeah, I'll take one . . .

CUT TO *Yonge Street as they all come out of the A.& A., giggling and moving with an urgency to get far away. Laughter from all except Peter who can't get his mind off the girl. They turn up an alleyway.*

22. Alleyway.

    JOEY: (*To Peter*) Hey did you buy a record?

    PETER: (*Embarrassed*) Yeah it was half price, so I thought what the hell.

    JOEY: Why didn't you tell Eddy, he'd of picked it up for ya free!

Eddy, wearing a big grin, produces about five LP's from under his sweater and begins handing them out.

    EDDY: There's the one you wanted Vince . . . Harold . . . yours Joey and two for me!

They all cheer him, except Peter who feels like a real cluck now.

    HAROLD: Come on you guys, lets hit the Edison.

23. Edison Hotel.

CUT TO *the setting of the Edison and the wail of lonesome Country and*

Western blues. This is Maritime music and where they will settle in for the night to do some serious drinking.

24. Yonge Street.

DISSOLVE TO A HIGH LONG SHOT: *the tiny figures of Joey and Peter swaggering up Yonge Street, arm in arm, just as the grey of dawn is breaking. The lights of the strip flicking off and on in the background, the streets empty. They stand on the corner singing and laughing and very pleased with themselves.*

Joey, with his arms outstretched to the buildings around him, yells out.

JOEY: Toronto . . . I Love You Baby!!

PETER: (*Tagging it*) Yeeeeeehaawwwwww!

CAMERA ZOOMS BACK SWIFTLY, *leaving them as tiny specks in a canyon of city all around them.*

ACT II

25. Montage.

Music comes up:

Joey and Peter exiting from the YMCA *and piling all their gear into the back of the car.*

Moving into a second storey flat of an old house. Joey's corner plastered in nude girls. Peter has giant poster of Marlon Brando on a motorcycle.

Coming out of the Rio Movie House where three horror movies are playing.

TIGHT IN *on Frenchy's face at work, screaming orders.* CUT TO *Peter dirty and covered in sweat staring back at Frenchy.*

The two of them staggering into the Brewer's Retail, laughing and struggling to balance about ten cases of empties.

Clowning about on the subway late at night. Trying to pick up girls.

Cruising for pickups. Two girls tell them to get lost. Peter yelling and waving his fist. Joey gives them the finger.

Sitting in the Edison again. Nostalgic and lonesome.

Music fades.

26. Factory.

CUT TO the factory the next morning. The heavy machines screaming and banging away, as they pound out the produce.

CUT TO the warehouse where Joey and Peter move with the same quick precise movements as the machines, piling the heavy crates on small wooden platforms. Fork lift trucks quickly move in and whisk away the platforms as they are ready. Peter stops to wipe sweat away from his face. He is pissed off.

    PETER: Whew! . . . what time is it?

    JOEY: (*Puffing*) Just a little past eleven.

    PETER: Hell I feel like I've been working ten hours already! Hell, this isn't any better than being back home! (*He walks over to one of the waiting fork lift trucks*) . . . Hey how do you operate this thing?

    MAN: (*Sarcastic*) Come on — I'm waiting for a load.

    PETER: (*Making a kiss off gesture with his hand*).

Three or four fork lift trucks are lined up waiting now.

    FRENCHY'S VOICE: Mills, Robinson! What is this? A holiday?!

Peter and Joey leap back into their work looking once more like two human machines.

27. Lunchroom:

CUT TO the lunch room crowded and humming with activity. Harold, Vince, and Eddy play cards at one table. Freddy reads a comic book by himself. Joey and Peter enter. Peter kicks chairs aside and makes a general ruckus getting settled. He is thoroughly pissed off.

    EDDY: Where you guys been? It's 12:15 . . .

JOEY: Ah, we had to go to the office about some pension or something. Boy you should see the broads up there!

Peter flops back and begins to rip at a sandwich like an angry animal. His eyes catch sight of Stella on the far side of the room sitting with the same group of junior executives. This irks him.

CAMERA HOLDS ON *Peter.*

HAROLD: (*Reading from "Flash"*) Hey listen to this . . . "Horseman's daughter was hot to trot."

MIKE: (*Reading over his shoulder*) Or this one . . . "G string snaps back after uprising."

HAROLD: (*Effeminate*) And for all you gay guys, "Rape in the rear can be a bum steer!"

PETER: (*Who has been staring intently at Stella*) Boy — doesn't that broad think she's something.

JOEY: Ah, that kind is only out for what she can get.

PETER: I could take her out if I wanted . . .

JOEY: Ah, forget her. Listen I met this real nice chick Betty a week ago. Took her home. I'm suppose to meet her again tonight. She's got this friend. You interested?

PETER: (*Coolly*) I dunno. What does she look like?

JOEY: Nice, real nice. No kidding!

28. Danforth Ave.

CUT TO *the two of them sitting in the car that night, parked outside a small Chinese restaurant somewhere on the Danforth. They watch the girls as they move back and forth inside, working as waitresses.*

JOEY: . . . What do you think?

PETER: She looks kind of fat.

JOEY: Naww, that's just the uniforms they're wearing.

PETER: What's her name?

JOEY: (*Thinking*) Ah . . . Selena.

PETER: (*Slouching back and wearing a sheepish smile*) Okay-y, we'll see what Selena's got . . .

29. Drive-In.

CUT TO *the setting of an A & W Rootbeer Drive-in. The four of them are drinking cokes and passing around a bag of potato chips. Peter and Joey sit slouched back listening to the girls who keep a running conversation going. Betty and Selena are plain and rather chubby girls, who wear high teased bleached blonde hair-dos, chew gum constantly, and are very dull.*

BETTY: So help me. God strike me dead right here, if I'm not telling the truth. Isn't that right Sellie?

SELENA: She's not kidding Joey. Every time Grace gets a little headache, she goes home.

JOEY: (*Yawning*) Well ya gotta say something! What about this Wong guy? Don't he say nothing?

BETTY: Nothing! Besides I told you what I thought was going on there.

JOEY: (*Explaining to Peter who is very bored*) Old Wong's the Chink who owns the restaurant. He's making out with one of the broads there.

SELENA: I'd rather die . . .

30. Cherry Beach.

QUICK CUT TO *the serene setting of Cherry Beach. Several cars are scattered about in the moonlit parking area and soft late night music oozes from all the car radios. The four of them are all in their respective positions as they sip cokes and the conversation continues . . .*

BETTY: I don't care what she does. It's her business, only we gotta make up for her. Now that ain't fair. Look at tonight: Agnes was off at eight, and there was just me and Selie.

JOEY: (*Yawns*) Well ya gotta stand up more. (*To Peter*) Come on let's take a walk. We'll be right back.

BETTY: Want somebody to hold your hand?

The two girls burst into giggles as Joey and Peter make their way through the darkness of the bushes to a place where they begin to relieve themselves.

JOEY: Well?

PETER: Well what?

JOEY: What do you think of her?

PETER: She hasn't said anything to me except "Hi" when I met her. All they do is yak with each other.

JOEY: Shhh, they'll hear ya! Look just play it cool, it's no sweat. It'll go easy from here.

They make their way back to the car where they are greeted with more stiffled giggles. Joey gets in and heaves his empty pop bottle into the trees where we hear it smash.

CUT TO *interior of the car. Joey puts his arm around Betty drawing her over.*

BETTY: Jeeze Joey, take it easy eh? I'm still drinking my coke.

JOEY: (*Impatient*) Well come on Bets come on. What the hell.

BETTY: (*Annoyed*) In a minute eh . . . (*Slurp from the Coke bottle*).

JOEY: (*Crumbling*) Throw it away if ya can't finish it.

BETTY: Can't you wait!! (*Joey takes the coke from her*) Ah Joey . . .

Her sounds are muffled as Joey kisses her, and gradually transform from anguish to moans of pleasure.

CUT TO *a two shot of Peter and Selena sitting self-consciously apart in the back seat. They both look out their respective windows. Peter takes out a mickey.*

PETER: (*Offering the bottle*) . . . Want some?

SELENA: (*Shakes her head*) . . . I'm full of coke.

CUT TO P.O.V. SHOT: *the silhouettes of Joey and Betty in the front seat, locked in an eternal kiss . . . rocking back and forth, and finally sliding down and out of view.*

CUT TO L.S. *of the convertible top slowly billowing into the sky with a lot of creaking and groaning . . . It seems to hang there for a second, then drops with a thud.*

CUT TO ENORMOUS C.U. *of the moon. A "Hank Snow" ballad starts in the background.* SCENE FADES OUT.

31. Montage.

Music holds as:

DISSOLVE TO MONTAGE *of leaves turning from green to various colors* INTERCUT WITH MONTAGE *of Betty, Selena, Joey, and Peter on various dates: Stills from a 25¢ picture machine. Goofing off at a driving range. Joey and Peter wildly missing balls, yukking it up. Girls yakking away to one another. Dancing at the Horseshoe Tavern.*

Peter grows progressively more and more bored as montage continues.

Betty's friend Selena (Cayle Cherrin) and Peter (Doug McGrath) get to know each other.

32. Rosedale.

CUT TO *a quiet residential street in Rosedale: beautiful mansions, lush full trees, etc. Joey's car comes up the street and stops.*

CUT TO CLOSER SHOT. *The four of them are dressed in their Sunday best and out for an afternoon drive. Peter is ecstatic with excitement while the other three could care less.*

PETER: (*Getting out*) Wowww, will you look at this place! Now these people know how to live! Some of these places must be worth a couple hundred thousand each! Where are we anyway?

BETTY: Rosedale. You gotta be a big mucky muck to live here . . .

PETER: Look at the one over there with the limousine in the driveway and everything! Think of what it would be like to live in a place like that Joey!

JOEY: (*Wet blanket*) Lotta upkeep: lawns to mow, hedges, all those flower beds. I hate doing that kind of stuff.

SELENA: Yeah I had a girlfriend who worked as a domestic around in here somewhere. She said it was an awful lot of work.

PETER: (*Angry*) I ain't talking about working there. I said live!

The three of them laugh, all heckling him at once.

JOEY: Are you kidding Pete! You ain't never gonna have a place like that.

BETTY: Fat chance!

33. Flat.

DISSOLVE TO *the flat early one morning. The alarm goes off and Joey mechanically gets up and turns it off. He sits on the bed a long time trying to shake off the sleepiness and wake up. Peter in the next bed continues to sleep.*

JOEY: Come on Pete. (*Waits*) . . . Pete!

PETER: (*Groans*) Piss off.

JOEY: It's six thirty, come on.

PETER: I'm not going to work today.

JOEY: Okay suit yourself . . . (*He shuffles down the hallway to the bathroom. We hear the toilet flush then . . .*) Get outta here ya bastards! (*He comes flying out slapping at the floor in every direction with his slipper*) Jesus bugs are everywhere! (*Wanders into bathroom, runs the water*) . . . Listen you can't take no day off. We only been there a month. You think they won't know?

PETER: I don't give a damn. Can't go horsing around with broads half the night, then drag my butt out of bed a couple of hours later . . . (*Grumbling*) I wouldn't have minded if it had been worth while. All that dumb Selena does is talk. Last night, she told me about her old lady, her brother's hernia operation, and Christ knows what.

JOEY: (*Wandering back into the room*) I thought you were getting to like her?

PETER: (*Sarcastic . . . Groans*) What I need is somebody like that Stella. (*Suddenly grabbing the pillow*) Auch, if I had that dame in bed here — boom! boom! Boom! (*Takes a deep breath, and flops over again, muttering*).

JOEY: Come on you crazy bugger, what are you doing? Get up!

PETER: Something inside me says, "You don't feel like piling boxes today Peter." And I agree. So you convey my regrets to dear old Frenchy and tell him . . . tell him . . .

JOEY: (*Sarcastic*) . . . Yeah, tell him what?

PETER: Tell him to go kiss my ass! I don't care what you tell him . . .

HOLD ON *Peter's face: having second thoughts.*

34. Warehouse.

CUT TO *Joey and Peter working very fast side by side later in the morning. Frenchy stands nearby wearing a big scowl and watching them.*

>**PETER:** (*Hushed anguish*) What the Hell did you tell him anyway?
>
>**JOEY:** (*Squirming*) Just what you said, "You weren't feeling so hot." And he said, "Get on the phone and tell him to get his ass down here or else."
>
>**PETER:** (*Groaning*) Joey, Joey, you should have said I was sick! Real sick!

CUT TO C.U. *of Frenchy's silent burning look.*

35. Warehouse.

DISSOLVE TO *Joey and Peter eating their lunch in the warehouse. They sit on the platform outside enjoying the sunshine. Peter is busy figuring something out on a piece of paper. He keeps muttering to himself.*

>**PETER:** Listen to this, I figured it out. Takes about 5 seconds to lift a crate and stack it? Right?
>
>**JOEY:** Yeah, I guess so . . .
>
>**PETER:** Okay, now get this! That's 12 every minute . . . 720 an hour . . . 5760 in a day! Which means that in the two months we've been here, we've piled 230,400 crates! Each!!
>
>**JOEY:** (*Bug-eyed*) Wow, no kidding?! Jeeze think if ya had a buck for every crate huh? Hell even a penny! How much is that??
>
>**PETER:** (*Searching for the answer*) . . . Ah . . . $2300!
>
>**JOEY:** (*Whistles*) Throw in my car and I could get a '68 XL! Hey I gotta go tell the guys about this!

Joey gets up and excitedly heads for the lunch room to tell the others. Peter just sits staring out at the bright sunny day and freedom. His eyes then turn to the long endless rows of crates waiting. He rolls up the piece of paper, chucking it at them in defiance.

36. Warehouse.

CUT TO the silent forklift trucks. Peter looks around, then walks over to one. He walks around one examining it from every side, then looking in all directions to make sure he is alone, he climbs up on it. He studies the controls for a few seconds.

    PETER: *(To himself)* . . . Forward . . . Backward . . . Up . . . Down . . . Start.

Slowly he reaches for the switch. He flicks it and the engine comes to life. He sits debating with himself, then ventures the next step. Slowly the car creeps forward. His confidence growing, he puts the machine through a series of gentle stop-go routines.

    STELLA'S VOICE: Can you tell me where Mr. Langlier is?

Peter's head swings up to see Stella standing there with some papers in her hand. He goes blank momentarily then starts sputtering directions to her.

    PETER: Langlier? Oh yeah, Frenchy. Ah yeay, yeah, ummm, he should be straight down the end of this lane. It's just a small office you can't miss it.

    STELLA: *(Smiles)* Thanks.

Peter sits spellbound watching her as the truck wanders straight into a pile of crates sending them flying in every direction.

37. Flat.

CUT TO the flat later that night. Joey stands in front of a mirror getting ready for a date. He has stopped to listen as Peter relates the whole event over. Peter relishes each detail and tells it with suspense and drama.

    PETER: So there I am . . . just lying there see. Crates all over the place . . . my head spinning round and round . . . I open my eyes and there they are! Those great big beautiful things just hanging there . . . "Are you alright?" she says . . . *(Long pause)*.

    JOEY: *(Not able to stand the suspense)* . . . What'd ya say???

    PETER: *(Peeved at himself)* Ah, I couldn't think of anything so I just said "Yeah."

Peter continues to prepare his supper at the stove. Joey gives a big sigh of disappointment.

JOEY: Jeeze Pete, that was your big chance! You should have moved in!

PETER: (*Confident*) Ah look, never mind the ice is broken now. (*Reflecting back*) In fact I think she kinda likes me . . .

Joey goes on primping for his date. He begins to sprinkle generous quantities of Old Spice all over himself.

JOEY: So what did the frog say to ya?

PETER: Aw, he just chewed me out, told me to keep my ass off the machines!

JOEY: What about the truck, any damage?

PETER: Pranged up the front a bit. You can't win Joey! You'd think they'd show a little appreciation for me trying to improve myself.

JOEY: (*Admiring himself*) . . . Hey Pete, you think my eyes are too close together? Betty don't . . .

PETER: Take it easy, you'll smell like a whore house!

JOEY: Betty really likes this stuff.

PETER: (*Pause*) . . . What, her again tonight?

JOEY: Sure, a few laughs, what the hell.

JOEY: You want me to get her to phone Selena, make it a foursome?

PETER: (*Scoffing*) Aw, that piece of fluff never shuts her mouth long enough for you to get near her. (*Final*) Naww, I'm tired of her . . . (*Thinking aloud in a dreamy tone*) . . . I think I'll ask out Stella tomorrow . . .

JOEY: (*Wide-eyed*) Really?!

38. Lunchroom.

CUT TO *faces of several of the guys staring across the lunch room the next day. Peter is talking to Stella. Joey watches with a big grin on his face.*

VINCE: I don't believe it.

EDDY: Who ever thought Pete had it in him?

Joey still grins. Peter leaves Stella and comes back to the table. The guys gather round him.

ALL: (*Together*) Aww, gowan! Did you really ask her?!

Peter is suddenly the hero as they all crowd around him asking questions at once.

PETER: Yep — Friday night.

VINCE: Hey, he really did it.

HAROLD: (*Shaking his head*) Well I'll be . . .

VINCE: Pete . . . you son of a gun . . .

EDDY: Hey I'll lend you my Mustang Pete. You can't take her out in Joey's old heap!

VINCE: Yeah and you gotta get some new clothes! She's a real dresser! Something really way out!!

ALL: (*Agreeing*) Yeah yeah!! Boy oh boy! Take notes eh Pete! Don't forget a thing.

39. Clothing Store.

CUT TO *cheap clothing store. Peter triumphantly emerges from changing room in outlandish mod suit — with cuffs three inches above his ankles. The boys let out a cheer.*

40. Flat.

They all gather round Peter, their excitement growing as the time draws near.

HAROLD: Jeeze, just look at him! Old Stella's gonna wet her pants when she sees you!

JOEY: How do you feel? Are you nervous?

PETER: (*Playing it real cool*) . . . Nawww.

EDDY: Boy I'd be! Where you going to take her?!

PETER: I don't know. Maybe to a movie.

VINCE: No – no, take her dancing somewhere. Get all snuggled in! (*Gasping*) Ohhh jeeze, just thinking of it!

EDDY: And and, don't forget now, get her to play the old "hands up" game. (*Demonstrating*) Put one boob under this arm and the other boob under that arm. Then put your face right here in the middle and say . . . "Hands Up" B-R-R-R-R!!

41. Car (Mustang).

CUT TO *Peter driving along in Vince's flashy hot Mustang, stealing glances at Stella's lush figure, while she busies herself gazing into her compact checking her makeup. Peter suddenly is caught by something he sees in the rear view mirror.*

STELLA: What's the matter.

PETER: Oh nothing.

Peter's eyes flash to the rearview mirror: where he sees all of the guys in Joey's car following behind them. They are all grinning and waving.

CUT TO SHOT *of doggy with eyes lit up in back of Vince's car.*

42. Car.

CUT TO P.O.V. SHOT *from Joey's car. Peter's hand hangs over the side, frantically waving them off. Joey pulls over and we watch Peter's car disappear. They all sit lost in their own vicarious dreams of Stella.*

VINCE: (*Clicking his tongue*) Well, he did it . . .

HAROLD: . . . Yes sir, he sure did.

JOEY: . . . Lucky dog.

EDDY: . . . Yep . . . ole Pete's going to have one fine time tonight . . .

43. Trinidad Club.

QUICK CUT TO colorful setting of the "Trinidad Club" alive with twisting, churning bodies, dancing to a fast Latin beat.

CUT TO Peter seated all alone at a table nursing a drink. The set is over and A colored guy brings Stella back to the table. She is panting, struggling to catch her breath.

> **STELLA:** Oh wow! I'm all out of breath! You don't mind me dancing so much like this do you?
>
> **PETER:** No no.
>
> **STELLA:** It was real swell of you to bring me. I always come here on a Friday night and I'd sure hate to miss it. These guys are just the greatest dancers. I mean they got such rhythm, you know?!

Music starts again.

> **VOICE OFF:** Come on Stella baby!
>
> **STELLA:** (*Getting up*) Here we go again! They're just not going to let poor Stella catch her breath!

44. Car (Mustang).

CUT TO the car as it pulls up in front of Stella's house later.

CUT TO interior of car. Stella is trying to give Peter the quick goodbye.

> **STELLA:** You don't have to see me to the door Petie (*Starts to get out*).
>
> **PETER:** (*Jumping out and shipping around to open the door for her*) No no, it's okay.

She gets out and walks quickly up to the sidewalk, Peter right on her heels.

45. House.

CUT TO interior stairway. Peter's P.O.V. of Stella's behind swaying back and forth as they climb the stairs.

> **STELLA:** I really had a super time tonight.
>
> **PETER:** (*Nervous*) Me too, yeah. Have to learn to do a few of those dances myself one of these days.
>
> **STELLA:** (*Reaching her door on the second floor, She does a quick disappearing act*) Okay, thanks again Petie. I'd invite you in for a cup of coffee, only I got this girlfriend staying with me for the night . . . (*Throws him a kiss*).
>
> **PETER:** Hey well that's okay, I . . .
>
> **STELLA:** Night! (*She slips in, shutting the door in Peter's face*).

Long pause.

> **PETER:** (*Quietly*) . . . Bitch.

He raises his hand to bang on the door, but instead slowly trudges back down the stairs. He opens the front door, then quickly ducks back in.

CUT TO *Joey's car sitting parked across the street.*

46. Car.

CUT TO *the interior of the car. Joey, Vince, Harold, and Eddy all sit eyeing the place.*

> **EDDY:** There goes the last light. The whole place is dark now . . . (*Groans*). That lucky dog.
>
> **VINCE:** Yeahhh . . .
>
> **HAROLD:** I bet she's just standing there . . . letting him slip her clothing off, piece by piece . . .
>
> **JOEY:** (*Adding*) And it's just dark enough, so he can still see everything.
>
> **ALL:** (*Murmurs*) Yeahhh . . .

CUT TO *Peter sitting in the darkness of the stairs. He lights up a cigarette to help pass the long wait before him.*

47. Beach.

Quiet musical sequence:

The setting is a picnic on the island. Betty and Selena sit with their hair up in curlers, sipping cokes and talking.

Joey lies back in peaceful bliss, strumming his guitar. Peter is slightly off from the group, laying on his stomach, watching a beautiful blonde nearby, sunbathing on the sand. After a while the blonde gets up, gathers up her things, and begins to walk off down the beach.

INTERCUT C.U. *of Peter's face and the girl as she grows smaller and smaller . . . A dream disappearing.*

Music ends: Peter suddenly rolls over . . .

PETER: (*To Joey*) Come on, lets take a walk.

JOEY: Okay (*Looks to Betty for approval*).

BETTY: What's the matter don't you like our company?

SELENA: Yeah Peter, what's with you? For a guy who only calls a girl once a month, you sure don't knock yourself out to be sociable.

PETER: (*Hint of sarcasm*) I've been lying here thinking of you.

BETTY & SELENA: Sure, tell us another one!

JOEY: (*Still waiting*) . . . Is it okay Bets?

BETTY: Why can't we come?

SELENA: Yeah?

PETER: (*Throwing his hand in the air in exasperation*) Okay, okay, come on then if you have to!

BETTY: Who wants to if you're going to act like that?

SELENA: That's for sure!

PETER: (*Groaning to Joey*) Ohhh, come on let's go (*They begin to walk away*).

BETTY: (*Calling after them*) Don't be long, cause we're making the sandwiches now.

JOEY: Yeah, yeah.

The two of them walk briskly along, Joey having trouble keeping up to Peter, who is very moody and pissed off.

JOEY: . . . What's up?

PETER: (*Bugged*) They never shut up Joey, they just talk talk talk. How can two broads talk at the same time and know what the other one's saying? You know how? They're not saying anything, that's how.

JOEY: What's the matter with you?! What are you going on about anyway?

PETER: Everything! When we first came here, things were really great. We had some good times, together . . . then you met her, and you can't keep your nose out of it for a minute.

JOEY: What else you gonna do?

PETER: I think we should blow the place. Go to Vancouver.

JOEY: But we haven't got any money, remember?

There is a long pause as the two of them just walk. Then Joey attempts to cheer up Peter.

JOEY: Hey look Pete, lets you and me take off ourselves tonite eh?! And live it up a little, just the two of us, no broads — nothing! What'd ya say?!

PETER: Now you're talking!

48. Nashville Club.

CUT TO *Aunt Bea's Nashville Club: a cheap dance hall featuring Country and Western music and situated on the second floor of an old building on Spadina Avenue. It is jammed with faces from the Maritimes: crooked teeth, old hair styles, and fashions from the fifties.*

Salty, earthy types who drink a lot of beer and raise a real sweat dancing to good old fashioned music.

CUT TO *several sequences of Joey and Peter dancing and clowning around.*

CUT TO *the men's washroom where the two of them are passing a mickey back and forth. They are both very drunk. Peter sings off key and Joey stands teetering on the verge of falling any second. They discover the French safe machine and put a couple of quarters in. They begin trying to blow them up, laughing hysterically and falling all over the place like a couple of kids. Joey puts his under his jacket like a pair of breasts . . . They burst into another session of hysterical guffaws, then begin trying to burst each others. They both break with loud bangs. Gradually the laughter tapers off.*

    PETER: (*Affectionately*) Joey boy . . . Joey Joey Joey!
    (*Laughs*) Hey how ya doing baby?!

Joey slides slowly down the wall to a sitting position where he sits wearing a silly grin.

    JOEY: You know something Pete . . . You're the best bloody old friend I ever had! You know that now don'tcha?!

Drunken laughter.

Long pause.

    JOEY: (*Maudlin*) I'm going to telephone Bets and tell her how much I love her . . .

    PETER: (*Sourly*) Now what the hell do you want to go and do that for? Can't you leave that broad alone just one night??

    JOEY: (*Shrugs*).

    PETER: You're slipping Joey. That's what it is, you're slipping!

    JOEY: I really love her . . .

    PETER: Oh bullshit!! (*Softer approach*) . . . Listen Betty's a great gal, but we got a lot of things to do buddy boy. Remember all the things we talked about?

    JOEY: (*Nods*).

    PETER: Sure ya do!

    JOEY: (*Quietly*) We're going to get married . . .

    PETER: (*Stunned*) . . . You're what?

JOEY: Yeah, I want you to be the best man.

PETER: What the hell for?! I mean, Christ, Joey we just got here! Three months ago! We ain't even started yet. We haven't done anything!

JOEY: I want to wait. It's her! She's knocked up . . . going to have a kid.

PETER: (*Hushed*) You crazy bastard . . . (*Shaking his head in disbelief*) You crazy bastard.

JOEY: (*Shrugs and tries to rationalize*) We all have to go sooner or later Pete. What the hell . . .

Peter completely loses his composure now, and with his fist smashes at the French safe dispenser on the wall.

Joey sits slumped and cowed like a puppy dog. Peter stands in fuming knotted silence, white with anger. Slowly he pulls himself together, then speaks in a very controlled and precise manner.

PETER: . . . Listen, it ain't too late. So we just . . . go to Vancouver a little earlier, that's all.

JOEY: Huh?

PETER: We take off Joey. She ain't the first dame to pull this kind of stunt just so she can get married! Only we're wise to her and we'll beat her at her own game!

JOEY: But what's going to happen to her, to the kid?

PETER: Lots of dames get knocked up! They got agencies to take care of this kind of stuff! You just gotta stall her.

JOEY: I can't do that.

PETER: You gotta do it! What about us! We made a lot of plans remember?!

JOEY: But this is different . . . I just can't do that. Why don't you go yourself Pete?

PETER: (*Stunned*) . . . Myself?

JOEY: Yeah. I mean it ain't no sense you changing all your plans cause of me.

Peter stands in the doorway trembling. He is fighting to hold back the instinct to cry.

> **PETER:** (*Choked*) . . . Okay. You screw your life up if you want buddy boy . . . Me, I'm on the move. I gotta lot of places to go and things to do and plans see? You think I need you?!

49. Wedding.

> CUT TO *small very inexpensive wedding cake.*
>
> CAMERA PULLS BACK *establishing Joey's wedding reception a few days later. It is a typical brawl in which the men measure their worth by the amount of booze they consume, while the girls huddle together near the buffet of sandwiches, talking on at great length about nothing. Most of the gathering consists of fellows from work and their wives and girlfriends, and Betty's Aunt Ethel and Uncle Art. The old uncle is a legion type, who is acting as M.C. and enjoying every moment of it.*
>
> *The reception is being held in a small storeroom in back of the restaurant where Betty works. An attempt has been made to decorate the room, but soda pop cases, etc. can still be seen stored at one end.*
>
> **UNCLE ART:** (*Clanging his glass with a fork*) Can I have everyone's attention please . . . thank you. I'm ah, Betty's Uncle Art for those that don't know me, and I've been asked to sort of officiate the proceedings. It's not every day I have the chance to do most of the talking . . . (*Few polite chuckles*). Now before you all start filling your faces with food, I'm going to make a toast . . . (*Raising his glass*) To the Bride and Groom, Ladies and Gentlemen.
>
> **EVERYONE:** Here, here!
>
> **UNCLE ART:** And now we'll hear a few words from our best man . . .
>
> **JOEY:** (*Very drunk*) Point of order, point of order!
>
> **BETTY:** (*Embarrassed*) Aw, Joey shut up.
>
> **JOEY:** I have to say a few words!
>
> **BETTY:** (*Pulling at him*) You don't HAVE to.

UNCLE ART: You'll get to say them in a few minutes Joey, but first we're supposed to hear from the best man . . . (*To everyone*) Never seen a groom so anxious!

Chorus of dirty snickers.

PETER: Well I don't have a lot to say (*Cheers*). I hope Toronto will be as good to all us Easterners, as it's been to Joey. So I'd like everyone to join me in a toast to a very beautiful bride, and I hope all their days be as happy as this one.

ALL: Here, here!

After the toast all eyes go to Joey waiting for his response. He sits there in a stupor.

UNCLE ART: Okay Joey, Now you can say your bit!

Laughter.

JOEY: Huh? Oh yeah, right ya are captain!

He wanders up to the front and stands looking out at them briefly. Betty is in agony watching him.

JOEY: Thank you there Peter . . . ah, me and Bets . . . (*Motioning*) Come up here with me Bets!

BETTY: (*Embarrassed*) Oh Joey . . .

CHORUS TOGETHER: Up you go! Go stand there with your husband! Show her who's boss Joey!

Betty reluctantly joins Joey, who puts his arm around her and gives her a good pat on the behind. The group cheers with approval.

JOEY: Isn't she a sweetheart?! . . . I don't have a hell of a lot to say. I know what some of you have been thinking . . . (*Few giggles*). Well let me tell you, I don't mind a bit anybody knowing.

BETTY: (*Embarrassed*) Joey don't.

CUT TO *the pained expression of Peter's face. He shakes his head trying to signal Joey.*

JOEY: No I don't care, I want to say this. It's true we are going to have us a little family — but that is not the reason we are getting married! Me and Bets would have made it anyway, cause that is how we feel for each other!

Becoming emotional, Betty suddenly hugs him, and gives him a kiss. Again we get a chorus of cheers.

UNCLE ART: By golly I think you've said enough! And I don't think I've heard it said better. How about cutting the cake you two?

Joey and Betty are swept over to the buffet table, as everyone gathers around them. One of Betty's maids of honor shoves her up front to get some pictures with her box camera.

CUT TO *Peter watching all of this from the side lines. His only involvement is a loyalty to Joey.*

UNCLE ART'S VOICE: After the cutting of the cake, the bride will go change and there'll be some dancing. And don't everyone stay half the night, because needless to say, our bride and groom will be wanting to get away as soon as possible . . . (*He gives a dirty chuckle*). And we all know why that is, don't we!

General smutty laughter.

CUT TO *Betty in a small room nearby. She has changed from her gown into a simple going away suit, with corsage, etc. Joey enters. He is tipsy and happy to the point of being maudlin.*

JOEY: Howww you doing kid? Heyyy look at you! Mrs. Joey Mills! (*Laughs*).

BETTY: (*Concerned*) Joey you going to be able to drive okay? Look at you.

JOEY: Listen don't worry about the kid here! Hey, come on give us a kiss huh?

BETTY: (*Pulling away*) I don't feel so good. I've been nauseated all night . . .

JOEY: Nauseated? What for?

BETTY: (*Annoyed*) I'm pregnant Joey, remember? It's not like ordinary you know. Everything gets funny inside you . . . and you feel like going and throwing up . . . (*Her eyes fill up*) . . . and why did you go and tell everybody?

JOEY: (*Simple logic*) Listen kid, seven months from now and they're going to know anyway. (*Shrugs*) Now the air's clear, and everything's out in the open.

BETTY: (*Sniffling*) It's just all so . . . It isn't the way I thought it was going to be. I don't even feel married.

JOEY: Hey don't go starting to get all upset now eh? We'll be leaving soon, go to some place where you can lie down. I just got to see Pete for a second.

Joey goes to the door and signals to Peter outside.

PETER: You just about ready to leave?

JOEY: (*Nervously*) Yeah yeah!

PETER: (*Grinning*) Well it's your big night! Tonight you get to do anything you want with it.

Punches him good naturedly.

JOEY: (*Loud laugh*) Ha haaaaaa, Hey ya hear that Betty?! I been filling her up with passion food all week, ain't I!!

Joey's laughter tapers off quickly and he winks to Peter to talk in hushed tones.

JOEY: Say ah . . . how ya fixed? Any money on ya?

PETER: Yeah about twenty bucks I guess.

JOEY: (*Embarrassed*) Yeah well see I kinda blew a little more than I intended on the booze . . . Think ya can spare it?

PETER: (*Quickly*) Sure sure . . . (*Gets out his wallet*).

JOEY: Careful careful, I don't want her knowing. She'll start worrying and everything . . . Thanks Pete . . . (*Pause*) . . . Hey ah, no hard feelings ey?

PETER: Beat it ya Hamburger.

JOEY: (*Coming over and taking Betty's hand*) Come on Bets. Thanks a million Buddy. See ya in about four days!

BETTY: Bye Pete.

They are greeted with loud yells and teasing about why they are leaving so early, etc.

CAMERA HOLDS ON *Peter soberly listening. There is a lost emptiness in his look.*

> **CROWD:** Throw the flowers Betty!! Yeah and you gotta throw her garter Joey!

Laughter and yelling and finally they break into a nostalgic song.

DISSOLVE OUT.

ACT III

50. Blues Montage.

CUT TO *Peter moving along Yonge Street at night. He looks in all the old familiar haunts. But just keeps walking.*

CUT TO *the Edison where all evenings seem to end. He sits at the bar alone, soaking up Country and Western blues. Later we see him coming out of the bar, the last person to leave. He is drunk and still has a chip on his shoulder. He moves up the street rather unsteadily.*

THE BLUES MONTAGE CONTINUES, *with a* SEQUENCE OF SCENES *establishing repetition and the limitations of Peter's life without Joey around.*

DISSOLVE TO *a shabby old house on one of the rundown streets east of Yonge. Peter paces across the street for a long time looking it over. He doesn't like it. He crosses the street and enters.*

CUT TO *a dark hallway crowded with junk. A crying child is heard. There is a musty smell of a dozen suppers cooking. Peter knocks on one of the doors. Betty answers.*

51. Apartment.

> **PETER:** (*Shy*) Hi, how's the bride?
>
> **BETTY:** (*Warmly*) Hi Peter, come on in. (*He enters*) Well it's about time. I told Joey to have you over for dinner two weeks ago.

PETER: Yeah, he mentioned it but, I figured you'd still be getting settled and everything.

BETTY: Come on in, see the place . . .

They enter the living room: a conglomeration of cheap junky furniture and knick-knacks fill every corner. A blanket hides one item from view. Peter slowly scans the setting . . . he feels Betty waiting for approval.

PETER: (*Nodding*) . . . Nice . . . real nice.

BETTY: Oh we're still moving things around, and there's a few things to come yet, but we're getting there.
PETER: Uh-huh . . . Where's Joey?

BETTY: He went down to get some beer. He'll be back in a minute. How you been keeping? Selie says she ain't seen you since the wedding?

PETER: (*Lamely*) . . . I been kind of busy. Meant to give her a call one of these days.

BETTY: Just sit down and make yourself comfortable. I gotta get back to the supper. (*Goes into the kitchen*) . . . Hope you like Kraft dinner?

PETER: (*Wandering slowly about the room examining things and just shaking his head*) . . . Yeah. I make it all the time.

Joey enters carrying a large case of beer.

JOEY: Petie! How's it going man?!

PETER: Oh hi Joey . . .

JOEY: (*The host*) Haven't you got a beer?! Betty?! How come you didn't give Pete a beer??!

BETTY: (*Off*) How can I give him one when you ain't brought them home yet?

JOEY: There's some in the frig still! You think I'd ever let the place go that low, so there ain't even a beer in the house?! (*Laughs*) (*Notices Peter's sour look*) . . . Hey what's the matter.

PETER: Where'd you get all this stuff Joey?

JOEY: (*Proudly*) Saw it on the back of a TV guide. "Five rooms of furniture — $479.00 and change." Not bad eh!

PETER: (*Moans*) Are you crazy? That's a hell of a lot of money.

JOEY: Money??? Who needs money? It's on time. Don't even have to make the first payment until October!

PETER: What's under the blanket?

JOEY: Ahhhhhh, big surprise. First a beer! You're going to need it, when you see this baby!

PETER: (*Big sigh*) Yeah okay. (*Sits heavily on the sofa*) I hope you know what you've done, buying all this stuff . . .

Betty appears from the kitchen; Joey gets a beer for Peter.

JOEY: What'd ya mean?

PETER: Well — it really ties ya down Joey. Getting in so deep so fast. I know, "you got it on time," but sooner or later you still gotta pay for it.

JOEY: Who's worried? I'm working, what the hell!

PETER: Sure, but don't ya see you're stuck in that dumb job now, whether you like it or not? I mean it's okay if you want to go on doing that all your life — piling crates all day, every day.

JOEY: (*Shrugs*) What's the difference? Work's — work. Jeeze I had lot worse jobs than that place. Remember when I had that roofing job back home and the tar kept making me break out in a rash?!

PETER: That's what I'm saying! All these jobs are rotten. You work like an animal and get paid nothing!

JOEY: I don't call $121.50 a week nothing Pete. Who do you know back home clearing that much?

Betty, cooking, listening.

PETER: How much is yours?

JOEY: Alright, $73.46. But with what Bets makes, that ain't bad. We'll do okay.

BETTY: (*Yelling from the kitchen*) Yeah Peter, I think you're kind of nervy telling Joey his job is no good.

PETER: I said all those kinds of jobs are lousy!

BETTY: (*Coming out, angry*) It's the same thing. Joey has to do it for his living. So do you, so I don't know what you're getting so uppy about!

JOEY: Okay Betty, cool it.

BETTY: Well I don't think he should come in here talking like that. You have him over for dinner and right away he insults you!

JOEY: Pete ain't insulting me. He can't help it if he don't like the job.

BETTY: That don't matter. It's my house and I don't want people talking like that!

JOEY: Alright alright! Let's drop the whole thing eh!

Betty goes back inside kitchen.

JOEY: Don't mind Betty. She's a bit up tight. Worried about the kid coming, living on one salary, you know . . . (*Going over to the item under the blanket*) Are you ready for this?! (*Fanfare*) La-ta-ta-taaaaahhhh!! (*Sweeps the blanket off, producing a new console color TV*) HOW ABOUT THAT MANNNN!!

PETER: Jeeze color yet! (*Teasing*) If the folks down home could see Joey Mills now (*Laughs*).

Betty stands in the doorway again.

BETTY: (*To Peter sarcastically*) Yeah, that ain't *so bad* for a guy who *has* to work in a warehouse . . . *Joey* — come on let's eat.

52. Warehouse.

CUT TO *the shocked faces of Joey and Peter and three others at work.*

PERSONNEL MAN: There is usually a slump at this time of the year, however, sales have been down for a considerable period of time, the result being we are forced to make cutbacks throughout the plant. Of course it is our policy in compliance with union agreements, to maintain a seniority system . . .

CUT TO Joey and Peter walking across the grass toward the parking lot. Peter pulls up the "keep off" sign and flings in the direction of the factory.

> **PERSONNEL MAN'S VOICE:** It was on this basis and this alone that you were selected, yourselves being the people employed by us for the shortest period of time . . .

They get into Joey's car and leave the parking area with screeching of tires and a lot of noise.

> **PERSONNEL MAN'S VOICE:** We hope to return to a full time production basis in the not too distant future, whereupon you'll be notified . . . if and when your services are needed.

53. Joey's Flat.

QUICK CUT TO Peter opening two bottles of beer in Joey's flat. The kitchen counter has about ten empties already, and the two of them are feeling quite cocky and confident.

> **PETER:** Screw their bloody job!

> **JOEY:** Right, what the hell! There are lots jobs around. Eddy was saying they were looking for guys at the tire factory just last week!

> **PETER:** They don't hire Maritimers there.

> **JOEY:** Whose a Maritimer? I come from North Bay. No sweat.

> **PETER:** You don't understand, we gotta find something better than these kind of lousy jobs! Who are ya if you're a factory worker? Nobody! Part of the machinery. Things get a little slow, they shut you off for a while . . . Who gives a damn how you're going to make out?! If you've got any money?! I mean just look where this leaves you. You're gonna have a kid soon . . . all this bloody furniture to pay for . . . This is a hell of a mess Joey!

Long pause. Joey sits very depressed now.

JOEY: Maybe we could start our own business.

PETER: What kind of business?

JOEY: Must be a lot of things guys can start up themselves . . . How about a hamburger stand? They do real good!

PETER: That takes too much money.

JOEY: (*Enthusiastic*) I read about this guy the other day, just started collecting junk. Today he's a millionaire, has his own plane, everything! (*Suddenly thinking of something*) Hey wait a minute! (*Goes over and gets a "True Detective" magazine*) Take a look at some of these. "$100.00 a week selling shoes in your own neighborhood!" or this, "Need More Money? A Better Job? A Business of Your Own — 17 Kits Sent to You. Professional Testing Equipment." Electronic stuff huh? Here's one you can make up to $12.00 an hour "Plastic Laminating at Home."

PETER: (*Uninterested*) . . . I dunno Joey, if it was that easy everybody'd be doing it . . . (*Long pause*). Course if you weren't tied down, it would be a breeze. We would just hop in the car and head for the west coast. They're crying for guys on the docks. Sure it's the same kind of work, but they pay a hell of a lot more money! You can afford a layoff . . .

Betty enters.

BETTY: What's going on??

JOEY: Hi hon, me and Pete are just having a couple of brews.

BETTY: Yeah I see that. Why aren't you at work?

JOEY: (*Hedging*) We got off early.

BETTY: (*Sarcastic*) Well there are a lot of things you could help out with around here Joey . . . (*Goes into kitchen*).

Joey looks to Peter.

PETER: You better tell her.

Joey shuts his eyes and sighs. Gets up and walks over to the kitchen doorway.

JOEY: (*Hesitant*) Kind of had some bad luck today Bets. We ah . . . got let off work for a while . . .

BETTY: (*Shocked*) Your job?

JOEY: We didn't get fired, just laid off. Hell, they'll probably call us back in a week or so!

Joey (Paul Bradley) tries to reassure Betty (Jane Eastwood). "We didn't get fired, just laid off. Hell, they'll probably call us back in a week or so!"

BETTY: Joey we can't afford you off work for a couple of weeks. What are we going to do?

JOEY: I'll find something. Don't worry, we'll be okay!

BETTY: Well, you'll have to Joey cause I can't go on working much longer!

JOEY: Take it easy! Me and Pete were just talking about it. There's lots of jobs floating around. Hell we may even go into business for ourselves, eh Pete?!

PETER: (*Evasive*) Yeah well, we were talking about it . . .

BETTY: (*Scoffing*) What kind of business can you guys go into?

JOEY: I told you, we don't know yet! But there's lots of things — lots!

Betty just looks at him. She is very upset and goes into the bedroom. She has made Joey very nervous and he instinctively clings to Peter now.

PETER: I better blow.

JOEY: What's your hurry. She'll be okay. Stick around, have another beer. (*He paces back and forth*).

PETER: (*Peter quietly puts his jacket back down*) . . . Okay. (*He opens two more*).

JOEY: (*Suddenly*) You know what? First thing tomorrow we should go look for a job together! Huh, what do you think?!

PETER: Sure Joey, I'm easy. Maybe you can find us another like you did before.

JOEY: (*Nervous laughter*) Yeah sure, I got us that one without even trying!

PETER: Okay, what time will we meet?

JOEY: Well . . . Listen why don't you just hang around here tonight? Save you going home and us having to meet somewhere in the morning . . . You can sleep on the sofa. Look, it makes out into a bed.

PETER: (*Shrugs*) Okay, sure.

JOEY: (*An idea slowly begins to form in his head*) Heyyyy, wait a minute . . . (*He walks over to the sofa and measures the room with a glance*) I got it! You could move in with us!

PETER: Huh? (*Reluctant*) Well I don't know about that Joey. Look, you're married now.

JOEY: (*Very excited*) Sure come on Pete! Listen it would be great. Living like that together, we could make a go of things! Cut down on expenses — you know, one rent, share food bills! I mean it would only be until things were okay again and everything!

PETER: Well I dunno . . . I guess it would be cheaper alright . . . (*Looking toward the bedroom where Betty is*) . . . But three of us?

JOEY: See what we do is . . . is put a blanket or sheet up . . . and then ah, then you got some kind of privacy. It'll be a little crowded, but there won't be nothing Betty ain't seen already! (*Laughs*) Come on, it'll be a real gas! Like old times, you and me living together again!

PETER: (*Motioning to the bedroom*) What about Betty? I don't think she'll be too hot on the idea.

JOEY: Are you kidding? She'd love to have you!

PETER: Okay, just be sure she knows it's your idea.

54. Joey's Flat — Later.

CUT TO *Peter lying awake in the semi-darkness that night. Joey's and Betty's voices can be heard inaudibly from the bedroom.*

CAMERA MOVES OFF *Peter toward the bedroom. The voices becoming clear as we enter the bedroom.*

BETTY: I said I don't want him here . . . We should be alone.

JOEY: Look we're in a tough spot! Christ it's only for a while! (*Sighs, reaches over to touch her*) Come on now eh . . .

BETTY: Don't.

JOEY: I don't get it? Everything was fine, you said okay. And now you're acting funny like this?

BETTY: You didn't ask me, you came and told me!

JOEY: Look, I promise as soon as things are okay, Pete'll be gone. I swear it.

BETTY: But what good is he going to be? He hasn't got a job either.

JOEY: Pete and me, we've been through a lot of things together — we always make out . . . We all gotta stick together right now.

55. Montage.

CUT TO *the two of them going from factory to factory in the heavy industrial area of the West End.*

CUT TO *them sitting in a small greasy spoon, studying the want ads. They share a cup of coffee.*

CUT TO *Manpower at six a.m. A clerk with a clipboard moves through the group of men huddled in the faint grey of early morning. He selects the day's quota, sends the rest away. Peter and Joey are in the group which is dispersed. They walk away down the quiet empty streets.*

CUT TO *a carwash early in the morning.* CUT TO *Joey and Peter working on the car wash assembly line later that day. They are in the pits where they clean the wheels. Occasionally they communicate to each other concerning the appeal of a certain car, but they must keep working full speed to keep up. It is hard, dirty work, and the noise is almost unbearable.*

DISSOLVE TO *them lying on the grass for a lunch break. There is a long pause as they smoke their cigarettes and savor the rest . . .*

56. Car Wash Lawn.

PETER: How'd we do last week?

JOEY: I figure about 50 bucks between us . . .

PETER: (*Moans*) Gotta do better than that Joey.

JOEY: You're not kidding. The Chink told Betty she has to quit on Saturday. Says she's getting too big . . .

A thin kid wanders over. His hair is greasy and his face covered in pimples.

KID: (*Amused*) You guys look beat. Can't take it huh?

PETER: We can keep up to you anyday.

KID: (*Laughs*) That's a good one! You are the slowest ones on the line! Everybody's gotta wait for you all the time!

PETER: You only have to wait for important people kid!

KID: (*Scoffs*) Hah!! Hey you got a butt?

JOEY: (*Hands him one*) You're one of the steadies ain'tcha?

KID: (*With pride*) That's right.

JOEY: How long you been here?

KID: (*Bragging*) Two years. When I started, I was first one here every morning. Got on every day! I worked the pits for about three months, then I didn't have to go in the pit no more . . . they made me a jock. All the jocks are steadies.

PETER: The rest these guys do this for a living?

KID: Yeah, an other odd jobs: snow clearing in the winter, picking tobacco in the summer, pushing handbills.

PETER: (*Enquiring*) Handbills?

KID: Yeah, you know advertising sheets to all the houses. That use to be a good go, you could dump half of em in the garbage. Now they got all these guys going around in cars watching though . . .

PETER: Where's it at?

KID: You gotta go real early to this place on Dundas. Get there before the winos . . . (*Shrugs*) . . . get a couple of loads you can make yourself seven or eight.

Shop boss comes over.

BOSS: Okay okay we working today?! Let's move it huh!!

Peter gives him the finger.

All the men get up and slowly make their way back to their positions.

57. Rosedale.

CUT TO a quiet residential street in Rosedale: beautiful old mansions, full, lush trees, etc. A van stops letting Peter and Joey off. They wear handbill bags over their shoulders and begin moving up each side of the street depositing circulars in the mail boxes. Joey, wrapped up in his own troubles, moves along in a sluggish depressed manner. Peter is impressed and taken by the surroundings. He is busy peering into every open window, grabbing every opportunity to see how the other half lives. They meet on the corner.

PETER: (*Looking back*) Mannn, will you look at this place Joey! Now these people know how to live! Some of these places must be worth a couple hundred thousand apiece!

JOEY: (*Not impressed*) . . . I guess so . . .

PETER: See that one over there with the limosine in the driveway and everything?! I took a look inside. There's a chandelier hanging in every bloody room! Think of what it would be like living in a place like that Joey!

JOEY: (*Wet blanket*) Lotta upkeep: lawns to mow, hedges, all those flower beds. I hate doing that kind of stuff.

PETER: So does the guy who lives there Hamburger! He's got a gardener, a maid, people to do it for him! He doesn't do anything but live! (*Taking a longing look at it*) You live in a place like that Joey . . . you're somebody. You don't worry about things like money . . . a job. That's what I want.

JOEY: (*Sympathetic*) Pete are you kidding? You ain't never gonna have a place like that. Look at ya!

PETER: (*Defensive*) You mean, YOU ain't never gonna have a place like that!

JOEY: Pete . . . come on. We must of been to every factory in the west end, filled out a hundred application forms. Did anyone call us?

PETER: I ain't interested in factories! You don't get to live in a place like this working in factories!

JOEY: (*Sarcastic*) Huh, then how you gonna do it on 8 bucks a day, delivering circulars?!

PETER: Yeah, well look I happen to know where I can earn 50-60 bucks a day, just like that!

JOEY: (*Doubting*) Where?

PETER: West man — the prairies! They're crying for guys to work the harvest! Someone could make himself a 1000 bucks out there in four weeks! (*Sarcastic*) But little Joey couldn't go, because his Betty wouldn't let him!

JOEY: (*Defensively*) That's bullshit!

PETER: Is it Joey, is it?! Aw come on Joey, I been watching you: you can't go to the can without asking her if it's okay. So don't you tell me! Because it ain't me who got himself in a mess! Look at you — you owe so much money, you don't know which way to turn! You got a kid coming! A kid! That's a real joke! What the hell kind of father are you going to make?!

CUT TO A LONG SHOT *as the two of them start to cross one of the many bridges which span ravines . . .*

JOEY: Don't worry about me. I'll do okay.

They both stop and empty their bags, sending the circulars like confetti over the ravine below.

PETER: Sure you will! One of these days one of those dumb little factories'll call you up and give you another nothing job. But not me. I'm gonna do a hell of a lot better than that!!

JOEY: Okay Pete.

58. Montage.

QUICK CUT TO *the rear of a bowling alley. Peter is dirty and covered in sweat, as he hustles back and forth, between alleys as a pinsetter. The noise is constant, as the balls rumble down, crashing the pins in every direction. The games are finally finished and it is suddenly very quiet. Peter flops back on the walk way and just lies there.*

CUT TO *Peter traveling home on the subway. It is nearly empty at this late hour. A pretty young girl sitting nearby moves, to a seat further away, obviously because of the appearance of him. He scoffs to himself and just looks out the window into the darkness.*

CUT TO *Joey sitting and watching television alone. He drains the last of his bottle of beer, belches, and gets up and gets another from the fridge. He is lethargic with a "could care less" attitude. Peter enters. He is quiet and moody.*

59. Joey's Flat.

JOEY: (*Trying to be chipper*) Hey, how'd she go tonight Pete!

PETER: Okay I guess.

Peter tosses his jacket on his couch, walks over to the fridge, which is practically empty except for a couple of bottles of beer and a carton of milk. He stares at the emptiness . . .

PETER: Is this all we have?

JOEY: Yeah, she's pretty low . . .

Peter takes the last of some bologna, rolls it up and eats it. He walks back over to the couch, draws the blanket closed and flops back.

JOEY: Ain'tcha gonna have yourself a beer?

PETER: . . . maybe later.

Betty comes out of the bedroom. She goes over to Joey. He shrugs, making a face. She walks over to Peter and pulls the blanket aside.

BETTY: Peter you got any money?

PETER: (*Long pause*) . . . couple of bucks.

BETTY: Well there isn't anything to eat.

PETER: I gave you three dollars yesterday. I thought you were going to get some stuff.

BETTY: I did and it's gone . . .

Peter looks over to Joey for some kind of explanation. Joey watches television.

PETER: . . . it's gone?? Gone where??

BETTY: Well you don't get much for three dollars you know . . .

PETER: (*Digging into his pocket and handing her a five*) Well that's it, there isn't any more.

There is a long pause: Betty and Joey watch Peter . . . waiting . . . hoping he has some kind of answer.

PETER: You hear anything from that unemployment office yet?

JOEY: Yeah some letter came today . . . (*Shrugs*) . . . but I don't know what the hell they're talking about . . .

60. Unemployment Insurance Office.

CUT TO *Peter as he steps up to the wicket in the Unemployment Insurance Office the next day.*

CLERK: Yes?

PETER: Yeah, we filled in the application for insurance a few weeks ago, and we get this letter back saying we're not eligible! How come?

CLERK: (*Routine voice*) Let's have a look at it . . . (*Examines it*) Um-hmmm, quite simple: you weren't employed long enough to receive benefits.

PETER: (*Angry*) What're you talking about?! I worked there 4 1/2 months! There's the book, the stamps!

CLERK: You must be employed a minimum of 30 weeks and 25 of them must be within the last 52 weeks period.

PETER: Look, we paid into it and we been layed off! What the hell good is it if we can't get it when we need it?! What do we do now, just go hungry?!

CUT TO *Joey and Betty sitting on a bench nearby.*

Peter storms away from the wicket, yelling back at the clerk.

PETER: This is one hell of a great organization you got here man!!

CLERK: I told you to discuss it with one of the officers . . .

PETER: And I told you to shove it right up!! (*He stops in front of a bewildered Italian who stands watching*) Hey you got 30 weeks huh buddy?! I hope so, cause if you ain't then you're out of luck see!!

The Italian just stands there with his mouth hanging open, as Peter swishes past, and signals Joey and Betty to follow with a gesture of his hand.

61. Joey's Flat — Exterior.

CUT TO *the three of them sitting on the front steps of the house several hours and many beers later. Joey and Peter have their shirts off and wear vacant looks, as they watch the traffic go by. All three of them are very drunk. They have reached such a low, they are now oblivious to their problems. It is typical of the scenes around the slum streets east of Yonge.*

Peter takes a swig of rye and then some beer for a chaser.

PETER: (*Wincing*) Ahhhhhh! Woooo, does that stuff burn going down! (*Shakes his head*).

Joey suddenly bursts into a fit of hysterical laughter. Peter and Betty just stare at him.

PETER: What the hell you laughing at?

BETTY: Yeah what's so funny Joey.

JOEY: (*Struggling to get it out*) I . . I was just thinking of that crazy guy in the unemployment office . . . when Pete told him "If he didn't have 30 weeks, he was outta luck!" Did . . . did you see his face?! (*Convulses with laughter*).

Betty and Peter look at one another bewildered . . . soon Joey's laughter becomes infectious and they are chuckling . . . then laughing . . and soon in hysterics. They are relieving themselves emotionally.

BETTY: Jeeze you're a goof Joey!

JOEY: (*Still laughing*) . . . And that guy! You got him so flustered, he started dancing around like he was gonna pee himself!

PETER: A ding-a-ling! Work or no work, you couldn't give me his job!

JOEY: (*Delighted scream*) That's good, that's good!!

They are all laughing again. Peter and Betty more at Joey than what has been said. Gradually it slacks off . . . and they just sit there again for a while, drinking.

JOEY: Wow, am I hungry! All that laughing really worked me up!

BETTY: We didn't do any shopping remember?

Joey bursts into laughter again.

BETTY: Now what's so funny?

JOEY: You said we couldn't buy no beer remember? So what'd we do? Bought beer and forgot all about food!!

They all laugh.

BETTY: (*Suddenly*) I don't know why I'm laughing. All of us sitting around getting drunk like it don't even matter!

JOEY: Ah, it ain't gonna do no bloody good worrying about it! Gotta have your fun today! Eh Pete?!

PETER: Right right! (*A twinkle coming to his eye*) Hey Joey . . you an me . . we'll go down and do the shopping for Betty huh?!

JOEY: (*Knowing laugh*) Yeah . . yeah okay. Why not. Might be fun.

BETTY: You guys don't know what to get.

JOEY: (*Waving her off*) Relax relax . . you just leave it to us kid. Me and Pete know how to do it . . .

62. Supermarket.

CAMERA TRUCKS ALONG *rows of food in a supermarket — thick juicy steaks, barbecued chicken, etc.* PAN TO *the shopping cart filled to the top with groceries. Joey pushes the cart while Peter reaches at random for whatever meets his fancy. It is very late and the market is almost deserted.*

JOEY: (*Giggling*) Pickled eggs, stuffed olives, shrimps. Artichokes??! Ain't we gonna be living high on the Hog!

PETER: You damn right! Always wanted to try some of this stuff! Might just as well hang for caviar, as hot dogs!

JOEY: Okay okay, take it easy, the bloody cart's full! Just get a couple of bags of them potato chips for Betty and we'll make it!

Peter walks over to the potato chip shelf. He carefully takes in the setting of the store . . . he returns.

PETER: Okay there's only a couple of old women over there and a clerk putting stuff in the shelves way at the back . . . He's just a skinny kid on the cash register, shouldn't be any trouble. After the first cart, you go for the car, and I'll keep him busy after that.

JOEY: Right-oh Pete-oh! (*Giggles*).

Joey heads for the cash register while Peter grabs another cart and begins to pile things in as quickly as possible.

CUT TO *the cash register as it totals $57.83.* CAMERA PULLS BACK *establishing a gawky clerk with thick glasses. He has just finished processing Joey's cart as Peter wheels up.*

CLERK: $57.83 please . . .

JOEY: Huh, oh you shouldn't have totalled it yet. (*Motioning to Peter*) We're together . . .

CLERK: (*Flabbergasted*) Gee all that stuff together??

JOEY: Yeah. Aw look it don't matter. Just bag this stuff and I can start taking it out to the car. Then you can put his through, and he'll settle for everything! (*To Peter*) Be right back Fred . . .

PETER: (*Woodenly*) Okay Art . . .

Joey exits to get the car while the clerk just stands there still amazed.

CLERK: Boy that sure is a lot of groceries!

PETER: Yeah we're having a big party tonight! A loo-ah or low-ah or whatever you call them!

CLERK: (*Nods*) . . . Oh . . .

CUT TO *the outside of the store as Joey pulls up in the car. He gets out leaving the motor running . . .*

CUT TO *the counter where the clerk has bagged everything and starts to put through Peter's cart now.*

PETER: Here let me give you a hand Art.

He and Joey both take an armful. They casually return for another load. The clerk has finished putting the second lot through.

> **CLERK:** Wow, that's a total of $97.16! That's the biggest I've had yet!
>
> **PETER:** Right, catch you in a minute . . .

They exit. The clerk begins to bag the next lot.

CUT TO *the outside as they put the last of the groceries into the back. The motor stops. They both look at one another.*

> **PETER:** The damn thing's stalled! (*Hushed*) Don't panic, just get in and get it started . . .

Joey quickly jumps in. He tries several times but the car won't start. The clerk has stopped bagging the rest of the groceries now and watches them suspiciously.

> **PETER:** Come on Joey, he's getting suspicious!
>
> **JOEY:** (*Frantic*) I'm trying but it won't start!
>
> **PETER:** (*Panic creeping into his voice*) Well keep trying!

The clerk has gone to the doorway now and stands watching.

> **CLERK:** Hey, you better come and pay for this stuff, eh?
>
> **PETER:** Yeah yeah, in a minute! . . . Jooooey?

The clerk starts to come out. The engine sputters, hitting on a couple of cylinders.

> **CLERK:** (*Leery*) What are you guys doing anyway?

Peter leaps into the car.

> **PETER:** Come on move it! Let's go!!

The car moves away chugging and lurching . . . The clerk runs after them yelling to stop.

> **CLERK:** Hey where are you going?!! Stop!!

63. Streets.

CUT TO *the interior of car. Joey is covered in sweat.*

> **PETER:** Joey, you've driven this crate a thousand times, what happened??

JOEY: I don't know! She stalled that's all!

PETER: She stalled?? You stalled it you mean!!

JOEY: I wasn't even near it! I was with you, you saw me!!

PETER: Well you sure as hell did something wrong!! You know what could have happened if you hadn't got it going?!

The clerk keeps running, catches up to the sputtering car, grabs the door handle.

PETER: Christ it's that stupid kid! Move it Joey — move it!!

JOEY: (*Frantic*) I can't! I got it to the floor now! She's still only hitting on about four cylinders!!

PETER: You gotta lose him! He's making enough noise to wake up the whole city!!

JOEY: I can't Pete, I can't!! She just won't go any faster!!

The car sputters, stalls.

The clerk jerks the door open, hollering, indignant.

CLERK: Get out of there! You clowns aren't going to pull a fast one on me!!

He drags Peter out, pummeling him, in a rage.

PETER: Joey!!

Joey jumps out, runs around the car, tries to pull the clerk off Peter.

JOEY: Hey! You bastard!!

But the clerk turns on Joey, swinging wildly. He catches him flush in the face, knocks him down, stunning him.

The clerk and Peter continue to tussle violently, slip to the ground. The clerk is on top, out of control, pounding Peter . . .

PETER: Joey!! Grab his arm!!

Joey gets up, staggers to the car.

PETER: Take him!! Take him!! Take him!!

Joey grabs a tire iron. The kid is still hitting Peter. Joey whacks him, once, hard, on the head.

For a second everything stops. The clerk lies on the ground, not moving.

JOEY: Okay! Come on! Come on!

But Peter remains kneeling over the clerk.

PETER: (*Stunned, gasping*) You stupid dumb kid! What do you care about a couple of lousy groceries!?

JOEY: Come on! Get up!! Come on!

Peter gets up and they both stumble into the car.

PETER: Get in! Go! Go!

They take off, leaving the kid lying on the ground — not moving.

CUT TO *interior of the car. They drive in tense silence, as if neither knows what to say.*

PETER: (*Finally*) What'd you have to go and hit him with that iron for — You see what you did to him?

JOEY: Jesus! He was clobberin' us! Besides, I didn't mean to hit him that hard.
PETER: Stop at the first phone you come to . . .

JOEY: What for?

PETER: So we can call somebody. We can't just leave him laying there. He could die you know.

CUT TO *a phone booth on a dark street.*

PETER: (*On phone*) Yeah, Yeah. He's just laying there in the parking lot. He's hurt pretty bad.

Peter gets back in the car.

PETER: Won't be able to go home tonight — In case somebody got the license number. We'll just hide out for tonight and go back in the morning . . .

Joey just sits there, dazed, shaken.

PETER: Let's go. Let's go. I know a good place down by the lake.

They drive off into the night.

64. Waterfront.

CUT TO *sunrise on the waterfront. The car sits in an ugly industrial area of the waterfront, oil tanks, factories. The rising sun beats on the faces of Joey and Peter, asleep in the car. We see traces of dried blood, remnants of the events of the previous night.*

Joey stirs awake. He pokes Peter. They look at each other.

Nothing is said.

65. Joey's Flat — Exterior.

DISSOLVE TO *Peter moving slowly up the street toward Joey's. He sees something, and stops . . .*

CUT TO *the house while several pieces of furniture sit on the sidewalk. A husky worker comes out carrying another piece. Betty plunges out after him, clawing and punching at him.*

BETTY: (*Screaming hysterically*) Give me that! Give it to meeee!! You bastard! You son-of-bitching bastard!!

MAN: (*Trying to shake her off*) Lady let go!

Joey appears. He tries to grab Betty, who still holds onto the workman.

JOEY: Betty, don't!

BETTY: Stop Him, Stop Him! He's taking everything away!

MAN: (*To Joey*) Mac, will you please get your wife away!

JOEY: (*Pulling her aside*) Betty, Betty come on. It ain't gonna do no good . . .

BETTY: You dirty bastard! Bastarrrd! They're mine! Mine!! (*She bursts into tears, nearly collapsing*).

Joey grabs ahold of her and guides her to the car. She is in a state of shock.

JOEY: Come on now, that's right . . .

BETTY: (*Sobbing*) Joey what are they doing? Where are they taking everything . . . ?

JOEY: (*Trying to soothe her*) Come on, sit in the car now.

Joey places Betty in the car and gets in the other side. He draws her over, holding her and protecting her while she quietly sobs. He just sits watching the workmen bring the things out . . .

CUT TO *Peter coming up the street. He goes over to the car.*

PETER: What the hell's going on?

JOEY: (*Choking up*) They've thrown us out Pete. Yeah no kidding! Just putting us out on the street.

PETER: Whadda ya mean? They can't just throw you out?? How come?

JOEY: (*Ashamed*) I owe them for a long time . . . three months.

PETER: (*Pained*) Oh Christ Joey . . .

JOEY: Pete, I gotta take Betty away from here. Will you stay and watch the stuff . . . ?

PETER: (*Nods*) Yeah yea, go ahead . . .

JOEY: (*Sitting her up*) Bets, come on Hon, I'm gonna take you to your aunt's an uncle's place.

BETTY: (*Still sobbing*) What about all our things Joey . . . ?

JOEY: They'll be okay. Pete'll watch them . . .

BETTY: Don't let them take anything Peter.

PETER: Go with Joey Betty, everything'll be okay.

Joey starts the car and they drive off. Peter walks over to the steps and sits down. The two guys carry out the last of it.

MAN: Come on fellow, you're in the way.

PETER: (*Slowly moving aside*) You like your work?

MAN: I do my job, okay?

They put the stuff down, and get in their car and drive away. Peter sits on the steps watching the cars go by. It is the morning rush hour and hundreds of curious eyes turn his way. Defiantly he stares straight back at them. He walks over to the fridge and takes out a bottle of beer, and opens it. He sits back on the steps to wait for Joey . . . Joey drives up and gets out. He wanders slowly through the furniture, just touching things. He looks very awkward and helpless. Peter just watches him . . .

PETER: . . . How's Betty?

JOEY: (*Frightened*) She's real bad, just keeps crying and talking about the kid coming . . . asking me what we're gonna do. I don't know what we're gonna do . . . ?

PETER: What did you do with the money Joey?

JOEY: (*Shrugs*) Oh how the hell do I know? There were so many things I guess I just used it for something else . . . (*Suddenly frightened*) Christ look at all this stuff! What am I gonna do Pete?!

PETER: (*Shrugs*) I dunno . . . (*To some people who stand curiously watching them*) What's the matter, ain't you ever seen anyone out on the street before?? (*Gets up and walks toward them*) . . . What do you think we are, some sort of freaks or something?! (*He stands challenging, waiting for an answer. They stare back at him with blank faces*) . . . Gowan beat it!! (*He makes a sudden movement and they quickly fan in every direction*). I said move it!! The show's over!!

Slowly they all wander off in their own direction, pausing only to glance back. Peter turns and walks back to Joey who sits on the steps fighting to hold back the tears. The shock of the whole situation has overcome him now and he sits frightened.

JOEY: I guess I should call one of these welfare places huh? (*Breaking down*) God, what am I gonna do Pete?! What am I gonna do?!

PETER: You're forgettin' what the hell happened last night! Come on, pull yourself together! We gotta get outa here. Now! You wanta go to jail over some crummy furniture?! Leave it all behind you! Listen I heard of a guy who'd give you a couple hundred bucks for a color TV like that, no questions asked. That would stake us to the coast! (*Quiet urgency*) Joey Joey you didn't come here to end up like this . . . living in a broken down dump . . . being kicked out onto the street. You gotta have some pride Joey. You ain't good to nobody like this! . . . Betty would be okay. In fact the mess everything's in, she'd probably be better off. Her aunt and uncle will keep her, won't they?

JOEY: I dunno, I guess . . .

PETER: (*Pressing*) Sure they would. Sides it ain't like you're leaving her . . . it's just til you can get something going, some money behind you. Man this is a tough town! . . . So there are other towns. We just gotta find them. You an me. If we stick together we're bound to hit! (*Long wait*) . . . Well?

JOEY: (*Torn between*) I don't know, I don't know . . .

PETER: (*Final*) You gotta man!! You're backed up against a wall! There ain't nowhere else to go!! (*Long pause as these words sink into Joey*) . . . (*Quietly*) It's as easy as just getting into that car Joey . . . Come on! We gotta go!

66. Montage.

CUT TO *the car on the expressway.*

The faces of Joey and Peter, lost in thought, as they drive out of the city.

As they go, images of the city — factories, office towers — give way to images of the snow-covered countryside.

Peter is gesturing, grinning, trying to cheer Joey up, although we can't hear what he's saying. Joey, however, still seems dazed, disconsolate.

Peter persists, finally elicits a trace of reaction from Joey.

And the car continues on — down the road.

MON ONCLE ANTOINE

BY CLEMENT PERRON
Translated by Wayne Grady

I can think of no better way to introduce this screenplay than to say that it wouldn't surprise me in the least if certain scenes from *Mon oncle Antoine* have become as indelibly inscribed in my memory as are the older ones that actually inspired the film. Writing this screenplay was my first important attempt at bringing back to life the various and problematical events that made up my native village. East Broughton, Beauce County, Quebec, situated in the province's asbestos-mining region, was a sort of company town. It was run by a single man — the mine owner, always an Anglophone — who held sway over a group non-unionized workers, many of whom suffered, as an extra bonus, from a deadly industrial disease, asbestosis. This screenplay was written, however, in the late 1960s, before the famous revelations from Mount Sinai Hospital concerning that terrible disease.

Fortunately I had, at the time, enough maturity, recollection, and information to identify dramatically the long, complicated, quasi-epic journey that was my adolescence. This story came directly out of my life, and the magic of its director, Claude Jutra, did the rest. The film's reception in many countries confirms, if confirmation were needed, the universality of the themes it explores. In a single day — an ever memorable Christmas Eve — young Benoît discovers suffering, death, and the multiple traps of love, revolt and, ultimately, submission. In this cinematic monograph, if I can call it that, the authenticity of the characters and situations stands as their benevolent trade mark, and the fact of their having been ground up by life confers on them, brought together in one story as they are, a sort of undistorted aspect.

Meeting the cinematist Claude Jutra was, for me, an unforgettable event. The year was 1968, a watershed year around the world and from many points of view. It was a very special year for me, too.

Clément Perron

MON ONCLE ANTOINE

1. Title and Credits.

Superimposed over images of Quebec's asbestos-mining district, followed by the following inscription:

> Somewhere in Quebec's asbestos region,
> not too long ago.

2. Exterior. Day. Autumn.

A schoolyard. Children playing as they would anywhere in the world. The sun is behind us, and its light seems weaker than natural.

3. Exterior. Day. Autumn.

A sparse stand of spruce trees above which rises a strange sort of mountain; at its summit, a gigantic conveyor pours out a continuous stream of white powder that spreads and, flake by flake, forms the mountain itself. The local people call it "the dump."

Near a sharp drop, a small red truck backs up and stops dangerously close to the edge. The driver, Jos Poulin, gets out. Mario, his young helper, remains in the truck looking nervous. Jos raises the hood and leans in to inspect the engine.

JOS: Goddamn son-of-a-bitchin' clutch! I told them to fix this thing two fucking months ago. Jesus Christ! For two cents I'd push this shit-box of a truck over the side and leave it there.

Jos lies down on the ground and slides under the truck to get a better look at the gearbox.

JOS: Hey, Mario!

> **MARIO:** Yeah?
>
> **JOS:** Gimme the wrench, will you?
>
> **MARIO:** We don't have one.
>
> **JOS:** Well, a piece of pipe, anything. Everything's covered in grease down here, I can't see a goddamned thing.
>
> **MARIO:** Okay, okay.
>
> **JOS:** No one ever cleans anything around here. And they call themselves a maintenance department.
>
> **MARIO:** Watch it, Jos. Here comes the boss.
>
> **JOS:** Tell him to go eat shit.

A car stops beside the truck and a man gets out. He's tall, strong-looking, very aggressive. He speaks English.

> **FOREMAN:** Hey, Joe, are you crazy, you stupid fool? What's the matter with you. You want this truck to roll over the edge? It's gonna go down the dump, I told you a hundred times. Hey! Jos Poulin! Get up out of there!

Despite the order, Jos continues working under the truck. Mario prudently gets back into the truck and closes the door.

> **JOS:** Look at all this shit. Call themselves a goddamned maintenance department.
>
> **FOREMAN:** Look at that!

Jos grips the bumper and pulls himself out from under the truck. He stands up and looks defiantly at the foreman, who has been his boss for many years.

> **FOREMAN:** Hey, Joe, what's the matter with you? You gotta understand . . . . It's not my truck. It's the company's property, and you know . . . I've got my job to do, that's all . . .

Turning away from him, Jos drops the hood back into place, gets into the truck and starts it up. Mario looks at him anxiously. The foreman makes a menacing gesture at them:

> **FOREMAN:** I'm telling you for the last time, Jos. Do you understand . . . ? The last time . . . !

>   JOS: (*To himself*) You could be more right about that than you know.

By now the truck is rumbling down the slippery incline.

>   MARIO: What'd he say, anyway?
>
>   JOS: (*Sarcastically*) How should I know? I don't speak English.

4. Exterior. Day.

The truck leaves the road to the dump and turns onto an asphalt highway. High above it, the conveyor belt continues to make its eternal hill of white asbestos.

5. Interior. The Living Room of a House.

A corpse is lying in an open coffin, and a priest in a white surplice is administering the last rites. Several relatives are watching the ceremony. At the foot of the coffin, Antoine, the village's funeral director, is admonishing Fernand, his assistant, whose attention is wandering.

>   ANTOINE: Your hat . . . Fernand, your hat!

Snapping out of it, Fernand holds his hat properly in front of him. The priest finishes his oration and hands the prayer book to one of the two choirboys standing beside him. Then he turns to the other and holds out his hand, as though waiting to be given something. This boy has also drifted off. The priest nudges him with his elbow, and the boy hands him an aspergillum. The priest shakes it mechanically above the body, then leaves the room, followed by the deceased's family. A woman hangs back and makes a final sign of the cross, and before she is even out of the room Fernand begins taking down the decorations. Benoît, one of the two choirboys, stays in the room. The funeral director turns to him:

>   ANTOINE: Shut the door, Benoît.
>
>   BENOIT: Yes, Uncle.

Benoît closes the door and watches Antoine and Fernand go about their business. Apart from the corpse, there are just the three of them left in the room. Antoine takes off his suit jacket and gets to work.

6. Interior. Kitchen.

Family members are offering their condolences to the widow. The priest goes up to the her and shakes her hand ceremoniously.

>**PRIEST:** Madame Vachon, Euclide was a good Christian, as everyone in the village will tell you. They have offered fifteen High Masses and twenty-five Low Masses. After that, you'll be able to rest easy.

The widow sits wearily down on a chair. Someone brings her a plate of cold-cuts. Maternally, she turns to her youngest son and straightens his tie.

7. Interior. The Living Room.

Antoine is taking down the decorations and undressing the body. The coffin is still open. Fernand is examining the row of cards arranged along the sideboard.

>**FERNAND:** Hey, psst . . . listen to this one: Oscar Moisan, one Low Mass . . . (*Slyly*) I guess he couldn't stand the guy.

He laughs. While Fernand goes on looking at the cards, Antoine takes the crucifix and wreaths down from the wall. Fernand picks up another card.

>**FERNAND:** Oh, here's a good one. The widow Théodore Pelletier, one three-dollar High Mass. We can figure out why, eh? Ha-ha!

This is the first time Benoît has taken part in a funeral service. Fernand gives him a conspiratorial wink and goes on reading.

>**FERNAND:** The women of the congregation of Sainte-Anne . . .
>
>**ANTOINE:** (*Interrupting him*) Enough clowning around, Fernand. The priest is waiting for us.

Fernand takes his time getting back to work, humming to himself. Antoine tries to remove a rosary that is threaded through the fingers of the dead man. It proves to be a difficult job.

>**ANTOINE:** Here . . . Fernand, wake up. Take this.

He passes the rosary to Fernand, then unfolds a winding-sheet that

Fernand hands to him. Carefully, Antoine grabs the lapels of the suit jacket on the body and lifts. Everything comes off in one piece: jacket, shirt, collar, tie, sleeves, etc. It was all a false front, which they take off this body to be ready for the next one. Benoît looks on, fascinated. Fernand is now whistling merrily. Antoine is becoming impatient.

    ANTOINE: Stop it, Fernand. You're giving me the willies.

With an exaggerated shrug, Fernand stops whistling.

    FERNAND: Sorry.

Embarrassed by the naked body, Benoît hides his eyes behind his prayer book. Antoine and Fernand set the lid on the coffin and begin screwing it in place. After a moment, Benoît looks up cautiously.

When their work is finished, the three of them get ready to leave. Benoît stops them at the door.

    BENOIT: (*Maliciously*) Fernand, your tie is crooked.

Fernand stops to straighten his tie. Antoine has had enough.

    ANTOINE: Fernand! That's enough!

8. Interior. Day. A Small Rural Tavern.

A table covered with beer bottles: all quarts, all empty. The tavern is nearly empty, as well, and looks forlorn. In one corner, a customer is playing an old song on a badly tuned piano.

9. Interior. The Washroom of the Tavern.

Jos Poulin is relieving himself at a urinal while reading the usual sad but humorous grafitti that graces the walls: Duplesis Can Kiss My Ass; Yvette Loves It; Lucette, Janine, Rita, Laurence's Cat House. *There are also a few telephone numbers, some crude drawings of male and female sexual organs; and a greatly simplified portrait of Adolph Hitler.*

10. Interior. Tavern. Day. (Same as Scene 8).

Jos comes out of the washroom, returns to the table, and sits down with his cronies.

JOS: What are you talking about now? You're still going on about Euclide!

FIRST CRONY: Yeah, well, he died kind of sudden, all the same.

JOS: Oh, for Christ's sake, he's been working in the pit for the past twenty-five years. You call that sudden? It's gonna happen to all you guys too, one of these days. You look like a bunch of cadavers already.

SECOND CRONY: Not me, that's for sure.

JOS: Me either, you can bet your life on that.

Jos picks up his quart and pours the rest of his beer into his glass.

JOS: Well, there's another one the English won't get. They can all kiss my ass! The fucking English, Euclide, the bloody embalmer, the priest, the fucking foreman, the whole goddamn bunch of 'em. I'm getting the hell out.

He looks around the table defiantly.

FIRST CRONY: If you go off one more time, Jos, you know damn well they won't take you back at the mine again.

Jos bangs his glass down on the table in anger.

JOS: The mine can go fuck itself. I've spent my whole life kissing ass at that fucking mine. I'm fed up, and I'm fucking off. Hey, Gus, how much do I owe you?

Without waiting for a reply, he stands up and tosses a bill on the table.

JOS: There . . . Keep the change. So long!

He leaves. The piano continues to play. Through the window, a small white church rises over a motionless landscape that seems frozen in time.

11. Interior. Stable. Day.

A bare stable with three thin cows lined up in their stalls. Jos Poulin is leaning lazily against a wall while he does the chores. The sound of milk being poured from one pail to another, of rubber boots walking through straw. Then the cadence of two alternating jets of milk hitting a pail.

> **MADAME POULIN:** There's the housework . . . and the chores . . . ? Who's going to do those every morning?

She speaks slowly, but her voice is charged with anger.

> **MADAME POULIN:** And what about the children? You won't see them for six months . . .
>
> **JOS:** I can't do it. I've gotta get away. (*Pauses*) I'll be back in the spring.

They don't look at each other, each of them absorbed in their separate problems.

> **MADAME POULIN:** As usual . . . ! It's always you who gets to make these decisions.

Exasperated, Jos throws down the straw he's been playing with and leaves the stable.

> **MADAME POULIN:** Jos . . .

12. Interior. Barn. Day.

Jos' wife catches up with him as he is about to open a large door to go outside. She holds him back, and he turns toward her. She looks imploringly at him. She opens the collar of his shirt and rubs her hands along his skin. Moved, Jos takes his wife's face in his hands and looks into her eyes. A kind of smile passes between them. Gently, he leads her to a corner of the barn, where they lie down on a pile of straw and, in a bright ray of sunlight, begin to make love.

13. Exterior. Day. House and Yard.

Through the front window we can see Madame Poulin, her face unmoving, unyielding. Outside, Jos looks at her, his lumberman's axe on his shoulder. It is a form of leave-taking. Then he turns and walks resolutely away. He is obviously in a hurry. His only luggage is a cloth bag which he carries over his shoulder.

14. Exterior. Day. Autumn. A Country Road.

When Jos reaches the main road, he sees his five children — four boys between the ages of eight and sixteen, and one fifteen-year-old girl. The two younger boys are sitting in a miniature horsecart pulled by a small horse.

    ONE OF THE KIDS: 'Bye, Dad.

    JOS: Goodbye, kids.

Jos walks shyly up to his oldest son, Marcel, and tries to explain why he is leaving.

    JOS: Look. I'm going up to the lumbercamp. You'll have to look after things while I'm gone. Give your mother a bit of a hand, eh?

Jos begins to walk away. Marcel falls in beside him.

    JOS: I've gotta go, you understand that, eh? I've had it with that mine. Up at the camp it's . . . different. Quiet. The woods . . . snow . . . no boss on your back all day.

A delivery cart rumbles by along a cross-road, and a box of groceries falls off the tailgate. The children quickly dash over and pick it up.

    A CHILD: Hey, Dad! It's a case of beans!

Jos stops, turns around, and laughs.

    JOS: Bring it in to your mother. You'll be eating beans for a week!

The children laugh with him and lift the box onto their own cart. Jos and Marcel start walking again, but after a few steps the boy stops.

    MARCEL: I'll go back with the others.

Jos stops and looks his son in the eye.

    JOS: Listen. Next year I'll send you to college, okay?

He puts his hand on Marcel's shoulder. The boy doesn't seem to understand.

    MARCEL: I don't know . . .

There is nothing more to be said.

JOS: Goodbye, son.

They both turn and walk off in different directions. The other children are already a long way off, but the youngest turns and takes a few steps toward his father.

YOUNGEST SON: Bye, Daddy!

JOS: Goodbye, Serge.

Serge turns back and joins the others, and together they walk off into the autumnal countryside. The scene is calm, but filled with sadness.

15. *Exterior. Early Morning. Winter.*

The land is covered with snow; the sky is an unbroken white surface on which are etched the thin black outlines of fir trees. In the background rise the smoking mountains of asbestos, which now look like huge glacial volcanoes spitting out cinders. The miners are on their way to work. The factory siren barely disturbs the silence; the church bells, ringing out the hour, are muffled by the snow. Their sound is somehow reassuring. It is eight o'clock. Benoît is seen entering the church through the side door.

16. *Interior. Early Morning. Church Vestry.*

Benoît is late. He takes off his winter coat and yawns. His right arm is in a cast, but it hardly impedes his movements. He goes to the cupboard and takes the ciborium, from which he takes one of the hosts from it and, imitating a priest, raises his eyes to heaven before placing the flat, white wafer in his mouth and eating it. Then he takes a bottle of holy wine from the cupboard and washes down the wafer with a drink from it. He barely has time to replace the bottle before the priest enters. The priest seems in a bad mood.

BENOIT: Good morning, Father.

PRIEST: Morning.

17. *Interior. Church. Morning.*

Low mass on an ordinary weekday. Benoît's heart doesn't seem to be in it.

He gives the responses distractedly, by rote. Whenever the priest turns his back, Benoît takes a piece of string out of his pocket and plays with it, or carves a notch in the railing with his pocket knife.

18. Interior. The Door between the Vestry and the Main Part of the Church.

After the mass, as he leaves the vestry, Benoit sees the priest taking a long drink from the bottle of holy wine. With a smile, unseen by the priest, Benoît lifts his hand in benediction. Then, climbing up on a pew, he leaves the church by hopping from one pew to the next until he reaches the door.

19. Exterior. Day. Winter.

Benoît is racing along the main street of the village. He is very happy, for he is going to work in the general store owned by his Uncle Antoine. It is a sort of privilege.

Director Claude Jutra discusses a scene with Benoît (Jacques Gagnon) and Antoine (Jean Duceppe).

20. Exterior. Day. Winter.

Shivering with cold, the regular clerk, Fernand, arrives at the front door of the store, takes out a huge ring of keys, and unlocks the door.

21. Interior. Day. The Main Room of the Store.

The room is in semi-darkness because the curtains are still closed. Fernand begins to get the store ready for the day. Antoine's wife, Cécile, still in her nightgown, comes down the stairs. She doesn't see Fernand, and when he turns on the lights she jumps.

    CECILE: Fernand?

    FERNAND: Good morning, Madame Cécile.

    CECILE: You're here early.

    FERNAND: We have a lot of work to do this morning. The decorations aren't finished. We still have the window to do, and the crèche . . .

    CECILE: Oh yes, that's right. Would you please hand me a box of tea. We've run out upstairs.

    FERNAND: What kind do you want? We have all the popular brands. Lipton, Salada, Red Rose . . .

    CECILE: Come on, Fernand, hand it over. Salada, Salada.

    FERNAND: Excellent choice, Madame.

Fernand slides backwards over the counter and holds the box of tea out to Cécile, but just out of her reach. She is not amused by his teasing.

    CECILE: Fernand . . . !

He pretends to be sorry. She notices something on the floor.

    CECILE: What's that?

    FERNAND: A keg of nails. It came in yesterday.

Fernand kicks at the small barrel on the floor at the foot of the stairs. It seems quite heavy.

    CECILE: Well, I'm going up for breakfast.

FERNAND: See you later. Have fun.

Cécile goes back upstairs. She is still a very attractive woman. Fernand watches until her slippers disappear onto the second floor. Then the door opens and Benoît comes in.

FERNAND: (*In a nasty tone*) Well, look who's here.

BENOIT: Good morning, Fernand.

FERNAND: See that keg of nails, Benoît? It has to go up to the storeroom right away.

BENOIT: You could at least say good morning.

FERNAND: Good morning. Now take the keg upstairs.

BENOIT: (*Raising his hand*) I can't. I've got a cast on my arm.

FERNAND: Excuses, excuses.

Fernand busies himself behind the counter. When Carmen comes down the stairs, he turns toward her.

FERNAND: Well, if it isn't the little clerk who thinks she's a princess!

CARMEN: You're the little clerk, Fernand.

Carmen is about thirteen years old, dressed in a bathrobe and still sleepy. Like Cécile, she is looking for something for breakfast. She goes up to one of the shelves.

CARMEN: You didn't get any jam?

FERNAND: What's that look like? Chopped liver?

CARMEN: I don't like that kind. I like Raymond's.

FERNAND: You could at least say good morning to Benoît.

BENOIT: (*Matching the words with the gesture*) Good morning, my beauty.

CARMEN: . . . same to you! (*To Fernand*) Okay, give me the jam, but get some Raymond's in, okay?

She tries to go back upstairs, but Benoît blocks her way. She feints to go around him and then ducks under his arm.

FERNAND: You're coming back down to help Benoît, right?

CARMEN: (*On the staircase*) If I feel like it.

Benoît is ready to start work.

BENOIT: What do I do?

FERNAND: All this . . . the decorations . . . there are some lights over there. And some garlands. A few of these presents, some wrapping paper. Spread it all around the store, and when you're finished give me a shout.

BENOIT: Okay, boss, I'll get right to it!

22. Interior. Fernand's Office.

Fernand enters the small, windowed room at the back of the store. He sits down at his desk and, taking out his account book, starts his accounts. In the background, Benoît holds up a box of Christmas bulbs.

BENOIT: Some of these are broken.

FERNAND: So throw them out.

Cécile can be heard humming to herself. Fernand turns and sees her sitting in her own small office, doing her own accounts. Slipping his pencil behind his ear, he takes his book and joins her.

23. Interior. Cécile's Office.

Cécile is surprised to see him. Defensively, he explains:

FERNAND: I just came in to do my books.

CECILE: What's wrong with your own office?

FERNAND: (*Slyly*) Too much noise.

Cécile says nothing. Fernand sits down. She tries to concentrate on her work, but he makes his presence felt by turning pages and adding up his columns out loud.

FERNAND: Two and two are four and three are seven and two are ten, carry the one . . . .

She interrupts him with a reproachful voice:

    CECILE: Fernand!

    FERNAND: (*With false sincerity*) Oh, sorry.

They go back to work. Fernand mumbles to himself quietly, which is even more irritating than before. He turns a page . . . taps the desk with his pencil . . . his thoughts are clearly elsewhere. He wants Cécile to look at him. He whistles between his teeth. Finally, she looks up.

    CECILE: What's the matter?

    FERNAND: I was just looking at your dress. It's very pretty.

    CECILE: Do you think so? (*Falsely modest*) This old thing?

She goes back to work. She tries to sit up straight, but her near-sightedness forces her to lower her head closer and closer to her book until her nose is practically touching the paper. Fernand lowers his head as well, to get a better look at her face.

    FERNAND: Have you considered getting glasses?

    CECILE: (*Annoyed*) Who, me? No!

She lowers her nose to the book.

24. Interior. The Store.

Antoine, the last to get up, descends the staircase in his stocking feet, wearing pants, braces, and longjohns and not completely awake yet.

    ANTOINE: Isn't anyone here this morning?

    BENOIT: I'm here, Uncle.

Benoît jumps up like a jack-in-the-box from behind the counter.

    ANTOINE: Why hasn't anyone taken these nails up to the storeroom?

    BENOIT: I can't. I've got this cast on my arm.

    ANTOINE: Where's Fernand?

    BENOIT: I haven't seen him.

    ANTOINE: What about your aunt?

BENOIT: Her either.

ANTOINE: (*Grumpily*) Aaaaaah! Another day off to a good start!

He waddles over to the bottom of the stairs and disappears toward the back of the store. Benoît removes a plastic reindeer from its wrapping and holds it up against the wall to study the effect.

25. Interior. Cécile's Office.

Cécile and Fernand are still doing their accounts. She begins to hum an old song.

CECILE: Are you sleeping, are you sleeping,
Brother John, Brother John?

Fernand picks up the line and repeats it as Cécile sings the next one.

FERNAND: Are you sleeping, are you sleeping,
Brother John, Brother John?

So that they are singing a round together:

CECILE AND FERNAND: Morning bells are ringing,
Morning bells are ringing,
Ding, ding, dong,
Ding, ding, dong.
Are you sleeping, are you sleeping,
Brother John, Brother John?
Morning bells are ringing,
Morning bells are ringing,
Ding, ding, dong.
Ding, ding, dong.

Boldly, Fernand tickles Cécile's hand with his pencil.

CECILE: . . . Good heavens, Fernand! What's gotten into you this morning?

FERNAND: (*Brightly*) Anyway, those figures just don't add up at all. Look at them: they come to more than thirty dollars and fourteen cents.

CECILE: What are you talking about?

Fernand's change of tone has been caused by Antoine, who has just entered the office. Cécile hasn't noticed him.

FERNAND: There must be a bill missing somewhere. Look around. Check the figures yourself.

CECILE: Fernand, what's the matter? I don't understand a word you're — (*Jumping*) Oh! Good lord, Antoine, you scared me.

Cécile is short of breath. Slouching back in a chair, Antoine enjoys the the commotion he has caused. Cécile quickly regains her composure and begins to treat Antoine as if he were in the wrong.

CECILE: Look at you, Antoine. Not dressed at this hour of the morning. Don't just sit there like that. You know how much work we have to do today. We have to call the tinsmith, we have to bring the vegetables up from the root cellar . . .

Antoine remains unmoved by this flood of words. Cécile pulls him up and drags him out of the office. Fernand pretends to ignore the goings-on and to be concentrating on his account book.

FERNAND: It can't be thirty dollars and fourteen cents. There must be another bill around somewhere. I *know* it!

26. Interior. The Store.

Carmen and Benoît are fooling around. Carmen gets the better of Benoît because of the cast on his arm. Antoine enters, dragging his feet.

ANTOINE: Come on, you kids. We've got to get this stuff up.

BENOIT: Hello, Uncle. Did you find Aunt Cécile?

ANTOINE: Yes. Thirty years ago.

Aunt Cécile herself enters.

CECILE: What's going on in here? You're not working? Do I have to do everything myself? Please, Antoine, get a move on. We have to open the presents, get out the crèche, put up the tree, hang the bells. Come on, now. We've got to hurry!

>   **ANTOINE:** (*Insinuatingly*) You weren't in such a big hurry a few minutes ago, eh?

Cécile brings a box up from under the counter and puts it down with a scornful thump.

>   **CECILE:** I can't find the figurines for the crèche.
>
>   **ANTOINE:** (*Sarcastically*) Be careful with the Virgin Mary! She breaks easily.
>
>   **CECILE:** Where's the Baby Jesus?

Enter Fernand.

>   **ANTOINE:** Here comes the Holy Ghost. Why don't you ask him? He seems to know a lot.
>
>   **CECILE:** Come on! Let's get busy . . .
>
>   **ANTOINE:** I think I'll go into the office. I have some things to do there.
>
>   **CECILE:** (*Sarcastically*) Why don't you do them here!

Antoine shrugs his shoulders and moves off. Fernand signals to Benoît to come and help him, and everyone begins to look busy.

27. Exterior. Day. Winter. A Field near the Village.

It is snowing, windy, and cold. Madame Poulin, with three of her children, is cutting down a small, meager-looking Christmas tree.

28. Exterior. Day. Winter. The Bush.

Jos Poulin is swinging his axe at the trunk of a huge pine tree.

29. Interior. A Bedroom in the Poulin's House.

Marcel, the oldest Poulin boy, is lying sick in bed. He has a high fever, and he's breathing with difficulty. His eyes look haunted.

30. Exterior. Day. Winter. The Bush. (Same as Scene 28).

Jos chops furiously at the tree.

31. Exterior. Day. A Field of Snow.

To the great delight of the children, Madame Poulin succeeds in bringing down the little tree. They begin to drag it toward the house. Madame Poulin steps in a hole in the snow and falls down: the children find this extremely funny. Then the daughter comes out onto the porch and shouts:

DAUGHTER: Mom . . . Marcel is sick . . .

Mme Poulin lets go of the tree and hurries toward the house. The children, unaware of her anxiety, run after her laughing and playing.

32. Interior. The store.

Carmen brings Benoît an armload of boxes.

CARMEN: Here, Benoît, you have to put these sweaters on the shelf.

BENOIT: These are girls' sweaters. I don't have to touch girl's sweaters, do I? (*Looking at her more closely*) What's that you've got all over your face?

Carmen looks at herself in a mirror. She has tried to put on some makeup, without much success.

BENOIT: Idiot! I thought you were crazy before . . .

Disappointed by the effect of her effort, Carmen runs to the washroom to scrub the makeup off her face. Sitting on the counter, Fernand lights a cigarette. When Carmen comes out of the washroom, he pats her behind.

CARMEN: (*Greatly offended*) Stop that!

Fernand leers at her lecherously.

33. Interior. The Store.

Cécile is in a better mood. She is busy at the fabric counter, humming "Are you sleeping" quietly to herself.

Benoît is perched at the top of a step-ladder. Carmen is removing artificial flowers from a cardboard box and handing them up to him. Benoît takes them and hangs them from a silver paper bell.

BENOIT: How many more have you got?

CARMEN: Seven.

She removes them delicately, one at a time. Then she places one of them in the opening of her blouse, like a corsage. Fernand is watching from a distance. They exchange a conspiratorial glance. Benoît suspects nothing. He reaches behind him for the last flower. Thinking he is touching the flower, he touches Carmen's breast. He withdraws his hand quickly, as if he had burnt it. The others laugh. He is upset, happy, shy. The only way he can think of to regain his masculine dignity is to insult Carmen. He touches his forehead with the flower and looks at her disdainfully.

BENOIT: You're crazy in the head, you.

FERNAND: Watch yourself, Benoît. You might break your other arm. Or something else . . .

34. Interior. The Windowed Office.

Thinking he is unobserved, Antoine takes a bottle out of the desk and pours himself a drink. As he raises the glass, he sees Benoît watching him reproachfully through the window. But he drinks anyway. Benoît turns away and goes to help Fernand, who has called him.

35. Interior. Store Window.

Fernand has strung up a bed sheet to act as a curtain, as if the window were a theater.

FERNAND: We're going to try this curtain to make sure it works okay.

BENOIT: What do you want me to do?

FERNAND: Pull it open. You're the one who has to do it.

Benoît pulls it open.

FERNAND: Not now, you idiot! Wait till I tell you! (*Muttering to himself*) Little jerk . . . !

Fernand goes outside to view the window as a spectator.

FERNAND: (*Shouting*) Okay, go!

Benoît yanks on the cord. The curtain opens. Everything works well.

FERNAND: (*Shouting*) Good! Now close it!

Benoît closes the curtain. Fernand comes back inside.

FERNAND: Perfect! Now that's what I call a window display. Get that ladder out of there.

36. Interior. Store Window.

The crèche is almost in place. Carmen is spreading artificial snow over it.

CECILE: No no, don't put the snow on yet. Wait till I get the Baby Jesus in place. I think I'll put Joseph over here . . .

CARMEN: Madame Cécile, I want to move the bulls. Can I put them over here?

CECILE: Yes, that's a much better place for them. You've got a good eye, Carmen. Okay, the Virgin Mary . . . and the Baby Jesus here in the center. I think the crèche looks lovely, this year.

CARMEN: The Baby Jesus doesn't look very good.

CECILE: No, he's the only one who doesn't. But what can we do. He's been through a lot. Someone dropped him last year. But it doesn't matter. He's too small for anyone to notice. All in all, I think it looks pretty good.

They put the final figurine in place and stand back to admire their masterpiece.

37. *Interior. Windowed Office. (Same as Scene 34).*

Antoine is still sitting at his desk. Cécile walks in humming.

ANTOINE: What are you looking for?

CECILE: Some sticky paper.

ANTOINE: It's right there, where it always is.

CECILE: Ah!

She finds the paper and begins to unroll it loudly, with great flourishes.

ANTOINE: Need any help?

CECILE: No, I can manage.

While she works, Antoine takes out his bottle and refills his glass. She sees him.

CECILE: Don't I get some?

ANTOINE: Oh, by all means . . . Excuse me.

He takes out a second glass and fills it. They touch glasses and drink.

CECILE: Not bad.

ANTOINE: I've always said it does a person good.

Another drink. They both smile.

ANTOINE: (*Gently*) You're wearing your brooch?

CECILE: Yes, I thought it would look good with this dress. And I shortened it, too. I still have good legs, don't I?

ANTOINE: Of course you do. You know you're not what I would call ugly, eh? Wife of mine?

CECILE: (*Slightly embarrassed*) Oh, stop.

Antoine pulls her gently toward him and kisses her on the cheek. From a distance, Benoit watches them through the window. Cécile begins to return her husband's kisses.

CECILE: And you're not exactly what I would call an old man, either.

ANTOINE: (*Pretending to be gruff*) Old man, old man. You wouldn't mind having an old man for a husband, would you?

CECILE: (*Serious*) No . . . no . . .

ANTOINE: Old . . . . ! Yes . . . ?

They continue kissing.

ANTOINE: Here . . . Let's have another drink.

CECILE: (*Reluctant*) It's stronger than I thought.

ANTOINE: It won't hurt you. It'll warm you up.

CECILE: I'm not used to it.

ANTOINE: Here . . . it'll help you relax.

CECILE: Is that what I need to do?

ANTOINE: Hmmm . . .

They joke as they kiss.

38. Interior. Store.

Fernand, walking through the store with a huge garland in his arms, trips over the keg of nails.

FERNAND: Goddamn nails!

He begins to lose his temper, but Benoît shushes him, pointing to Antoine and Cécile in the office. The two of them watch the couple affectionately. Then Fernand notices the calendar, which still shows December 23. Humming "Are You Sleeping," he changes the date: it's Christmas Eve.

39. Exterior. Day. Winter. A Schoolyard.

Children running out of school, shouting joyfully. Christmas holidays have begun.

40. Interior. Mine Office.

The miners punch out their time cards and collect their paycheques.

THE PAYMASTER: Merry Christmas. Don't drink it all, eh?

41. Exterior. Day. Village.

The villagers have begun to celebrate the holidays. In the middle of the village, mineworkers and schoolchildren alike jostle each other playfully, roll in the snow, wrestling, laughing, and shouting. Snowballs fly through the air.

42. Exterior. Day.

A small crowd of curious onlookers has gathered in front of the store window. For the moment, they can see nothing but the blank curtains. Antoine peeks around one end to see how big his audience is. He seems satisfied. He comes out of the store and takes his place among the crowd. Everyone greets him.

ANTOINE: (*To an onlooker*) Can't wait to feast your eyes, eh? Well, you can't see it yet: it's a surprise.

Carmen's face peeks around the curtain.

ANTOINE: You're really fascinated, aren't you. You know I've got some good stuff this year . . . . some really nice stuff for the ladies . . .

YOUNG BOY: Do you have anything for kids?

ANTOINE: For kids? Of course I do. I've got toys for kids.

YOUNG BOY: What kind of toys?

ANTOINE: Well, what kind do you like? Don't by shy, now, speak up.

YOUNG BOY: I want a train.

ANTOINE: You want a train? Well, ask your father, then. He'll buy you a train. I'll give him a good price.

The crowd laughs. Encouraged by his success, he tries to build on it.

> **ANTOINE:** No, I'm not going to be hard to get along with this year. I'm even willing to give credit. You can see how well the store's doing, eh?

Antoine, master of his world.

43. Interior. Store Window.

Behind the curtain, Benoît gets ready for the big event. Cécile opens the shutters and calls in a low voice:

> **CECILE:** Ready?

Benoît nods his head: ready.

> **CECILE:** Carmen . . . pull your dress up a bit . . .

Carmen obediently adjusts the neck of her dress. Cécile approves. Outside, the public is waiting. The curtain jiggles slightly.

44. Exterior. In Front of the Store.

> **ANTOINE:** Okay, everyone. Pay attention. The curtain's going to open.

Cécile gives the signal to Benoît, who yanks on the cord. But instead of opening, the curtain falls onto the floor. The spectators laugh uproariously. The whole thing is a disaster. Antoine is mortified. Benoît looks as though he would like to disappear. Carmen is on the "stage," tangled up in the curtain, which has fallen on top of her. Cécile strides on and hurries Carmen and Benoît off, then leaves herself after giving the audience a small, apologetic smile. In the ensuing levity, Antoine's expression turns to one of anger.

45. Interior. Lumberjack's Cabin. Day.

A huge cross-cut saw hangs from a wall. Morning light pours in through a window. Jos Poulin is lying on his plank bed, fully dressed. He looks at his watch, then gets up quietly. In the background, we can hear other lumberjacks talking and laughing as they play cards. One of them calls to Jos:

FIRST LUMBERJACK: Hey, Jos, don't be crazy, eh? You leave now they'll never take you back here again.

JOS: So what.

FIRST LUMBERJACK: You idiot. You never learn, do you?

SECOND LUMBERJACK: Go ahead, Jos, run away. It'll catch up with you one day, and then you'll be a sorry man.

JOS: What can I do? It's the way I am.

He puts on his jacket and cap, picks up his bag, and leaves camp.

46. Exterior. Winter. A Forest.

Two lumberjacks, one of them Jos Poulin, walk steadily on snowshoes through the bush. The snow is deep, and the bush is very quiet.

47. Interior. The Store.

Things have returned to normal. A few villagers are gathered around Antoine, who is telling risquée stories.

ANTOINE: Have you heard about the Scotchman whose kilt was too short?

A VILLAGER: No, what about him?

They already find it funny. Even Benoît.

ANTOINE: Well, you see, his kilt . . .

Fernand calls Antoine from the other end of the store.

FERNAND: Antoine . . . Can you come here for a minute, please?

Reluctantly, Antoine gets up to go.

ANTOINE: I'll tell you later.

A VILLAGER: Don't be long!

48. Interior. The Store, Men's Wear Department.

Fernand is busy with a not-too-bright-looking man named Ti-Mignon, trying to sell him a pair of pants that are at least five sizes too large for him.

FERNAND: That's a nice pair of pants, that is. They look good on you.

TI-MIGNON: They're not really my style.

FERNAND: Not your style? What do you mean?

TI-MIGNON: They're too big.

FERNAND: Yeah, well, you're sucking in your stomach.

TI-MIGNON: No, no, no. They're too big.

FERNAND: Turn around a bit. Look. We'll take in a tuck here . . . another one there . . . they'll fit you perfect, no problem.

Fernand, matchstick stuck in the side of his mouth as usual, turns Ti-Mignon around and with a rough gesture and tries, without success, to hoist up the trousers so they'll look as though they fit. Antoine comes over.

ANTOINE: Ah, Ti-Mignon. Is it true your wife's pregnant?

TI-MIGNON: No.

ANTOINE: Everyone says she is. Even she says she is.

TI-MIGNON: Well, she's not. They're crazy.

ANTOINE: You'd think she'd know. Go ask her.

Fernand is still tugging at the pants.

FERNAND: No sir, I think they're fine. With one of our belts they'd look great.

ANTOINE: You've lost weight. Marriage wearing you out?

TI-MIGNON: A bit.

FERNAND: Are you going to take them or not?

TI-MIGNON: I'll take them.

FERNAND: That'll be eight-fifty, okay?

TI-MIGNON: Okay.

FERNAND: Cash.

TI-MIGNON: Cash.

ANTOINE: (*Surprised*) Cash?

TI-MIGNON: Cash!

ANTOINE: The man's a saint! We'd better drink his health.

49. Interior. Office.

Everyone is laughing. Antoine pours a round of drinks and goes up to an old man.

ANTOINE: What always amazes me is that Thomas here never swears. When you think that he's been in two world wars . . .

THOMAS: One. Just one.

ANTOINE: . . . and been married three times . . .

THOMAS: I was only in one war, and I spent half of that under house arrest.

ANTOINE: Under house arrest? What did you do?

THOMAS: They put me in prison. The army prison.

ANTOINE: The army prison! Ay-yi-yi!

Fernand has written up the sale. He points Ti-Mignon to a corner.

FERNAND: You can change over there.

Antoine proposes a toast.

ANTOINE: A little drink never hurt anyone. To your very good health!

They all drink up.

ANTOINE: (*Looking for Fernand*) Where the hell did he go?

50. Interior. The Store. Ladies' Section.

Carmen is measuring a length of cloth for a customer. Fernand comes up to her.

>   **FERNAND:** Carmen . . .

Carmen turns to him, somewhat surprised.

>   **FERNAND:** There's someone to see you.
>
>   **CARMEN:** Who is it? My dad?
>
>   **FERNAND:** Yes.

She looks around for her father, who is standing in the crowd with his eyes lowered. Carmen goes over to him. Cécile watches her. Fernand chews angrily on his match stick.

>   **FERNAND:** (*To Cécile*) When are you going to adopt that kid? What are you waiting for?

Cécile doesn't answer. Carmen places a dutiful kiss on her father's cheek. He looks away.

51. Interior. Office.

Carmen brings her father into the office, where Antoine is waiting for them. She sits down to one side, as though not wanting to hear what the two men have to say to each other.

>   **ANTOINE:** So, you've come to collect your daughter's wages?

The man says nothing. Carmen lowers her head. Antoine looks gently at her, then takes a roll of bills out of his pocket.

>   **ANTOINE:** Ten . . . twenty . . . thirty . . . thirty-two . . . thirty-four . . . thirty five!

He slaps the last bill down deliberately. So far, Carmen's father has studiously avoided meeting Antoine's eyes. But now he looks up at him.

>   **THE FATHER:** Isn't it supposed to be forty?
>
>   **ANTOINE:** I'm keeping the other five for her.

FATHER: That isn't what we agreed on.

ANTOINE: I know. But I'm doing it anyway.

Resigned, the father pockets the money and goes out without a word or even a glance at his daughter.

52. Interior. The Store.

Antoine looks around to make sure Carmen's father has left the store. He notices the keg of nails still on the floor.

ANTOINE: Maurice! How many times do I have to tell you?

Maurice is the second clerk, a boy of seventeen who is neither good at his job nor keen on becoming so. He shrugs his shoulders without paying the slightest attention to the keg of nails.

Antoine whispers something into Cécile's ear.

53. Interior. Office. (Same as Scene 51).

Cécile enters the office to speak to Carmen, who hasn't moved from her chair. She looks sullen. Cécile bends over her, strokes her hair, and very tenderly suggests she come out and join the others. Carmen gets up and they both leave, but the girl's face as well as her demeanour betray unrelieved sadness and anger.

54. Interior. The Store. Ladies' Wear Counter.

A young customer goes up to the counter, where Cécile is standing.

YOUNG WOMAN: Excuse me . . .

Cécile puts on the warm smile of the accomplished salesperson. The young woman bends shyly toward Cécile and speaks in a low voice:

YOUNG WOMAN: Do you have any wedding veils?

Cécile is astonished.

CECILE: Why, Mademoiselle Brière, this is wonderful news. Congratulations. We've been wondering when this would happen . . .

She is speaking so discreetly that everyone in the store is listening. Several women come over.

SEVERAL WOMEN: You don't say, Lise . . .
Oh, isn't that wonderful . . .
Congratulations . . .

Cécile turns to Carmen and gives her explicit instructions.

CECILE: Go on up to the storeroom and on the third shelf on the left you'll see a grey box with blue printing on it. It's a wedding veil . . . Mademoiselle Brière needs it now. (*To the other women*) Lise is getting married!

Murmurs of approval. Fernand grabs a young man by the arm and pushes him into the center of the crowd.

FERNAND: Hey, here's the lucky groom.

The other young men surround him, pushing him playfully and ruffling his hair. Antoine brings a bottle and glasses, and everyone laughs and jokes.

Fernand kisses the bride-to-be. So does Thomas. Then it's Antoine's turn. He raises his arms high in the air and gives a joyous shout. The other women exchange smiles.

ANTOINE: Ladies, there is only one thing to do: crack a bottle.

When Antoine has finished kissing everyone within reach, there is a general applause. He feigns shyness. A man goes up to Cécile and asks her for a song. She demurs, but he insists. She gives in, but asks for help from the crowd:

CECILE: Everyone sing along with me, okay? It's a round.

ANTOINE: (*Impatiently*) Let's have it! Begin, begin!

Cécile takes a deep breath, opens her mouth . . . but gets out nothing but a nervous little laugh. Finally, she begins:

CECILE: My father he did me wed
To a merchant from St. Mâlo

(*Everyone sings along merrily*)
That night when we went to bed
My luck it did run shallow . . .

Someone in the crowd begins to tap his foot on the floor. Antoine looks at his wife with a strong pride burning in his eyes and hugging a quart bottle of de Kuyper's gin in his arms.

EVERYONE: Gai lon la vive la houlette
Gai lon la vive la houlée

CECILE: That first night when we were wed
My luck it did run low
For we no sooner went to bed
Than the cock began to crow . . .

The young boys and girls in the crowd exchange embarrassed glances, but their eyes are shining.

EVERYONE: Gai lon la vive la houlette
Gai lon la vive la houlée

CECILE: The cock said in his towering voice
It's time we did get up . . .

Benoît is looking around for someone. He moves off.

55. Interior. The Attic of the Store.

Carmen is trying on the wedding veil. Sounds of singing rise up from downstairs. She looks at herself in a mirror and places the veil on her head. She is still young and rough-edged, but her beauty shines through in her eyes and her wide smile. Suddenly, she sees Benoît spying on her from a corner.

CARMEN: I see you.

Benoît goes up to her. Carmen lets him get close, but her attitude is defiant. He stops and makes a face at her. His smile is troubled. Her next words are more an invitation than a warning:

CARMEN: Don't touch me, you little jerk.

BENOIT: I'm going to, you know.

Benoît continues to advance toward her. She runs. There follows a chase among the coffins lined up in the part of the storeroom used for the funeral business. They stop. . . start again . . . run out of breath. Then, at last, in a race, Benoît launches himself at Carmen and grabs her by the waist. They roll on the floor. Body against body. The wedding veil falls to the floor. Carmen lies stiff, immobile. Benoît places his hand on her breast. They stare into each other's eyes. She turns her head, then begins to cry in short, quiet sobs. A tear runs down her cheek. He doesn't move; he is fascinated, transfixed, horrified. He doesn't know what to do. Carmen shakes him off, gets up, and leaves the room. Disappointed, Benoît remains stretched out on the floor. Suddenly, something catches his eye. Fernand is on the staircase. He has seen everything. He walks over to join Benoît, picks up the veil and puts it back in its grey box. They look at each other for a moment, but neither speaks. Fernand goes back downstairs with the box, but on the staircase he stops for an instant and thinks about what he has just witnessed.

56. Interior. Store.

Carmen has returned to the main room. She sulks, sitting at the bottom of the stairs, apart from the others. Fernand comes back down and sees her. He goes to Cécile and hands her the box. Cécile is surprised.

    CECILE: Fernand? What were you doing with this?

Fernand doesn't reply. She sees Carmen and goes over to her, perturbed. She kisses the top of Carmen's head.

    CECILE: Carmen, what's the matter. In a bad mood?

    CARMEN: (*Furiously*) Yes, that's it. A bad mood.

Carmen gets up and walks off. Cécile looks questioningly at Fernand, but he doesn't seem to know what to say.

The siren at the mine is heard, warning of an explosion. Carmen covers her ears and hides behind a counter. Thomas grins and looks at his pocket watch.

    THOMAS: Ten to four, Fernand. That clock is ten minutes fast. They're gonna blast.

Fernand goes over to the clock to check the time, but on the way he trips over the keg of nails.

    FERNAND: Damnit!

He chews furiously the matchstick in his teeth and makes the momentous decision to move the keg of nails. However, just as he's about to pick it up, he freezes in his tracks.

Alexandrine, the beautiful Alexandrine, has just opened the front door and is standing silhouetted in the sunlight. The store literally lights up as she enters. As if that weren't enough, since it is now exactly four o'clock, the explosion at the mine coincides with her entrance. The very walls and decorations in the store tremble as she passes. Every head looks up and every eye follows her. Young boys and old men alike have a glint in their eyes. The older women cannot hide their distaste. Maurice and Fernand stand there like two mummies. Finally, without taking his eyes off Alexandrine, Fernand passes the keg of nails to Maurice.

Alexandrine (Monique Mercure) makes her dramatic entrance at the general store. "Alexandrine, the beautiful Alexandrine . . . is standing silhouetted in the sunlight . . . Every head looks up and every eye follows her."

FERNAND: Here Maurice . . . you take it.

Maurice nods, takes the barrel, but keeps his eyes rivetted on the beautiful woman. He begins walking toward the stairs, and when he reaches the spot where the keg had been, makes an exaggerated step as if the keg were still there, even though it is now in his arms. As he walks away looking back over his shoulder, he bumps into the post.

Alexandrine makes her round of the store, making a wide path through the crowd. She looks at various articles one by one, squeezing this one, stroking that one. Back-handed comments trail in her wake. Alexandrine is aware of this and overhears most of them. Neither the women's jealousy nor the men's drooling excite her as much as the fact that she is being talked about.

One of the men squeezes a pair of invisible breasts.

THE MAN: Holy jeez . . . !

ANOTHER MAN: The lawyer must be crazy to let her out on her own like that.

A THIRD MAN: He's out of town.

A FOURTH: Poor Alexandrine . . . all alone in that big house. Over here, honey, I'll keep you company. Heh?

A young man with wide eyes swallows loudly. The women murmur amongst themselves. Alexandrine stares daggers at them, then goes up to Cécile, who listens to her attentively. They talk in low voices.

ALEXANDRINE: Has it come in yet?

CECILE: Yes. I have it upstairs. You want to try it on?

Alexandrine smiles yes. She moves toward the staircase, still causing a stir.

A MAN: Wouldn't it be funny if we just spoke to her like a normal person? Then again, what would she have to say to us . . . ?

ANOTHER MAN: Not a thing. All she could say is: Excuse me, but I believe you are a man.

Alexandrine climbs the stairs in regal fashion, stopping near the top to cast a last, lingering, seductive glance at her crowd of admirers.

57. Interior. The Staircase and Upstairs Room.

Maurice crosses carrying the keg of nails. Benoît is still sulking on the staircase.

    MAURICE: Hey, Benoît, did you see who just went upstairs? Alexandrine. I think she's going to try on a new girdle. Come on, we gotta get a look at that.

Benoît is reluctant, but Maurice gives him a little kick and changes his mind. They go up. On the second floor, Maurice puts the keg down carefully so as not to make any noise.

    MAURICE: (*Very quietly*) Over there.

They tiptoe up to the door. Maurice bends down and looks through the keyhole. We can hear the women talking within. In order to get a better look, he half-opens the door.

    CECILE: Anyway, about the girdle, it came in yesterday. I told you it was beautiful. Just wait till you see it.

    ALEXANDRINE: It's so hot in here.

She takes off her coat. Maurice and Benoît exchange lascivious smiles. Alexandrine, standing in front of a full-length mirror, checks her waistline. Then, through the window, we see a man's legs going down the outside staircase. Alexandrine jumps.

    ALEXANDRINE: Hey, there's a man out there.

    CECILE: I'm sorry. Here, let's have a little privacy, shall we? How's that?

She lowers the blind on the window, then goes back to helping Alexandrine, who is struggling with the zipper at the back of her dress.

    CECILE: Here, let me help you.

    ALEXANDRINE: I hope it's the same one I saw in the catalogue.

    CECILE: Oh, it is. Exactly. It's a Triumph, in black lace with a bit of pink and a little flower on the hip. It's very pretty.

    ALEXANDRINE: I hope it fits me.

CECILE: You know, Alexandrine, you haven't gained an ounce this year. Are you still doing your exercises?

ALEXANDRINE: (*Brusquely*) Give me a hand.

CECILE: (*Hurrying*) Certainly . . .

The big moment arrives. Alexandrine unfastens her brassiere and takes it off. At the partially-open door, Maurice and Benoît jockey for the best view. Alexandrine's breasts are clearly seen through the crack, and their excitement mounts.

CECILE: Look at this and tell me it isn't a beautiful sight. It's exactly what you wanted.

58. Interior. Staircase.

Below, Carmen crosses the back of the store and begins to climb up the stairs, taking the same route as the two boys did earlier.

59. Interior. Changing Room.

Alexandrine is looking at herself in the mirror and shaking her head.

ALEXANDRINE: I don't think it's a very good fit.

Cécile tries her best to adjust the girdle.

CECILE: Don't move, don't move . . .

She pulls again, this time a bit more roughly.

CECILE: There, that's better. You see?

ALEXANDRINE: You're hurting me. You're pinching me.

60. Interior. Upstairs Room.

We can hear rapid footsteps on the stairs and then a loud thud. The two boys turn around and see Carmen stretched out on the floor: she has tripped over the keg of nails.

Alexandrine is startled. Very quietly, the boys close the door.

61. Interior. Changing Room.

    ALEXANDRINE: What was that noise?

    CECILE: What noise?

    ALEXANDRINE: There's someone at the door.

62. Interior. Upstairs Room.

Carmen is still lying on her stomach. She has obviously hurt herself in the fall. She is also quite humiliated. She looks at the two boys in a black rage.

    CARMEN: Pigs!

From behind the door, the voices continue:

    CECILE: (*Reassuring*) It must have been outside.

    ALEXANDRINE: (*Not convinced*) No, I heard something.

    CECILE: Really, Alexandrine . . .

63. Exterior. A Street in the Village.

The village seems frozen into an icy immobility. The "dump" is a gigantic bulwark with huge drifts of snow clinging to its sides.

The village's two-storey houses, each with its front porch, are neatly arranged in two rows along the street. They exude an aura of peace and order. On several of the porches, people have come out and are watching down the street as a horse and buggy, driven by a single man, follows the curving street near the curbside. In the quiet of winter, the sound of the horse's hooves, even from a distance, are loud and disturbing.

An old woman looks on from her window holding the curtain aside and muttering to herself:

    OLD WOMAN: Hmmf. So the mine owner is tossing out his trinkets again. I guess that means there'll be no pay increases this year, either.

The buggy stops in front of a door.

    MINE OWNER: Whoa!

Cheap toys in plastic Christmas stockings rain to the ground. A small child runs out to pick them up.

From a window, a woman watches her.

The buggy moves along.

Men in dark clothes are leaning against the porch railings. The children crouching behind them seem frightened, then suddenly dart out into the street to collect their gifts.

The mine owner sits alone in his buggy. He is wearing large glasses, a coat of lynx fur, and a black sheep-skin cap. A pipe is clenched in his teeth. He throws off presents to the right and left without the slightest regard for them, as though it were some irksome task he has to perform.

From time to time, as the presents hit the snow, two or three children pounce on them and begin to tussle over them with muted laughter. Once the prizes are distributed, the children disappear into their houses.

On the porches, or from their doorways, the adults of the village look on without moving a muscle. Only the occasional child, too young to appreciate what is going on, makes a small wave of goodbye as this bizarre Santa Claus moves away. Behind the implacable faces of these villagers seethes a barely controllable rage.

64. Exterior. The Second-floor Balcony of the Store.

Maurice and Benoît are waiting in ambush on the balcony, the only two in the village to be showing a bit of life. They have something of the air of spies.

MAURICE: Hurry up . . . make a few snowballs. We'll scare the shit out of him.

BENOIT: I can't throw with this cast.

MAURICE: Throw with your left hand, dummy.

They crouch down behind the railing.

65. Exterior. Village Street.

As soon as the buggy reaches the store it is hit with a hail of snowballs.

The horse rears up, the mine owner shouts and yanks on the reins. Two more snowballs hit the horse. The owner has a great deal of difficulty keeping the horse under control.

Suddenly, the villagers seem to wake up. People come out of their houses to get a better look, some with expressions of satisfaction, others looking frightened.

The mine owner succeeds in turning his horse around, and the buggy races off down the street at a gallop.

A man watches them disappear with a smile of contentment on his face. He takes a deep drag on his cigarette.

66. Exterior. Village Street.

Maurice and Benoît leave their hiding place, go down through the store and come out onto the sidewalk. At first, they strut around like a pair of heroes, but gradually they realize that, far from applauding them, people are avoiding even looking at them. Doors close as they pass. In the end, the street is completely empty. They have never felt so alone.

Suddenly, at the end of the street, Benoît sees Carmen. She is looking him straight in the eye and smiling. She gives him a nod of approval, even admiration. For Benoît, this is the ultimate reward. He glows with happiness.

67. Exterior. Winter. A Railway Track in the Woods.

Jos Poulin and his companion are waiting beside the tracks. A small supply train chugs in, and Jos jumps lightly onto the rear platform of the caboose as it moves slowly along. He is on his way home for Christmas. He is happy.

JOS: So long! Merry Christmas!

He waves to his companion, who returns his wave.

His back against the wall of the caboose, Jos pulls up the collar of his jacket and watches the countryside roll by.

68. Interior. A Bedroom in the Poulin House.

The sick boy has been moved into the large bedroom. Madame Poulin is asleep in a chair beside the bed. On the wall, above the sick boy's head, hangs a crucifix.

There is no sound, no movement.

The two youngest children prance around the bed and begin to act up. Madame Poulin wakes.

MADAME POULIN: Stop it, you two. This minute.

The children laugh nervously.

MADAME POULIN: Have some sense. He's very sick. Go on out now.

They move slowly toward the door, smothering their laughter. Madame Poulin takes a cloth from the bedside table and wrings it out in a basin of water. She places the damp cloth on her son's forehead. Then she jumps back.

MADAME POULIN: Oh my God!

She brings her hands to her mouth to keep from crying out, to stifle her sobs. She looks at her son. He is dead.

69. Interior. The Store Office.

There is still a lot of activity in the store. Fernand has gone back into the office to work on his accounts. The telephone rings: two short and one long — the store's ring. It rings again. Fernand picks it up absently.

FERNAND: Hello.

A woman's voice is heard coming feebly over the line.

VOICE: Is this Monsieur Antoine?

FERNAND: No, it's Fernand, his clerk. Who's speaking, please?

VOICE: This is Madame Poulin . . . from Saint-Pierre.

FERNAND: Madame Jos Poulin?

VOICE: Yes.

FERNAND: What can we do for you, Madame Poulin?

VOICE: It's about my son . . . he's . . .

FERNAND: Hello! . . . Hello!

Static on the line drowns out what the woman is saying.

FERNAND: Speak louder, Madame. I can't hear you. We've got a bad connection. There's a hell of a lot of static.

MADAME POULIN: My son Marcel . . . you know, the oldest one. The one who was sick . . . He died this morning.

A new burst of static drowns out her words.

FERNAND: What was that?

Fernand's expression becomes completely professional.

FERNAND: Oh! I am extremely sorry to hear that.

MADAME POULIN: Do you think Monsieur Antoine could come . . . ? Can you hear me? Hello . . . !

FERNAND: (*Very loudly*) I said I am extremely sorry to hear that, Madame Poulin.

MADAME POULIN: My husband is away, you see, up at the lumber camp. I need someone to . . . Can Monsieur Antoine come right away?

FERNAND: Don't worry about a thing, Madame Poulin. We'll take care of everything. We'll come out right away.

MADAME POULIN: Good. That's good. Thank you. I'll wait for you, then. Goodbye.

She hangs up. Fernand thinks for a moment, then calls out:

FERNAND: Monsieur Antoine!

No answer. He leans over and taps on the office window with his pencil.

FERNAND: (*Loudly*) Monsieur Antoine! There's been a death in Saint-Pierre.

This draws Cécile's attention. Antoine goes over to talk to Fernand. Benoît looks on.

ANTOINE: Who is it who died?

FERNAND: The oldest Poulin boy, in Saint-Pierre.

ANTOINE: How old was he?

FERNAND: Fifteen, about. Not much more.

ANTOINE: We'll take the small coffin, then. It should be big enough.

FERNAND: Okay.

Antoine responds to the situation with calm authority. He looks at his pocket watch.

ANTOINE: It's a fairly long way. It'll take us a while.

FERNAND: I know. I'll go hitch up the wagon right away.

But first he takes a bottle from the desk drawer and pours a drink into Antoine's glass. He does not take a drink himself, however.

70. Interior. Store.

Benoît leaps over the counter and runs to his aunt, who has overheard everything.

BENOIT: (*Pleading*) Can I go with them, auntie?

Cécile is taken by surprise by this. But he is insistent.

BENOIT: Please!

She considers for a moment, then nods her head. Benoît is overjoyed.

BENOIT: Oh, thank you.

He runs to the stairway, but is stopped by his uncle.

ANTOINE: Where are you off to, you?

BENOIT: I'm going with you this time. Aunt Cécile said it was all right.

Antoine looks questioningly over at Cécile, who nods.

ANTOINE: Okay, but calm down.

Benoît gives Cécile a look of gratitude, then follows his uncle upstairs to get ready for the trip.

71. Interior and Exterior. The Stable.

In front of the stable, Fernand has finished harnessing the horse and throws a blanket over the animal's back. Maurice, leaning against the stable's door post, looks on without interest.

    FERNAND: Maurice, go in and get the box, will you?

Maurice slouches inside and begins to bring out a large coffin.

    FERNAND: No, not that one.

Maurice drops the end of the coffin loudly. Fernand looks at him impatiently and points his finger.

    FERNAND: The small one, over there.

With ill grace, Maurice puts the large coffin back in its place and takes out the small one. Fernand lends him a hand, and the two of them hoist the box onto the back of the wagon.

72. Interior. Upstairs in the Store.

Carmen is helping Benoît get ready. Because of his cast, he cannot wear a glove on his right hand, so Carmen is wrapping it up in a bright red woollen scarf. Fernand comes in.

    FERNAND: Okay. Red Fly is all hitched up. Everything's all set. Whenever you're ready . . .

Cécile comes in.

    CECILE: Wait. Here's your hat.

Antoine puts it on.

    CECILE: There. Are you cozy now?

    ANTOINE: Oh yes, very.

Cécile leaves. Fernand makes a small sign to Antoine and shows him the large bottle of gin he had hidden behind his back. Antoine opens his coat and Fernand slips the bottle into an inside pocket. Antoine thanks him with a gentle tap on the shoulder, then looks around quickly to make sure no one has seen the exchange. Cécile comes back and hands Antoine a small mickey of the same gin.

    CECILE: Here . . . in case you get cold.

Antoine pockets the mickey with a glance at Fernand.

    ANTOINE: Thanks, that's not a bad idea!

Fernand nods approvingly. Cécile also hands Antoine a small brown paper bag.

    CECILE: These are some candies. You can give them to the other Poulin children.

    ANTOINE: You think of everything.

He pecks her affectionately on the cheek.

    CECILE: Have a good trip. Take care . . . Come back safe and sound.

She reaches out to touch Antoine's coat. Antoine is impatient to get going.

    CECILE: Are you ready, Benoît? Your uncle is going.

She goes over to where Benoît is standing next to Carmen.

    CECILE: Do you have everything you need?

They walk in a group toward the front door. The men go out. The women stay behind.

    CECILE: Take care! Be sure to get back in time for midnight mass!

73. Exterior. Dusk. Village Main Street.

Antoine and Benoît are in the wagon, going down the main street of the village. As they pass a house, a young girl runs out and calls to Benoît:

    YOUNG GIRL: Hi, Benoît!

Benoît smiles back at her with the look of someone who has just has just been knighted.

74. Exterior. Dusk. Deserted Road Outside the Village.

The road is a thin, dark line between high banks of snow. Antoine is in a good mood and, if the truth be known, happy that Benoît is sitting beside him. With a fatherly gesture, he hands Benoît the reins.

ANTOINE: Here, you be the driver!

Benoît hesitates, then gives in to the pleasure of responsibility. He feels in charge of the whole operation.

Night falls quickly, and fatigue begins to set in. Antoine takes the mickey out of his pocket. Benoît eyes him without objecting.

ANTOINE: You want some?

Benoît shakes his head.

ANTOINE: It's up to you. You'll feel the cold later on.

With an habitual gesture, Antoine wipes the neck of the mickey with the back of his glove, takes a long drink, then throws away the empty bottle. He rummages under the blanket and comes up with the large bottle. He takes another long gulp. Benoît is becoming less tolerant. He looks reproachfully at his uncle, then stands up and shakes the reins.

BENOIT: Giddyup, Red Fly! Hya, hya!

A sharp turn comes up. The horse shies. It is quite dark now. Antoine was right: Benoît is beginning to feel the cold. He takes the glove off of his good hand and blows on his fingers. Snow is falling. Antoine, who has been dozing, opens his eyes.

ANTOINE: Leave the reins, Benoît. Red Fly knows this road better than you do.

His voice is thick. He sounds grumpy.

ANTOINE: Sit down, get under the blanket. I've seen tougher guys than you before.

Benoît pays no attention to him, but remains standing and driving the horse. Antoine goes back to sleep, which is fine by Benoît: now he is in charge again. Standing up in front of his seat, he feels like the captain of a ship standing on his bridge.

But the road is long and the night is dark and cold. Benoît gives in.

Burrowed under the blankets, he falls asleep. Luckily, Red Fly has no need of a driver. The good horse continues plodding along the solitary road, slowly but steadily.

75. Exterior. Night. Approaching the Poulin House.

Instinctively, Antoine wakes up the moment the wagon reaches their destination. He takes the reins and turns the horse into the laneway leading to the farm, between two long rows of trees.

With his elbow, he gently nudges Benoît to awaken him. He nudges him a second time. At last, Benoît opens his eyes, but he doesn't seem very sure of where he is.

The Poulin house is small and isolated, its black outline barely discernable in the darkness except for twin shafts of light coming from two windows. A strong wind has come up, creating great flurries of snow. The large trees stretch their limbs desperately toward heaven. The travelers descend from the wagon and hastily remove the box. Benoît moves stiffly.

Benoît and his uncle unload the coffin at the Poulin house, "its black outline barely discernable except for twin shafts of light coming from two windows."

ANTOINE: What's the matter, Benoît? Are you afraid?

Benoît stares at him briefly, then replies defiantly:

BENOIT: No, I'm cold.

ANTOINE: (*Skeptical*) Whatever you say. Okay, grab your end.

Carrying their burden between them, they struggle through the storm toward the house. The strong wind makes them stagger drunkenly. They climb up the three steps to the front porch and Antoine goes in without knocking. The door is not locked.

76. Interior. The Poulin's Kitchen.

When they get inside, Antoine and Benoît put the coffin down on the floor. Madame Poulin approaches them. They look silently at one another for a moment. Antoine is the first to speak.

ANTOINE: I tried to call your husband up at the camp, but the lines were down. I'll try again tomorrow.

Madame Poulin helps him take off his heavy coat. This is Benoît's first visit to the house. At the far end of the kitchen, the daughter is sitting in a rocking chair, watching him. She gets up, comes toward him, and, like her mother, helps him take off his coat. The atmosphere is heavy and solemn. Two small children have commandeered the stairs to the attic as an observation post. Antoine sits down at the table. Madame Poulin brings over a large platter.

MADAME POULIN: I've made you some dinner. (*To Benoît*) There's enough for both.

Benoît sits down. Antoine digs in to his meal, but neither Benoît nor Madame Poulin seem interested in food.

ANTOINE: He was your eldest boy?

She nods her head.

ANTOINE: I thought he looked pretty healthy.

MADAME POULIN: He started coughing a couple of days ago. I thought he was just catching a cold.

ANTOINE: He was just a kid. A good boy. And so young.

They fall silent. Benoît looks around him carefully, noticing everything about the room. Then he finds what he's looking for: the door to the room in which the body lies. The door is half-open; the room inside is completely dark. Antoine, following Benoît's gaze, places his hand reassuringly over the boy's.

    ANTOINE: Plenty of time for that. Eat your dinner.

But Benoît looks down at his plate without the slightest appetite. He pushes it away gently.

    ANTOINE: I almost forgot. My wife sent along some treats for the children.

He walks over to his coat, which has been folded over a chair, and searches in the deep pockets. He takes out the small paper bag and, with a big smile, holds it out to the daughter.

    ANTOINE: Here, pass these around to your brothers.

    GIRL: (*Calling*) Serge . . . Robin . . .

The boys are delighted. They look at each other and giggle. Antoine takes the bottle out of his coat and brings it over to the table. The children come to get their candies, but Madame Poulin finds the noise too much to bear. They hurry out, calling, "Thank you, Monsieur Antoine . . ." Antoine takes a drink of gin and lets out a belch. He eats like a pig. Benoît watches him, disgusted. Antoine takes huge mouthfuls. Chunks of meat fall on the table near his plate; he picks them up with his bare hands and shoves them back in his mouth. He chews noisily. He licks his fingers. He pours himself more gin. He pays absolutely no attention to Madame Poulin, who is distracted, shattered, and immobilized by grief. All this torments Benoît. At last, Madame Poulin looks up, emotion contorting her face. Her lips begin to tremble. She gets up, murmuring:

    MADAME POULIN: I'll make you some tea.

She moves away, turning her back, but while she is making the tea she makes a nervous movement and the teapot falls to the floor and breaks. She holds her face in her hands and leans against the cupboard, crying loudly, huge tears falling from her cheeks. Benoît and Antoine watch her without knowing what to do.

Antoine finishes his meal. It's now time to get on with the business at hand. He heaves a great sigh and addresses his young assistant:

    ANTOINE: Are you ready, Benoît?

    BENOIT: I'm ready.

Antoine himself doesn't appear to be ready: the half-open door seems to terrify him.

    ANTOINE: Excuse me.

He leaves quickly by the back door.

Benoît and Madame Poulin are left in the kitchen. She looks at Benoît for a time, then lowers her eyes and retreats into her own thoughts.

Benoît feels helpless before such misery. He sighs, then lets his eyes sweep over the room. The clock strikes nine-thirty. The chimes are not loud, but they make him jump. He sighs again. A small, gently humming voice draws his attention; it's the young girl, still in her hiding place in the corner, watching him with her chin resting in her hands. She is beautiful. When Benoît's eyes meet hers, she leans back in her rocking chair and disappears into the shadows. Then Benoît sees two small legs hanging down from the top of the stairs: a small body without a head. The other child is on the floor, absently turning a plate around with the tip of his finger.

Antoine comes back inside. He appears to have got hold of himself in one way or another. He leans on the table, appearing very weak.

    ANTOINE: Élise, do you have his baptismal certificate?

    MADAME POULIN: (*Nonplussed*) His what?

    ANTOINE: His baptismal certificate. I need it.

    MADAME POULIN: I'll go look upstairs.

She goes upstairs.

    ANTOINE: Benoît, drag that box over to the bedroom door, will you?

Benoît gets up and moves toward the box. Antoine grabs the gin bottle, fills his glass, and takes such a long drink that it leaves him breathless.

77. Interior. The Death Room.

As the door opens, a shaft of light penetrates the gloom and illuminates the bed. Antoine and Benoît drag the box to the foot of the bed. Antoine turns on a light, signals to Benoît, and they lift off the box's lid. They take a white sheet from the box and unfold it, each holding an end. They then put the sheet back in the box so that it forms a lining. Reluctantly, Antoine approaches the bed. Benoît is frozen in place. Antoine pulls back the bedclothes and reveals the body. Benoît looks at the blanched, unmoving face of the boy, who was about his own age and who now is dead. He cannot move. He doesn't even blink. His uncle lifts the head of the corpse and gives a brief order.

ANTOINE: Come on . . . get to work.

Benoît moves. He isn't sure what he has to do. He takes the sheets and pulls them completely off the bed, revealing the corpse's feet. He looks up and waits for another order from his uncle. He knows he's supposed to grab the body by the ankles, but it's as though his hands are paralyzed. This time, Antoine speaks to him more gently, paternally:

ANTOINE: Go on . . . go on . . .

Benoît finds his courage, and they lift the body up and carry it to the box. One stiff arm remains sticking up in the air, then suddenly falls as if the body has moved by itself. Benoît jumps. To calm himself, he takes a deep breath, then turns to his uncle as if to apologize.

The door opens a crack and Madame Poulin appears. She looks at her son for the last time. Little by little, the corpse disappears as Antoine folds the ends of the sheet over it. When the boy's face is finally hidden, Madame Poulin sobs loudly. Benoît's heart is also on the point of breaking.

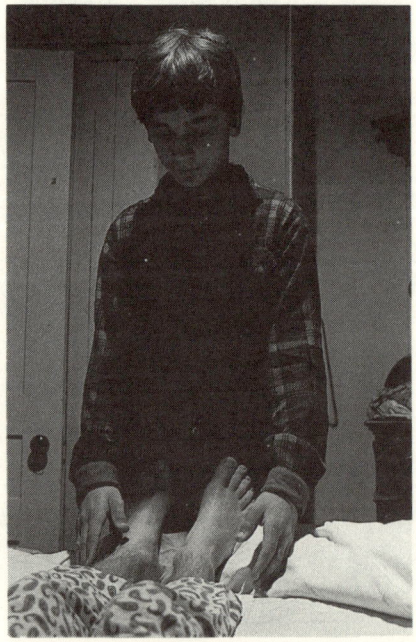

Benoît (Jacques Gagnon) experiences death first-hand. "He knows he's supposed to grab the body by the ankles, but it's as though his hands are paralyzed."

78. Exterior. Road. Winter.

Under a full moon, the wagon returns along the road. The trees cast their long shadows on the silvered snow. Antoine is sound asleep; once again, Benoît is in command.

They enter a small stand of pine trees. In his sleep, Antoine leans over onto Benoît's shoulder, and Benoît pushes him roughly back upright. He shakes the reins and makes the horse go faster.

Now they are passing through a clearing. The neck of the gin bottle is poking up through the collar of Antoine's fur coat. Benoît reaches over, pulls the bottle out of the coat, opens it and takes a huge gulp. The gin gives him a surge of courage, and he stands up and whips the horse with the end of the reins, shouting:

BENOIT: Let's go, Red Fly . . . Hya, hya!

They race madly through the darkness. Both horse and driver seem transported, in a kind of exalted state. The cold air is pure and still, the night itself transparent.

Suddenly they hit a bump, or perhaps a hole . . . Benoît turns his head and sees that the box has fallen off the back of the wagon. He pulls on the reins with all his strength.

BENOIT: (*Shouting*) Whoa . . . !

The horse stops. Benoît looks around: his uncle is fast asleep, the countryside is deserted. He gets down from the wagon and walks resolutely back to the box, which lies some thirty feet behind the wagon. He tries to lift it, then he tries dragging it, but it's impossible. He thinks for a while, then runs back to the wagon. He shakes his uncle, gently at first, and speaks to him in a low voice so as not to awaken him too abruptly:

BENOIT: Uncle Antoine . . . Uncle Antoine . . .

Then he shakes him more roughly, slapping him on the shoulder.

BENOIT: Uncle Antoine, wake up!

Antoine lifts his head and looks at Benoît in bewilderment. Then, without warning, he smacks the boy so hard he falls back on the ground. Lying on his back, Benoît calls up to his uncle:

BENOIT: We lost the body, uncle. We have to go get it.

Antoine is too stupefied to know what's happening.

ANTOINE: Huh?

BENOIT: (*Shouting*) The body! It fell off! We have to go get it!

ANTOINE: Body? What body?

Benoît points to the box.

BENOIT: That body! Back there!

With a tremendous effort, Antoine turns around and sees the box.

ANTOINE: What the hell's it doing back there?

BENOIT: Get down. Come and help me.

ANTOINE: Hey! Hang on a bit, eh? How did it get back there? I've never seen anything like this before.

BENOIT: Are you coming down or not?

ANTOINE: (*Blearily*) Only a little whippersnapper like you could get us in a fix like this. You're always sticking your nose in where it doesn't belong. You look for trouble, you do. You get everyone into a real state. Why'd you want to come here for anyway?

Antoine doesn't wait for an anwer to his questions. His head sinks back down on his chest. Benoît looks at him angrily, then, with a sudden movement, he returns the blow that Antoine had given him earlier. Antoine jumps. He struggles to come to terms with where he is, then slowly gets down from the wagon. Benoît makes no move to help him. His uncle turns to him anyway.

ANTOINE: Let me alone . . . let me alone.

He takes a few steps, then turns and comes back.

ANTOINE: I wish Fernand was here.

Benoît watches him for a few moments, then takes the horse by the bridle.

BENOIT: Let's go, Red Fly . . . Walk!

He tries to turn the horse around so he can get the wagon closer to the box, but the horse resists and stamps. It is unbearably cold. Clouds of vapor stream out of the horse's nostrils. Antoine is hunched over, having trouble staying on his feet. He groans, staggers, goes down on all fours.

ANTOINE: Jesus, it's slippery.

He lies down on the snow, still a long way from the box. Benoît goes up to him. The wagon has plowed a furrow in the snow that shines like silver in the moonlight. Antoine groans again. The wind sends up clouds of powdery snow around them. Antoine turns painfully toward Benoît.

ANTOINE: Okay . . . I'm coming. Come and help me.

Benoît doesn't move.

ANTOINE: Okay, okay, forget it!

He stands up and staggers to the box, lurching through the snow. The wind howls. Benoît joins him and goes to the opposite end of the coffin. He unrolls the scarf from around his cast. They each grab an end of the box and try to lift it up, but Antoine can't manage his end. He lets it drop.

BENOIT: (*Shouting*) Don't let go!

Antoine looks up tearfully at Benoît.

ANTOINE: I can't do it, Benoît. Sometimes there are some things we just can't do.

BENOIT: You can do it. I've got a cast on my arm, and I can do it.

Antoine slumps over beside the box. Benoît goes up to him and kneels down, trying with all his might to convince his uncle not to quit.

BENOIT: We're almost home, Uncle. Don't give up now. You can do it.

Antoine begins to whimper, falling into a state of shameless self-pity.

ANTOINE: Would someone mind telling me what the hell I'm doing out here? I hate my life, Benoît. I hate living out here in the sticks. I feel . . . like I'm suffocating. All I want is to buy a nice little hotel in the States somewhere. But oh, no. Your aunt won't let me. She won't let me do anything. I hate . . . I'm . . . scared to death of corpses. (*Sobs*) I do everything for everyone. Your aunt . . . she never wanted to have children. I've spent my whole life looking after other people's kids. I raised Carmen . . . I raised you, I did the best I could for you, you know that, don't you?

Benoît is unmoved by all this melodrama. Barely controlling his anger, he rejects Antoine's appeal.

> **BENOIT:** Drunkard!

Antoine accepts the insult and starts crying again. He hides his face in his mittens.

> **BENOIT:** (*Shouting*) Drunkard!!

The storm has reached its apotheosis. Benoît feels completely alone. The snow is a blank screen that his eyes can barely penetrate. He can see nothing around him, finds nothing to give him courage. With the fingers of the hand that has the cast on it, he picks up a clump of snow, forms it into a small ball, and hurls it furiously to the ground.

> **BENOIT:** (*Muttering*) Goddamn it!

79. Exterior. Night. The Supply Train.

The train on which Jos Poulin has stowed away to get home for Christmas is nearing the asbestos region. Jos is cold, but happy. He looks at the mountains of asbestos silhouetted against the night sky as if they were his closest friends. On the top of one, a huge machine continues to dump its endless load of white powder. Jos is home.

80. Exterior. Night. Village.

The funeral wagon returns to the village, but in place of a box lying in the back of it, there is only Antoine, stretched out and dead to the world. The jolting disturbs his sleep, and he rolls and grumbles to himself. Christmas Eve is in full swing. Many windows along the street are lit up. People are singing hymns; the whole village seems joyful . . . except for Benoît. He is hurrying to get to the store. He whips the reins.

> **BENOIT:** Giddyup, Red Fly . . . Hya!

Somewhere in the village, people are singing "O Holy Night" with single-minded tenacity.

81. Interior. Cécile's Bedroom.

The sound of a jazz recording is heard, then the voice of a radio announcer.

    ANNOUNCER: Good evening, ladies and gentlemen. Direct from the ballroom of the magnificent Lasalle Hotel in Montreal, on this most beautiful of Christmas Eves, this is CKAC, North America's foremost French radio station. Tonight, it is our intense pleasure to bring you the very latest in music from Harry Trueblood and his famous orchestra . . .

Applause; a trombone adds to the merriment. The music is coming from a small radio on the night-table beside the bed. Fernand wakes up, looks at the alarm clock and gets sleepily out of bed. He pulls on his shorts and a shirt. Someone turns on a light, revealing a large and well furnished bedroom. Fernand is in a triumphant, supercilious mood. He flops down on the sofa and begins pulling on his boots. He shakes his head incredulously:

    FERNAND: I don't believe it.

Cécile, wearing a nightgown, comes over and sits down beside him. She has just come back from checking to see if Antoine is in his own bed. Her face is still flushed. She is brushing her hair coquettishly.

    FERNAND: I just don't believe it.

He bends over to her, laughing, and kisses her neck. Then he pours drinks for both of them from a carafe of cut glass. Cécile has a hairpin in her mouth and Fernand one of his matchsticks. He takes the hairpin and matchstick and tosses them on the floor. Then he raises his glass. They clink, smile, and drink. The liquor makes Fernand cough.

    CECILE: A very smooth drink, eh? It comes from France.

    FERNAND: It's good just the same.

They both laugh. He puts his hand on her neck and pulls her toward him. A few drops of liquor spill on the rug. She admonishes him lightly.

    CECILE: Careful, Fernand, it's very dear . . .

    FERNAND: So am I, madame. So am I.

They laugh again. Fernand puts the glasses on a pedestal table and, taking Cécile by the hands, pulls her down on top of him on the sofa. They lie in an embrace, kissing, caressing.

CECILE: Tell me honestly, Fernand, have you been thinking about this for a long time?

FERNAND: I don't know. I wasn't going to think about it at all until the morning.

She laughs. He runs his fingers through her hair. They kiss again.

FERNAND: What about you?

CECILE: Me?

FERNAND: Who else?.

They laugh and kiss again. Suddenly, she jumps up.

CECILE: Fernand!

Unaware of her seriousness, he continues laughing. She hits him gently with her hand.

CECILE: Shhh! Listen!

FERNAND: What is it?

CECILE: I heard something.

FERNAND: Not me.

CECILE: I'm sure I did . . .

FERNAND: Maybe it was Carmen.

CECILE: It might have been them.

FERNAND: No, we would have heard the back door.

CECILE: But what if they came in through the front?

A shaft of light suddenly blinds them. She leaps up and shields her eyes.

CECILE: Oh my God!

Benoît, still wearing his fur coat and hat, is standing in the doorway. Embarrassed, Cécile turns away from him. Fernand puts on a hypocritical smile and tries to pretend nothing is going on.

FERNAND: Benoît! Hello! What took you so long?

82. Interior. Hallway.

Fernand leaves the bedroom and closes the door behind him, out of consideration for Cécile. He buttons up his shirt.

> **FERNAND:** Carmen's been waiting up for you all night, but I think she fell asleep. I wouldn't waken her now, if I were you.

He motions Benoît to be quiet.

> **FERNAND:** I tried to get to sleep, myself, but I wasn't tired. I came up here to wait for you.

Benoît stares fixedly at him, not believing a word he says. Fernand realizes this.

> **FERNAND:** Where's your uncle?
>
> **BENOIT:** He's outside. You can go bring him in.

Fernand begins to suspect that something is wrong.

> **FERNAND:** Outside?

He goes down the stairs to the main store. Left alone in the hallway, Benoît turns away in disgust and looks at the door behind which Cécile is hidden.

83. Interior. Cécile's Bedroom.

Cécile is in a bad state. The smile that lit up her face a few moments ago has given way to an expression of intense anxiety. She walks nervously over to the bed, straightens the covers, turns off the radio and the bedside lamp, glances quickly at the mirror, smooths her hair and adjusts her nightgown, then walks resolutely to the door.

84. Interior. Hallway.

Cécile opens the door and leaves her bedroom. Benoît is still there, and he stares at her. She does her best to keep calm.

> **CECILE:** You are very late. You must have run into trouble,

eh? Saint-Pierre is a long way . . . the roads are terrible . . . and with this storm . . . !

Benoît continues to stare at her.

 CECILE: Are you hungry?

 BENOIT: No. Just tired.

He is indeed exhausted, and it shows. He leans back against the wall.

 CECILE: (*Stammering*) Fernand has gone up to bed, he's asleep . . . poor Fernand.

This explanation so flagrantly contradicts what Fernand himself has just said that all Benoît can do is stare at her with contempt.

 CECILE: Carmen hardly left the doorway all night, waiting up for you. She really wanted to talk to you when you came home.

Benoît doesn't react: he can only take so many lies in a row.

 CECILE: Take off your coat.

She reaches out to help him off with it, but he pushes her hand away gently but firmly.

 BENOIT: Don't touch me.

His reaction dumbfounds her. She tries to smile.

 CECILE: Maybe you should go to bed . . . I'll make you some hot milk, would you like that?

Benoît's frigid stare finally unnerves her. She begins to lose control.

 CECILE: Benoît . . . at least . . .

She takes a step, then comes back.

 CECILE: Is Fernand downstairs?

Benoît smiles sarcastically. Cécile persists. She is babbling anything that comes into her head.

 CECILE: He went down to help your uncle, I suppose. I'll go bring them in . . .

85. Exterior. Night. In Front of the General Store.

The porch light illuminates the wagon on which Antoine is still sleeping. Fernand is desperately trying to wake him up.

> **FERNAND:** (*Lowly*) Monsieur Antoine, what's going on, eh? Where the hell is the body? (*Silence*) Shit!

Fernand grabs Antoine by the collar and tries to lift him up.

> **FERNAND:** Hey! Wake up! Did you get to the Poulin place or what? What the hell is going on?

The only answer he gets from Antoine is a low groan. Cécile appears at the door in her nightgown. She half opens it, covering her throat with her hand to protect it from the cold.

> **CECILE:** Fernand, what's going on?
>
> **FERNAND:** I don't know. He's drunker than usual and the body's missing. I don't understand a thing.
>
> **CECILE:** Sweet Jesus! Well, do something . . . bring him inside!
>
> **FERNAND:** What do you think I'm trying to do? Got any bright ideas?

He gives a fierce tug on Antoine's coat.

> **FERNAND:** Come on, Monsieur Antoine! Get yourself up, goddamn it! Let's go!

Cécile gestures to him to hurry up.

86. Interior. Night. The Main Staircase.

Benoît comes down the stairs and sees Carmen sleeping near the front door, curled up on a chair with a pillow and quilt. Benoît watches her sleep for a while, then calls to her gently.

> **BENOIT:** Carmen . . . Carmen . . .

He touches her hand with his fingertip. She turns in her sleep. Benoît heaves a sigh. He takes off his coat and climbs weakly up on a counter and lies down. Cécile and Fernand are heard dealing with Antoine.

FERNAND: Come on, Cécile, give me a hand.

CECILE: Please, Fernand . . .

FERNAND: Bloody hell . . . I've never seen him so drunk . . . Why the hell did he get like this?

CECILE: Poor old man.

FERNAND: He's poor and old, all right. Maybe too poor and old to keep running things around here, eh?

CECILE: Never mind, Fernand. His boots are still far too big for you.

FERNAND: His boots, eh? Watch that step. All I want to know is where's the goddamn body?

CECILE: I can't imagine what happened.

FERNAND: Should I call the Poulins?

CECILE: Are you out of your mind? What if they lost it on the way back?

FERNAND: Jesus Christ!

CECILE: If somebody finds it, the whole village will know about it. We've got to go look for it.

FERNAND: *Who's* got to go look for it?

CECILE: You do, of course.

FERNAND: Me? I don't even know which way they came!

CECILE: You can take Benoît.

FERNAND: Benoît? He's sleeping.

CECILE: Then wake him up!

FERNAND: That won't be easy.

CECILE: I don't care! You have to!

Benoît tosses in his sleep. He hears Fernand's and Cécile's voices as if they are coming through a thick fog. His eyes flutter. The green lamp just over his head dims. In the display of women's clothing, a new brassiere reveals the wooden breasts of a headless mannequin. Beside it, a silken dress with printed flowers suggests the outlines of an invisible corpse.

87. Benoît's Dream.

Dressed like a choirboy, Benoît is lying in a field of flowers. He gets up slowly. The flowers have become gigantic. Uncle Antoine's hands begin to disentangle a rosary clutched in the fingers of a corpse. He removes the funeral clothes from the mortal remains, and the body of Alexandrine is revealed, sleeping in the flowery silk lining of the coffin. Her breasts are visible through a black-lace corset. She stands up, looks at Benoît, smiles at him, and begins to jump up and down in the coffin. He wants to touch her breasts: he reaches out his hands, one bare and the other encased in a cast. He tries to follow her movements, but her breasts remain just out of reach . . .

Fernand goes up to Benoît, who is deep asleep, his two hands covering his crotch.

> **CECILE:** You have to wake him up.
>
> **FERNAND:** Benoît . . . (*Insistent*) Benoît! Benoît!

Fernand shakes him gently. Benoît wakes up with a start.

88. Exterior. Day. In the Wagon.

The two of them, Benoît and Fernand, are back in the wagon in a worse snowstorm than the one last night. They can hardly see through the lattice-work of huge flakes tossed madly about by the wind, flying nearly horizontally. The horse is ploughing through snow up to its knees and is hardly making headway. The wind is relentless. Fernand is worried, but Benoît seems indifferent to his surroundings. He is numb.

> **FERNAND:** Try to remember. Did you go this way? I can't see a goddamned thing . . .

Fernand tries unsuccessfully to protect his eyes with his hand. He pulls hard on the reins.

> **FERNAND:** Whoa, boy! Did you take the south line or take the shortcut?

No answer. A blast of wind hits them harder than before.

FERNAND: Goddamn it, Benoît. Try!

BENOIT: I don't know.

FERNAND: Jesus!

Fernand pulls on the reins. The Poulin house appears through the snow. The wagon stops.

FERNAND: We're here, Benoît. Get a move on.

Benoît, wrapped in his blanket, has no desire to get down.

89. Exterior. Day. Outside the Poulin House.

Fernand approaches the house, struggling through the storm. Benoît follows at a distance. Fernand staggers up onto the porch and looks through the window in the door. He calls out:

FERNAND: Madame Poulin . . . Madame Poulin . . .

The house looks deserted. He ploughs around to the back. Benoît goes up to one of the front windows and peers in.

The snow and ice on the windowpane obscures his vision.

But what he sees is not real.

He sees the coffin lying on the floor in the middle of the kitchen. The lid is off, and the boy's body is still in it, the head bent a little sideways as if he is sleeping in an uncomfortable position.

Kneeling on the floor beside the coffin, Jos is staring at his dead son.

Jos' wife is standing beside him, as still and lifeless as a statue. She holds a hand to her mouth as if to keep from crying out. She is looking far off into the distance, into the void.

Also on the floor, two young boys are rocking mechanically back and forth. They look bored.

On a chair, another child is playing with two sticks of wood.

The daughter, the beautiful one, is sitting very still and looking very thoughtful.

Through the frost-covered window, Benoît's face looks frozen.

THE GREY FOX

BY JOHN HUNTER

The Grey Fox was an unusual screenwriting experience in that only four months after I started work the film was in production. In feature films a four-year timespan is more usual. In fact *The Grey Fox* project had been around for five years before I got involved. It had generated six screenplays by five different writers but none of these had satisfied potential investors.

There was an abundance of archival material on Bill Miner's train robbing career and his time in Canada, and I felt it would make a terrific film. The problem with the existing versions, as I saw it, was that every screenplay had utilized a documentary approach. The facts were on the pages but characterizations were minimal and the story was cold. I decided to try a more intimate approach, which would involve some departure from truth. I spent a week kicking it around with director Phillip Borsos (who had originated the project in the first place) and we decided to plant a fictitious love affair in the middle of the story. I then wrote the new screenplay in eleven days. I don't normally work that fast but the material was needed to pin down an actor and meet the timetable for an October-November shoot. The actor, Harry Dean Stanton, crapped out to do *One from the Heart* but the screenplay was good enough to put the investment in place. I wrote three more drafts between then and the end of production. The version published here is the last of those — the shooting script.

Readers familiar with the film will notice there are scenes that didn't make it to the finished film and considerable re-ordering of sequences, the reasons for which would take a long article to explain, but which are part of the normal production process. The dialogue was recorded almost word for word as I wrote it. I am grateful that the actors and the director did not feel compelled to improve it as its slightly formal style is part of the film's charm.

The Grey Fox is the most successful project I have worked on, so it's appropriate that it was also the most pleasurable experience. Skill is never quite enough. A production also needs luck. Fortunately, all of us working on *The Grey Fox* wanted and needed to make that film at that time, which resulted in heroic effort by all hands and an absence of poisonous ego displays. I wish I felt half as good about some of my other working experiences.

By making *The Grey Fox* we mythologized Bill Miner. Such is the power of film that I have since come across published items about Miner which quote little facts about him that I invented for the screenplay. I like to believe old Bill would enjoy this, as he was quite a liar in his own right.

John Hunter

THE GREY FOX

1. Int. Miner's Cell. Day.

The screen is BLACK. *The following* SUPER FADES IN:

"On June 17, 1901 after thirty-three years in San Quentin Prison, stagecoach robber Bill Miner was released into the twentieth century."

SUPER FADES OUT. BLACKNESS *remains. Miner's impatient sigh is heard. He stirs restlessly in the dark. Then, distant, the noise of a key in a heavy lock, a heavy door squeals open, slams shut. Then the sound of boots approaching from the distance. Close by, Miner's voice is heard, muttering to himself in the dark. It is a soft, southern voice.*

    MINER: (*Off*) Here they come, Bill.

The bootsteps draw closer.

    MINER: (*Off*) Sounds like Walsh and Fishburne.

The bootsteps draw very close, then stop. The sound of a bolt pulling back. A sudden bar of light slashes the darkness as a little window in the solid cell door is opened. The bar of light slants across Bill Miner's eyes — old, wise, blue-colored eyes. His eyes dart sideways to the light source.

    GUARD #1:   (*Off*) On your feet, Miner.

The sound of the cell door being unlocked and opened. Miner stands as the door is opened and more light seeps into his small, dank cell. Miner is visible now — a thin, slightly stooped man of fifty-five clad in a filthy prison uniform of horizontal stripes. On the chest is a faded number: 10191. Miner's white hair is cropped close but a full white moustache adorns his upper lip. He squints as if even this pallid light is too bright for his eyes.

    GUARD #1:   (*Off*) Let's go.

Miner shuffles out of the greasy cell, leaving its grimy walls and the dirty straw-matted cot.

2. Int. Cellblock Corridor. Day.

TRACKING *in front of Miner as he moves along a dimly-lit stone corridor past rows of cell doors — solid wooden doors with closed iron grates covering the little windows. The corridor is not unlike some mineshaft deep beneath the surface of the earth. The two uniformed guards walk behind Miner, their boots echoing. Miner is barefoot and walks like a man with permanently sore feet, but he walks quickly, his eyes fixed straight ahead.*

3. Int. Cellblock Stairway. Day.

A VIEW *of Miner climbing up from the dimness below, followed by the guards.*

4. Int. Warden's Office. Day.

A high, cavernous room with prison stone walls. An expressionistic shaft of daylight slants in from one tall, barred window, spotlighting Miner who sits on a hard chair clad only in a suit of long underwear. He is in the process of putting on a suit of civilian clothes. One of the guards and Warden Kelly (about fifty-five) stand watching him.

In one dim corner of the office another guard sits at a desk, pecking away on a cast iron typewriter.

Kelly has a solemn face and his expression is mirrored by the standing guard.

A series of TIGHT SHOTS *of Miner's hands as they do the job of clothing himself: buttoning the shirt/pulling up the pants/buttoning a vest/pulling on heavy work socks/lacing up a pair of high-top shoes. The hands are mottled but strong. On one of them, in the bridge between thumb and forefinger, is a tattoo of a bluebird with wings spread. These* SHOTS ARE INTERCUT *with the watching faces of Kelly and the guard.*

Miner now stands up, fully dressed except for suit-coat and hat. The guard holds the suit-coat for Miner like a sullen valet. Miner slips his arm into it. The whole outfit is slightly too large for his lean frame.

    KELLY: Don't you look the gentleman?

Miner looks at Kelly, detecting sarcasm in Kelly's tone.

KELLY: Unfortunately, it would take more than a new suit of clothes to make a good citizen of you.

Miner fixes Kelly with his kindly blue eyes.

MINER: I might surprise you, sir.

KELLY: (*Snorts*) I'll be surprised if you aren't back within a month.

Miner does not reply. Kelly moves to his desk where he picks up a hat. It is a stetson similar to the kind worn by Mounties. He returns to face Miner.

KELLY: You've spent more than half your life in here, Bill. Even the crime for which you've served your terms has ceased to exist. You're a relic. The only proper place for you is this museum.

He hands the stetson to Miner who takes it and holds it politely against his chest. Although the outfit is cheap and ill-fitting there is now something courtly in his appearance.

MINER: There's some life in me yet, sir.

KELLY: (*Derisive*) What can you make of it? How will you live?

MINER: I will adjust to what's dealt.

KELLY: Rot. All you know is prison and robbing stage-coaches. If I had the authority I would keep you here.

MINER: I have served my full sentence.

KELLY: I would keep you here for your own good.

MINER: With respect, sir, I have had my fill of San Quentin's charity.

Kelly glares at him then motions at his desk top.

KELLY: There are your personal effects. You'll have to sign for them.

Miner moves over to the desk and stares down at the objects.

What he sees: a couple of flashy, cheap rings, an old pipe, a pearl-handled brush, and a tattered Holy Bible.

151

Miner looks at Kelly, slightly troubled.

KELLY: Is something missing?

MINER: (*Nods*) My pocketwatch and my diamond ring.

KELLY: (*To Guard*) Mister Walsh?

The guard immediately produces and scans a sheet of paper.

The Grey Fox himself (Richard Farnsworth) and the tools of his trade — a Colt .45 revolver and a guileless expression. "Although the outfit is cheap and ill-fitting there is something courtly in his appearance."

GUARD #1: They ain't on the list, sir.

MINER: There was no list when I turned them in.

KELLY: That was long ago. Perhaps you are mistaken?

Miner seems about to protest but his eyes catch the cold, murderous stare of the guard. Miner shrugs and nods.

MINER: Perhaps I am.

The guard thrusts the paper and a pencil at Miner.

GUARD #1: Sign.

Miner tucks his hat under one arm, takes the sheet and signs it.

5. Int. Main Corridor. Day.

In foreground an old guard mans a desk. Kelly and Miner approach from the far end of the corridor, past high windows along the left side which admit pools of daylight. Miner carries his stetson and walks as if the shoes hurt his feet. They approach the guard at the desk.

KELLY: Bill Miner is going out now.

GUARD #2: Sign beside your number.

Miner leans on the desk and signs a sheet of paper. Kelly produces an envelope and hands it to Miner.

KELLY: You'll find twenty dollars in there. We issue release money as part of the new system.

GUARD #2: You have to sign for it.

Miner shrugs and signs the top sheet again. He then looks at Kelly who offers an official handshake. Miner shakes. Kelly is staring at him.

KELLY: I'll be seeing you soon.

Miner does not reply. He simply stares at Kelly with his alert blue eyes.

6. Ext. San Quentin Prison Yard. Day.

TRACKING behind Miner and Kelly as they walk toward a huge set of wooden gates mounted in a high stone wall.

Kelly stops, gives Miner a final clap on the shoulder, and Miner trudges onward toward the gates. He dons his stetson as he walks.

As he gets close to the gates a guard moves across and opens a small door that is set within one of the gates. It admits a tremendous, dazzling blast of sunlight as if from the mouth of a blast furnace. Miner pauses then steps over the sill through the door to the outer world where he is immediately swallowed by the blinding glare. The guard shuts the door after him.

7. Ext. San Francisco Bay. Day.

VIEW of a longboat that is being rowed by six prisoners. It carries a guard at the stern and the figure of Miner is visible, riding up in the bow as the boat plows across open water under a blue sky and clouds. Seagulls swoop around the boat.

8. Ext. A San Francisco Street. Night.

Solid fog. A narrow street. A foghorn moans. The figure of Miner emerges through the fog, making his way carefully, footsore.

He stops, hearing something, turns and looks back into the fog. Some kind of engine is heard. A dim light begins to cut the mist.

Suddenly the shape of a motor car comes hurtling through the fog, rattling down on Miner. Miner steps aside as the auto rattles past him with a toot of its horn.

Miner watches as it vanishes into the fog, then he continues walking along, peering into the occasional illuminated window.

He stops outside an illuminated shop with a protruding shingle that advertises GUNSMITH.

9. Int. Gunsmith's. Night.

A small, narrow shop with display cases of weapons along the side walls and a single display counter across the back. Miner is at the counter, across from the gunsmith who is showing him a tray of shiny little Derringer pistols.

GUNSMITH: . . . These Derringers are highly popular, sir.

They fit the pocket without any bulge or pull. There's a choice of ivory or pearl handles.

MINER: Well, I'd prefer something with more heft to it.

GUNSMITH: (*Slightly snotty*) Compactness is the fashion, sir.

Miner has spotted something in the display counter.

MINER: (*Points*) I'd like to have a look at that one.

GUNSMITH: (*Looks*) The Colt?

Miner nods. The gunsmith looks as if he might protest the choice but decides to acquiesce. He opens the back of the counter and takes out the gun — a black Colt .45 revolver. He hands it across to Miner.

GUNSMITH: Careful, sir. It's heavy.

But when Miner takes it the weapon looks natural in the old man's hand. In a quick series of efficient motions Miner snaps open the cartridge chamber, spins it, cocks the hammer, checks the bore, shuts the chamber, checks the balance, sights out the window, and pulls the trigger. Click.

He then turns back and puts it down in front of the now-impressed gunsmith.

MINER: I'll need some bullets to go with it.

The gunsmith nods.

10. Ext. San Francisco Alley. Night.

Fog. Miner makes his way along the narrow alley, looking for an address. Two Chinese wearing coolie hats emerge from the fog and scurry past him in the other direction. Miner almost stumbles over another Chinese who is sleeping huddled against a wall. He eases past, sees the doorway he is seeking, and goes inside a building.

11. Int. Oriental Baths. Night.

VIEW *of Miner luxuriating in a large wooden tub of soapy, steamy water while two Chinese girls bathe his body. It is a dimly-lit room with plain wooden walls. The girls wear light robes. One is scrubbing Miner's back while the other works on his white, knobby legs.*

>**MINER:** Scrub away, ladies. Cleanliness is next to Godliness, or so I'm told, and I'd like to get closer than I've been.

The girls giggle at this although it's obvious they neither speak nor understand English. Miner's shoulders and arms are visible. In addition to the bluebird tattooed on his hand there is a large tattoo of a ballet girl on his right forearm. One of the girls points this out to the other and they giggle and speak in Chinese. Miner smiles and waggles his thumb and forefinger, making the bird tattoo 'fly'. The girls giggle with delight. In addition to his tattoos, a ragged white knife scar runs from shoulder to chest. Miner rubs at it absently.

One of the girls moves to the bottom of the tub and lifts out his feet to wash them. She is startled by what she sees and calls the other girl in Chinese. The other girl joins her and they look at Miner's soles.

What they see: Across the soles of both feet are numerous white scars, some of which still look recently acquired.

Miner sees them looking at his soles and smiles at them.

>**MINER:** A legacy of San Quentin, ladies. A man can't run far on whipped feet. No sir.

The girls begin to wash his feet gently. Miner sinks back in the hot water, shuts his eyes, and begins humming softly.

12. Ext. A Seawall in a Park. Day.

VIEW of Miner standing alone on a rough, stone seawall. Gulls swoop, the sun shines down, the Pacific laps against the wall.

Miner is leafing agitatedly through the pages of a hardcover book. The title inscribed on its cover is "Outlaws of the American Frontier."

>**MINER:** (*Muttering*) . . . The James Brothers, the Dalton boys, Billy Bonney, Jack Slade . . . But not a word about me.

Miner slams the book shut and stares at its cover.

>**MINER:** And I'm still here.

He tucks the book under one arm and marches off along the seawall.

13. Int. A Waterfront Bar. Night.

A long, narrow, low-ceilinged dive in which the coal oil lanterns barely cut the shadowy gloom. The shapes of men are visible, hunched at tables. Some seem to have passed out. A few others stand at a crude trencher bar, tossing back shots of whiskey. The air is smokey, conversation is negligible here. Outside, the sound of a foghorn, distant.

ANGLE ON *a hard, dirty-looking man of about thirty (Danny Young) who is standing at the bar. He is unshaven and has bad teeth. He is peering sideways toward the back of the bar.*

What he sees: Bill Miner is seated alone at a small table with a bottle of whiskey and a glass in front of him. Young leaves the bar, carrying his shot glass, and walks down to Miner's table.

YOUNG: Miner. Bill Miner. Right?

Miner looks up at him slowly, without recognition.

MINER: Do I know you, sir?

YOUNG: I'm Danny Young. I was in San Quentin four years back . . . when you got knifed by Billy Hicks. Remember?

It's obvious that Miner wants no part of Young.

MINER: I don't remember you.

Young looks offended, then grins, revealing rotten teeth.

YOUNG: I thought you'd died.

MINER: As you can see, I did not.

Young laughs — more a mirthless tic than a laugh — then he pulls out a chair and sits down without being invited.

YOUNG: You just got out, right?

MINER: Last week.

YOUNG: So what're you up to?

MINER: (*Non-commital*) Looking for work, seeing the sights.

YOUNG: You're in luck, Miner . . .

He glances around then leans forward and lowers his voice.

    YOUNG: . . . I'm putting a gang together.

    MINER: (*Smiles*) Like Jesse James?

Young misses the sarcasm and pours himself a drink from Miner's bottle.

    YOUNG: D'ya mind?

He tosses off the drink in one gulp then winks at Miner.

    YOUNG: I figure we'll do some hold-ups. That's your line, right?

    MINER: I only robbed stagecoaches.

    YOUNG: (*Grins*) Try to find one these days. Anyhow . . . stages, banks, stores . . . They're all the same.

Something goes hard in Miner's eyes but he maintains his polite demeanor.

    MINER: They are not the same. A professional always specializes.

Young senses a put-down. He half-grins, half-sneers.

    YOUNG: Well, your's is gone with the buffalo, Miner. Maybe I can teach you something new?

    MINER: Oh? I would be interested in how you plan to rob banks?

    YOUNG: Simple. All I need is four or five guys with guns and guts.

    MINER: (*Smiles*) That is simple.

    YOUNG: (*Nods/grins*) Right. So, you want to throw in with me?

    MINER: No thank you.

    YOUNG: (*Offended*) Why not?

    MINER: I don't work for anyone.

Although Miner says it pleasantly, Young senses his contempt.

    YOUNG: You're kind of old to be choosy ain't you?

    MINER: That is exactly why I've got to be, son. Now I must be going.

Miner moves to stand but Young plants a hand on his forearm.

    YOUNG: Miner . . .

Miner remains still and meets Young's glare. Suddenly Young drops the bravado and a wheedling tone comes into his voice.

    YOUNG: . . . Lend me a couple of bucks willya?

    MINER: I have no money.

    YOUNG: Bull! You must've got twenty or thirty bucks in your release envelope.

Miner stands, pulling his arm from Young's grasp.

    MINER: A professional never begs.

Suddenly Young leaps to his feet, knocking over his chair. He has a knife in his hand and he presses the glinting blade against Miner's throat.

    YOUNG: I ain't' beggin', grampa.

In one fast, fluid motion Miner's arm snakes down, snatches up the whiskey bottle, and whips it into the side of Young's head. The bottle explodes in a shower of glass and whiskey and Young goes down with a crash.

The bartender and customers all freeze.

Miner drops the neck of the bottle and immediately makes his way toward the door, forcing himself to move calmly.

Behind him, Young struggles to his feet, his face streaming whiskey mixed with blood. He looks around, sees Miner moving away, and lunges after him clutching the knife.

    CUSTOMER: *(Off)* Look out!

Miner turns, as if expecting Young's rush, and his hand comes out of his pocket gripping the Colt .45. The gun arcs up, aiming right at Young, who skids to a halt.

The customers immediately dive for cover amid a great clatter of overturning furniture.

Miner's thumb cocks the hammer with an efficient double click.

Young sees certain death in the muzzle of the Colt and his expression goes blubbery. He drops the knife and sinks slowly to his knees, raising his hands to protect his face.

YOUNG: (*Meek*) Please . . .

MINER: You aren't worth killing but if you come after me again I most certainly will put a window through your head.

Young doubles over, all the fight gone out of him. Miner backs away slowly and pauses at the door to survey the room.

MINER: I apologize for this disturbance.

Then he pockets the Colt and goes out. There is a beat before the bartender and a couple of customers hurry to the aid of Young. They haul him to his feet.

YOUNG: He comes in here again, I'll kill 'im.

Young shakes them off, staggers to a chair and plops down on it. He wipes at the blood and whiskey.

14. *Ext. Railroad Track. Day. (Travel).*

P.O.V. *from the front of a fast-moving steam locomotive. The whistle squeals as it rushes along the gleaming tracks through lush farmland with a range of mountains visible along the right.*

15. *Int. Railroad Coach. Day. (Travel).*

VIEW *of the coach interior with its sash windows and wicker seats.* SHOT *moves back along the aisle of the coach revealing the passengers — a cross-section of western American humanity — men, women, children, babies. This is not a first class coach so its passengers do not look prosperous. Luggage is stowed on the racks over the windows.*

SHOT *finally reveals Miner. His hair has grown out some and he looks spiffy in a new, cheap suit. Facing Miner is a salesman (Al Sims) in a checked suit. On the seat beside Sims is a large rectangular sales case with "Topeka Housewares" emblazoned on the side of it. Sims (about thirty-five) has an open, hopeful face and he is talking to Miner with sincere enthusiasm.*

SIMS: . . . I tell you, Bill, with electrification coming along there's going to be a revolution in the American kitchen. Right now our company has designs for an electric toast-making machine . . . and I hear stories about a stove that'll heat up with the flip of a switch. Think of it.

Miner nods. Hard to tell if he's impressed or not.

> **SIMS:** Yessiry, I'd say the future in houseware sales is unlimited, Bill, and I feel darn lucky to be part of it.
>
> **MINER:** Sounds fine, Mister Sims . . .
>
> **SIMS:** Al. (*Nods*) Darn tootin' it's fine.
>
> **MINER:** . . . Of course to a man my age the future doesn't mean much unless you're talking about next week.

Miner rummages in a paper bag beside him and produces an apple, which he polishes on his sleeve. Sims's eyes light up.

> **SIMS:** Here . . . Gimme that.

Miner hands him the apple. Sims snaps open his sales case and lets the front lid down, revealing a dazzling array of housewares nestled inside. He raises the top tray to reveal another layer beneath it and extracts a black, cast-iron device with a crank handle. Miner watches this, perplexed, as does a young boy who is seated with his parents across the aisle. Miner and the boy watch with interest as Sims sticks the apple on a spike and cranks the handle of the device. An arm with a fine blade begins to rotate, peeling the skin neatly off the apple. Then another small arm kicks the apple off the spike into Sims's hand. Sims holds it up proudly.

> **SIMS:** What do you think of that?

Miner takes the peeled apple and looks at it, impressed.

> **MINER:** Real nice workmanship, Mister Sims.
>
> **SIMS:** Al. (*Nods/grins*) I tell you, Bill, in the next few years we're going to see new products that'll make our heads swim.

Miner notices the young boy staring at the apple. Miner reaches across and offers it to him. The boy is hesitant about taking it. Miner smiles and nods. The boy takes the gift and begins to eat it. Miner produces another apple from the bag. Sims hands him the mechanical peeler.

> **SIMS:** Try it yourself, Bill.
>
> **MINER:** (*Dubious*) I would hate to break it.

SIMS: (*Laughs*) No chance. This baby is made to last a lifetime.

Miner takes the peeler and positions the apple on the spike and cautiously cranks the handle — pleased to see that the blade performs for him. Sims is noticing the bird tattoo on Miner's hand. He gestures at it.

SIMS: You a seafaring man, Bill?

MINER: Pardon?

SIMS: I notice that tattoo you've got.

Miner smiles and keeps peeling the apple.

MINER: I have never been to sea.

The little arm kicks the peeled apple into Miner's hand and he looks at it, pleased.

SIMS: (*Grins*) What is your line, Bill?

MINER: I am between careers, Al.

SIMS: No kidding? What'd you used to do?

Miner takes a big bite out of the apple and chews it.

MINER: I robbed stagecoaches.

Sims stares at him then laughs weakly. Miner smiles/chews.

16. *Ext. Johnson House. Day.*

VIEW of Miner trudging along a rutted road toward a distant farmhouse that is partly hidden by trees.

17. *Ext. Side of Johnson House. Day.*

SHOT TRACKS with Miner as he approaches the house. The sound of an axe chopping kindling is heard from somewhere nearby. Miner stops walking and stares off.

What he sees: A woman (Jenny Johnson) is standing near a woodshed attached to the house. She is putting logs on top of a stump and chopping them into kindling with an axe. Her back is turned. She wears a cheap *smock and has a kerchief tied around her head.*

Miner says nothing. He smiles, takes something out of his pocket — it is the mechanical apple peeler — and holds it out of sight behind his back. Jenny stops to catch her breath. She turns and sees Miner. She is pretty but her face, at forty, shows the strain of years of hard work.

MINER: Hello, Jenny.

He removes his stetson exposing his grey hair.

Jenny's expression flickers from startled, to pleased, to joyous, then she drops the axe and moves toward him, faster and faster until she is running. She throws herself into his arms and they hug.

Jenny finally pulls her face back and stares up at him. She is half-laughing, half-crying.

JENNY: Oh god . . . It's been so long . . . I never thought . . .

Miner, uneasy with her emotionality, extricates himself and brings out the apple peeler from behind his back.

MINER: Brought you this little gizmo from San Francisco.

Jenny takes it, barely noticing what it is, and keeps staring at Miner.

MINER: (*Uneasy/smiles*) I suppose I have aged some.

Jenny suddenly becomes animated, grabs him by the hand, and begins leading him off toward the sheds and the fields at the back.

JENNY: Come . . . You must meet Tom.

They move off, hand in hand.

18. Int. Johnson Dining Room. Night.

VIEW *of Miner, Jenny, and Tom Johnson seated at the dinner table. Tom (forty-five) is a dour-looking working man who is concentrating on his food. The room is clean but spartan and the mood is formal, strained. Miner and Jenny share several slightly nervous glances as if conspiring on something. Jenny finally puts down her fork and looks at Tom who continues eating, looking down at his plate.*

JENNY: Tom . . . I have some good news.

Tom glances up at her, glances at Miner, then returns to eating. Jenny now looks intimidated, but Miner encourages her with a smile and a nod.

    JENNY: (*Forced gaiety*) I've been talking with Bill and I've persuaded him to stay with us.

Now Tom stops eating and looks up at them — his expression far from pleased.

    MINER: I will pay my share of course.

    JENNY: It will be nice to have Bill here . . . And there's lots of room now that the kids are gone.

Tom says nothing for a moment and then stares at Miner.

    TOM: What can you do?

    MINER: I will find some work.

    TOM: Doing what? You haven't got any skills and you're old.

    JENNY: (*Hinting*) They're hiring over at the oyster beds.

    MINER: (*Nods*) I can pick oysters.

    TOM: (*Snorts*) That's for Indians, Chinamen, and bums.

Miner's face reveals a flash of anger then he is calm again.

    MINER: It's money, Tom, and I'm willing to work for it.

    TOM: (*Dubious*) You are, huh?

    MINER: (*Nods*) It will be easy compared to where I've been.

Tom measures him with dour eyes.

    TOM: I've heard about where you've been and what you done to get there. I frankly don't have much use for your kind.

    JENNY: Tom . . .

    MINER: (*Calm*) I hope I will have the chance to soften your opinion, Tom.

Tom glances at Jenny, then looks at Miner again.

    TOM: What I think of you is neither here nor there.

You're Jenny's brother. You can stay if she wants it.

Jenny looks very relieved. Tom returns to eating. Miner smiles at Jenny.

MINER: Tomorrow I will look for work.

19. *Ext. Samish Bay Oyster Farm. Day.*

A sweep of dirty, kelpy beach facing onto a shallow bay. The tide is out far and the figures of workers are visible on the tidal flats, picking oysters and putting them into baskets. Other workers are carrying loaded baskets up to a horse-drawn wagon and carrying empties back out to the flats. The glassy water is misty and the far side of the bay is shrouded in fog.

20. *Ext. On the Flats. Day.*

ANGLE on Miner who is picking oysters. Like the others he is wearing rubber boots but he looks damp and chilled. Working near him is a young, blonde man of twenty (Charles Hoehn) who picks up an oyster, cracks it open with a knife, and gulps down the contents as Miner watches. Hoehn then tosses the shell away. He and Miner exchange a brief glance, then they return to picking.

21. *Int. A Movie 'Theater'. Night.*

A smoke-filled room where the audience (all men) are hunkered on rows of folding chairs. Gas lamps give off a wan illumination. The men are all staring ahead — intent — as the music of a piano bangs out a silent movie score.

ANGLE on the pomaded piano player, staring up and ahead as his fingers dance over the keys of an upright.

CLOSE on Miner entering the theater — a look of dubious curiosity on his face. He registers surprise as he looks ahead toward the screen, then quickly finds himself a seat on one of the folding chairs and stares ahead — rapt.

VIEW of the movie screen on which we see a moustachioed bandit aiming a pistol right at us in grainy black-and-white. A puff of smoke emits from the barrel as he fires, then the title card pops up: "Edwin S. Porter's The Great Train Robbery.*" The piano trills.*

INTERCUT between scenes from "The Great Train Robbery," the piano player, and Miner. At first Miner displays a child's amazement at what he is seeing — an amazement that quickly turns to absorption, then inspiration. On the screen he sees the movie bandits invade the mail car, steal the loot, commandeer the locomotive, cut it loose, and run it to a spot down the line where their horses are tethered.

But all is not well. The bandits are pursued by a posse. Silent shots are exchanged. A bandit falls. Miner's delight turns to concern. The bandits in a sparse copse of trees begin to divvy the loot. The posse creeps up through the trees. A gunfight. The bandits die.

CLOSE on Miner, not enjoying the ending. Blam! A real gunshot makes him jump and look.

VIEW of an over-excited man who has jumped up and fired his revolver into the ceiling. The piano segues into exit music.

The men rise and begin to file out. Miner sits for a moment, pensive, then rises and joins the outgoing men.

22. Int. Miner's Room. Night.

A clean, spartan room in the Johnson house containing only a bed and a bureau. Miner is sitting on the edge of the bed in his longjohns, his bare feet soaking in a pan of warm water. He has a school exercise book open on his lap and is writing in it with a pencil. Rain splashes on the window.

> **MINER:** (*Mutters*) . . . There was cunning in my choice of target . . . A stagecoach could be waylaid in an isolated place . . . lessening the risk of outside interference and providing time for a clean getaway.

Miner pauses, thinking, then writes again.

> **MINER:** Today I would choose a train.

He puts down the book and the pencil, thinking, then stands up and walks over to the window, where he stares out at the night and the rain.

23. Ext. Oyster Farm. Day.

VIEW of Miner and Hoehn groping around in the water, lifting oysters and dumping them into baskets on the walkways. It is pouring rain and Miner is wearing his soggy stetson. Hoehn is, as always, grinning.

MINER: What's your name, son?

HOEHN: Charlie Hoehn.

MINER: You like this work?

HOEHN: Hate it with all my heart.

Miner laughs. They go on digging up oysters.

24. Ext. Railroad Track. Night.

CLOSE on Miner standing in darkness. A train whistle moans. Miner drags on a cigarette, the glow illuminating his features. In the distance the locomotive's headlight comes into view. Miner turns to face it.

A WIDER ANGLE reveals that Miner is standing in the middle of the railroad track, facing the onrushing train. His body is silhouetted by the headlight. The whistle blasts a warning. Miner stands his ground.

The massive locomotive is approaching fast, whistle blaring now, the sound of its pistons growing loud.

As the train roars down on him Miner calmly steps off the track at the last moment and the monster locomotive thunders past.

25. Int. Johnson Kitchen. Day.

Jenny is hard at work doing the family laundry in large tubs on the kitchen counter. She is perspiring from the steam.

Suddenly she hears orchestrated music and the voice of an Irish tenor singing "My Wild Irish Rose." She picks up a towel and moves cautiously toward the dining room.

26. Int. Johnson Dining Room. Day.

Jenny enters the room and sees Miner seated at one end of the dining table. He is still wearing his work clothes. On the table is a gleaming new *gramophone with a record playing on it. Jenny is confused and delighted.*

JENNY: Bill . . . Where did that come from?

MINER: I bought it in town. Like it?

Jenny goes over, starry-eyed, and touches the wondrous machine.

JENNY: It's magnificent. It must have cost the earth!

Miner turns a small knob and lowers the volume.

MINER: This little knob adjusts the loudness . . .

He picks up a couple of other records from the tabletop.

MINER: . . . And these are some extra records for it . . . "My Department Store Girl" and a Sousa piece.

JENNY: (*Enthralled*) I never dreamed we'd have one of these in our own home!

The tenor sings on. Miner shifts uneasily.

MINER: Well, I would be very grateful if you would keep and use this one while I'm away.

Jenny's delight is instantly cross-cut by a look of dread.

MINER: (*Nods*) I have decided to move on.

JENNY: (*Hurt*) Why?

MINER: I am no oyster picker, Jenny.

Jenny is trying to absorb this but doesn't comprehend.

JENNY: I thought things were going so well. You had work . . . and a place with us.

Miner knows he is hurting her. The music ends and he busies himself with lifting the record arm and placing it in its cradle.

JENNY: What will you do?

MINER: Oh, I'm going to head down Portland way. Maybe I will do some prospecting.

Jenny knows he is lying. A tear wells in her eye.

JENNY: The gold rush is over, Bill.

Miner nods, looks down, and smiles.

    MINER: Seems I've missed out on all the big opportunities.

Jenny moves to him and places a hand on his shoulder.

    JENNY: Please. Stay.

Miner looks up at her, stands, and puts his arms around her. She hugs him tightly.

    MINER: Can I tell you something?

Jenny, her head against his shoulder, nods.

    MINER: In the months since I came out of prison I have realized something about myself and I must act on it. (*Pauses*) I am simply no good at work planned by other heads. No good at all.

Jenny does not reply. Miner raises a hand and strokes her hair.

27. Ext. A Pond. Dusk.

Mist rises off a glassy body of water bounded by darkening woods. A rowboat glides into view carrying three men. One of them, standing in the bow like George Washington crossing the Potomac, is Miner. The boat glides out of view.

28. Ext. Railroad Track, Oregon. Dusk.

A railroad track stretches away, flanked on both sides by deep evergreen forest. The sound of crickets fills the darkening air. Bill Miner stands waiting, listening, on the tracks, a boot resting on one of the rails.

A CLOSER ANGLE. *Miner is now wearing his Colt in a holster that is belted around his suit-coat on the outside. At his feet on the cross-ties sits an unlit hurricane lantern and two bundles of dynamite.*

29. Ext. In the Trees, Oregon. Dusk.

Two men (Harshman and Hoehn) are using knives to cut a couple of long branches. Harshman is bearded (thirty-five), Hoehn is blonde (about twenty). They carry revolvers in their belts.

30. Ext. The Track, Oregon. Dusk.

VIEW of Hoehn and Harshman emerging from the forest to join Miner on the track. Each of them is carrying a long, pole-like branch.

    HOEHN: These do?

Miner nods. Harshman and Hoehn kneel down and busy themselves tying the sticks of dynamite to the ends of the poles. Miner watches them with his arms folded.

    MINER: Let's review the whole procedure one last time.

Harshman and Hoehn exchange disgruntled glances.

    HARSHMAN: (*To Miner*) We already done it fifty times!

Miner's expression becomes dangerous — fleetingly — then he frowns.

    MINER: There are never enough times.

    HOEHN: Aw, Bill . . . We're ready!

    MINER: (*Snorts*) We will soon find out.

Miner turns on his heel and walks away a few paces, then stands with his back to them. Harshman and Hoehn shake their heads and grin.

31. Ext. Along the Track, Oregon. Night.

A big locomotive, headlight glaring, sweeps around a curve and highballs past. It pulls a baggage car, a mail car, and two coaches.

32. Int./Ext. Locomotive Cab, Oregon. Night. (Travel).

The engineer is in the right-hand seat, his hand on the throttle bar, his eyes on the track ahead. The fireman is in the left-hand seat, taking a breather. The glow from the boiler is visible through the grates in the firebox door. The engineer reaches up and yanks on the whistle cord. The whistle moans.

Suddenly the engineer and fireman both spot something ahead.

ENGINEER'S P.O.V. *along the right side of the boiler. Ahead, a bright light glows on the right-of-way.*

The engineer immediately yanks on the whistle cord, closes the throttle, and starts braking the enormous train.

33. Ext. Along the Track, Oregon. Night.

TIGHT *on the hurricane lantern glowing bright.* SHOT WIDENS *to reveal Miner, Harshman, and Hoehn all standing behind it on the track. They now wear bandannas that mask the lower halves of their faces and they have their guns drawn.*

The headlight of the approaching locomotive bathes them as it squeals and hisses to a stop. Miner immediately heads for the locomotive while Hoehn and Harshman stoop to retrieve the long poles with the dynamite now tied to the ends.

34. Ext. Beside the Train, Oregon. Night.

The engineer peers down from the cab at Miner.

> **ENGINEER:** What's this about?

Miner aims the Colt up at him.

> **MINER:** Hold-up! Get down here now!

The engineer looks confused but he doesn't argue with a gun. He climbs down from the cab, followed by the fireman. Miner keeps his gun trained on them. He is very tense.

Harshman and Hoehn come into view carrying the dynamite-laden poles. They are about to hurry past when Miner stops them.

> **MINER:** No! Keep the engine crew in front of you!

Miner gestures for the engineer and fireman to walk toward the rear of the train. They obey. Harshman and Hoehn follow them. Miner waits by the locomotive.

As the foursome walks back to the mail car, a conductor pokes his head out the vestibule door of a coach farther back. Harshman aims his revolver and fires a shot. The conductor ducks back inside.

At the door of the mail car Hoehn produces a match and lights the fuses on both bundles of dynamite. He quickly plants one end of each pole in the earth and leans the dynamite-laden ends against the sliding door of the mail car. The fuses are sputtering down. Harshman and Hoehn hurry the engineer and fireman back toward the locomotive.

The dynamite explodes with an enormous flash and boom — shattering the door of the mail car. Splinters fly.

Hoehn cheers, then starts running back to the mail car with Harshman. Miner is alarmed.

>MINER: Use these men as shields!

But Harshman and Hoehn are going. Suddenly a mail clerk appears in the shattered doorway with a Winchester rifle. He pumps off two shots.

Harshman falls heavily on his back, legs jerking.

Hoehn and Miner fire several shots and the mail clerk ducks back in. Hoehn, panicky, shouts back to Miner.

>HOEHN: What now?

Miner motions at Harshman's fallen form.

>MINER: Check him!

The clerk leans out and fires again. Miner fires back and the clerk ducks in. Hoehn is crouched over Harshman.

>HOEHN: They've kilt 'im!

>MINER: Damn!

The clerk fires again. The fireman, standing beside Miner, goes down with a bullet in his arm. The engineer flattens himself against the side of the car.

>ENGINEER: Stop shooting before you kill the lot of us!

>MINER: (*To Hoehn*) Let's get out of here!

Hoehn comes running right past Miner. Miner takes a final look at the shambles of his operation then runs after Hoehn with a speed spurred by fear.

ON *Hoehn and Miner as they vanish, crashing into the dark forest.*

ON *the engineer, waving his bandanna toward the mail car like a flag of surrender.*

ENGINEER: Don't shoot! Don't shoot!

35. Ext. A Trail, Oregon. Day.

VIEW *of Miner, alone now, as he trudges footsore along a wooded path. He looks crumpled and dirty and he listens for sounds of pursuit as he moves along.*

He stops and looks down at some berries on a low bush. He kneels, picks them off, and stuffs them into his mouth — very hungrily. He picks off more, stuffs them into his pockets, then stands and forces himself to move on.

36. Ext. The Forest, Oregon. Night.

Miner squats beside a low fire, his posture suggesting some prehistoric man. He is munching on a handful of roots.

37. Int. An Interrogation Room. Night.

CLOSE *on Hoehn, seated on a chair. His eyes are puffed and his face is bloody. A big fist arcs down and smashes into his jaw, snapping his head sideways. He moans.*

VIEW *of the room. A husky detective is administering the beating, watched by a well-dressed, hard-eyed man of about forty-five (Detective Seavey) who has mutton-chop sideburns and looks impassive as he watches the beating.*

SEAVEY: Give us his name, son.

Hoehn, half-crying from pain, does not speak. The husky detective smashes him again.

Seavey now comes over, grasps Hoehn's hair and — almost tenderly — turns his face upward.

SEAVEY: Save yourself some pain, son. We'll get him anyway.

HOEHN: (*Thickly*) Bill . . . Miner.

Seavey releases his hair and turns to the husky detective.

SEAVEY: Get this lad some water.

38. Ext. A Rural Store, Washington. Day.

A wood-frame store in the middle of nowhere. A flat expanse of fields stretches off in all directions. The figure of Miner approaches along the dirt road toward the store. He carries his coat slung over his shoulder and as he gets closer it's obvious that he is very tired now. He is unshaven and his clothes are dirty. As Miner draws even with the store he pauses on the road and looks at the store — thinking of food.

The elderly storekeeper then emerges onto the porch. He has a bad limp. He stares at Miner for a moment.

STOREKEEPER: Mornin'.

Miner nods "hello" and summons up some weary charm.

MINER: Is this the road to Olympia?

STOREKEEPER: Ten miles more'll get you there.

Miner nods, looks ahead, looks back, and sees a horseman approaching from the distance — riding slowly toward them. Miner isn't sure what to do so he stands still.

STOREKEEPER: Chew tobacco?

MINER: Pardon?

The storekeeper produces a package of plug tobacco from his pocket and displays it.

STOREKEEPER: Tobacco?

Miner nods. The horseman is getting closer.

MINER: I don't have any money.

STOREKEEPER: No charge.

Miner walks over to the porch and takes the tobacco.

MINER: Thank you.

He looks back at the approaching horseman as he bites off a wad and tucks it into his cheek.

    STOREKEEPER: Looks like you've been walkin' some. Not the best for a fella your age.

Miner glances nervously as the horseman nears them.

    MINER: I have no choice. My brother is dying in Olympia.

    STOREKEEPER: Couldn't walk a mile on this leg of mine.

The horseman now rides right up. He does not seem to be a lawman but a rancher. He dismounts and ties his horse to the hitching post. He glances at Miner then nods to the storekeeper.

    STOREKEEPER: Afternoon, Mister Lawton. Guess you're wantin' your mail?

The horseman nods and follows the storekeeper inside.

Miner stares covetously at the saddled stallion, then glances at the door of the store, then looks at the stallion again. It snorts and paws the dirt.

Miner stands up grandly and slips on his suit-coat. He then walks boldly to the stallion, unties it, plants a foot in a stirrup, and swings himself aboard with the ease of a practiced horseman. He turns the horse and moves off along the road at a stately canter.

39. Ext. A Mountain Ridge. Day.

EXTREME WIDE SHOT *of a ridge. High mountains are visible in the distance beyond. The figure of Miner aboard the stallion enters view, riding quickly along the spine of the ridge.*

40. Ext. Beside a Road. Day.

TRACKING PARALLEL *to a dirt road. Miner is riding the stallion at a walking pace — moving out and into view as he passes a long row of evenly spaced trees. His back is straight. He now looks proud, heroic.*

41. Ext. On the Road. Day.

Miner reins the stallion beside a raised stone marker.

What he sees: Lettered on the stone is: INTERNATIONAL BOUNDARY: U.S.A. — CANADA.

Miner stares ahead into Canada and pats the horse's neck.

MINER: New lands to conquer, Pat.

He spurs the horse into motion and rides forward into British Columbia.

42. Ext. A Barrel Factory Yard (Vancouver). Day.

A large, open enclosure where rain drizzles down on rutted dirt. Miner emerges from a row of squalid, joined cabins on one side of the yard and follows the boardwalk around the back perimeter where new barrels are stacked high on pallets. He hurries to escape the rain and goes into a dingy factory along the other side of this yard.

43. Int. The Barrel Factory. Day.

MOVING with Miner as he hauls a flatbed cart laden with new barrel staves across a Dickensian expanse of rattling machines, pulleys, belts, and steam, past other workers making barrels in this industrial gloom. In background, blasts of flame are visible from the area where the barrels are fired.

44. Ext. An Alley between Buildings. Day.

Miner emerges, hauling the cart. In this gloomy alleyway a short, stocky man of about thirty (Shorty Dunn) is standing in front of two whirring circular saw blades. He places staves on a holding bar and guides them forward, letting the blades cut both ends at once, then places the cut staves on a cart.

Miner begins to unload his cart of staves for Shorty, who turns and grins at him. There is a slightly crazed look in Shorty's eyes. He motions for Miner to watch. Miner looks on, horrified, as Shorty puts his fingers dangerously close to the whirring, steam-driven blades.

SHORTY: (*Grinning*) Sharp!

Miner shakes his head and returns to unloading staves.

45. Int. Miner's Cabin. Night.

Room for two cots. On one, Shorty snores. Miner sits on the other, fully dressed for warmth, writing in his exercise book.

MINER: (*Muttering softly*) . . . Train robbery is a difficult proposition. The mail car is a fortress that must be separated from the train before it is breached.

Miner pauses, thinking, then nods to himself.

46. Ext. Paymaster's Office. Day.

At the other end of the alley from the stave saw. Raining still. Workers are lined up in the drizzle, collecting their pay from a paymaster at his office door.

Miner takes his envelope and trudges away along the alley.

47. Int. The Barrel Factory. Day.

MOVING *with Miner as he enters and crosses the now shutdown factory, past silent machines. Steam hisses softly from some unseen valves. Miner goes out the other side.*

Now Shorty enters, walking quickly to catch up to Miner.

48. Ext. Barrel Factory Yard. Day.

Miner is crossing to his cabin when Shorty comes hurrying out of the factory.

SHORTY: Hey, George . . . What say we go buy ourselves a bottle?

Miner stops and turns to look at Shorty, who hurries over. Miner looks unhappy about something. He displays his pay.

MINER: They deducted me for food and bed, Shorty. They even deducted me for using the gloves and apron.

SHORTY: (*Grins*) The railroad shaves us six ways from Sunday, George.

Shorty realizes that Miner doesn't understand.

SHORTY: Who d'ya think owns this factory? (*Nods*) The railroad owns everything both sides of the tracks!

Shorty spits on the ground to emphasize his point.

49. Ext. Railroad Track. Day.

VIEW *of Miner and Shorty walking slowly along the deserted track somewhere near the factory (an edge-of-town feeling). Shorty has a bottle of whiskey and he gulps at it liberally.*

SHORTY: . . . Guess I hate the railroad about as much as most. Makes us work like dogs. (*Grins wildly*) 'Course when there wasn't no railroad in these parts there wasn't no work either. (*Shrugs*) Thing I do like is hearin' the steam whistle and the sound of those wheels . . . Chocka, chocka, chocka, chocka!

MINER: (*Smiles*) You have a good attitude, Shorty.

Shorty seems surprised but pleased by this apparent compliment.

SHORTY: Sure. A man can't hate everything about the railroad, eh?

Shorty pauses and looks both ways along the gleaming track.

SHORTY: Fact is it's kinda amazing to think this here track we're walkin' on stretches clear across the whole country.

MINER: A sure sign of man's progress.

SHORTY: They say you can get aboard in Vancouver 'n' ride like a king all the way to Montreal without ever gettin' off. I hear those trains got dining rooms, toilets, real beds!

MINER: You ever been to Montreal, Shorty?

SHORTY: Me? (*Laughs incredulously*)

MINER: A man can afford such things if he's willing to take some chances.

SHORTY: (*Puzzled*) How's that, George?

Miner puts a friendly arm around Shorty's shoulders as they pass and walk on.

MINER: Well . . . The first thing we'd need to get you is a good horse . . .

FADE TO BLACK. FADE IN.

Director Phillip Borsos and Richard Farnsworth appear to be enjoying the film-making process, and it shows on the screen.

50. Ext. Beside the Track (Mission). Night.

TIGHT on the locked drive wheels of a big locomotive as it squeals and hisses to a halt.

ANGLE on the cab as the fireman clambers down, followed by Miner who is disguised in his duster, kerchief over face and a pair of round driving goggles. Miner is clutching his Colt. The engineer remains in his seat, covered by the recognizable figure of Shorty Dunn, who has a kerchief over his face. Miner calls back up.

> MINER: Wait for our signal then pull ahead!

Miner prods the fireman into a trot and they hurry back alongside the train, past the baggage car and the mail car.

51. Ext. Rear of Mail Car (Mission). Night.

VIEW of the space between the mail car and the first passenger coach, coupled together by steel and hoses. The fireman and Miner appear in the space.

> MINER: Hurry up, son. Break it.

The fireman, who is scared, disconnects the air hoses with a loud whoosh then breaks the coupling open.

Miner waves forward for the engineer to start moving, then motions the fireman to get on the ladder up the back of the mail car. The train lurches into motion and the mail car pulls away from the passenger coaches.

Miner and the fireman get on the ladders.

52. Int. Locomotive Cab (Mission). Night. (Travel).

Shorty stands with a revolver against the back of the engineer's head. Shorty's eyes look wild and scared.

> ENGINEER: What do you want me to do?
>
> SHORTY: Stop 'er at the Silverdale Crossing!

53. Ext. Silverdale Crossing (Mission). Night.

The locomotive and the baggage and mail cars ease to a stop, straddling a rutted, narrow road.

The engineer climbs down, followed by Shorty, and they move toward the back of the train.

54. Ext. Mail Car (Mission). Night.

The engineer and Shorty join Miner and the fireman beside the doors of the mail car.

> **MINER:** Tell them to open the door and throw out any weapons.
>
> **ENGINEER:** (*Loud*) Open up, Herb!
>
> **CLERK:** (*Off*) That you, Nat?
>
> **ENGINEER:** Yep!
>
> **CLERK:** (*Off*) What's going on?
>
> **ENGINEER:** I think we're being robbed!
>
> **MINER:** (*Loud*) You are being robbed! Now open the door or we'll blow it off with dynamite!
>
> **CLERK:** (*Off*) Do they have dynamite, Nat?

Shorty quickly pulls three sticks of dynamite from his coat and shows them to the engineer.

> **ENGINEER:** They most certainly do, Herb!

There is a pause, then the sound of the door unlocking. Miner immediately shields himself behind the fireman, and Shorty does the same with the engineer.

But the door slides back to reveal a scared looking clerk who raises his hands high.

> **MINER:** (*To Shorty*) Cover them.

Miner then goes over and clambers into the mail car.

55. Ext. Silverdale Crossing. Night.

The engineer and fireman return to the locomotive, followed by Miner and Shorty, each of whom is toting a loaded mail bag. Miner motions the engineer and fireman to get aboard. They hurry up the ladder to their cab.

Miner and Shorty watch as the engineer reverses the locomotive and begins to back it up.

MINER: (*To engineer*) Goodnight, sir! Be careful when you are backing up!

The engineer nods as the train backs away along the track.

Miner and Shorty carry the bags down the embankment and into a field where their horses stand tethered. They tie the bags onto the saddle pommels and mount up and ride away into the darkness.

56. Ext. A Clearing in the Forest (After Mission). Night.

Miner and Shorty are squatting by a bonfire. Open envelopes and packages lie strewn around. Miner is examining little sacks of gold dust while Shorty is counting currency.

SHORTY: (*Excited*) Whooee! There's more'n a thousand dollars real money here!

MINER: (*Shows a sack*) Gold dust. Must be worth five to ten thousand.

SHORTY: We could buy our own railroad!

MINER: For the time being we aren't going to buy anything.

SHORTY: (*Disbelief*) Whaddya mean?

MINER: We would draw attention to ourselves. We will take some of the cash and bury the rest in a safe place.

Distant, an owl hoots. Shorty jumps to his feet and pulls his revolver.

MINER: Settle down, Shorty. It'll be midday before they can get men and horses to the crossing . . . And they won't know which way we went.

Shorty looks at Miner, suddenly puzzled.

SHORTY: Where *are* we goin', George?

MINER: Up-country. I have an old friend in Kamloops who won't ask questions.

Shorty nods, satisfied. Miner stands up and gestures at the litter.

MINER: While we're at it let's bury this evidence too.

57. Ext. A Trail. Day.

It's raining. Miner's stallion walks into view with Miner in the saddle. He is humming softly. Some distance behind comes Shorty on a mare. Shorty is pulling drinks from a bottle of whiskey.

Miner rides past, out of shot. Shorty abruptly topples off his mare.

SHORTY: Damn stupid horse!

58. Ext. A Canyon. Day. (To Kamloops).

The journey to Kamloops. Miner and Shorty ride along the narrow bottom of a canyon.

59. Ext. A Slope. Day. (To Kamloops).

In the distance the figures of Miner and Shorty ride slowly up a slope. Miner, tall and lean, Shorty, short and squat, form the image of Picasso's "Don Quixote."

60. Ext. A Mountain Trail. Day. (To Kamloops).

Miner and Shorty let their horses plod along a trail etched in the side of a steep hillside, high above a winding river.

61. Ext. Plateau of Barren Rock. Day. (To Kamloops).

Miner and Shorty cantering their horses across a high plain dotted with boulders. High grey sky.

62. Ext. Chinese Settlement Outside Kamloops. Day.

The road skirts a squalid collection of shacks, huddled together outside the town proper. These hovels have been constructed out of every kind of material that could be scrounged. Wisps of smoke trail up from stovepipes. A few Chinese stand watching outside the shacks.

At roadside, a discrete distance from the shacks, a photographer stands shrouded under the cloth hood of a large box camera on a wood tripod. The photographer's arm is extended, thumb pressing the shutter valve, exposing a shot of these shacks and the watching Chinese. The photographer's legs, clad in a skirt and riding boots, reveal that it is a woman.

Miner and Shorty ride into view. They rein to a halt when they spot the photographer and her horse hitched to a Democrat wagon.

> **SHORTY:** (Whispers) Who'd want a picture of that lot?

The photographer completes her shot and emerges from under the hood. Miner and Shorty register surprise that it is a female (Kate Flynn). She is about thirty-five and has loose, wild, auburn-colored hair that frames a curiously strong but delicate face. She is very thin, almost frail-looking but her movements are strong and deliberate.

Miner, fascinated by this singular-looking person, immediately smiles and doffs his stetson. Kate nods, then busies herself unloading the glass plate from the side of the camera.

Miner notices a small shingle hanging from the back of her wagon which advertises: K. FLYNN, COMMERCIAL PHOTOGRAPHY.

Miner flicks his reins and moves on, followed by Shorty.

63. Ext. Kamloops Main Street. Day.

A fairly settled, prosperous-looking small town that still bears a frontier appearance. There is a short main street flanked by stores and other establishments. The pedestrians look well-dressed. Mountains are visible in the distance.

ON Miner and Shorty as they ride slowly along the main drag and rein-up in front of a three-storey frame hotel called the TULAMEEN.

They dismount and hitch their horses. Miner motions Shorty to wait while he goes into the hotel.

64. Int. Tulameen Lobby. Day.

Miner enters and looks around at the paneled, horsehair, and chintz lobby. He then crosses to the front desk which is manned by a young clerk.

CLERK: Good afternoon, sir. May I help you?

MINER: Does Mister Jack Budd manage this hotel, son?

CLERK: Yessir. Shall I get him?

MINER: I would be grateful. Would you tell him George Edwards is here?

The clerk nods and goes through a door to the office. A few moments later he emerges followed by Jack Budd. Budd is a big man of about fifty-five who wears a shirt, vest, and matching pants. The first thing one notices about him is his lidded, watchful eyes which are set in a craggy, opaque face that hides everything behind it.

MINER: Hello, Jack.

When Budd looks at Miner there is a moment of non-recognition, then a slight, fleeting surprise in his eyes.

BUDD: Ah, yes . . . George Edwards.

Budd comes out from behind the counter with a slow efficiency of movement and extends his hand. He and Miner shake but there is some edge between them. Budd fixes Miner with his watchy eyes.

BUDD: Been a long time but I've been expecting you.

Miner's expression reveals slight surprise. Budd nods slightly to emphasize the point — never a superfluous motion — then indicates a doorway to the restaurant.

BUDD: Let's have some coffee.

65. Int. Tulameen Restaurant. Day.

A paneled room with windows facing the street. Shorty is visible out there with the horses. There are only a few customers in the place. In spite of this, Budd and Miner converse very quietly at their isolated table near the front windows.

BUDD: ... So when I read about that Silverdale train robbery I figured you might show up on my doorstep.

MINER: They know it was me?

BUDD: (*Nods*) The Pinkerton guys identified you to the CPR. Seems they're still chasing you for that messy business down in Oregon.

MINER: My partners forgot to use the engine crew as shields.

BUDD: You didn't make that mistake at Silverdale.

MINER: No. I followed the Chapman method there. It's the only reliable way.

Budd takes a sip of his coffee, keeping his eyes on Miner.

BUDD: They say you got away with seven thousand in gold dust.

MINER: (*Lying*) A fraction of that, Jack. They always stretch the truth. Shorty and I need a place to lie low for a while.

BUDD: Mmmm. What's in it for me, Bill?

MINER: (*Smiles*) I'm sure you'll think of something, Jack.

BUDD: (*Smiles*) You bet I will.

66. Int. Hotel Corridor. Day.

A long, dark hallway that looks like a tunnel. Budd comes along this passageway followed by Miner and opens the door of a room. Light floods into the corridor. Budd goes in and Miner follows.

67. Int. Hotel Room. Day.

A plain room with two creaky-looking beds. The window overlooks the main street. Budd moves to the window while Miner glances around the room.

>   **BUDD:** You'll be safe here. The law thinks you went south, back into Washington. I'll have to invent some cover story to explain you and your partner.
>
>   **MINER:** I appreciate it, Jack.

Budd is staring through the dirty lace curtain down to the street.

What he sees: Shorty with the horses.

ON *Budd. His mouth forms a slight, disdainful smile as he stares down at Shorty.*

>   **BUDD:** I see you're still working with idiots.

Miner senses the insult but responds gently.

>   **MINER:** Don't mark Shorty down, Jack. He's got plenty of spunk.

Budd turns and looks at Miner.

>   **BUDD:** Good. I've got some work for the both of you.

68. Ext. A Field (Whatcom). Dawn.

Vapor rises off wild grass. Cows graze. A grey day. A motor car — a Rambler — chugs into view along the road in distant background and stops. Three men in suits, bowler hats climb out. They are all carrying rifles.

The men immediately begin to approach across the field at a brisk walk. Cows move aside. As they come closer it is possible to recognize one of them as Detective Seavey.

69. Ext. Side of Johnson House. Dawn.

A VIEW *along the side of the house. Seavey and the other two detectives approach along the road from the back. It is only now that their whereabouts (i.e. Whatcom) becomes clear. Seavey positions himself beside the kindling shed and motions the other detectives forward.*

The other two immediately make their way up the porch steps and position themselves near the door. One of them aims his rifle at the door-lock assembly and fires — blasting it open. They rush inside.

Seavey watches from his position near the kindling shed.

70. Ext. Side of Johnson House. Day. (Time Cut).

Jenny Johnson now stands on the porch wearing a smock and a sweater. She looks cold and frightened and angry. Seavey is leaning against a porch pillar, smoking a small cigar and asking her questions. The other two detectives are loitering around at the side of the house, their rifles now crooked in their arms.

SEAVEY: When did he last contact you?

JENNY: He hasn't since he left here. You had no right to invade my home, Mister Seavey.

SEAVEY: Your brother is a dangerous criminal, Missus Johnson. Did you expect us to knock on the door and ask if he was here?

JENNY: Bill has never done violence to anyone! He's a gentle man.

SEAVEY: (*Drawing her out*) Is he indeed?

JENNY: Oh, yes . . . He loves children and he bought us a . . . (*She tails off, sensing a trap*).

SEAVEY: Yes? Go on.

JENNY: I'll thank you to get off my property now.

SEAVEY: You know where he's hiding, don't you?

Jenny shakes her head no vigorously.

SEAVEY: Missus Johnson, harboring a fugitive is a criminal offense . . . even just knowing where he is and not telling us can put you in a mess of trouble.

Jenny is thoroughly frightened now but says nothing.

SEAVEY: It stands to reason that he's hiding out somewhere in Whatcom County. After all, you're the only person he can turn to.

JENNY: My brother has many friends! And even if I did know where he is I would never tell you!

Seavey drags slowly on his cigar and shifts to a gentler tack.

SEAVEY: Missus Johnson . . . His capture would be best for everyone . . . including him. He's a tired old fox.

JENNY: (*Angering*) You know nothing about Bill Miner! There is more life in him than most men half his age!

SEAVEY: (*Smiles*) He's just been lucky so far . . . but we'll soon run him to earth, with or without your help.

JENNY: Without my help you can be sure!

Seavey stares at her then tips his bowler slightly.

SEAVEY: Good day, Missus Johnson.

He leaves the porch and strides off in the direction from which he came, followed by the other two detectives. Jenny watches them depart, hugging herself against the chill.

71. Ext. Budd's Mine. Day.

VIEW *of Budd, Miner, and Shorty riding up to the dilapidated entrance of a mine in a rocky hillside. A pair of rusty rails leads out of the mine's entrance. A sign on the side of Budd's wagon reads* TULAMEEN HOTEL.

MINER: You own this?

BUDD: I won it in a card game a few months back. The assay office says there's gold traces.

Budd stops the wagon and climbs down, followed by Miner and Shorty.

BUDD: (*Shouts*) Louis!

MINER: I don't know anything about mining, Jack.

BUDD: You do now. I'm telling the story around town that you're a couple of mining engineers up from Idaho.

MINER: (*Slightly angry*) So we have to work our behinds off in your mine?

BUDD: Would you rather be known as a couple of train robbers?

Before Miner can respond they are interrupted by deep coughing from inside the mine. They look over as Louis Colqhoun emerges. He is about thirty, thin, has a scruffy growth of stubble and an unhealthy pallor.

BUDD: (*To Louis*) Brought you some company, Louis. This is George Edwards and that's Shorty Dunn. Louis Colqhoun, boys.

Louis nods hello and coughs into his hand. Miner immediately motions for Budd to come with him and they walk a discrete distance, out of Louis's earshot.

MINER: That man's working your mine?

BUDD: (*Nods*) He works in return for room and board at the hotel. Same as you.

MINER: I know that cough, Jack. He's got the consumption.

BUDD: (*Nods*) He used to be a school teacher in the east. Came out here for his health. He's a good worker.

MINER: (*Concerned*) The dust will kill him fast.

BUDD: It's a tough old world.

Miner looks as if he'll object again but he restrains it. Budd then picks up a mining pick and hands it to him.

BUDD: (*Smiles*) So you might as well get to work . . . Mister Edwards.

72. Int. Mineshaft. Day.

A ragged tunnel lit by flickering coal oil lanterns. Miner is planting a dynamite charge in the rock face while Shorty chops away at another spot using a pick. The clanging is enormous. Louis, coughing, is loading shattered rocks into a mining cart. Miner turns to Louis.

MINER: Take that out, son, and get yourself some fresh air.

Louis nods and pulls the cart away along the little track.

As Louis vanishes, a small piece of rock falls and hits Shorty on the head. He yelps and retaliates with the pick against the rock face.

SHORTY: Goddamn stupid mine!

Miner glances at him then continues working.

73. Int. Hotel Room. Night.

Shorty lies on one bed — still in his dirty clothes — and fast asleep. Miner sits on the edge of his own bed clad in longjohns, his sore feet resting in a basin of water. He looks old and fatigued as he writes in his exercise book.

MINER: (*Muttering*) . . . It is ironic that even with success my independence must be deferred . . . and I find myself, as always, doing work planned by other heads.

Miner stops writing and slowly eases himself down on the bed. He is bone-tired and his eyes flicker, fighting sleep.

MINER: (*Sighs*) Soon, Bill . . .

The pencil and booklet drop from his hand and he sleeps.

74. Int. Barber Shop. Day.

VIEW *of Miner reclining in the chair of the town barber, who is busy lathering his face in preparation for the shave. It is Miner's day off and he is dressed in his good suit.*

BARBER: So, Mister Edwards, how are you enjoying Kamloops?

MINER: It seems to be a fine town.

BARBER: It is that. It's a place with a real future.

Miner's eyes glance up at him at the mention of that word.

BARBER: (*Confidentially*) A man would be smart to consider planting his roots right here.

MINER: I will keep that advice in mind.

The barber nods and winks as he strops the razor.

75. Ext. General Store. Day.

A young town boy with large eyes and poor clothes stands on the boardwalk fronting the general store, staring at a basket of oranges which is prominent among baskets of apples and vegetables.

Miner comes walking along, fresh from the barber shop. He looks every inch the gentleman today. Miner doffs his stetson to a passing lady. He then sees the boy staring covetously at the oranges.

Miner smiles, then goes over, selects two oranges from the basket, and goes into the store without acknowledging the boy. The boy stands there.

A moment later Miner emerges from the store. He looks down at the boy, then offers him one of the oranges. The boy can barely contain his delight but is hesitant to accept the gift.

> **MINER:** *(Smiles)* Don't you like oranges, son?

The boy nods. Miner motions him to take it. The boy does. Miner turns and strolls away with the other orange.

76. Ext. Newspaper Office. Day.

ANGLE *on Miner munching the orange as he strolls along to a small building with* KAMLOOPS PROSPECTOR *emblazoned on the front window. He also notices a familiar horse and Democrat tethered outside. It bears the shingle:* K. FLYNN, COMMERCIAL PHOTOGRAPHY.

77. Int. Newspaper Office. Day.

As Miner enters he spots Kate Flynn standing at the front counter in the midst of an argument with editor/publisher Roy Wilks. Both are on the verge of real anger. Kate is flushed as she brandishes a hand-written letter in front of his face.

> **KATE:** . . . I must insist you publish it. Your "Letters to the Editor" section is supposed to be a forum for public opinion and I am a member of the public!
>
> **WILKS:** Miss Flynn . . . As I've told you already, I reserve the right to publish such letters as I deem to be of interest

to our readership. Your letter is of no interest to people around here.

Miner stands politely by the door, his stetson off. Kate is getting furious.

KATE: Mister Wilks . . . I refuse to allow your editorial stance against the National Women's Trade Union League to go unopposed! Your readership should be informed that women working in factories are earning one-third the wages being paid to men for the same jobs! Your editorial failed to mention that!

WILKS: My editorial was directed against the Bolsheviks who are manipulating that union, not against the women who have joined it.

KATE: Your editorials see Bolshevism behind every new instrument for social betterment!

WILKS: (*Angering*) In the case of the Women's Trade Union League it is a fact!

KATE: (*Angering*) But you ignore the point that this union is needed! My letter simply outlines the facts!

Wilks, feeling cornered, makes a dismissive motion.

WILKS: People around here don't share your passion for trade unions.

KATE: Mister Wilks . . . Kamloops is not the planet Mars! There is a transcontinental railway on the edge of town and it brings ideas here as well as people and goods. Besides, it is the role of your paper to lead public opinion, not simply to curry its favor!

WILKS: I will not be told my role in life by someone who obviously does not know her own!

Kate now looks as if she might hit him. She crumples up her letter and glares at Wilks.

KATE: Mister Wilks . . . You have the mentality of a grocery clerk!

With that, she flings the balled-up letter against Wilks' chest. He looks astonished as it bounces off his vest and drops on the counter.

Kate turns on her heel and stomps toward the door. Miner quickly reaches out and opens it and holds it for her as she goes storming past him.

> **KATE:** (*Angrily*) Thank you!

Miner closes the door behind her. Wilks, embarrassed, grins at Miner and shrugs "What can I say?" Miner walks over to the counter.

> **MINER:** I would like to purchase some back-copies of the paper.
>
> **WILKS:** Certainly, sir.

Wilks moves away to find the papers. Miner leans an elbow on the counter and stares out the front window.

What he sees: Kate moving away on the Democrat.

ON *Miner — interested.*

78. Int. Hotel Room. Night.

Miner is propped up on one bed, reading aloud from a copy of "The Prospector." Shorty, wearing only his long underwear — dirty — is perched on the edge of the other bed, listening intently.

> **MINER:** ". . . Law enforcement agencies in British Columbia and the States of Washington and Oregon confirmed that the search for William Miner and his accomplice is concentrated on the Whatcom County, Washington area where Miner is known to have resided following his release from San Quentin . . ."
>
> **SHORTY:** (*Cackles*) Wow! They think Bill Miner robbed that train and it was only us!

Miner glances at Shorty, his vanity insulted.

> **MINER:** I don't believe Miner could have planned it any better than I did.
>
> **SHORTY:** Don't get me wrong, George . . . You did great for a nobody.
>
> **MINER:** (*Reads*) ". . . The identity of Miner's accomplice remains unknown. The train crew described this man as short, dirty, nervous, and unintelligent."

SHORTY: (*Angering*) I ain't never been nervous in my life!

Miner looks at him and smiles.

79. Ext. Budd's Mine. Day.

VIEW *of the mine entrance. From within can be heard the distant clanging of pick axes on rock.*

A rider appears and slowly approaches the mine on his horse. The rider (Corporal Fernie) wears the blue tunic with gold buttons of the B.C. Provincial Police. He is a sturdy, good-looking man of about thirty-three. He reins up at the mine entrance, hearing the clanging, then dismounts, glances around at the boxes of dynamite, then goes into the mine.

80. Int. Mineshaft. Day.

VIEW *toward the entrance as Fernie enters, silhouetted against the daylight. He makes his way forward into the darkness which is broken by a glow of light that seems to emit from a spot along one rocky wall of the shaft. The clanging is louder.*

As Fernie nears the glowing spot he stoops slightly and peers into a side shaft.

What he sees: A hacked-out area in which Shorty is crouched on his knees, hacking away at the rock face.

FERNIE: (*Off*) Hallo there!

Shorty swivels, spots the blue uniform, immediately loses his balance and half-tumbles, half-slides down the incline to the main shaft. Fernie catches him.

Shorty immediately gets to his feet, his eyes wide with fear, and hurries away deeper into the mineshaft.

FERNIE: (*Surprised*) Hey . . .

81. Int. T-Junction. Day.

A widened out area where the main shaft branches off in two directions.

Miner and Louis look up from their task of preparing dynamite charges as Shorty comes hurrying out of the darkness.

SHORTY: (*Hushed/gesturing*) A Provincial!

MINER: Where?

SHORTY: He's comin'.

FERNIE: (*Off*) Hallo in there!

SHORTY: (*Panicky*) What'll we do?

MINER: Relax. We aren't breaking the law.

Fernie now comes into view and looks at the three of them. Miner notices the Corporal's chevrons on the sleeve. He stands.

MINER: Good afternoon, Corporal.

FERNIE: (*Nods*) You must be the men who are working for Jack Budd?

MINER: We are. I am George Edwards. This is Louis Colqhoun and that is Shorty Dunn.

FERNIE: (*To Shorty*) Gave you a start back there, eh?

Shorty looks rigid with criminal apprehension. Miner spots this and takes Fernie's attention away.

MINER: And you must be the local law enforcement officer?

FERNIE: (*Nods*) I am Corporal Fernie.

He indicates some ore samples in the mine cart.

FERNIE: Are you having any luck with this old mine?

MINER: Only lead and zinc traces so far.

FERNIE: I told Jack Budd this ridge runs the wrong direction for gold veins. But I suppose there's no reasoning with a man and his hunches.

MINER: (*Chuckles*) You're right about that, Corporal . . . But they have had some success down Idaho way with ridges placed like this one.

FERNIE: Jack told me you were up from Idaho. Where exactly?

MINER: (*Flawless*) Kellogg.

FERNIE: (*Nods*) Well, I was passing and thought I should meet you. I hope you'll take care with those dynamite charges.

MINER: Oh, yessir. Caution makes for a longer life.

FERNIE: (*Smiles*) That it does. Well, good day, gentlemen.

MINER: Good day, Corporal.

Fernie turns and makes his way along the shaft, out of sight. Miner visibly relaxes. Louis, who has been taking it all in, glances from Miner to Shorty.

LOUIS: Are you men in some trouble with the law?

MINER: No. Shorty hates policemen.

Miner returns to work, as does Louis. Shorty watches, still tense.

82. Ext. Along a Range Fence. Day.

Two riders appear and canter forward along a range fence. As they approach it becomes clear that they are Miner and Budd. They rein up and Budd gestures beyond the fence.

What they see: A herd of horses grazing in the distance.

BUDD: (*Off*) Douglas Lake Range.

Miner leans on his pommel and stares at Budd.

BUDD: At any one time there's five to ten-thousand horses on that spread.

MINER: You brought me all the way out here to see some horses, Jack?

BUDD: I know a man over in Cache Creek who'll pay a nice price for good horses.

MINER: Rustling is not my line.

Budd seems unperturbed. He keeps staring at the herd.

BUDD: You'll probably enjoy it more than working in that mine, Bill.

Miner does not respond.

BUDD: I'll cut you and Shorty in for twenty-five percent of whatever we get for the horses.

MINER: (*Smiles*) Are you going to help us steal them?

Budd simply glances at him then looks away. Miner nods.

MINER: I didn't think so. You're good at figuring out the angles, Jack, but you've never had much stomach for the risky parts.

Budd now looks at Miner with his watchy, lidded eyes.

BUDD: That's why I've spent more time out of prison than in it.

MINER: A three-way split between Shorty, me and you.

BUDD: Fifty-fifty.

MINER: A three-way split. Take it or leave it.

BUDD: Alright. It's a deal. When'll you do it?

MINER: (*Smiles*) Patience, Jack. I have to plan it out first.

Miner turns his stallion and rides off at a gallop. Budd watches him go as he takes out and lights a small cigar.

83. Ext. Countryside. Day.

ANGLE *on Miner as he rides down a gentle slope on his stallion. His ears hear some sound and he reins up, listening.*

Faint, from some distance, comes the singing voice of an Italian basso in the middle of some aria.

Miner listens and looks around, trying to locate the source of this singing. He then nudges his horse into motion and moves down toward a copse of trees.

84. Ext. By the Copse of Trees. Day.

The singing is louder and clearer here — obviously from a record. Miner reins up and dismounts, then moves toward the trees and peers through them.

What the sees: A view through the sparse trees to the country-side beyond. Kate Flynn's horse and wagon are visible on the other side of the copse and, resting on the wagon deck, is a gramophone. The opera music is flowing from the speaker.

    KATE: (*Off/distant*) Fore!

Miner moves into the copse and almost right through it to where he has a better view of the countryside beyond.

What he sees: On a gentle rise, about a hundred yards away, Kate Flynn is half-stooped, holding some kind of stick in one hand.

85. Ext. Countryside. Day.

ANGLE *on Kate. What she is doing is teeing up a golf ball and the stick in her hand is a hickory-shafted 5-iron.*

She straightens up, addresses the ball, assumes a golfing stance, crooks the club somewhat awkwardly, and swats the ball. Thwack. It lifts out, slicing badly, and bounces down the slope toward the trees.

Unsatisfied, she tees up another ball and adjusts her stance.

    KATE: (*Hollers*) Fore!

She swings the club and catches the ball nicely. It lifts off in a good arc and sails downward into the copse of trees behind the wagon, where Miner is concealed.

Kate, now out of balls, walks down the slope with the club slung over her shoulder. She stops to retrieve a golf ball, walks some more, stops to retrieve another, then heads for her wagon where the gramophone is winding down, giving the opera singer a sour sound.

Kate stops at her wagon, cranks up the gramophone and moves the needle arm back to the start of the recording. The basso begins with new vigor.

Kate then reacts with a slight start as she sees Miner stepping out of the copse, holding one of her golf balls. Miner looks apologetic, as if he knows he is intruding.

    MINER: I was attracted by the sound of your music.

KATE: (*Sudden recognition*) I know who you are!

Now Miner is startled — not sure what that means.

KATE: You were in the newspaper office last week!

MINER: (*Relieved*) My name is George Edwards.

KATE: How long have you been lurking in those trees?

MINER: I was not lurking, Miss. (*He indicates the record player*) Is that the Lovers' Aria from "Martha?"

KATE: (*Nods*) You know opera?

MINER: Not well, but I attended that one in Chicago . . . long ago.

Kate hesitates before deciding that he is okay.

KATE: My name is Katherine Flynn.

MINER: (*Removes his stetson*) It is a pleasure to meet you. Would it be an intrusion if I stayed to hear your record?

KATE: (*Shrugs*) I suppose not. You could help me find my balls.

86. Ext. Countryside. Day. (Time Cuts).

While the basso sings, Kate and Miner are visible collecting golf balls. They are carrying on a conversation from a considerable distance apart.

MINER: (*Calls*) I was taken with the way you handled that publisher!

KATE: (*Calls*) A lot of good it did me, Mister Edwards! In this country you are not taken seriously unless you are Protestant, Caucasian, and male!

MINER: (*Calls*) Sometimes even that is not enough, Miss Flynn!

KATE: (*Laughs/calls*) You have a point, Mister Edwards!

They continue searching for golf balls.

87. Ext. Countryside. Day. (Time Cut).

ANGLE on Kate and Miner standing close together. She holds a knit bag while Miner places golf balls into it. The aria continues. Kate looks more relaxed now — she seems more girlish without her usual intensity.

    KATE: . . . So you left Kentucky at the age of twenty?

    MINER: (*Nods*) Farm work was kind of dull. I wanted adventure.

    KATE: I'll bet you found it.

    MINER: Some. I was with the U.S. Cavalry during the Arizona Indian wars.

    KATE: On the side of the oppressors.

    MINER: (*Frowns*) I didn't see it that way at the time. (*Smiles*) Of course I was young and not so wise as you.

    KATE: (*Forgiving him*) Then you entered the mining business?

Miner nods "yes."

    KATE: Odd. You don't seem like a man who's spent his life underground.

    MINER: (*Smiles*) Thank you.

88. Ext. Countryside. Day. (Time Cut).

Kate and Miner are now seated on the grass near her wagon. A lunch she had prepared for herself is now spread out on a picnic blanket and Miner is chewing on a chicken leg while Kate cuts cucumbers.

    KATE: . . . Of course my parents were mortified that no young man asked to marry me but I was ecstatic at such good fortune.

    MINER: (*Curious*) Ecstatic?

    KATE: Of course. I never wanted to be like everybody else.

    MINER: Well you certainly are not.

KATE: (*Delighted*) Thank you. (*Offers a cucumber*) Cucumber, Mister Edwards?

MINER: (*Takes some*) Thank you.

KATE: You see, I found my passion in the art of photography and, much to my father's horror, I elected to make my own way in this world. So . . . five years ago I boarded the train west.

MINER: There isn't much to take pictures of around here.

KATE: Oh, you're wrong, Mister Edwards. This is a frontier in transition, filled with beauty and despair. You yourself might be shocked by some of the injustice I've recorded with my camera.

MINER: Perhaps you would be kind enough to show me your pictures sometime?

KATE: (*Nods*) Perhaps I shall. Some pie, Mister Edwards?

MINER: Yes, please.

Kate begins to serve him a slice of pie, using the plate she had packed for herself. Miner is watching her, fascinated by her.

MINER: Don't you find it lonely out here? A single woman like yourself?

KATE: (*Looks at him*) Not at all. I don't need anyone.

MINER: (*Smiles*) You are very brave, Miss Flynn.

KATE: (*Pleased*) Really? You know, I often feel I was born thirty years too soon . . . if you know what I mean.

MINER: No, I don't.

Now Kate really looks at him for the first time, unsettled by Miner's note of disagreement.

KATE: You know, Mister Edwards, your face has fascinating planes. It would photograph well.

MINER: I am superstitious about having my picture taken.

KATE: (*Laughs*) A man who knows opera?

MINER: I am much less worldly than you think.

KATE: (*Laughs*) Are you indeed?

89. Ext. Kate's House. Day.

Kate reins her wagon to a halt in front of her house, with Miner riding on the seat beside her. His stallion is tied to the back of her wagon. A printed wood sign on Kate's front lawn advertises K. FLYNN, COMMERCIAL PHOTOGRAPHY. Miner climbs down and assists Kate to alight from the wagon.

KATE: Thank you for seeing me home, Mister Edwards.

MINER: I thank you for the fine lunch.

KATE: My pleasure. Perhaps you'd like to come for dinner this Sunday? I'll show you my photographs.

MINER: Sunday? (*Quickly*) Yes, I would like that very much.

KATE: (*Smiles*) Fine. Please come by about three.

Miner nods. Kate offers her hand. Miner takes it briefly.

KATE: Good day, Mister Edwards.

Kate then turns and walks quickly to her front door and goes inside. Miner stands there, staring, then a slow grin spreads across his face. He goes and unties his stallion, swings into the saddle, and gallops off along the street looking very spry.

90. Ext./Int. Tulameen Bar. Night.

Light spills from windows at the side of the Tulameen Hotel. The young town boy to whom Miner gave an orange is standing on tiptoes, staring in the window of the bar.

What he sees: Miner, Shorty, and Budd are seated at a round table with drinks. They are all smoking and conversing in quiet, intense tones. Miner seems to be stressing some point to Budd and Budd nods and makes some reply. Then Miner tosses off his whiskey, pushes his chair back, and stands up, motioning Shorty to come to him. Shorty does so and they stride toward the side door.

The town boy crouches down against the wall. Light spills out as the side door is opened and Miner and Shorty emerge. They don't see the boy.

    SHORTY: First sign of a range guard 'n I'm cuttin', George! I ain't gettin' myself shot for no lousy horses!

Shorty and Miner are walking away. The town boy watches them go.

91. Ext. Douglas Lake Range. Night.

Snowing lightly. TIGHT *on a barbed wire fence. A gloved hand comes up with snippers and cuts one strand, then another one — snick, snick. Nearby, the sound of horses nickering.*

VIEW *of the herd. The figure of Miner is among them, cutting horses from the herd and shooing these toward the fence.*

ON *Shorty at the gap in the fence as several horses are trotted through, followed by Miner. They glance around, furtively, then set to work re-tying the cut wire to disguise the theft for as long as possible.*

92. Ext. Open Country (Douglas Lake). Night.

Miner and Shorty ride at walking pace. The stolen herd follows them easily. Muffled clatter of hooves.

93. Ext. Small Railroad Station. Day.

A small station/telegraph office in the middle of nowhere with the railroad track going past.

Miner rides up to the little building alone. He dismounts and goes inside.

94. Int. Station Office. Day.

The telegraph operator sits at a desk, manning his telegraph key, which is silent. He nods as Miner enters.

    MINER: 'Morning. I've got to move some stock across the tracks.

At that moment the telegraph starts to clatter. The operator listens, then taps out a reply.

>	MINER:	Did that say "early?"

>	OPERATOR:	You know "Morse?"

>	MINER:	(*Cautious*) A little.

The whistle of an approaching train. The operator grins.

>	OPERATOR:	It said "early."

Outside, the train thunders past, rattling the windows, then is gone.

>	OPERATOR:	What've you got? Cows? Horses?

>	MINER:	Cows.

>	OPERATOR:	You can take 'em across anywhere. But don't trail the right-of-way.

Miner nods.

95. Ext. Railroad Track. Day. (With Horses).

VIEW of Miner as he comes riding along beside the tracks. Patches of snow cover the ground.

Miner reins up and waits as Shorty rides out of the adjoining forest with the stolen herd.

>	MINER:	(*Calls*) The tracks will lead us right to Cache Creek.

Shorty nods and turns the horses onto the right-of-way. The horses get the easy-travel idea quick. They string out, trotting alongside the track. Hooves clatter on gravel.

96. Ext. A Railroad Cut. Day. (With Horses).

The track curves through a cut bounded by steep, blasted rock along both sides. The herd comes around the curve into the cut with Shorty riding point and Miner riding tail.

A distant train whistle sounds.

ON Miner as he reins up and listens. The whistle again. He looks both ways then dismounts. He touches one of the rails. Then he kneels down and puts his ear against it. What he hears makes him stand up quickly and re-mount. He gallops after Shorty and the herd.

    MINER: (*Yells*) Move them along!

ON Shorty, who looks back and hears the whistle. It is behind them. Shorty spurs his mare into a gallop.

VIEW of Miner, Shorty, and the herd galloping to get through the cut.

97. Ext. Beyond the Cut. Day. (With Horses).

The curve of the track comes out of the cut along a steeply banked hillside. On one side the rocky fill drops away precipitously. On the other side the berm rides almost vertically.

The horses begin to emerge from the cut, urged on by Shorty who is spurring forward, trying to get into the lead.

Miner rides out last, waving his hat.

    MINER: (*Yells*) Run 'em! Get 'em off!

The whistle blows again — getting close.

Miner stops his stallion on the narrow shoulder between the track and the steep drop. He waves his hat frantically as the locomotive rounds the curve, rumbling out of the cut. The whistle toots a series of short warning blasts which echo against the rock face.

Ahead, Shorty and the herd are galloping in panic, feeling the thunder of the overtaking train.

Behind, Miner's stallion rears as the locomotive thunders past. Miner fights the horse to keep it from going over the lip.

Ahead, Shorty opts out and takes his mare over the edge. Several of the horses follow; others continue straight ahead, trying to outrun the train.

98. Ext. Steep Rocky Slope. Day. (With Horses).

Dust billows, rocks clatter, horses whinny as they slide, struggling for footing, *down the rocky slope. Shorty fights to control the plunge of his mare.*

Above, the train roars past, whistle screaming.

99. Ext. Beyond the Cut. Day. (With Horses).

Miner calms his stallion as he looks over the lip, then he coaxes the horse over the edge and eases him downward to join Shorty and the herd.

100. Ext. Bottom of the Slope. Day. (With Horses).

A crippled horse lies breathing in short panting bursts.

Shorty and Miner have dismounted. Shorty watches grimly as Miner pulls out his Colt .45, trudges over, and fires a shot into the horse's head.

    SHORTY: (*Subdued*) Damn railroad.

    MINER: (*Re-holsters gun*) It was a work train. That's why she was running so close behind the other.

Miner begins counting the remaining horses. Two others lie dead at the base of the slope. Shorty uses his own hat to knock dust and shale off his clothing.

    SHORTY: Tell you this . . . Robbin' trains is a whole lot easier than rustlin' horses. What say we get back to that?

    MINER: (*Nods*) In the spring.

    SHORTY: (*Incredulous*) You mean we got to stay under Jack Budd's thumb all winter?

    MINER: It's safe in Kamloops. (*Smiles*) Besides, I am growing fond of the place.

Shorty looks as if he wants to argue about that but he decides not to.

    SHORTY: (*Grumpy*) Just bothers me . . . Us stealin' horses and slavin' in that stupid mine when we got a fortune buried in the ground down at Mission.

Miner smiles and mounts his stallion.

MINER: A man's got to think of the future, Shorty. Meantime, let's get these animals over to Cache Creek.

Shorty slowly boards his mare and they begin to re-herd the horses.

101. Int. Hotel Bathing Room. Day.

VIEW *of Miner soaping himself in a large tub of hot, steaming water. He is singing "Sweet Betsy from Pike" in a raspy, off-key voice.*

102. Ext. Kate's House. Day.

VIEW *of Miner as he comes strolling along the boardwalk towards Kate's house, dressed in his good suit, cleanly shaven, hair slicked down. He is carrying a huge box of chocolates. He stops and slicks the tops of his boots against the backs of his trouser legs before striding to the front door.*

103. Int. Kate's Parlor. Day.

TIGHT *on a stack of photographic prints in Miner's hands. His hands are sorting through them. They are good-quality black and white prints depicting people at work: Chinese Coolies working on track gangs — their opaque faces captured by Kate's camera; ranch hands branding calves; construction workers erecting a frame building; a family of settlers arrayed for the camera in front of their crude dwelling.*

MINER: (*Off*) These are fine images, Kate.

ANGLE *on Kate and Miner, seated side by side on a small sofa. Miner is wearing his checked suit, Kate looks quite lovely in an empire dress — her hair done up. Other framed photographs she has taken are visible on tabletops and on the walls of the little room.*

KATE: The camera is an instrument of truth in a way that history books are not. Imagine if we could see a photograph of Leonardo da Vinci or Boswell's London?

The idea has obviously never occured to Miner. In fact he seems more interested in looking at Kate, but he nods sagely. Kate suddenly stands up and offers her hand.

KATE: Come. I'll show you how it's done.

Miner accepts her hand and stands up.

Bill Miner shows an interest in photography — and the photographer, Kate Flynn (Jackie Burroughs). "The camera is an instrument of truth in a way that history books are not."

104. Int. Kate's Darkroom. Day.

Kate and Miner stand side by side, close, illuminated by a red-coated lantern. Kate wears a pair of elbow-length rubber gloves and is pressing a plate into a tray of developing solution.

KATE: . . . The photographic plate is sensitive to densities of light . . . This chemical solution brings out all the recorded tones and you end with an accurate photograph.

Miner is enjoying standing so close to her in this intimate dark space. Her hair brushes the side of his face.

KATE: See.

Miner looks down.

What they see: A photographic image forming on the plate. It is a shot of the local railroad station.

    MINER: (*Off*) That is amazing, Kate.

ON *Kate and Miner. He looks at her. She turns her head to look at him and their faces are very close — almost touching.*

    KATE: It's very simple really.

    MINER: Yes. So I see.

105. Int. Kate's Kitchen. Night.

Kate is at the counter, basting a roast.

106. Int. Kate's Parlor. Night.

Miner, alone, moves slowly around the room, looking at Kate's photographs and bric-à-brac. When he touches anything he does so respectfully, as everything is an extension of her. On a small table sits a beautiful thing: an ornate, enameled and gold globe. Miner picks it up gently. He sees that it is hinged across the middle. He lifts the lid.

Inside, an ornate mechanical bird mounted on a pivot begins to chatter loudly and rotate on the pivot in rhythmic clicks. Miner is astonished by the sight of something so ornate that seems to have no practical purpose.

    KATE: (*Off. Laughs*) Do you like it?

Miner looks over, embarrassed, and sees her in the doorway.

    MINER: Yes. What is it for?

    KATE: (*Smiling*) Itself. Dinner is on.

She goes out. Miner closes the lid and puts the globe back in its spot on the table.

107. Int. Kate's Dining Room. Night.

Miner is seated on one side of the linen-covered, candlelit table. There is silver, china, and bowls of steaming vegetables. Kate enters from the kitchen carrying the roast on a platter. Miner watches how the candlelight catches her face as she places the platter on the table. She looks very beautiful.

108. Int. Dining Room. Night. (Time Cut).

Kate sits watching admiringly as Miner — his shirtsleeves rolled up — carves the roast. Kate notices the strong tendons in his wrists and forearms. From under the rolled-up right sleeve, part of his ballet girl tattoo is visible.

109. Int. Dining Room. Night. (Time Cut).

A VIEW of Miner and Kate as they eat. Miner's table manners seem exaggeratedly formal on this occasion. They say nothing but keep looking at each other between mouthfuls — somewhat shy and awkward.

110. Int. Kate's Parlor. Night.

Miner is adding some wood to the Franklin stove, which is burning brightly. Kate is standing at the front window, looking out.

    KATE: (*Pensive*) It looks like it will snow.

Miner closes the stove door and stands up.

    MINER: Yes. I should be going.

    KATE: Yes, I suppose so.

Miner just stands there. Kate's eyes meet his. HOLD.

111. Int. Kate's Bedroom. Night.

Flickering light and shadows from a coal oil lamp. Clothes draped over a chair. Miner and Kate naked under the quilt. He is caressing her gently with his rough hand. She seems fascinated by his scar and his tattoos. She traces the scar with one finger.

    KATE: (*Soft*) How did you get this?

    MINER: I got knifed in some saloon.

    KATE: (*Concerned*) Why?

> **MINER:** I have spent too much time among men who need no reason.

Kate puts her hand on the ballet girl tattoo.

> **KATE:** Where did you get this?
>
> **MINER:** Denver.

She lifts his hand to display the bird tattoo.

> **KATE:** And this?
>
> **MINER:** San Francisco.
>
> **KATE:** (*Awed*) You have lived.

Miner smiles, gently pulls her face to his, and kisses her. She responds and they begin to make love in the flickering half-light.

112. Ext. A Skating Pond. Day.

Many skaters — a lot of them kids — now glide around on the frozen pond. A big bonfire burns on the bank where a few people stand to get warm. Shorty is among these, sipping from a bottle of rum.

THE SHOT then picks out Kate and Miner on ice skates. Neither of them is any good and they attempt to hold each other upright as they try to glide along. They are followed by the town boy who always seems fascinated by Miner.

Miner and Kate suddenly fall down in a spray of arms and legs.

Shorty spots this and points and laughs.

On the ice, Wilks stops to help them to their feet.

113. Ext. Kate's House. Day.

Kate emerges from her house, carrying a basket, and begins walking along the board sidewalk toward town. Another woman comes out of the house next door and moves to the sidewalk as Kate approaches. Kate and the woman greet each other and stand chatting.

At this moment Miner comes into view from the other direction, carrying a small Christmas tree.

As he approaches Kate and the woman he doffs his hat and nods "Good day." Kate and the woman smile and say "Good day," then Miner continues past them as if he is merely an acquaintance of Kate.

Miner continues to the front of Kate's house where he puts down the tree and busies himself as if re-tying his shoelace. In the background, Kate and the woman begin to walk away side by side. Miner then picks up the tree and hurries it into the house.

114. Ext. Anglican Belfry. Day.

TIGHT *on the steeple of the church as Xmas bells ring out.*

115. Ext. Catholic Belfry. Day.

TIGHT *on steeple as Catholic bells chime loudly.*

116. Ext. Tulameen Hotel. Day.

The area is deserted except for Shorty and Louis who are standing on the porch of the hotel, passing a bottle of whiskey back and forth. From a distance the church bells ring.

> **SHORTY:** Listen to that racket. Never had no use for church stuff.
>
> **LOUIS:** Back east I used to go every Sunday. Our church was always warm in winter and after service the ladies served cakes.

Shorty stares at him, then takes another swig from the bottle.

117. Ext. Kate's Street. Day.

A VIEW *of Miner, Kate, and Fernie walking along the sidewalk from Kate's house. Miner and Fernie are carrying Kate's camera and photographic equipment.*

> **FERNIE:** . . . I really do apologize for having you do this, particularly on Christmas day, but I do think it's necessary.

MINER: Are they all dead, Corporal?

FERNIE: I'm afraid so. The husband ran off somewhere after he did it.

SHOT PANS with them as they pass. They are walking toward the Chinese settlement in distant background.

118. Int. Chinese Shack. Day.

CLOSE on the upturned face of a dead Chinese woman of about twenty-five. Her eyes are open and her hair and face are matted with dried blood. SHOT WIDENS to reveal that she is lying on a dirty cot. One dead child is sprawled across her body and another dead child lies crumpled on the dirt floor. Their bodies are also bloodied — victims of a violent, pathetic death.

SHOT WIDENS more to reveal a view of the dark, fetid shack with furniture made out of old crates. Fernie and Miner are standing there looking down at the corpses. Miner is covering his mouth and nose with his hand.

FERNIE: (*Sadly*) They hate the cold weather. Every winter one or two will suicide but this is the first murder here.

Miner tears his eyes away from the broken child on the floor and forces himself not to run from this dark cell of a dwelling. Fernie kneels down and scans the floor looking for the murder weapon.

FERNIE: He used a knife but he must have taken it with him. Do you see it anywhere?

Miner says nothing and does not move.

119. Ext. Chinese Shack. Day.

Miner and Fernie emerge. Several Chinese are gathered a respectful distance away, watching stoically. Kate stands isolated in front of the shack near her set-up camera. She looks stricken and stands very still with her hands covering her lower face. Miner goes to her and puts his hands on her arms, comfortingly.

MINER: I had better take you home.

Kate shakes her head "no."

KATE: (*Muffled*) I'll be alright.

FERNIE: I regret bringing you to this, Miss Flynn, but these people won't tell me what it means.

He gestures at the front wall of the shack. THE SHOT *now reveals that some message has been hastily swathed there in Chinese symbols with red paint. The hand that painted the symbols did so with jagged rage or pain. They look powerful, aggressive.*

KATE: (*To Fernie*) I'm ready.

Miner would clearly like to take her away but he resists imposing himself on her. Kate goes to her camera.

FERNIE: (*Apologetic*) I need the photograph for evidence. These people might erase the thing before I can get it deciphered.

KATE: You're blocking my shot, Corporal.

Fernie immediately moves away to a spot some distance behind Kate. Miner comes over to join him while Kate prepares to take the photograph. Fernie indicates the watching Chinese to Miner with a slight jerk of his head.

FERNIE: (*Quietly*) Look at them. You can never tell what's going on in their heads.

MINER: Don't be too harsh, Corporal. They are a world away from home.

Kate takes a picture and prepares to reverse the plate.

KATE: (*Calls to Fernie*) I'll take another one for safety.

FERNIE: (*Calls*) I really appreciate this, Miss Flynn.

Fernie then looks around, scanning the distant hills.

FERNIE: (*To Miner*) The husband can't have gotten far on foot. I'll ride after him when we're done here.

MINER: I would like to ride with you.

Fernie looks slightly surprised, then pleased.

FERNIE: Thank you, Mister Edwards. I would enjoy some company.

MINER: I will take Kate home, then get my horse.

Fernie now leans closer and lowers his voice. He seems awkward.

FERNIE: I'm, uh, sorry about knocking at Miss Flynn's door unannounced. I, uh, had no idea you were 'visiting', if you get my meaning.

MINER: I don't mind if you don't, Corporal.

FERNIE: Of course not. (*Winks*) As far as I'm concerned I didn't see a thing.

Miner nods.

ON *Kate as she snaps another shot of the Chinese symbols.*

120. Ext. Countryside (Kamloops). Day.

VIEW *of Miner and Fernie riding across an expanse of yellowed, windswept grass. They ride at a canter, spread apart, scanning the ground as they go along.*

Fernie suddenly spots something and reins up.

FERNIE: Here!

Fernie dismounts and stoops down while Miner rides up to join him.

Fernie picks up an object and stands, displaying it to Miner. It is a hunting knife — its blade caked with dark, dried blood. Miner stares at it without comment.

Fernie looks around and spots something else. He walks a few paces and kneels.

What he sees: Splotches and specks of dried blood are visible on the hard ground and blades of dead grass.

FERNIE: (*Off*) There's blood here.

Fernie stands and points off.

FERNIE: A trail of it going that way.

Fernie returns to his horse, mounts, and begins to follow the telltale traces. Miner rides behind him.

121. Ext. Farther Along. Day.

ANGLE *on Fernie and Miner approaching from the distance. The trail of dried blood leading to foreground is much more distinct now. They ride up and rein to a halt when they see something ahead.*

What they see: Some distance ahead the small shape of a man is visible, draped motionless against the barbed wire of a range fence.

Fernie and Miner exchange a look, then move forward on their horses at walking pace.

122. Ext. By the Range Fence. Day.

In foreground, the dead Chinese husband hangs caught on the barbed wire, his legs buckled awkwardly. Dried blood is caked on his throat and stains the entire chest of his clothing. Fernie and Miner ride up from background. Fernie dismounts.

Fernie walks over and looks at the corpse.

>**FERNIE:** (*Slightly shaken*) He must have slashed his own throat back there and run until he hit the fence.

Miner has removed his stetson out of respect for the dead. Fernie turns and looks to Miner.

>**FERNIE:** Well, at least he's saved us the bother of a trial.

123. Int. Kate's Front Hallway. Day.

ANGLE *on the front door as Miner comes inside.*

>**MINER:** Katie?

No reply. Miner goes upstairs.

124. Int. Kate's Bedroom. Day.

Kate lies curled up on her bed. She looks small and defenceless for the first time.

Miner enters the room, sees her there, then moves slowly to the edge of the bed, sits on it, and takes her in his arms. He wants to comfort her but feels awkward.

>**MINER:** (*Gentle*) I will make you some tea.

Kate murmurs a "no," her head buried against his shoulder.

MINER: You did well out there.

MINER: *(Soft)* No ... I always believed ... I wanted to believe ... that one could always find some reason to go on.

Miner does not reply. He simply strokes her hair. She now looks up at his face.

KATE: But it's not true, is it?

MINER: It is true for me, Kate ... and that is all I will ever know about it.

He kisses her gently and she responds.

FADE TO BLACK. FADE IN.

125. Ext. Countryside (Kamloops). Day.

A SINGLE, LONG LENS SHOT *of Kate and Miner riding together. It is springtime now. Miner rides western — a forward/back motion; Kate rides English — posting — an up/down motion. They are talking as they ride.*

MINER: *(V.O.)* ... When were you in Paris?

KATE: *(V.O.)* With my parents. We attended the World Exposition there.

MINER: *(V.O.)* Then you have seen the Eiffel Tower?

KATE: *(V.O.)* I stood atop it a few days after it was opened. You haven't been abroad?

MINER: *(V.O.)* No. I have never even been to New York City. I intend to get that far someday.

KATE: *(V.O.)* I was there too. They have a magnificent opera house.

MINER: *(V.O.)* I would love to see it.

KATE: *(V.O.)* I would love to show it to you, George.

MINER: *(V.O.)* I will be coming into some money soon. I am attracted by the comforts of the east. Have you considered moving back, Kate?

KATE: (*V.O.*) I've never ruled out the possibility.

They ride on.

126. Int. Hotel Room. Night.

Miner is sitting on the edge of his bed. His .45 — all taken apart — is spread out on the bedspread, and Miner is meticulously oiling the parts with a rag.

The door opens and Shorty lumbers in. He is visibly drunk.

MINER: I was looking for you earlier.

SHORTY: Me 'n Louis were sharin' a bottle down at the stables.

Shorty moves to the foot of the bed and glares at the spread-out .45 parts.

SHORTY: (*Hostile*) What's all that for?

Miner catches the tone and looks up at him.

SHORTY: I mean what's the point, George? You ain't gonna use it no more.

MINER: No?

Shorty is too drunk to spot the menace on Miner's face.

SHORTY: I mean it looks to me like you want to cozy with that picture-takin' lady.

MINER: (*Tight smile*) When did you become an expert on affairs of the heart, Shorty?

Shorty cackles, not sensing the warning in Miner's tone.

SHORTY: Fact is, I'd say she's just about made a gelding outta you.

Miner is suddenly on his feet and has seized Shorty by the lapels of his jacket. He is tremendously angry — slightly out of control — and the shock of seeing it causes Shorty to cringe in fear. For a long moment Miner glares at him, then he abruptly regains his control and releases Shorty, who immediately stumbles back from such wrath.

MINER: (*Tight*) I told you we would move at the right time and now it is the right time.

SHORTY: (*Relieved/hopeful*) A train?

MINER: Yes.

SHORTY: When, George?

MINER: As soon as we recruit another reliable man to assist us.

SHORTY: (*Nods*) Sure. Whatever you say.

MINER: (*Smiles*) Yes. I would appreciate your keeping that attitude in mind, Shorty.

Shorty nods.

127. Int. Church. Day.

A SHOT of the church interior. A wedding has just been completed. Miner stands watching among the crowd of guests all dressed in their Sunday finery, while Kate prepares to photograph the wedding party.

The bride, groom, and others all stand stiff and proud in front of the altar as Kate prepares to take a picture.

Miner watches Kate admiringly.

KATE: Hold still . . . and smile.

Stretched grins. She snaps the picture.

Fernie slides over to Miner's side. Fernie is wearing his dress uniform, his hair is neatly slicked, and he now wears Sergeant's stripes on one sleeve.

FERNIE: Afternoon, George.

MINER: Good afternoon.

Miner indicates the Sergeant's stripes.

MINER: My congratulations on your promotion. That is a fine accomplishment for a man so young.

Fernie is obviously flattered but tries to be offhand.

FERNIE: This detachment is expanding. Headquarters is placing two men under my command.

MINER: (*Nods*) I'm sure you will measure up to the responsibility, Sergeant.

Fernie gives him a tight little smile of pride. Kate takes another picture of the wedding party.

128. Int. Town Hall. Night.

Kate and Miner waltz at the wedding party. SHOT IS TIGHT *on the two of them, absorbed in their own dancing and each other. Miner dances surprisingly well. He holds a linen handkerchief against his left palm — between his own and Kate's palm. They are totally happy — the only two people in the world.*

129. Ext. Main Street. Night.

VIEW *of the deserted main street. The putt-putt of a motor car is heard, then the car appears around a corner and rattles along the main street toward the Tulameen Hotel. It pulls to a stop in front of the hotel and its driver shuts it off and climbs down.*

A CLOSER ANGLE *on the driver. It is Seavey. He takes a gladstone bag from the back of the auto and makes his way into the Tulameen.*

130. Int. Town Hall. Night.

ANGLE *on Kate and Miner as they dance.*

131. Ext. Tulameen Front Porch. Night.

ANGLE *on Seavey who stops and listens. Distant, from the town hall, can be heard the strains of dance music.*

Seavey goes into the hotel.

132. Int. Town Hall. Night.

ON *Miner and Kate as they dance.*

133. Ext. Police Office/Courthouse. Day.

VIEW *along the main street as Seavey comes driving from the Tulameen in his motor car. Various townspeople gawk at the passing car. Seavey pulls up in front of the Police Office, which is in the courthouse, gets out of the car, and goes inside the building.*

134. Int. Fernie's Office. Day.

Seavey is seated calmly in the visitor's chair. Fernie is pacing slowly, looking agitated.

> **FERNIE:** . . . You are mistaken. If Miner was hiding out in this area I'd know about it.
>
> **SEAVEY:** Not necessarily. He's clever at using false identities and this region is filled with people who seem to think that Miner is some kind of hero.
>
> **FERNIE:** My opinion stands, sir.
>
> **SEAVEY:** (*Caustic*) Indeed? I take it you are experienced in the apprehension of major criminals?

Fernie reddens at the insult but controls his anger.

> **FERNIE:** I am not . . . But this is my jurisdiction, Mister Seavey, and I'm not obliged to take your word for anything here.

Seavey realizes he has nudged too hard and retreats into a charming smile.

> **SEAVEY:** I apologize if I seemed condescending, Sergeant. It's just that I've been pursuing this particular criminal for some time and I know how tricky and dangerous he can be.
>
> **FERNIE:** Dangerous? That's not what I've heard about him.
>
> **SEAVEY:** (*Tight smile*) Now you're starting to sound like one of his admirers.
>
> **FERNIE:** (*Angering*) Not at all. But I have more realistic duties to attend than the whims of an American detective agency.

SEAVEY: Your Superintendent in New Westminster does not agree.

Seavey now produces a letter which he hands to Fernie.

SEAVEY: Its contents are explicit. You are to extend full and enthusiastic cooperation in this matter.

Fernie's face reddens as he scans the letter. He then tosses it onto his desk and glares at Seavey.

FERNIE: (*Angry*) Why didn't you simply show me that in the beginning?

SEAVEY: (*Smiles*) Cooperation is preferable to coercion, Sergeant.

FERNIE: (*Icy*) What do you want from me?

Seavey produces another sheet of paper, unfolds it, and puts it on the desk.

SEAVEY: That is an accurate description of Miner, provided by San Quentin.

FERNIE: And you would like me to circulate it?

SEAVEY: No, Sergeant. We don't want to set him running again. I simply want you to keep an eye out for anyone who matches that description and notify New Westminster if you spot him.

Fernie picks up the description and scans it.

FERNIE'S P.O.V. *of the page: Tight on the printed lines,* "Six feet tall, slim build, bluebird tattoo above right thumb, ballet girl tattoo on left forearm . . ."

CLOSE *on Fernie's face. He knows.*

SEAVEY: (*Off*) What is it, Sergeant.

Fernie immediately masks his surprise and looks at Seavey.

FERNIE: (*Flustered*) Nothing . . . He, uh, could be any number of older men around here.

Seavey holds up his right hand and indicates the spot between thumb and forefinger.

SEAVEY: I'll wager none of them have a bluebird tattooed right here.

FERNIE: (*Nods*) I don't recall seeing such a mark on anyone. In any case, I will start looking for you.

SEAVEY: Not for me, Sergeant . . . For us. (*Smiles*) We're on the same side, are we not?

FERNIE: (*Stiff*) Yes sir.

Seavey simply stares up at him, a small smile on his face.

135. Ext. Main Street. Day.

VIEW *of Seavey driving away in his motor car.*

136. Int. Fernie's Office. Day.

ANGLE *on Fernie, who is staring out his window, deliberating what to do. He looks troubled now.*

137. Ext. Budd's Mine. Day.

Miner is sitting on a dynamite box on the edge of the bluff where the mine cart is emptied down the slope. Budd is standing near him, his gaze scanning the valley below.

MINER: . . . So he's checked out and left town already?

BUDD: Yeah. He drove out right after meeting with Fernie?

MINER: Then we can stop worrying.

Budd turns to him, agitated.

BUDD: You must be getting soft in the head, Bill. That Pinkerton man wouldn't be sniffing around in Kamloops unless he has your scent.

MINER: That is a hasty conclusion.

BUDD: The hell it is.

Miner looks at him but does not argue this time.

BUDD: It's time for you to move on.

MINER: *(Sighs/nods)* I have been planning to move east anyhow.

BUDD: You'd best go tomorrow.

Miner shakes his head "no." Budd looks agitated, worried.

MINER: I have some important business to take care of first.

BUDD: What business?

MINER: Another train.

BUDD: When?

MINER: Shorty and Louis are waiting for me to set the date. The situation being what it is, I suppose we'd better go for it tomorrow.

BUDD: *(Angry)* Forget this train . . . Forget those idiots. Go east right now.

MINER: I'm going to need the money. It is my intention to retire from the profession.

BUDD: *(Worried)* You'll retire in a jail cell if you don't listen to me on this.

MINER: *(Smiles)* I never knew you were concerned for my safety, Jack.

Budd looks at him for a moment, then sighs.

BUDD: I'm only trying to protect my own situation.

Miner smiles and nods. He thinks for a moment.

MINER: I wouldn't want to harm that, Jack. So I will head straight for the border after I've done the job.

Budd stares at him, looking far from pleased.

138. Int. Kate's Parlor. Day.

Fernie sits posed on the piano stool, in uniform, with the new Sergeant's stripes on the arms. He holds his hat on his lap and sits stiffly, like one who is not used to having a photograph taken. Kate has her camera set up facing him and is under the hood focusing and lining up the shot.

    KATE: . . . Turn slightly more to the side so the stripes will show.

Fernie obediently adjusts his position.

    KATE: Perfect. Hold that.

She emerges from under the hood.

    FERNIE: I'm sorry about the rush but I'd like to get it off to my parents.

    KATE: I understand. One doesn't become a Sergeant every day.

    FERNIE: (*Smiles*) If I arrest Bill Miner I'll probably be kicked up to Inspector before that photograph is ready.

Kate doesn't twig to this. She is busy getting a plate ready to put in the camera.

    KATE: I can have a print for you the day after tomorrow.

Fernie looks uneasy now — not sure how to proceed.

    FERNIE: The Pinkerton's are certain he's hiding out in this area. Maybe right here in Kamloops.

Kate is sliding the plate into the camera.

    KATE: Well I hope you catch him.

Fernie looks surprised by Kate's response and turns his head slightly to stare at her.

    KATE: Please, Sergeant . . . You must not move.

Fernie resumes his pose.

    FERNIE: Sorry . . . Do you really hope that I catch him?

    KATE: (*Shrugs*) I suppose I don't really care one way or the other.

She has positioned the plate and is now sliding off the plate covers.

    FERNIE: A lot of people like him because he only steals from the railway.

    KATE: I'm just about ready now.

FERNIE: In a way I hope I don't get the chance to arrest him. It might make me unpopular around here.

Kate is ready to take the picture now.

KATE: Hold very still and give me a nice smile.

FERNIE: He shouldn't be difficult to identify . . . Not with that ballet girl tattooed on his arm.

Kate instantly realizes what he is talking about, but her reaction is little more than a moment of hesitation and a flicker of surprise in her eyes.

KATE: Very still, please.

She trips the shutter and takes the photograph of Fernie, who sits rigid and unblinking.

139. Ext. Kate's House. Night.

ANGLE *on Miner as he rides up to Kate's house on his stallion, dismounts, and steps onto the board sidewalk. He stands there looking at the front of the house, reluctant to move, then he strides to the front door and raps on it.*

A moment passes before Kate opens the door. For a moment, neither speaks.

MINER: I must talk to you.

Kate moves aside. Miner enters and she closes the door.

140. Int. Kate's Parlor. Night.

Miner enters the room and stands there. Kate enters behind him, closes the parlor door, and stands with her back to it. Miner turns to face her. It is obvious he feels tense and awkward about what he needs to tell her.

MINER: Kate . . . In two or three days I will be leaving Kamloops for good.

Kate says nothing. Miner shifts uneasily then continues.

MINER: You and I have made important plans together . . . (*He trails off*).

KATE: Yes?

MINER: But I left something out . . . Something I never intended to tell you . . . (*He trails off again*).

Kate remains silent, motionless.

MINER: I am not the man you think, Kate.

He and Kate look at each other in silence.

KATE: Have you lied to me about your feelings too?

MINER: No. You do mean more to me than I have words for.

KATE: Are you sure?

MINER: I beg you to believe that whatever else you may choose to think of me.

Kate lowers her eyes for a moment — deliberating something. Then she looks at him again.

KATE: I have been thinking about it all afternoon. I decided that I am certain too . . . So all else is of little importance.

Miner now registers slow surprise.

MINER: You know?

Kate nods "yes."

MINER: How, Kate?

KATE: From Fernie. I think he was hinting that you should go before he has to arrest you.

Miner attempts to absorb these surprises. Kate now moves across the room to her side table and picks up a CPR ticket envelope which she shows to Miner.

KATE: I went to the station and reserved two places on the eastbound Limited for tomorrow. We will get off at Winnipeg and make connections to Chicago . . . or New York if you prefer.

Miner is astonished and moved. He goes to her and puts his arms around her. Kate hugs him tightly.

MINER: I can't go with you . . . Not right now.

Kate, immediately anxious, looks up at him.

MINER: It would be too easy for the police to find me.

Kate pulls out of his embrace — wild, angry.

KATE: There's nothing to be done then!

She sits down hard on a straightback chair — glaring at Miner. Miner immediately places his hands on her shoulders and speaks firmly.

MINER: Listen to me . . . I want you to take that train. Go to Chicago.

KATE: Why?

MINER: I will go somewhere . . . Throw off any pursuit and join you when it is safe.

Kate becomes calmer — beginning to see the sense in what he is proposing.

KATE: Will you come?

MINER: Yes. You must believe me.

Kate says nothing — studies him.

MINER: Do you believe me?

KATE: I believe in you.

Miner embraces her. They kiss.

141. Ext. Kamloops Station. Day.

VIEW *of Miner and Kate as they stand facing each other on the railroad platform beside a waiting train. A late passenger hurries past and boards one of the coaches. Miner and Kate are looking at each other, oblivious to anything happening around them.*

CONDUCTOR: (*Off*) "Board! . . . Allaboard!"

Miner takes Kate's hand and ushers her to the steps of a coach. She gets onto the bottom step where she turns and looks at him. Her anxiety and fear is visible in her eyes.

MINER: Have a good trip. I will join you in eight to ten days.

Kate leans forward and kisses him. The kiss lingers until the train lurches into motion. Miner continues to hold her hand and walks along the platform as the train begins to move out. Kate looks frightened now but she says nothing. The train gathers speed.

ON Miner as he watches Kate carried away from him.

142. Ext. A Stream (Kamloops). Day.

ANGLE on Miner, Shorty, and Louis wading across a shallow stream. They are leading two pack horses that are loaded with provisions and prospecting equipment.

Shorty yanks impatiently at the lead of one horse.

SHORTY: This'd be a whole lot easier if we was ridin'!

MINER: Yes . . . But the lawmen will be looking for train robbers on horses, not prospectors on foot.

Miner trudges up the bank. Louis and Shorty follow, leading the horses.

The journey to meet the train: What follows is a SERIES OF CROSS-CUTS between Miner, Louis, and Shorty walking and the CPR Imperial Limited as it steams to meet them at Ducks. This sequence will be scored to The Chieftains' "Job of Journeywork."

143. Ext. Countryside. Day.

The figures of Miner, Louis, Shorty and the pack horses inching up a steep hillside.

144. Ext. Rail Line. Day.

A VIEW of the CPR Imperial Limited as it steams around a curve — fast and powerful — gliding along the track.

145. Ext. Countryside. Day.

Miner's group moving onward.

146. Ext. Rail Line. Day.

VIEW *of the Imperial Limited rocketing along to meet them.*

147. Ext. Countryside. Day.

Miner's group traversing rough terrain.

148. Ext. Rail Line. Day.

CLOSE *on the pumping drive bars of the Limited as it steams past at high speed.*

149. Ext. Countryside. Day.

ON *Miner's group walking quickly.*

150. Ext. Rail Line. Day.

ON *the Limited traversing a straight stretch of track. The whistle moans.*

151. Ext. Countryside. Day.

Miner's group making its way down a slope.

152. Ext. Rail Line. Day.

The Limited blasting toward and past as it heads for Ducks.

153. Ext. Beside a Water Tower. Dusk.

A VIEW *of Miner, Shorty, and Louis standing grouped on a deserted stretch of railroad track beside a huge water tower. Miner checks the time on his pocket watch.*

SHORTY: How much longer?

MINER: An hour and ten.

Shorty glances around at the deserted locale.

SHORTY: What if it don't stop?

MINER: It will. They need to take on water for the upgrade.

Louis picks up a small, loaded sack and slings it over his shoulder.

LOUIS: I'll go up to the one-one-eight mileboard now.

MINER: Before you go there's something I have to tell you both . . . It's not safe for me in Kamloops. I'm not going back. I'd advise you didn't go back either.

Shorty seems confused by this news. Louis simply smiles and looks at Miner.

LOUIS: You're Bill Miner, aren't you?

Miner looks at him, his eyes proud and strong.

MINER: I am.

Shorty reacts with dumbstruck astonishment.

154. Ext. Ducks Siding. Night.

ANGLE on the Imperial Limited sitting at Ducks Siding. The locomotive headlight is blaring bright, steam hisses from boiler vents. The baggage car, mail car, and three illuminated coaches stretch away behind. The conductor and two other men are visible, standing outside one of the coaches. The engineer is leaning out the window of his cab, looking back. The conductor waves a lantern.

CONDUCTOR: (Distant) "Allaboard!"

The whoosh of air brakes being released. The bell begins to clang.

155. Ext. Other Side of the Train. Night.

Two figures hurry out of the brush and run toward the side of the baggage car. They are Miner and Shorty.

They climb up a service ladder to the roof of the car as the train lurches into motion.

The train moves out, gaining momentum. The whistle moans.

156. Ext. Along the Tracks. Night.

VIEW *of the Imperial Limited as it rumbles past at running speed. Brightly lit coach windows.*

157. Int. Locomotive Cab. Night. (Travel).

Engineer Callum is at the throttle. His fireman is checking pressure gauges and adjusting valves.

They both turn to look as Miner and Shorty come scrambling down the gangway from the tender with revolvers in hand. Both are wearing coats and kerchiefs over their faces. Miner is also wearing driving goggles.

    CALLUM: What in the mischief are you two doing here?

    SHORTY: We're robbin' this train!

Callum and the fireman look at each other in disbelief.

    CALLUM: How are you going about it?

    SHORTY: Just do like you're told!

    MINER: Have you got any guns on you?

    CALLUM: We don't carry guns.

Miner seems satisfied. He moves over behind Callum so he can look forward along the track.

    MINER: We want you to stop at the one-one-six mileboard.

Callum nods.

158. Ext. Mile 116. Night.

VIEW *of the train as it slows and squeals to a halt along a deserted strip of track in an evergreen forest.*

The fireman and Shorty scramble down from the cab and hurry back to cut the express cars from the coaches.

159. Int. Locomotive Cab. Night.

Callum is leaning out his window, looking back. Miner is covering him with his Colt .45.

> **MINER:** When they're done I want you to pull ahead to mile one-one-eight and stop there.

Callum's attention is drawn by something below. He looks.

What he sees: Another figure hurrying out of the woods toward the locomotive. It is Louis, his face also masked, and he is carrying a loaded sack.

Louis tosses the sack up to the locomotive deck and climbs up to join Miner in the cab.

Callum resumes looking rearward along the train.

> **CALLUM:** They're on their way back.

160. Ext. The Locomotive. Night.

Shorty and the fireman return and reboard the locomotive. It chuffs into motion immediately and glides away, pulling only the baggage car now.

161. Ext. Mile 118. Night.

The Mile 118 marker is in foreground as the big locomotive eases to a stop beside it.

The fireman, Callum, Miner, Shorty, and Louis, carrying the sack, all climb down from the cab and trudge back toward the baggage car.

162. Ext. Beside the Baggage Car. Night.

As they near the baggage car, Miner, Shorty, and Louis are startled by the sound of the sliding door being unlocked. They take cover behind Callum and the fireman.

The door slides back to reveal a yawning clerk (McQuarrie) who looks out at them.

> MCQUARRIE: What's up? A hose bust?

Miner and Shorty come over, guns pointed.

> MINER: This is no hose bust, it's a holdup!
>
> SHORTY: Throw down your guns!
>
> MCQUARRIE: I haven't got any gun! This is the baggage car!

Miner immediately looks more closely at the car, then darts a hard look at Shorty.

> SHORTY: (*Defensive*) They all look the same in the dark!
>
> MINER: Have you got mail?
>
> MCQUARRIE: Some.

Miner goes over and climbs up into the car while Shorty and Louis cover the engine crew.

163. Int. The Baggage Car. Night.

A long, functional "box" with shelves and pigeonholes along the side walls. One half of the car is loaded with baggage and wrapped parcels. Some mail sacks are visible. There is a sorting table in the center and the car is lit by acetylene gas lamps.

Miner herds McQuarrie over near the table and scans the array of goods.

> MINER: I want the box, son.
>
> MCQUARRIE: What box?
>
> MINER: The express box.
>
> MCQUARRIE: I told you . . . It's on the car you left behind.
>
> MINER: Then give me the 'Frisco registered pouch.
>
> MCQUARRIE: We don't have one. It doesn't come this way.
>
> MINER: (*Sharply*) Which way does it come?
>
> MCQUARRIE: By the Mission Junction.

Miner seems frustrated and confused. He looks around, then back to McQuarrie.

>**MINER:** You've got some registered mail?

McQuarrie nods "yes."

>**MINER:** Put it on the table.

McQuarrie goes over to a shelf and returns with one small mail sack and a small, wrapped parcel. He deposits these on the tabletop.

Miner dumps out the mail pouch. He picks up all the letters and stuffs them into his coat pocket. He then uses his gun to point to the little wrapped parcel.

>**MINER:** Is this a money package?

>**MCQUARRIE:** I don't know, sir.

Miner motions for him to open it with a jerk of his head. As he does so his kerchief slips down, exposing his face. He immediately replaces the mask, but McQuarrie has had a look at him.

McQuarrie tears open the package to reveal its contents. It contains six little bottles. Miner picks one up and holds it to the light.

TIGHT *on the label: "Munyon's Kidney Cure."*

Miner snorts, then puts the bottle in his pocket.

>**MINER:** This could come in handy.

164. Ext. Beside the Baggage Car. Night.

Miner climbs down, watched by the others.

>**MINER:** *(To Shorty, Louis)* Let's go. I'm done.

Louis displays his sack.

>**LOUIS:** What about this?

>**MINER:** No need for it now.

Louis tosses the sack up into the baggage car.

>**MCQUARRIE:** What is it?

>**SHORTY:** *(Laughs)* Dynamite!

Miner heads off toward the trees. Shorty and Louis follow him. Callum, McQuarrie, and the fireman watch them vanish into the forest.

165. Int. A Telegraph Office. Night.

TIGHT *on a man's hand tapping out a message on a telegraph key.*

166. Ext. Rail Line. Day.

A hand-pumped speeder comes into view, moving quickly along a stretch of track. It is operated by two section hands and on it rides Fernie.

167. Ext. Mile 118. Day.

The train is now gone but the site of the robbery is swarming with men — most of them armed. There are ten ranchers, several tracking dogs, three railroad officials, many horses, a couple of wagons. Three indian trackers sit calmly on one of the rails. A bonfire burns; a tent has been set up, outside of which is a folding table and some folding chairs. Fernie is standing by the table talking to one of his subordinates (Constable Pearse), who has a map spread out on the table. Fernie scans this scene of activity.

FERNIE: So what have you got?

PEARSE: The Indians found three good sets of tracks, sir. Looks like they set off to the north . . . (*He gestures*).

FERNIE: Then they looped south?

Pearse registers surprise at Fernie's intuition.

PEARSE: Yessir. About a mile east of here.

Fernie nods and points casually at the map with one finger.

FERNIE: They'll head down past Douglas Lake and make for the border.

PEARSE: (*Nods*) We might need more men. That's rough terrain.

Fernie takes out his watch and checks the time. He seems very calm.

FERNIE: I phoned Calgary. A detachment of Mounties is

coming here by special train. (*Indicates map*) See how the line loops south to Quilchena?

Pearse looks at the map and nods.

FERNIE: I'm having them get off there and deploy eastward to Douglas Lake.

PEARSE: (*Impressed*) Head them off, sir?

FERNIE: (*Nods*) That's the idea.

168. Ext. In a Canyon (Douglas Lake). Day.

Shorty and Miner have unloaded the pack horses and are shooing them off. The horses clatter away.

SHORTY: (*Dubious*) So what now?

MINER: We'll hike south past Douglas Lake and make for the border.

SHORTY: Maybe we shoulda sold those pack horses on the way, 'stead of shooin' them off?

MINER: (*Dangerous*) Shorty . . . You cut off the wrong car and we ended up with seventeen dollars and a bottle of kidney pills . . . Leave the thinking to me.

Miner hoists a pack and moves away.

169. Ext. A Trail (Douglas Lake). Day.

VIEW *of Miner leading Shorty and Louis as they drag themselves up the slope of a brushy hillside. Miner moves with grim determination.*

170. Ext. In the Woods (Douglas Lake). Night.

While Shorty and Louis sleep, huddled in their coats, Miner sits watch with his back to a tree. He is still but alert.

171. A Ridge. (Douglas Lake). Day.

Miner lies on the crest of a ridge, scanning the distant hills through binoculars. Shorty is crouched nearby.

SHORTY: Anything?

MINER: No . . . But they aren't far behind.

Miner drags himself to his feet and picks up his pack.

MINER: Let's get moving boys.

Shorty looks beat. Louis drags himself up, coughing. They sling packs and trudge after Miner.

172. Ext. Another Hill (Douglas Lake). Day.

VIEW *of Miner clambering up a rocky slope. He looks tired but coldly determined. Shorty and Louis straggle behind.*

173. Ext. A Clearing (Douglas Lake). Day.

The Indian trackers have hold of the abandoned pack horses and Fernie is looking them over. Pearse leaves the posse and walks over to Fernie.

PEARSE: Prospectors are always losing their horses in these hills.

FERNIE: That may be, Constable, but these belonged to the robbers. They must have set them loose to leave a false trail . . . and it worked.

PEARSE: What now, sir?

FERNIE: We'll fan out. Keep going south.

Fernie returns to his horse, followed by Pearse.

174. Ext. A Drywash (Douglas Lake). Day.

Miner and Shorty stumbling along a dry, rocky stream bed. In the background, Louis sinks to his knees, coughing. Miner turns, sees him, and trudges back.

MINER: On your feet, son.

LOUIS: (*Coughing*) I'm done.

Miner reaches down and hauls Louis to his feet.

MINER: You will be if you stay here. Come on.

They start moving again.

175. Ext. In the Brush (Douglas Lake). Night.

Miner, Shorty, and Louis sit huddled together for warmth.

SHORTY: I'm damn near froze, Bill . . . What say to a little fire?

MINER: We will be hot enough in Hell if they find us. No fire.

They sit there in silence — listening to the dark.

176. Ext. Along a Stream Bed (Douglas Lake). Day.

A small stream wends through a copse of sparse trees. Miner comes trudging along, painfully, followed by Louis and Shorty. All three look dirty and tired. Miner stops, surveys the surroundings, then slings off his pack and gestures across the creek.

MINER: Douglas Lake is just east of here. We'll rest here, have some lunch. I figure they're at least half a day behind us now.

SHORTY: Can I brew us some coffee?

MINER: (*Nods*) Make it quick.

Now Shorty and Louis unsling their packs.

177. Ext. In a Gully. Day.

A VIEW of six uniformed men on horses. They are in a little gully, not moving.

A CLOSER ANGLE *reveals them to be Mounties. They are clad in brown tunics with Sam Brown belts and they wear the distinctive* NWMP *stetsons — similar to Miner's own. All of them look lean and tough.*

The leader (Sergeant Wilson) moves away from the group and eases his horse slowly up the sloping side of the gully.

178. Ext. A Ridge. Day.

ON *Wilson as he rides slowly up the slope to the top of a ridge. He is a stern-faced man of forty with a dark moustache. He rides with one fist resting on a hip, lending arrogance to his overall impression. He reaches the crest and looks around. The countryside is rolling and open, dotted with small copses of trees.*

Wilson takes out a pair of field glasses from a case and puts them to his eyes. He slowly scans the expanse. He freezes as he spots something.

WILSON'S P.O.V. *through the binoculars: a faint column of smoke rises from a distant copse of trees.*

ON *Wilson as he puts the binoculars back in their case, turns his horse, and rides back down the slope toward his men.*

179. Ext. A Clearing in the Trees. Day.

A VIEW *through the sparse trees of Miner, Shorty, and Louis seated around a tiny bonfire, eating and drinking coffee. Their packs are nearby.*

180. Ext. Near the Copse of Trees. Day.

A VIEW *of the Mounties as they approach slowly on horses. Wilson gives a couple of arm signals and his men deploy to surround the copse. Wilson continues straight to the treeline, where he dismounts and unsnaps the cover of his gun holster.*

181. Ext. The Clearing. Day.

Shorty and Louis are eating hungrily. Miner is sitting quietly, smoking a cigarette. He seems lost in his own thoughts.

182. Ext. In the Copse. Day.

ON *Wilson as he walks carefully, quietly into the copse, making his way between trees.*

ON *Wilson's boots as they move stealthily over underbrush.*

ON *Wilson's right hand, resting on his holster.*

183. Ext. The Clearing. Day.

Shorty puts down his tin cup and stands up. He strolls into the trees to urinate. Louis is still eating. Miner pays no attention — just sits smoking.

184. Ext. In the Copse. Day.

Shorty stops and begins to unbutton his fly. He hears something and peers ahead.

What he sees: Sergeant Wilson is visible — staring at him from about thirty feet away.

    WILSON: Hello there.

ON *Shorty, who registers shock then turns and hurries back toward the clearing.*

185. Ext. The Clearing. Day.

Miner and Louis look over as Shorty comes rushing out of the trees, gesturing.

    SHORTY: (Loud whisper) Mounties!

Miner and Louis immediately glance around. They then see Wilson walking to the edge of the clearing.

Shorty immediately goes and sits down beside his pack, looking terrified.

Miner and Louis remain seated, not moving. Miner slowly butts his cigarette in the dirt and looks around. Other Mounties are appearing on all sides of the clearing.

Miner returns his gaze to meet Wilson's. Wilson nods.

WILSON: Good day.

Miner affects a casual, friendly grin.

MINER: Good day, sir. We didn't hear you coming up on us.

WILSON: I am Sergeant Wilson . . . North West Mounted Police. I must ask you to identify yourselves.

When Wilson speaks it becomes apparent that he is British. His voice is casual, ironic.

Louis is staring. Shorty is glancing around, twitchy with fear. Miner looks calm.

MINER: You boys are kind of out of your territory, aren't you?

WILSON: (*Firmer*) I must ask you to identify yourselves.

MINER: My name is George Edwards . . . This is Louis Colqhoun and that is Shorty Dunn.

WILSON: What are you doing out here?

MINER: Prospecting.

WILSON: Prospecting? Where?

MINER: (*Gestures*) Over there. East of Douglas Lake.

WILSON: Not north?

MINER: No sir. East.

Wilson and his men stare at them in silence. Wilson takes a couple of steps forward.

WILSON: You answer the descriptions of the men we're hunting.

Shorty is looking very panicky now. Miner smiles.

MINER: And who might they be, sir?

WILSON: The train robbers.

Miner glances at Shorty and Louis then back to Wilson.

MINER: What train robbers?

WILSON: The ones who robbed the CPR at Ducks Siding.

MINER: (*Chuckles*) Do we look much like train robbers?

Wilson is now in doubt. His eyes scan their gear.

WILSON: Those gold pans . . . They don't look much used to me.

MINER: We weren't panning. We were surveying and staking. This is the first we have heard of any train robbery.

Wilson hesitates, deliberating.

WILSON: Nonetheless, we must take you for the robbers.

Suddenly Shorty rolls over, pulling his revolver as he scrambles to his feet.

SHORTY: It's all up, boys!

Shorty begins firing wildly at the Mounties as he runs toward the creek. Mounties go for their guns. Wilson pulls his service revolver and aims it right at Louis who has half-drawn his own.

Miner, Louis (David Peterson) and Shorty (Wayne Robson) feign innocence for the Mounties. "Do we look much like train robbers?"

WILSON: You do and I'll blow your brains out!

Louis freezes. Miner sits stoically, not moving a muscle.

Shorty is running for the creek, firing back. The Mounties return a fusilade of shots.

Shorty is hit and goes down in the creek. A couple of Mounties rush toward him, revolvers pointed. Shorty sits up, clutching his leg. Blood is staining his trousers.

MOUNTIE: That was stupid! You could have been hit in the head!

SHORTY: (*Anguished*) I wish to God I had been hit through the head!

The Mounties begin to haul him out of the creek.

ON *Miner who remains seated, staring at nothing — his mind on the future that has slipped through his grasp.*

186. Ext. Kamloops Main Street. Day.

Several people are waiting on both sides of the street as the Mounties ride in. They flank a farm wagon drawn by a team of horses. In the back of the wagon sit the figures of Miner, Shorty, and Louis — each of them covered by a blanket. Other townspeople appear and hurry to spots where they can have a view.

VOICE: (*Off*) They got 'em! They've caught Bill Miner!

ON *Budd as he emerges from the entrance of the Tulameen. He looks anxiously toward the procession.*

As the wagon passes the blanket slips off Miner's head and he is clearly visible to Budd and everyone.

VOICE: (*Off*) That ain't Miner! They got George Edwards!

187. Ext. Behind the Police Office/Courthouse. Day.

A male photographer is readying his camera as the Provincials and the

Mounties bring out Miner, Louis, and Shorty. Two Mounties have to assist Shorty and sit him in a wooden chair. His leg is bandaged and splinted.

The photographer signals that he is ready and a Provincial nudges Miner over to a spot against the building's wall and positions him for a photograph.

Miner stands there serenely — his expression giving no clue to his thoughts, as the photographer snaps his mug shot. Flash.

188. Int. Miner's Cell. Night.

Miner is sitting on the edge of a cot, his elbows on his knees, his head in his hands. High overhead a gas lamp burns. Miner looks to the sound of a key in the lock.

The cell door opens and Fernie enters, followed by Seavey. Fernie seems uncomfortable and is very polite.

> **FERNIE:** Are my men treating you well?

Miner stands up and smiles at Fernie. The pursuit and his fatigue make him looked stooped, older.

> **MINER:** Yes, Sergeant. Thank you.
>
> **FERNIE:** This is Mister Seavey. He's a Pinkerton agent from Portland.

Seavey offers his hand. Miner accepts it.

> **SEAVEY:** Hello, Bill. I've been looking forward to meeting you for a long time.
>
> **MINER:** My name is Edwards, sir. George Edwards.

Seavey, still clutching Miner's hand, turns it inward to better reveal the distinctive bluebird tattoo.

> **SEAVEY:** (*Smiles*) Is it indeed, sir?

Miner meets Seavey's eyes for a moment, then looks at Fernie. Fernie looks back at him briefly, then his eyes move to Seavey. Seavey looks at them both and smiles knowingly, confidently.

189. Int. Courtroom. Day or Night.

ANGLE on Miner, Louis, and Shorty seated in the defendant's box of a courtroom. *Behind them is the presence of people and the murmuring of voices in a crowded room. Miner, Louis, and Shorty all look impassive. A gavel raps.*

>**JUDGE:** (*Off*) The prisoners will rise.

The murmuring dies as Miner, Louis, and Shorty stand up. Shorty has to pull himself up by bracing his arm on the side of the box.

>**JUDGE:** (*Off*) Louis Colqhoun, William Dunn, and William Miner, also known as George Edwards . . . You have been tried and found guilty of the crime of armed robbery and this court sentences you as follows . . . Louis Colqhoun . . . ten years . . .

There is a murmur from the assembled crowd. Louis does not react, although Shorty glances at him, horrified.

>**JUDGE:** (*Off*) William Dunn, twenty-five years . . .

A gasp from the crowd and a look of shock on Shorty's face.

>**JUDGE:** (*Off*) And William Miner, also known as George Edwards, you are also sentenced to twenty-five years.

The crowd bursts into excited conversation. Miner's expression remains totally passive, revealing nothing of his reaction to what amounts to a sentence of death.

The music of a brass band playing "The British Grenadier" crossfades in and bridges to:

190. Ext. Kamloops Station. Day.

A big crowd of people line the railway platform, along with B.C. Provincial Police, Mounties, and other dignitaries. The brass band is visible playing "British Grenadier." The scene and its atmosphere are festive. Fernie and Budd are visible in the crowd. Both of them look grim. Seavey is also visible, looking content as he talks to a reporter.

CLOSE ON *Seavey and the reporter. Seavey has to shout to be heard above the music and other voices.*

>**SEAVEY:** . . . It will all fade into proper perspective soon enough. Miner and his likes are nothing more than victims of history. The railroads are forever.

ANGLE on the platform. The crowd looks, cheers, applauds as Miner, Shorty, and Louis are marched into view wearing handcuffs, chains, and leg irons. People move aside to form a channel as they are marched along by several constables and detectives.

ON Miner as his eyes catch the gaze of Budd, who is watching from the crowd. Miner manages a small smile before he is nudged along by a Constable.

They are ushered to the steps of a special passenger coach. Louis goes up first. Shorty, limping, has to be assisted up the stairs by constables.

As Miner waits his turn a small figure darts from the crowd. It is the town boy who always watched him. Miner looks down at the boy and smiles at him. The boy thrusts an orange toward Miner. Miner takes it in his manacled hands and, before he can acknowledge it, the boy darts back into the crowd. A Constable nudges Miner onto the train steps. He turns and takes a last look at the crowd, then he is nudged up the steps and out of view.

191. Ext. Rear Platform of Train. Day. (Travel).

VIEW of the tracks and the crowded platform as the train pulls away from the station. The whistle moans. The train gathers speed, gliding away from the station, from the cheering crowd, from the band.

The band music gets fainter and fainter as the station diminishes in the distance. Soon the rhythmic clatter of the train wheels takes its place. The track curves and the town and the station are lost from view.

FADE TO BLACK. THE FOLLOWING SUPER FADES IN:

"Thirteen months later..."

FADE IN:

192. Ext. Base of Prison Fence. Day.

ON Miner's hands — the tattoo prominent — as they claw up through the soft earth, tunneling from the inside of the fence.

193. Ext. B.C. Prison. Day.

VIEW of Miner clad in a mud-covered prison uniform, running away from the prison wall. He looks desperate and is moving as fast as he can on his sore feet.

On the distant wall, two guards can be seen — gesturing. The wail of a hand-cranked siren splits the air.

Rifle shots. Wet dirt sprays up near Miner's running feet. Miner is breathing raspy as he runs full-out toward the treeline.

194. Ext. On the Wall. Day.

A guard pumps his Winchester and sights it.

P.O.V. along the gunsight: lined up on Miner's small, fleeing figure. The rifle fires. Miner vanishes into the forest.

195. Ext. Along a Riverbank. Day.

ANGLE on the soft, muddy bank of a dark river. Rain is falling and the river is shrouded in mist.

Miner comes plodding out of the brush and makes his way along the muddy bank to where an empty rowboat sits nosed to the mud. Miner stops and listens. Distant — the barking of hounds. Miner is soaked and covered with mud.

Miner looks at the rowboat, deliberating, then climbs into it and shoves off from the bank. The boat slips out, is caught by the current, and begins to drift downriver.

Miner squats in the boat. He takes a final look back — his features fierce, his eyes sharp, alert, then he is carried in the little boat into the rising mist and is lost from view.

FADE TO BLACK. THE FOLLOWING SUPER FADES IN:

> "Bill Miner eluded an intensive manhunt and was never again seen in British Columbia. In 1911 he re-surfaced in the State of Georgia where he robbed a train near Gainsville. Miner, then sixty-six years old, was captured. He contracted swamp fever during a failed escape and died on September 2, 1913 at Milledgeville, Georgia . . . in prison."

TITLES AND CREDITS CRAWL.

MY AMERICAN COUSIN

BY SANDY WILSON

It all began with "The Battle of New Orleans" in August 1959 when Johnny Horton's hit song topped the charts and my American cousin George "Butch" Warren Jr. drove up in a big fancy convertible. Whenever "The Battle of New Orleans" came on the radio, Butch would turn the radio up and my father would shout, "Turn that damn noise off!" I couldn't believe I was related to anyone so bold, so glamorous, so American!

Then his parents came to take him home because he was a runaway and I never saw him again. I forgot all about him more or less, until mom wrote me that he'd been killed in a car accident a couple of days after his wedding. He hit a tree or something. But it was 1965 and I was all caught up in the 60s so his memory faded.

Until I heard "The Battle of New Orleans" on my ghetto blaster, first week of August 1982 with Phil Schmidt and our four-year-old son Willie. I started telling Phil about my American cousin and we both got very excited: "Let's make a movie!" we said. I wrote "My American Cousin" first in Hollywood Pink lipstick on the cabin window looking south down Okanagan Lake. It looked perfect. And then I began typing *My American Cousin* on a second hand Empire Aristocrat typewriter. Starting with what I remembered — my family and Butch's arrival and departure.

I knew the movie would only work if I could do it in the style of a documentary and with an obnoxious precocious girl about twelve or thirteen years old to play me. That's when I remembered Margaret Langrick, my neighbor who lived across the street from us in Kitsilano. She told ghost stories at night and we were held spell bound in the palm of her hand. Even as a little girl she had a generosity of spirit and a wisdom far beyond her years. So I wrote the script with Margaret Langrick in mind all the time. No doubt about it. And I'd get a big American star to play the cousin. Some skinny unhealthy dark broody boy, a boy to strike terror into a mother's heart if her daughter ever brought such a boy home.

Collecting the data is one of the best parts about being a documentary filmmaker. People tell you the most amazing things! And so I began collecting stories. My mom and my sister Elaine and my brother Guy told me what they remembered about our runaway cousin Butch and that glorious summer. Guy said Butch showed up with French safes and firecrackers in his wallet and he took Dad's speedboat without asking one night and dropped the brand new Evinrude engine into the middle of the deepest part of the lake. My mother said he had "bedroom eyes."

Phil made a lot of wonderful suggestions and everyone from that time had a story to tell. Jeanne Lamb told me she tried starching her crinolines by boiling them in sugar and water, but it was so hot that the crinoline melted and got unbearably sticky. We had a lot of laughs along the way. Telling stories about families, first loves and everyone's favorite American cousin. Stealing ideas shamelessly from photo albums, high school yearbooks, old magazines, books, movies, songs, everything anywhere. Alone for a couple of days, or for a few hours, in the cabin or squatting at the National Film Board after hours finally with no one to interrupt me, the exterior world would fall away and I was that kid again, only now I was also the observing adult. Playing house, re-creating my family and my friends, digging into my past like an anthropologist writing to make my dream life a reality on the silver screen.

It was a private affair at that point. But not for long. When Donna Wong Juliani at Telefilm would ask politely what draft was I working on, I'd say, "Pick a number, any number you're comfortable with," because the script was always changing. Jim Burt, then a reader for Roman Melnyck, wrote a wonderful reader's report urging the CBC to make *My American Cousin*. He suggested "more conflict," so I wrote the fight scene on the beach the way I remember fights — with us girls running to the washroom to cry while the boys got down and dirty.

Everyone kept saying "Nice little story but it's too soft. There's no big change. Where's the big revelation, the big conflict?" and I would think to myself but rarely say out loud, "But everything changes! The world changes! From inside her head. She is different! Things will never be the same!" When Lindsay Law at American Playhouse read the script and said,"Nice script but nothing much happens in it," I thought, "That's it. I'll open with Sandy writing 'Nothing ever happens' in her diary. Get it out of the way."

I was the producer/director/writer and Phil Schmidt was the associate producer and we had a second son during this whole episode but that's another story altogether. Suffice it to say that I was still taking meetings well into my ninth month of pregnancy, and I made sure to book a private room with a phone at St. Paul's Hospital when Matthew was born on April 30th, 1983, so that I could continue making calls because Telefilm had just announced the new broadcast fund and all the players were coming to town to talk it up.

After more than a year of cross-country negotiations Peter O'Brian signed on as producer and within two months we were tumbling into production. Peter would give me pages of detailed notes. He wanted to discuss every scene. At the time I wondered, "Why doesn't he leave me alone and stop asking all these questions!" But he knew what lay ahead and he wanted to make the whole much greater than the sum of the parts; he cared about the movie first and foremost and he challenged all of us to be the best.

After I first met John Wildman in a Toronto casting session, I said to Maria Armstrong, "Get him outta here! He's way too gorgeous," but she insisted on calling him back and I finally agreed. When I saw John Wildman read a tender scene with a very young actress I saw Butch as this California dreamboat. So John got the part and I re-wrote the script for him. And then the real Butch's real dad and his genteel sisters showed up in Penticton during pre-production. We talked late into the night about the real Butch — his kindness and charisma, his wild destructive streak, abiding interest in girls and fast cars and then of course his untimely death. It was a tragic story and we all wept that night to think of Butch Warren. I knew I was tampering with very painful memories but I shielded myself from doubt with the hope that they would like the final film.

Getting a film into production is like riding a runaway train on a steep mountain slope. Suddenly the words on the page were now flesh and blood people. All the actors were generous with their ideas and little bits of business and various suggestions. My real mother Kitty says Jane Mortifee made her look good. And she's right, Jane added some sweet lines and softened her up a lot.

Well into shooting, Richard Donat, who played Major Wilcox, kept suggesting a scene between himself and Margaret, so I wrote him the "Boys have uncontrollable urges" scene and we filmed it the next day. Margaret was always asking me, "How would you like me to read this line? Let me guess . . . bratty, right?" Margaret and I sort of became this other third person — looking and talking the same way and finishing each other's sentences. John Wildman became Butch. He added lots of crazy slang and bits of songs and gave his character an easy confidence I had never considered. Camille

Henderson added a frosty perfection to her part as Shirley Darling and TJ Scott as Lenny gave our Canadian boy a sexy wholesome charm.

On weekends I would hide out at the cabin and work on the script. Peter O'Brian remembers me writing in the middle of the production office, in the eye of the hurricane. And Jim Burt is still complaining that the CBC never saw any pink pages. Richard Leiterman saved my bacon and Ed Folger ran an easy set and we shot the film in twenty-five days with no overtime to speak of. The crew worked above and beyond the call of duty.

The changes to the script didn't stop once we finished shooting. Take the ending. I had generally insisted that we needed to know that Butch was killed in a car accident when he was only twenty-one. But somewhere at a rough cut stage that ending seemed like a kick below the belt. So we dumped it.

Finally we had all the tracks laid and a mix booked in Toronto, so Peter O'Brian arranged for a screening with Fred Roos and some other American producers. Sitting with them, I saw the film through their eyes and it looked so corny, so painfully slow to get started, so sagging limply in the middle and at least ten minutes too long and I wanted to die. But the editor Haida Paul and I brought the whole show back home to Vancouver and very quickly cut ten minutes out of the film. Even while we were mixing the final tracks, I was re-writing voice overs and shuffling lines around here and there, especially for the ending.

We had a wet answer print ready just hours before *My American Cousin* was screened at the Bumbershoot Festival in Seattle — with all of Butch's family and my parents in attendance. Lucky for me, they all loved the movie. The following Thursday, September 7, 1985, *My American Cousin* was finished and I was surprised to realize that it was really out there all on its own — delivered and I couldn't change it anymore.

Years later *My American Cousin* was shown on American Playhouse and the cut line was "'Nothing ever happens' — Tuesday night at 9 on American Playhouse *My American Cousin*, award winning . . ." and here I am today writing about writing *My American Cousin*.

So my mom was right about a couple of things, boys are like buses and only time will tell.

Sandy Wilson

MY AMERICAN COUSIN

FADE IN:

1. Ext. Long Shot Ranch House — Late Evening.

It is a hot summer night in 1959. The light has almost left the sky. We are looking down on a long, flat roofed wooden house, situated over the Okanagan Lake and surrounded by green lawns, pine trees, and a few fruit trees.

In the distance we can hear a radio playing Slim Whitman's "Suddenly There's a Valley." A screen door slams, the sprinklers and crickets round out the summer sounds.

The lights inside the house look bright and welcoming.

2. Int. Ranch House Office — Late Evening.

Queen's speech continues on the radio. Major John Wilcox, a handsome man in his late forties, sits behind a bare officious looking desk adding numbers on an old adding machine. The Major pauses to pick up a letter and look at it in a worried way.

Kitty enters from the living room, book in hand; she is distracted by a light on down the hall and with an impatient sigh she says:

> **KITTY:** You children are all supposed to be sleeping. Now stop playing and Sandra, turn off your light.

The Major quickly hides the letter.

CUT TO:

3. Int. Sandy's Bedroom — Late Evening.

Sandy, a plain twelve-year-old, in rollers and pink baby doll pajamas, is sitting up in bed, writing in her diary. She has written "Nothing Ever Happens." Her room is littered with clothes, toys, photos of Elvis going off to the Army, Marilyn Monroe, James Dean, and Tab Hunter.

SANDY: Aw, Mom. I'm still writing.

Kitty appears in the doorway.

KITTY: Lights off. Now.

Sandy looks very annoyed, sighs and puts her diary away and turns off the light.

Sandy (Margaret Langrick) tries to stay up just a little later. In her diary she has just written "Nothing Ever Happens."

4. Ext. Ranch House — Night. (Same as 1).

The ranch house is in the distance. We see the lights go off. Distant coyote cries fill the silent summer night.

5. Int. Sandy's Bedroom — Night.

Sounds of Sandy fumbling around in the dark. Sandy finally fishes out a flashlight from underneath her mattress and shines it on a small, Phillips radio next to her bed. She turns the dial until she gets an American station.

DJ'S VOICE: And now, KRKO, in Spokane, Washington, the heart of the great American Northwest, is pleased to spin that old, country classic, "Young Love, First Love." So pucker up, all you back seat Romeos, here we go.

Sandy sets up the flashlight under the sheet, fishes in her bed until she gets a "True Confessions" magazine out and sits up to do some reading. She pauses to look out the window.

SANDY'S VOICE: I'd always known we had American cousins. They sent us the biggest and the best Christmas cards of all our Canadian or English cousins.

6. *Ext. Ranch Road — Night.*

A Cadillac is driving past lush, green orchards. Sound of car radio in the distance, playing "Young Love, First Love." There is a metallic sound. The Cadillac looses its muffler. The Cadillac stops.

7. *Int. Sandy's Bedroom — Night. (Same as 2).*

Now Sandy is reading her magazine. The song on the radio ends.

DJ'S VOICE: Wasn't that romantic, kids? You bet it was. And now, to change the pace a little, the Number One hit from Coast to Coast again this week, Johnny Horton and you guessed it, "The Battle of New Orleans."

Song begins.

8. *Ext. Ranch Road — Night.*

In the distance we see the Cadillac start up again. A car door slams and the Cadillac drives on down the road. The car makes a lot of noise now.

9. *Int. Sandy's Bedroom — Night.*

"Battle of New Orleans" is still on and Sandy is reading. Suddenly there is

the loud noise of the Cadillac driving up outside and squealing to a stop. Car radio is playing "Battle of New Orleans" loudly. Sandy jumps in her bed and freezes for a moment.

SANDY'S VOICE: I first saw my American cousin in the summer of 1959.

Sandy quickly throws her magazine into the bed, switches off the radio, and tucks the flashlight under the mattress.

There is a loud knock on the screen door. Sandy goes to her bedroom door and opens it slightly. A light goes on down the hall.

MAJOR'S VOICE: I'm coming. I'M COMING.

10. Ext. Ranch House Front Porch — Night.

A front porch light goes on, car headlights shine on the front porch steps, a light at the corner of the house goes on. The Major, tying up a tartan gown, stands into the porch light.

MAJOR: What is it man, speak up.

BUTCH: Ah sir, Uncle John, I'm Butch Walker.

The Major relaxes a little and studies Butch.

MAJOR: Of course, Al's boy. Must be about seventeen. What a surprise.

The Major and Butch shake hands.

MAJOR: Are Al and Dolly with you?

BUTCH: No sir. I'm here alone. On a vacation.

MAJOR: I see. Alone. Well, you're family so you're welcome here son. Now please turn that damn radio and those lights off. You'll wake up the whole house.

Butch runs off to his car. Kitty steps into the light, tying up her dressing gown. She yawns.

MAJOR: It's Al and Dolly's boy Butch. Alone, on vacation. Were you expecting him?

KITTY: No one has written to me about it. But then there are a lot of things no one bothers to tell me. Now if we had a telephone . . .

The radio and lights go off.

MAJOR: Kitty we simply can't afford it.

Butch reappears.

BUTCH: Hello Aunt Kitty, sorry to get you up like this.

KITTY: Hello Butch. Does your mother know you're here?

BUTCH: Oh yes, I'm surprised she didn't write you a letter. But then she's been busy.

KITTY: Must be in the mail. I'll make you a bed in the spare room.

Kitty goes into the house.

KITTY'S VOICE: Maybe you can help pick cherries.

BUTCH: Glad to help out.

MAJOR: You're not in trouble with the police?

BUTCH: Oh no, Sir.

MAJOR: You could tell me if you were.

BUTCH: No, sir, I'm not.

MAJOR: Good.

The Major guides Butch inside the house.

MAJOR: Haven't got a girl in trouble have you?

The Major and Butch disappear. Sound of door closing and the lights go off.

The Major stops Kitty in the hallway.

MAJOR: Kitty, please, you go back to bed. I'll handle this.

Sleepily, Kitty shrugs, turns to go back to her room, pauses, turns to the Major.

KITTY: Perhaps Al could help us. They've got lots of money.

MAJOR: Absolutely not.

Sound of car radio stops. Screen door slams. Kitty shrugs and goes off to bed. The Major disappears into the doorway opposite the bedroom. Sandy, Eddie, and Danny reappear.

    KITTY'S VOICE: Maybe he can help pick cherries.

    MAJOR'S VOICE: Quietly, man. You'll wake up the whole house.

11. Int. Sandy's Bedroom — Night.

Sandy runs from the window to her bedroom door and peeks out.

12. Int. Ranch Hallway — Night.

There are three doors on one side of the hallway, two on the right. Sandy's middle bedroom opens and she peeks out.

Another door opens and out peeks Danny — fourteen and wearing pj bottoms. A third door opens and Eddie — twelve and wearing pj bottoms — stumbles out.

    MAJOR'S VOICE: Come this way son.

The three kids scoot back into their rooms. The Major walks by. Butch follows the Major. Butch looks terrific. As soon as the Major has walked by, the kids come out again. The Major turns, the kids disappear, the Major goes into the spare room, the kids come out again, Butch turns and grins at them. Sandy, Eddie, and Danny stop dead in their tracks.

    MAJOR'S VOICE: If the girls wake you up too early, you might be better in your car but you can sleep here for tonight.

The kids scramble out of the way, the Major crosses the hallway, lights go out.

    JOHNNY'S VOICE: Sandy?

    SANDY'S VOICE: Ya?

    JOHNNY'S VOICE: Who is it?

    SANDY'S VOICE: Our American cousin Butch.

JOHNNY'S VOICE: Wonder how long he'll stay.

SANDY'S VOICE: Forever I hope.

13. Ext. Ranch Driveway — Day.

Butch is standing next to an enormous gleaming red '57 Cadillac El Dorado Biarritz with Pixie — a six-year-old girl with an enormous doll — and Ruth, an eight-year-old girl with blonde hair. Sandy is posing the girls and Butch in front of the car and taking photos.

PIXIE: Are you really from California?

BUTCH: That's right. Drove up yesterday.

Danny comes out pushing Johnny in a wheelchair. Johnny is about sixteen and handicapped.

EDDIE: Wow. What kind of a car is that?

DANNY: Cadillac, El Dorado Biarritz. I saw a picture in a magazine.

JOHNNY: Can you take a picture of us too?

SANDY: Sure.

The boys pose with Butch for photos. The Major comes along, dressed in Khakis and carrying a clip board.

MAJOR: Well, Butch. This is a pretty big car, son.

BUTCH: My mom gave it to me.

SANDY: Dad, can you take a photo of me and Butch?

The Major smiles and puts down his clip board. Sandy gives him the camera and runs next to Butch.

SANDY: Alright you guys, get lost.

EDDIE: Why?

SANDY: Because if you don't I'll kiss you dipstick. Now go jump in the lake.

Danny wheels Johnny away, Eddie reluctantly stands back while Sandy and Butch pose in front of the Caddy. Kitty comes outside wearing an apron and carrying a wooden spoon.

KITTY: Ah, here you all are. Such an extravagant car for one so young. It's so American.

MAJOR: Now Kitty, I know they're Americans, but still, he's from a decent family.

The Major snaps the photo.

BUTCH: Can I take a picture of you altogether to send back home?

The Major and Kitty share a smile. Kitty takes off her apron, Danny pushes Johnny next to the car. Eddie, Pixie, Ruth, and Sandy all pose for Butch. The Major talks quietly to Kitty.

MAJOR: Kitty, Jim Van Weston is coming out today to examine the frost damage done last January.

KITTY: Is he here for lunch?

MAJOR: Yes and tea.

Butch snaps the photo and the family relaxes.

MAJOR: Come along Danny and Eddie. Butch, it's time to get up to the orchards.

KITTY: Alright Sandra, we have cherries to can this morning.

SANDY: Can't I stay outside a little longer.

KITTY: No dear. I need you in the kitchen, let's go.

Everyone leaves and the Cadillac is left alone, gleaming in the morning sunshine.

14. Int. Ranch Kitchen — Day.

The large kitchen table is covered with Mason jars, Mason lids, bags of sugar, and boxes of cherries. Huge vats of boiling water are steaming on the stove. Kitty is using metal forceps to lift the jars into the boiling water. Pixie and Ruth are putting fistfuls of cherries into the jars on the table. Sandy, wearing an apron, is measuring sugar and adding the sugar to the jars. Sandy catches something out of the corner of her eye. She goes to the window and looks out.

15. Int. Ranch House Kitchen — Day.

Still gazing out the window, Sandy asks her mother:

SANDY: Mom, how old were you when you started going out on dates?

Kitty pauses mid-movement to let her mind wander. She smiles to herself.

KITTY: Not until I went away to McGill. I went out with a boy from Trinidad. He was in my Contemporary Literature class. I wonder if . . .

Sandy turns around to look at her mother and grimace.

SANDY: You never went out till they shipped you off to university?

KITTY: I was not shipped off. Back to work.

Both Kitty and Sandy resume their duties. Sandy pauses.

SANDY: If you weren't allowed to go out on DATES, what did you DO?

KITTY: Well, your Aunt Lid and I were always putting on plays and . . .

SANDY: (*Disgusted*) Ew yuk. That is so dumb.

Kitty turns from the boiling vat of water to face Sandy, forceps in hand.

KITTY: (*Slowly*) Sandra. You really are the most unpleasant child I could ever imagine.

SANDY: (*Staring at her mother*) I am not a child.

As if on cue, Pixie and Ruth stand back together, holding hands. Kitty walks closer to Sandy, forceps raised. Sandy puts down the measuring cup filled with sugar and stands facing her mother with her hands on her hips. They glare at each other.

KITTY: Believe me, you most certainly are. You are the most selfish, self-centered . . .

Kitty points the forceps accusingly at Sandy, coming closer and closer. Sandy quickly throws up her arms, spins around, and moves quickly to the other side of the table. She rests her hands on the table and leans toward her mother.

SANDY: I know. I know. Let me see, "selfish, self-centered, sloppy, silly," oh yes, and "cheap" and let's not forget the old favorite, "inconsiderate" . . . Let me see, did I forget any?

Sandy pretends to consider, picks up a handful of cherries, and pops one in her mouth. Kitty glares at her. Now her hands are on her hips and she is shaking her head.

KITTY: (*Slowly*) That is IT. That is really IT. If you can't say anything nice . . .

Sandy puts her hands on her hips. They are facing each other over the table.

The timer rings and continues to ring.

SANDY/KITTY: (*In unison*) . . . DON'T SAY ANYTHING AT ALL.

Immediately Kitty spins around to grab the timer and turn it off. Sandy shakes her fistful of cherries at her mother's back and turns to go outside.

KITTY: (*Keeping her back to Sandy*) Get out. Get out. Before I . . .

SANDY: I'M GONE!

Sandy slams the screen door. Kitty slams the kitchen timer down on the counter and its alarm goes off again.

CUT TO:

16. Ext. Kitchen Porch — Day.

Sound of alarm ringing. Sandy throws her fistful of cherries at the kitchen door and screams out.

SANDY: I wish I lived anywhere else but here! This place is a PRISON. Some day I'll just run away. Then you'll be sorry.

KITTY'S VOICE: (*O.S.*) Go right ahead.

CUT TO:

17. Int. Cab of the Truck — Day.

Sandy is hanging around her father who is filling up cherry boxes and making notes on his clipboard.

MAJOR: Your mother grew up in a quiet house. She always thought she would be a librarian. So you must understand that she's not, well, she's . . . . it's just that you children are a bit much for her sometimes.

The Major walks away. Sandy throws her arms in the air.

SANDY: I'm not a child.

The Major returns to look at Sandy.

MAJOR: Oh yes you are.

Sandy looks disbelieving and shakes her head.

MAJOR: Exactly how old are you anyway? I lose track of you all.

SANDY: Oh Dad, really. I'll be thirteen in three months. I'm practically a teenager.

MAJOR: (*Surprised*) Really? A teenager. Oh dear.

The Major looks at his clipboard. He looks up at Sandy.

MAJOR: Perhaps you should come with me today, I think we'd better have a talk.

The Major walks to the driver's side of the truck. Happily Sandy heads for the truck.

SANDY: Okay Dad, I wasn't doing anything anyway.

CUT TO:

18. Ext. Cab of the Truck — Day.

The Major is driving, Sandy is lolling out the window catching the breeze.

MAJOR: I think the time has come to talk to you about males and females. Together. I'm afraid it's a very complicated bit of business. But it's been going on for years, centuries in fact. Lives have been made and shattered. Plays and poetry and novels have been written, songs have been sung. There's nothing new about it. Some people never seem to get enough.

SANDY: Ya. I know, me and Thelma and Sue and Lizzie talk about it all the time.

The Major looks taken aback. The truck stops next to the mail box. Sandy automatically jumps out and gets the mail.

MAJOR: Anything from California?

SANDY: Nope, a "National Geographic" and a letter from the bank. The rest is junk.

MAJOR: I'll keep the letter from the bank. Don't mention it to your mother, she needn't know the details.

Sandy comes back into the truck, the Major takes the letter and puts it in his pocket. Sandy flips through the "National Geographic."

MAJOR: As I was saying, the attraction between the male and the female is natural and necessary for the continuation of the species.

Sandy looks out the window to stifle a giggle.

MAJOR: The female excites the male and once excited, the male is overcome by uncontrollable urges.

SANDY: Uncontrollable urges!

The Major starts the truck up and drives some more.

MAJOR: It's difficult to explain. But you can see it when a bull knows there is a cow nearby. That bull will break through fences, barn doors, walls, anything that stands between him and that cow.

SANDY: You were like that? With mom?

MAJOR: No no no. Of course not. Not exactly. I am just trying to tell you that it's the female's responsibility not to allow theses uncontrollable urges to go to far.

SANDY: Why the female?

MAJOR: Because women are more intuitive. They know

more about these sorts of things and so they must have better control over their own urges. And consequently over the male urge.

SANDY: What if the female doesn't have better control?

MAJOR: Ah. Then the poor female is in trouble and the male goes off Scott free. Not very fair of course. But then there you are, these things aren't always fair I'm afraid.

SANDY: Sounds complicated Dad.

MAJOR: Yes, it is.

The Major glances over at Sandy.

MAJOR: It's good to talk with you like this. You're like your grandmother and your mother — strong-minded women. (*He sighs and shakes his head*) But you simply must learn to operate within the bounds of safety.

SANDY: Ya. Sure thing Dad.

Sandy resumes her quizzical observation of the passing scenery.

19. Ext. Granny's House — Day.

Granny's house is an old orchard house with a large, screened veranda going all around the outside of the house and a sloping roof. It is set in an orchard and surrounded by a large garden. There is a German Shepherd dog and puppies under the front porch.

Granny, a vigorous, healthy woman in her seventies, wearing a canvas type skirt and a silk shirt, is pouring tea on the steps of the veranda. Aunt Nell, Granny's companion, in her late sixties and rather timid, is pitting cherries for jam. Sandy looks bored. The Major looks troubled.

GRANNY: Tea, Sandra? No, I don't suppose so.

Nell gets up and goes into the kitchen. Sandy stands up and stretches.

SANDY: No thanks, Granny. I think I'll just have a glass of water.

Sandy starts to walk into the house but stops.

GRANNY: "WAD DER." What on God's great earth is "WAD DER?"

SANDY: Water, from the tap, in the lake, falls from the sky.

GRANNY: Gracious, you mean WAH TAH. Not "WAD DER." Really, what these young children do to the Queen's language makes me shudder. Now let me please hear you say "WAH TAH" as it is meant to be spoken.

SANDY: (*Softly*) Wadder.

GRANNY: (*Loudly*) Speak up, child. Speak up. Are you afraid of something?

SANDY: No.

GRANNY: Good. It doesn't do to be afraid. Now, let's hear it pronounced correctly.

SANDY: (*Loudly*) WAH TAH.

GRANNY: Very good. See, now that wasn't difficult, was it, dear? John? (*Offering him a plate*) Another bickie?

Sandy storms into the house, nearly colliding with Aunt Nell on her way out.

SANDY: Could I please use the phone?

GRANNY: Yes, but don't be too long. Party line you know.

CUT TO:

20. Int. Granny's Living Room — Day.

Sandy saunters into the living room, with a bowlful of cherries and a couple of Peak Frean cookies. The living room looks like an outpost of the British Empire. There is a large gramophone in the corner, an upright piano against the wall, a large brick fireplace, oil paintings of Cyprus and India, old Colonels and military and hunting scenes. The furniture is large, old, stuffed chintz with doilies, newspapers, and magazines all over the place. Swords and hunting horns decorate the mantle and wall above the fireplace. Plants are crowded into any available nook and cranny. Sandy clears off a chair next to the roll-top desk where the old telephone is situated, gathers up some "London Illustrated News" magazines, arranges her cherries and cookies and magazines, dials a number, and settles into the chair.

Throughout the phone conversation, she flips through the magazines, eats cookies and cherries, and spits the cherry pits in the general direction of the fireplace, but generally they fall on the heavily carpeted floor. She faintly whispers into the phone and keeps glancing up to see if anyone is approaching.

> **SANDY:** Sue? Ya, it's me, Sandy. Look, we got this American cousin staying with us. Ya. (*In a deep voice*) California. Honest. He's way cuter than Barry Bent. I am not joking! His car is so fabulous. I've never seen anything like it. No joke! I think he ran away from home.

Sandy spits out more pits.

> **SANDY:** Ya. He nearly looked at me, but he was sleeping. Anyway. I'm going to get him to take us for a car ride (*Giggles*).

Sandy glances up. The Major is staring down at her, watching her spit pits across the living room. He looks furious.

> **SANDY:** Sue, I gotta go. Talked to you last.

Sandy quickly hangs up the phone and scrambles down on her hands and knees to pick up the pits off the carpet. Nell comes in, carrying a plate of biscuits and looks at the scene in disapproval.

CUT TO:

21. Ext. Naramata Roads — Day.

In a LONG SHOT we see the flatbed truck driving along winding orchard roads. Glum faced, Sandy hangs out the window, looking up at the clouds.

> **SANDY'S VOICE:** My girlfriends and I only liked to talk about boys and make-up and boys and other girls and clothes and boys. My father had warned me that boys got "uncontrollable urges" and that girls got into trouble. It was a fascinating mystery to me.

22. Ext. Road by the Cherry Orchard — Day.

The Major parks the truck next to the loading dock. He and Sandy get out of the truck.

> **MAJOR:** I don't want you hanging around the pickers while they're working. Go see if you can help your mother.
>
> **SANDY:** All she does is yell at me.

Sandy slams the truck door.

> **MAJOR:** Sandra . . . (*He pauses*) . . . this is not the time for another childish tantrum. Now, run along and make yourself useful.

The Major strides purposefully off into the orchard. Sandy makes faces at him behind his back.

> **MAJOR:** Is Jim June here yet?

Sandy glares after her father, turns, and starts to walk off down the dusty road. Unbeknownst to her, Butch climbs down off a ladder perched against a cherry tree. He looks frazzled, glances over his shoulders, and sneaks out of the orchard to follow Sandy.

CUT TO:

23. Ext. Graveyard — Day.

The graveyard is situated with a fabulous view of Lake Okanagan. There is only one grave in evidence. It is made from the flat rocks taken from the nearly shale outcroppings. Sandy sits glumly on top of the grave.

> **SANDY:** One of these days I'll just run away.

She picks up a pine cone and throws it away with all her strength.

> **SANDY:** I'll just get out of here. I'll leave. No note or anything. Then they'll be sorry. Then they'll wish they were nicer to me. Maybe I'll leave a short note.

Suddenly she stops, turns around, and looks very startled and confused. Butch is casually leaning against a tree and looking rather amused. He is carrying his small transistor radio and watching Sandy.

BUTCH: Hi. Hope I'm not interrupting.

SANDY: (*With confused delight*) Oh, no. Hi.

BUTCH: (*Smiling*) So, ah, what're you doin' anyway?

SANDY: (*Very casually*) Nothing.

Butch turns on the radio and moves the dial until he gets "Memories Are Made of This" (Dean Martin).

SANDY: They only play rock 'n' roll from four til five.

BUTCH: No kidding? In the States we get rock and roll all day long.

SANDY: That'd be tops.

BUTCH: Ya, it's okay.

They both laugh a little.

BUTCH: You're Sandy, right?

SANDY: Ya.

BUTCH: Well, Sandy, I'm your cousin Butch (*He extends his hand*) and I'm very pleased to meet you.

SANDY: (*Shaking his hand*) And I'm very pleased to meet you, too.

BUTCH: I saw you getting mad at yer dad.

SANDY: They treat me like a child.

BUTCH: How old are you?

SANDY: Guess.

Sandy turns to catch her breath. Butch studies her from head to toe.

BUTCH: I'd say about fourteen to fifteen.

Sandy smiles at Butch.

SANDY: Can I go for a ride in your car?

BUTCH: (*Shrugs*) Why not?

Sandy's face lights up.

SANDY: When?

BUTCH: I dunno. I'm supposed to be picking cherries. But those ladders are dangerous. A guy could hurt himself on one of those things.

SANDY: Ya. A picker broke his leg last year. Was Dad ever mad.

They laugh a little.

BUTCH: So, how old did you say you were?

SANDY: I never said.

BUTCH: Girls. You're fourteen, right?

SANDY: Nope. I'm twelve.

Butch turns away in disgust.

BUTCH: (*Jumping up*) Oh, man. I'm talking to some kid. I figured you were at least fourteen or something. Jesus.

SANDY: (*Calmly*) What's the big deal? Everybody thinks I'm fourteen. Even me. I'll be thirteen in October.

BUTCH: And you're the oldest girl, right?

SANDY: Right.

BUTCH: (*With a smile, he sits*) Oh well, what the Hell, you're a cousin anyway, right?

SANDY: That's right.

BUTCH: Sounds like my luck has run out.

SANDY: Me too. I wish I could run away from home.

BUTCH: (*Surprised*) What are you talking about?

SANDY: It's so dumb out here on this ranch. There's *nothing* to do.

BUTCH: Seems pretty nice up here. Your folks are real nice.

SANDY: Maybe to you they're nice, but they never let me do anything.

BUTCH: At least they worry about you.

SANDY: You ran away from home, didn't you?

BUTCH: (*Getting up and walking away*) Jeez.

SANDY: Don't worry. I'd never tell.

BUTCH: No, I did not run away from home. I'm up here on a vacation. No big deal. A guy can take a vacation, can't he?

SANDY: I think you did.

BUTCH: (*Looks at her for a moment, then turns and walks away*) Ya well, you're just a chick. What do you know?

SANDY: (*Getting up and following Butch*) Lots. That's why everyone's so worried about me.

24. Ext. Ranch Road Scenics — Day.

The red Cadillac is seen skidding around narrow dirt corners lined with pine trees and sagebrush and zooming along roads carved out of clay banks, leaving a great plume of fine dust billowing up behind it and settling slowly in the hot summer air.

25. Ext. Ranch Orchard Roads — Day.

The Cadillac drives alongside rolling green orchards, trailing dust behind.

26. Ext. Cherry Orchard — Day.

And then the Cadillac drives into the cherry orchard itself. The radio in the Caddy is blaring a country and western hit, "Come Pickin' Time" (Johnny Cash), as Butch maneuvers through rows of large cherry trees, ladders, piles of wooden apple boxes, and assorted pickers. Finally, the car stops and Butch sits up on the back of his seat to look around.

BUTCH: You guys still need some help?

DISSOLVE TO:

27. Ext. Cherry Orchard — Day.

Quiet country sounds are heard amid the lush, green orchard. In the distance we see the Major driving the tractor down the road between the cherry trees. Jim June, a middle-aged man, with a weathered countenance, leans against the driver's seat of the tractor, talking to the Major. Behind the tractor is a low flat trailer with Kitty, Ruth, Pixie, Eddie, and Johnny riding on it.

As the tractor and trailer drive along the row, the pickers begin to appear from various trees. The pickers are Lenny McPhee, a tall, dark, preppy boy, about eighteen, wearing a white T-shirt and jeans; Mucker, a big, sloppy looking guy, about eighteen; and a young gypsy couple.

They follow the trailer until it stops at the edge of a gully. Butch and Danny stop picking and join the gang.

From the trailer, Kitty pours tea from a large china teapot.

KITTY: Tea, Jim?

Sandy appears in the orchard. She wanders about aimlessly, trying to catch Butch's attention.

LENNY: Fancy car you got there, Butch. What the hell kind of a car is it, anyway?

BUTCH: El Dorado Barritz.

LENNY: It's a Cadillac then?

BUTCH: Ya.

LENNY: Hmmm. Must have cost a pretty penny. But I bet the girls are really impressed.

KITTY: Sandra. I'm so glad you decided to join us. I baked your favorite cake.

Sandy is watching Butch. Butch is wandering off. Kitty points to the cake.

KITTY: See?

SANDY: (*Looking at the cake*) Looks good.

Sandy comes over to the trailer. Her mother cuts her a slice of cake. Sandy takes it.

SANDY: (*Takes a bite*) MMM. Good cake.

KITTY: Thank you, dear. Would you mind just . . .

Kitty gestures that Sandy should offer the cake around. With a disgruntled look, Sandy takes the cake and passes it around.

JIM JUNE: Sure is a beautiful spot.

MAJOR: It's almost impossible to think of livin' anywhere else.

JIM JUNE: Be a real shame to have to sell it.

KITTY: Sandra, could you help me with my lines after supper?

JIM JUNE: That's right. You're in the Little Theater aren't you, Kitty?

KITTY: Yes. And we're always looking for new members, Jim.

MAJOR: Now Katherine.

KITTY: He might enjoy it John. Where is that girl?

SANDY: I'm right here and ya I'll read your cues.

DISSOLVE:

28. Int. Ranch House — Early Evening.

Sandy is lounging on the kitchen table. Johnny is building with Meccano. Kitty is washing a great stack of dishes. Eddie and Danny run through the room taunting Sandy with one of her newly acquired "training bras" held high over their heads.

EDDIE: Wow wee. What a figure. Two more legs and you'll look like Trigger.

Sandy dives at Eddie, but he's too quick and makes his escape.

KITTY: Boys, boys, boys. Leave your sister alone.

SANDY: They are so immature.

KITTY: Where were we?

SANDY: "From now on you have a hold over me."

Kitty turns from the kitchen sink to look directly at Sandy. She dries her hands on her apron.

KITTY: "From now on you have a hold over me."

SANDY: "My dearest Hedda, believe me I shall not abuse the position."

Kitty walks up close to Sandy and fairly hisses at her.

KITTY: "In your power all the same. At the mercy of your will and demands. And so a slave. A slave!"

For a moment mother and daughter stare at each other. Then Kitty comes to, spins around, and walks to a small mirror by the door way.

KITTY: "No. That thought I cannot tolerate. Never!"

Kitty is combing her hair and putting on some mascara, eye liner, and lipstick throughout this scene.

KITTY: "I can hear perfectly well what you are saying. But how am I going to get through the evenings out here?"

Now Sandy, please make sure Ruth and Pixie get to bed on time. And don't forget to put away the laundry.

SANDY: Okay.

KITTY: And you're not to be hanging around the pickers.

SANDY: Ya. (*In a masculine voice*) "We shall have a very pleasant time together here, you and I" (*She grins at her mother*).

KITTY: "Yes, that is what you are looking forward to, isn't it, Mr. Brack? You, as the only cock in the yard" (*Pause*).

Kitty mimes the action of shooting herself in the head with a pistol. She and Sandy watch in the mirror. There is a brief pause, then Sandy hams it up and Kitty walks away.

SANDY: "Shot herself! Shot herself! In the temple! Think of it! (*Changing her voice*) But, merciful God! One doesn't do that kind of thing!"

KITTY'S VOICE: Goodbye Sandra. Don't forget, put away the laundry. Tell your father I'm gone, be back around ten.

SANDY: Bye, mom. "Break a leg! Knock 'em dead!"

Sandy sighs with satisfaction, bows to the mirror.

KITTY'S VOICE: It's only a rehearsal.

Sound of screen door slamming. Sandy studies herself in the mirror and puts on her mother's lipstick and talks to herself in the mirror.

CUT TO:

Sandy studies the unopened letter from California. "It's All in the Game" (Tommy Edwards) is playing on the little Seabreeze record player, pennies on the needle arm. When the song is over, Sandy carefully plays it over and over; meanwhile, she is applying a gooey black polish to her finger and toenails.

Sound of Butch's Cadillac pulling up outside. Sandy sits up straight and takes the record off. She quickly finishes up her nails and blows on them frantically.

Sound of Butch's car radio playing "Battle of New Orleans" (Johnny Horton); the Cadillac is turned off but the radio continues loudly. Sound of footsteps, screen door opening and closing.

MAJOR'S VOICE: Young man, turn that wretched noise OFF.

Still blowing on her nails and shaking her hands about, Sandy exits her bedroom.

CUT TO:

29. Ext. Ranch Driveway — Evening.

It is a beautiful hot summer evening. The cloudless blue sky is beginning to turn pink with the sunset. A light breeze from the mountains ruffles the flowers and trees. Sound of swallows and kildeer, children playing in the distance.

Butch is lounging in his Cadillac, singing along with the song, unaware of the Major standing there at the screen door with his hands on his hips. The Major walks to Butch's Cadillac, pauses, and then reaches over Butch to switch off the radio. Silence. Butch jumps up straight in his seat and looks at the Major nervously for a moment and then stares straight ahead.

The Major carries his war medals and polishing rag in his hands and continues his polishing.

BUTCH: Sorry sir, didn't realize you were here. I mean, uh . . .

Butch squirms uncomfortably and runs his fingers through his hair.

Sandy flies out of the house. Butch looks relieved to see her. The Major, however, looks very annoyed.

KITTY: Isn't it time you were in bed, young lady? You always look so sleepy in the mornings.

Sandy continues to walk up to the Cadillac.

SANDY: Oh Dad, it's nowhere near my bedtime. Anyways, I'm not at all tired.

The Major looks at her, sighs, then looks at his watch.

MAJOR: It is precisely eight thirty-five and you are to be in bed in your room in exactly twenty-five minutes, young lady. Understand?

SANDY: Yes, sir.

The Major looks at Butch and then turns and disappears into the house. Butch stays in his car and lights up a Camel. Sandy stands by the car, displaying her nail polish and trying to look nonchalant.

BUTCH: Hey. Where did you get that wild stuff? (*Indicating her nails*).

SANDY: Shirley Darling gave it to me.

BUTCH: Ya? She's gotta be older than you. Right?

SANDY: She's sixteen.

Butch sits up with interest and tries to charm Sandy.

BUTCH: So ah, you gonna be a real pal and introduce me to her?

SANDY: (*Shaking her head*) Nope.

Butch looks miffed.

BUTCH: Why not? Don't you think I'm a nice guy?

Sandy shrugs.

BUTCH: Come on. Be a pal.

SANDY: She's going steady with Lenny.

BUTCH: Lenny that guy picking cherries?

SANDY: Yup. Lenny McPhee.

Butch sinks back down in the car seat.

SANDY: I've never seen such a beautiful car.

BUTCH: Ya? These dirt roads are makin' a real mess out of it. Had to drive all the way to town this morning to get my muffler fixed. Cost me nearly $10.00 too.

SANDY: Maybe if you drove slower . . .

BUTCH: Ya. I'm gonna have to try that. What a road. Does Uncle John always polish up his medals?

SANDY: (*Giggles*) No, just for the parade.

BUTCH: What parade?

SANDY: Dominion Day Parade. On Sunday. He's the Parade Marshall.

BUTCH: Oh. (*Pause*) Ya, I'm gonna lower my car soon as I get home. (*Looking at Sandy*) You don't even know what that means, do you, kid?

SANDY: Sure. Some of the guys at High School have lowered their cars.

BUTCH: They do that up here too, huh?

SANDY: Of course.

BUTCH: I bet mine's gonna be lower.

Butch lazily gets out of the car, stands close to Sandy, takes a pack of Camels out of his shirt pocket, and holds it very close to Sandy's nose. Sandy stares at him.

BUTCH: See this?

SANDY: Ya. So?

BUTCH: "So" she says. (*He chuckles*) I show you "so."

Butch slowly kneels down on the ground and places the packet of Camels between the car and the ground.

BUTCH: That, little girl, is how low my Cadillac is gonna be. You wanna sit in it?

SANDY: (*Excitedly*) Ya.

Butch stubs out his cigarette and opens the driver's door for Sandy. She leaps in and starts to examine the knobs. Butch gets in and turns on the radio. "Catch a Falling Star" (Perry Como).

SANDY: Gee, I'd sure love to go for a ride sometime.

BUTCH: Tell you what. You got any girlfriends?

SANDY: Of course.

BUTCH: Preferably older than you?

SANDY: Ya, well sort of. Thelma's just about fourteen.

BUTCH: Thelma! What sort of a name is that?

SANDY: Well, her family's Catholic.

BUTCH: Oh, brother. Look, kid. Forget I mentioned it. It wasn't a good idea. Forget it.

SANDY: But you almost promised.

Butch leans across Sandy and opens her door.

BUTCH: I think it's time you went in. Your dad will be out here any moment now. Maybe when you're older.

Sandy gets out of the car, slams the door, and walks around to Butch's side. She glares at him.

SANDY: I think you are a conceited jerk and your car is a hunk of junk.

She turns to walk away but Butch grabs her wrist.

BUTCH: Hey, wait a second, wait a second. I thought we were friends. I'm sorry if I hurt your feelings. Honest. (*Silence*) Listen, let's be friends.

SANDY: Maybe.

BUTCH: Come on, look at me. Sandy. Come on.

Slowly and with a heavy sigh, Sandy turns around to look at Butch.

BUTCH: We're friends? Right?

SANDY: Okay. Friends.

BUTCH: You are some crazy chick. You know that?

SANDY: So if we're friends, can I go for a ride in your car?

BUTCH: Okay.

SANDY: (*Smiling now*) And can my girlfriends come too?

BUTCH: Oh brother.

SANDY: Come on, Butch. We won't hurt you.

BUTCH: Oh, what the hell. Sure they can come too. But they'd better be good looking. I don't let ugly chicks in my car.

MAJOR'S VOICE: Sandra. It is now one minute past nine and you are not in your bedroom.

SANDY: I'm coming. I'm coming.

MAJOR'S VOICE: IMMEDIATELY, child.

SANDY: (*Growling*) Ohh-h-h. So when are we gonna go for a ride?

BUTCH: I don't know. You'd better go in now or you're gonna be in trouble.

SANDY: Who cares. He just yells a lot, that's all. I have to know now.

BUTCH: Why right now?

SANDY: Because.

BUTCH: Because why?

SANDY: I don't know, so I can tell my girlfriends.

MAJOR'S VOICE: SANDRA. I DO NOT WISH TO REPEAT MYSELF.

SANDY: I'm COMING.

BUTCH: The Major wants me to help pick cherries and I need the money so I gotta work for a couple of days. I dunno, maybe Saturday?

SANDY: Saturday? That's two whole days away from now.

The Major appears at the doorway again, with hands on his hips. With a sigh, Sandy turns and walks into the house.

SANDY: 'Night, Butch.

BUTCH: 'Night.

30. Sandy's Bedroom — Evening.

Sandy sits at her window. The sun is setting over the lake. She writes in her diary. The unopened letter is next to her diary.

SANDY'S VOICE: He talked to me twice. I was so excited I almost puked. No kidding. He makes me so mad sometimes but I would follow him anywhere. We aren't first cousins so it's okay. I think. Sigh. I hope he stays forever.

CUT TO:

Sandy's American cousin Butch (John Wildman) lounges in his Cadillac. "He talked to me twice. I was so excited I almost puked."

31. Ext. Cherry Orchard — Day.

Butch, stripped to the waist, is trying to maneuver a long ladder into place under a big, leafy, cherry tree. In the trees around him, though not necessarily visible, are Lenny, Danny, the gypsies, and Mucker. Ladders in the other trees are partly visible. There are stacks of wooden apple boxes, some empty, some already filled with cherries. Butch staggers, backs into the limb of the cherry tree, and hits his head. He is generally having a very difficult time. Finally he gets the ladder in place, secures it, and then sits down to light a cigarette.

Sound of a tractor approaching. The Major appears behind Butch and lifts the full boxes of cherries to the waiting trailer behind the tractor. Sandy tags along after her father throughout this scene.

MAJOR: How many boxes, Butch?

BUTCH: (*Jumping up and hiding his cigarette*) Sir? Ah, two so far, sir.

MAJOR: I see. (*Louder*) How many boxes, Daniel?

DANNY'S VOICE: Six and a half, Sir.

MAJOR: (*Loudly*) How many boxes, Lenny?

LENNY'S VOICE: Eight, sir.

Butch goes up his ladder with his pail. The Major carries off the remaining full boxes. The tractor slowly inches forward.

MAJOR'S VOICE: How many boxes, Mucker?

MUCKER'S VOICE: Seven and a half, sir.

MAJOR'S VOICE: Good work. Keep it up. ONLY eight more rows to go.

Sound of tractor driving away.

Butch reaches to pick some cherries, nearly falls over, runs his fingers through his hair. He starts to climb down the ladder.

BUTCH: Well, I know two cherries on this ranch we won't be picking.

Butch doesn't notice Shirley Darling, an attractive, blonde girl, about sixteen. She is wearing short shorts and a pop top and carries a large, white, plastic purse. She is walking through the orchard.

BUTCH: One's green and the other's rotten.

There is general laughter at this remark. But when Butch gets to the bottom of the ladder and turns around, he sees Shirley Darling and stops dead in his tracks.

Shirley looks very embarrassed and continues walking. Butch watches her walk away.

LENNY'S VOICE: Shirl. You made it.

MUCKER'S VOICE: Hey, does this mean Rosie's here, too?

SHIRLEY'S VOICE: Uh hu. But she's waiting in the car. Afraid of rattlesnakes.

Butch looks very nervous and unhappy. He pulls out a cigarette and sits down carefully.

CUT TO:

32. Ext. Field by the Lake — Late Afternoon.

The lake sparkles in the late afternoon sun. Sandy, wet from swimming, is sitting with Johnny and Shirley and Shirley's friend, Rosie Hardman. Rosie is dark, cheerful, and sixteen.

ROSIE: Too bad we can't stay out late.

SANDY: At least you get to go out.

SHIRLEY: What's your cousin like, Sandy?

Sandy doesn't notice Butch come up behind her. Shirley only sees him when it's too late.

SANDY: (*Enjoying herself*) Well, it's kind of hard to say. I think he's pretty conceited and a little immature.

Sandy notices a hush in the conversation. She turns around and gasps in horror to see Butch standing there looking at Shirley.

BUTCH: I'll just pretend I never heard that.

Sandy gets up. Shirley and Rosie also stand up. Butch joins them.

BUTCH: (*Still staring at Shirley*) Aren't you going to introduce us.

SANDY: (*With a sigh*) Shirley Darling, this is my American cousin, Butch. And that's Rosie Hardman. I'm going for a swim.

Sandy walks into the water and calls out.

SANDY: I wish I was dead.

Sandy dives underwater and stays down for a long time. She finally springs up out of the lake.

SANDY: Maybe not completely dead. Maybe just sixteen and some place else.

She swims out into the lake.

CUT TO:

33. Ext. Lake — Late Afternoon.

Sandy has a bright, white rock that she throws for a distance into the water. Then she dives down to retrieve it. In the distance we see Butch and Shirley and Rosie sitting outside several pup tents where the pickers are staying.

Rosie wheels Johnny away. Sandy is intrigued and repulsed at the same time. She watches with horror as Shirley and Butch climb into a little pup tent. The tent starts to bulge out in various directions, then it's still, then it moves some more.

Sandy comes out of the lake.

34. Ext. Field by the Lake — Late Afternoon.

Still wet, Sandy sneaks out of the lake and quietly zips shut the little pup tent.

BUTCH'S VOICE: These things sure are small.

SHIRLEY'S VOICE: Ya. Maybe we'd better go outside.

BUTCH'S VOICE: Not just yet. Here, I'll move.

The pup tent bulges out on the sides again. Sandy picks up a snakey-looking twig and carefully slips it into the tent, and zips it shut.

SANDY: (*Yells out*) Oh, my God. It's a rattlesnake. It's in your tent.

The tent comes alive. Shirley and Butch are screaming and yelling.

Sandy pulls out the back ground peg and takes off at a gallop, laughing at the fun of it all. Butch and Shirley tumble out of the tent.

35. Ext. Field by Lake — Day.

Butch and Shirley stand facing each other. Lenny stands next to Shirley. Rosie tries to pick up the tent and put it back together.

LENNY: What the hell were you two doing in my tent?

SHIRLEY: We were just trying to find your radio.

LENNY: So you both had to go in? Is that it?

BUTCH: I think I'd better be going.

Butch starts to walk away.

LENNY: Shirley, don't you care about your reputation?

SHIRLEY: Of course I do. We didn't do anything.

LENNY: And what about my reputation?

CUT TO:

36. Int. Sandy's Bedroom — Night.

The flashlight is on under the sheet. Sandy is at her window staring out at the night and listening to the distant laughter and splashing down by the lake. Other night sounds include a garden sprinkler going around, an owl, and crickets.

Sandy practices kissing the back of her hand, looks bored, sighs, and then gets up and picks up her hand mirror and practices kissing herself in the mirror to see what she would look like kissing close up.

Throughout all this we hear Sandy's parents talking.

MAJOR'S VOICE: (O.S.) I'm afraid it doesn't look good at all.

Sandy stops her kissing exercises and goes to the door to listen.

KITTY'S VOICE: (O.S.) But John, what exactly did they say? What actual damage has been done to the trees?

Their voices are muffled by the sound of the bathtub draining and splashes. Sandy returns to her kissing exercises. She then tries out different lines into the mirror.

SANDY: (*Casually*) Hi, Butch. How you doin', Cous? Can I have a ride in your car today?

Well then how about tomorrow?

Maybe the day after?

The draining bathtub stops.

KITTY'S VOICE: (O.S.) Well, we have six growing children to consider in all this.

Sandy immediately puts the mirror down and goes to the door to eavesdrop.

KITTY'S VOICE: (O.S.) And they're growing up very quickly.

Sandy smiles proudly.

KITTY'S VOICE: (O.S.) I know, I know. They are the ones I'm thinking of. I grew up here. I want them to grow up here, too.

Sandy makes a face as though she were about to throw up and then she shakes her head.

KITTY'S VOICE: But John, we must face reality. We simply cannot go on like this.

Sandy nods in agreement.

Sound of the door opening.

Sandy leaps into bed, turns the flashlight off, and pretends to be asleep. Her bedroom door opens. Light from the hallway comes in. The Major and Kitty look at Sandy fondly and smile at each other. Sound of distant splashes and laughter rise up from the beach. Kitty and the Major exchange surprised, disapproving looks. Kitty moves out of sight.

MAJOR: (O.S.) Good God. Now what the dickens is that ruckus?

Sandy is struggling to hold back the giggles. She rolls over, away from her father.

KITTY'S VOICE: It's those pickers out swimming. Perhaps you should tell them . . .

Kitty moves away from Sandy's bedroom door.

MAJOR'S VOICE: (O.S.) Nonsense. I'd miss the News.

KITTY'S VOICE: Now if that was Sandra . . .

RADIO ANNOUNCER'S VOICE: Good evening. This is the CBC and now here's the News to ten o'clock. The Queen ended her five day visit to Canada today. In a "once upon a time" atmosphere and amid storybook settings, events of far-reaching modern importance took place.

MAJOR'S VOICE: I know, but it isn't Sandra.

KITTY'S VOICE: Any day now.

MAJOR'S VOICE: She's just a child.

KITTY'S VOICE: She doesn't seem to think so.

MAJOR'S VOICE: Please, I'd like to hear about the Queen's visit.

Sandy has been getting out the flashlight and her "True Confessions" magazine and setting up to do some reading in bed.

CUT TO:

37. Ext. Back Lawn of the Ranch House — Day.

Sandy is ironing furiously on an ironing board set up on the back lawn. She is wearing her bathing suit and her hair is in rollers. On one side there is a huge pile of unironed clothes; in a heap on the other side, a stack of pressed men's shirts. A large, pink transistor radio is playing "Yakity Yak" (The Coasters).

SANDY'S VOICE: (V.O.) In those days we ironed everything. I used to imagine the Olympics of Ironing and I'd iron those shirts faster than anyone else.

Eddie runs through the scene, wearing Sandy's training bra. Once again Eddie eludes Sandy. Pixie and Ruth are playing dolls on a tartan blanket. Suddenly Butch comes up to Sandy.

BUTCH: I was thinking of going into town, thought you might like to come, but I see you have a lot of work to do.

Pixie and Ruth put down their dolls and stand next to Sandy. Sandy looks around for a moment then furiously unplugs the iron.

SANDY: I'm coming with you. You promised. I can do this later.

Sandy heaps all the laundry into a pile and stuffs it into an apple box. She runs into the house.

Pixie and Ruth stare at Butch. He smiles at them, looks over his shoulder, and lights up a cigarette. Sandy comes quickly out of the house. Her hair is done; she is wearing peddle pushers and a pop top and carrying a large plastic purse.

RUTH: Can we come too?

SANDY: Of course not. You guys are just babies. Come on Butch, I'm ready.

38. Ext. Ranch Driveway — Day.

Sandy stands by the passenger's door, Ruth and Pixie stand together watching. Butch opens his door then looks at Sandy.

BUTCH: Get in.

SANDY: My grandmother says the boy is supposed to open the door.

BUTCH: Oh really?

Sandy and Butch stare at each other.

SANDY: Yes really.

Butch shakes his head, gets into the Cadillac, and starts it up. He stretches across the front seat to open the door from the inside.

BUTCH: There. Now get in if you want a ride.

Sandy gets into the car.

SANDY: Thank you Butch. Girls like to be treated with respect.

BUTCH: Tell me about it.

Butch slides the car into reverse, backs up, and they drive off.

PIXIE: Is she going to get into trouble?

RUTH: I think so. Let's go for a swim.

PIXIE: Okay. I'm hot.

39. Ext. Ranch Road — Day.

Butch and Sandy are driving along the road next to the lake. Sandy is putting on bright pink lipstick in the rear view mirror. Danny is pushing Johnny along the road. Butch pulls up to stop alongside them.

BUTCH: Hi. Can I give you guys a lift?

DANNY: Thanks but we have to go swimming. I'm too hot and dirty.

JOHNNY: Maybe tomorrow?

BUTCH: Sure thing Johnny. You let me know when you're ready.

JOHNNY: Good idea.

DANNY: (*To Sandy*) Mom know where you are?

SANDY: Who cares, we're coming right back.

DANNY: Have a good time.

Butch immediately guns the engine and the Cadillac spins off. Danny, Butch, and Johnny all give cowboy yells and whoops of joy.

40. Ext. Ranch Road — Day.

Sandy and Butch are driving fast and dusty along the roads. Sandy ties a bright red chiffon scarf on her head. Butch is lighting up a cigarette.

BUTCH: Will Johnny ever walk?

SANDY: I don't think so.

BUTCH: What happened to him?

SANDY: I don't know. He's just always been like that. I think it was the birth.

BUTCH: (*Startled*) The birth.

SANDY: Ya. They had to use forceps.

BUTCH: (*Butch appears to be visibly horrified.*) Oh my God. That's horrible.

SANDY: Ya. I know. But he told me that in his dreams he can walk.

CUT TO:

42. Ext. Field by Lake — Day.

Lenny and Shirley are sunbathing outside Lenny's tent. Lenny's car is parked next to his tent. Butch's Caddy drives by, Sandy is tying her red scarf on her head. She jumps up in the Caddy.

SANDY: Hi Shirley, Hi Lenny.

Sandy waves. Shirley looks ticked off, Lenny waves.

LENNY: Hey, Butch, don't do anything I wouldn't do.

The Cadillac disappears. Shirley looks mad, Lenny sees her look. Shirley quickly recovers, smiles at Lenny, and shrugs her shoulders. Lenny smiles.

LENNY: He's got a nice car but he's no cherry picker. I'll bet he's never worked a day in his life.

SHIRLEY: He thinks he's pretty hot in that fancy car.

LENNY: Hi kiddo, have I told you lately that it's heaven when you're out here? I keep thinking about how it's gonna be when we're married.

Shirley and Lenny kiss with passion and warmth.

42. Ext. Ranch Gate — Day

The Cadillac stops at the closed gate. Sandy jumps out of the car, opens the gate; Butch drives the Cadillac through with a smile and a wave. Sandy curtsies, closes the gate by jumping on it as it swings shut.

    BUTCH: Back in the States we don't have roads like this. Everything's paved.

    SANDY: Ya? You like living in the States?

    BUTCH: Are you kidding? Of course I like the States. They're the most. Everybody loves the States.

    SANDY: Then why are you up here? In Canada?

    BUTCH: For a girl you sure ask a lot of questions.

    SANDY: How is a person supposed to find out anything unless you ask questions?

    BUTCH: See, another question. Look, why don't you just sit back and enjoy the scenery? Huh?

CUT TO:

43. Ext. Country Roads — Day.

Sandy and Butch are driving along in the Cadillac.

    SANDY: The scenery is so boring. I've seen it all before a million times.

    BUTCH: Well, see it some more.

    SANDY: Besides, I want to know why you ran away from home. (*Silence*) Well?

    BUTCH: Well what?

    SANDY: Why did you run away from home?

    BUTCH: Who says I did? And anyways, it's none of your business, okay?

SANDY: I'm considering it myself.

BUTCH: What? Are you retarded? Girls don't run away from home. Not unless they're tramps or something. It's too tough for a girl.

SANDY: Girls never get to do anything. It's not fair.

Butch, still shaking his head and looking a little serious, turns up the car radio. It is playing "Summertime Blues."

SANDY: I just love this song, don't you?

BUTCH: It's okay.

CUT TO:

44. Ext. Peach Concession — Day.

The Peach is a round concession stand made in the shape of a large peach. There are two families sitting on the blankets. A young couple is carrying a canoe into the lake. A gang of teenagers frolics in the water. There is a Chevy with three cruising guys leaning up against it. Butch's Cadillac is parked next to the Chevy. Butch combs his hair in the rear view mirror of his car. He puts the comb away and strolls over to the Big Peach. A blonde smiles at Butch, he looks very pleased and watches her with interest as she walks off with a hot dog. Still grinning, Butch follows her until he sees her tend a small baby.

Butch looks disgusted and turns to walk back to the Big Peach. He catches sight of Sandy and her three friends and looks even more horrified. He tries to disappear by leaning into a counter of the Big Peach.

45. Ext. Lakeshore Drive — Day.

Sandy is walking along very excitedly with her friends, Sue, Thelma, and Lizzie. Sue is handing out gum. They are all wearing white peddle pushers and pop tops. Lizzie is wearing white glasses that fly up a little at the corners. Thelma is wearing black glasses — very plain. They all carry large white plastic purses with brightly colored chiffon scarves tied to the straps. They are giggling and laughing.

THELMA: Wouldn't you just die if Barry Bent saw us in that car?

SUE: I just can hardly believe it.

SANDY: It's true. It's all true.

The girls look at Butch and stop giggling and talking.

THELMA: THAT's him?

LIZZIE: Holy cow.

CUT TO:

Sandy Wilson (right) directs "Sandy Wilcox" and the girls.

46. Ext. Peach Concession Stand — Back — Day.

Amid empty cases of Cokes and Pepsis, garbage and broken chairs, Butch is leaning against the Peach and smoking a cigarette and looking very disappointed. Sandy walks up smiling, then loses her smile and looks very concerned.

SANDY: What's the matter now?

BUTCH: Look, I can't be seen with you girls in my Cadillac.

SANDY: Why not?

BUTCH: I don't want to hurt your feelings. But you are all ugly.

CUT TO:

47. Ext. Peach Concession Stand — Back — Day.

Thelma, Sue, and Lizzie are standing around the Cadillac.

THELMA: Should we get in?

LIZZIE: No, not yet.

SUE: What're they doing, I wonder?

LIZZIE: Don't know. Is that Barry Bent over there?

SUE: No, I saw him already. He's working at the A&W.

THELMA: Should we go look? I mean for Sandy?

LIZZIE: No, let's pretend we're busy doing something.

SUE: I'm starting to feel kinda weird.

LIZZIE: Ya, me too. Let's pretend we're talking about something.

THELMA: Okay, what'll we talk about?

SUE: Let's talk about Barry Bent.

48. Ext. Peach Concession Stand — Back — Day.

Sandy and Butch are staring at each other in a silent stand off.

BUTCH: Okay, okay, just a minute. Let me think about this for a minute. (*He takes a couple of drags off his cigarette. Sandy watches intently*) I tell you what.

SANDY: Ya?

BUTCH: If you girls all sit in the back we'll go for a drive up to Kelowna and back. Okay?

SANDY: But what about the A&W?

Butch walks away.

BUTCH: Forget the A&W. That's the deal. Take it or leave it.

SANDY: (*Cheerfully*) Okay we'll take it.

Sandy follows Butch.

49. Ext. Lakeshore Drive — Day.

TRAVELING SHOT following Butch's red Cadillac as it cruises along the lakeshore. The four girls are in the back of the Cadillac quite cheerfully tying on their bright chiffon scarves. They are avoiding Butch's eyes in the rear view mirror. Butch is sitting very low in the driver's seat, self conscious and unhappy. His left arm rests on the open window frame and shades his face. He reaches into the glove compartment and fishes around a little and finally brings out a flashy pair of black reflector sun glasses and puts them on. The girls chatter to themselves.

THELMA: She's got the cutest pink cashmere sweater I've ever seen. I wonder if she's a virgin.

SUE: Hey, look what I found.

She holds up a beautiful earring she has found under the seat. Butch looks very excited.

BUTCH: You found it. Terrific.

Butch stretches out his hand. Sue gives him the earring.

SANDY: Whose earring is it?

BUTCH: Aw. Mary Kay's.

SANDY: Who's Mary Kay?

BUTCH: My girlfriend. She lost it the night of the prom.

The girls giggle in the back seat. Butch looks very puzzled, then annoyed.

BUTCH: She lost the earrings you twits. Grow up.

The girls are immediately sobered, but not for long. They giggle. Butch drives faster.

    SANDY: (*Smiling*) Hey Butch. Can you turn up the radio a teensy bit?

Butch turns up the radio. It's playing "Won't You Let Me Take You on a Sea Cruise." The girls all start wriggling around and singing to the tune. Butch sinks further down into the driver's seat. As they head out of town and hit the open highway, Butch starts to drive very fast. The girls look at one another and grin bravely. They continue to chatter.

A wedding car drives by in the opposite direction. It is decorated with paper flowers and crepe paper streamers and tin cans off the back bumper. Inside the bride and groom are necking in the back seat. The driver is laughing and honking the horn.

    THELMA: That's Donny and Diane.

    SUE: Don't they look happy.

    LIZZIE: They had to get married.

    SANDY: She was starting to show.

Butch drives even faster.

    BUTCH: Why don't you girls clam up.

CUT TO:

50. Ext. Valley Highway Scenics — Day.

We see the red Cadillac whiz through various claybank, lakeside, and winding highway situations. Radio is playing loudly. Butch is slowed down by a tractor and leans on the horn until the man driving the tractor pulls over to the side of the road and Butch screams past. The girls in their bright scarves are huddled together in the back seat looking a little terror stricken.

CUT TO:

51. Ext. Valley Highway Scenics — Traveling Shot — Day.

TRAVELING with the Cadillac, Butch is driving like one possessed and the girls huddled together in the back. Thelma starts rummaging in her purse and eventually pulls out a pink, plastic rosary and starts saying "Hail Marys."

SANDY: Slow down, Butch.

Butch answers her in the rear view mirror.

BUTCH: Look Sandy, you guys were the ones who wanted to go for a ride. Maybe you want me to stop and let you out or something?

Sandy looks out at the desert countryside as they zoom past. She looks worried.

SANDY: Well no. But just slow down a little.

Sandy sits back onto the back seat and stares out at the speeding scenery. She then turns to her girlfriends and smiles bravely. Thelma is lost in prayer, Lizzie seems to be enjoying herself, and Sue shares a look of hopelessness with Sandy.

The Cadillac starts tailgating a large orchard flatbed truck with a load of empty apple boxes. Butch honks the horn a couple of times, but the truck driver takes no notice.

LIZZIE: *(Cheerfully)* Gee, I sure hope we don't crash. I told my mom I was at Sue's house, and if she found out where I was, she'd kill me.

SUE: Oh, Lizzie, if we crash, we'd probably all get killed anyway.

THELMA: My mom always told us kids to make sure we were wearing clean underwear in case we got into an accident.

SANDY: Well, I hope you've got it on today.

CUT TO:

Butch honks his horn again and pulls up to pass the orchard truck.

SANDY: You're a maniac.

BUTCH: Damn farmers.

There is a corner up ahead. The girls scream and dive down onto the floor of the back seat of the Caddy. The orchard truck slows down and pulls over to let the Caddy go by. Butch sails through and keeps going, a worried look on his face.

52. Ext. Cadillac Traveling Shot — Day.

Butch is lighting another cigarette. There is no sign of the girls in the back seat.

Sound of girls sobbing.

BUTCH: (*Looking in the rear view mirror*) Hey girls? Where'd you go? Anyone back there?

After a long pause, slowly Sandy reappears, then Sue, Lizzie, and Thelma, with her rosary clutched tightly to her heart, climb up from the floor of the Cadillac.

LIZZIE: What happened?

BUTCH: (*Smiling*) Nothin'. Where you girls been?

SANDY: (*Seriously*) Very funny.

CUT TO:

53. Ext. Highway Scenics — Day.

The Cadillac continues careening along the winding valley roads.

BUTCH'S VOICE: You girls were the ones who wanted a ride. Hell, this is nothin'.

The car radio is playing "Maybelline" (Chuck Berry).

BUTCH'S VOICE: Nobody's hurt so what the heck?

A souped up black Mercury appears behind Butch's Cadillac. It, too, is traveling fast and recklessly.

54. Ext. Cadillac Traveling Shot — Day.

The girls in the back seat are now sitting quietly and staring straight ahead. Lizzie is the only one who seems to be enjoying herself. Butch notices the Mercury in his rear view mirror. He slows down. The girls seem relieved. Lenny McPhee is driving.

THELMA: Gee, I don't think I've ever gone so fast.

SANDY: Boys are such show offs.

BUTCH: You little girls ain't seen nothin' yet.

Butch is looking in the rear view mirror as the Mercury catches up. The girls turn around and see the Mercury.

SUE: Oh my God. It's Lenny McPhee.

THELMA: Oh no.

LIZZIE: Is it really? Who's with him?

SANDY: Nobody. Shirley's babysitting today.

55. Ext. Highway Scenics — Day.

The two cars are driving side by side. Then, suddenly, Butch guns the Cadillac and it goes flying ahead. The girls scream and we see their bright scarves dive down onto the floor to bob up occasionally, only for brief moments. The Mercury quickly takes up the chase and soon the two cars are dragging along the highway. They speed past tourists stopping to take photographs and the occasional oncoming car and orchard truck off the road. Sound of a police siren.

56. Ext. Cadillac Traveling Shot — Day.

Butch, who has been enjoying the drag race with the Mercury, hears the siren and suddenly appears terror stricken. He begins to look to the side of the road. Then he sees the police car in the rear view mirror. He hunches his shoulders and takes a deep breath. The girls are screaming "Stop! Stop!"

The Mercury is still right behind him and Butch steps on the gas to speed up over the top of the hill. Once over the hill Butch slams on the brakes and spins off the road, then continues to drive fast down a very narrow bumpy dirt orchard road. Meanwhile, the Mercury speeds past.

57. Ext. Orchard Road — Day.

Butch turns off the orchard road and into a large, old orchard. He knocks over a couple of long orchard poles used to support the limbs of fruit trees, careens around the big old apple trees, and eventually comes to a stop surrounded by fruit trees. Sound of the police siren stopped nearby.

58. Ext. Cadillac in the Orchard — Day.

The girls slowly emerge from the back floor of the Cadillac. They look like a real mess and they're hugging each other and crying and laughing at the same time. Butch looks annoyed.

> **BUTCH:** Shhhh. Please, shut up. Come on. Nothing happened, you're okay. Shhhh.
>
> **THELMA:** I wanna go home.
>
> **LIZZIE:** What happened? Did we crash?
>
> **BUTCH:** Aw come on. Will you girls grow up.

The sound of the police car siren stops. We hear sprinklers, a car door slams, and then distant voices.

Butch looks very worried and slinks down into his seat and reaches into his pocket for a cigarette.

> **BUTCH:** Just my luck. (*Turning around quickly to look at the girls*) Listen you gorks, SHUT UP. The cops are real close and if they hear you, you are gonna be in big trouble, so just be good little girls and everything will be just fine. Got it?

The girls are immediately frozen silent as Butch shakes his left index finger violently at them in a warning gesture. Suddenly a sprinkler showers the entire car. Where the water hits the hot car, puffs of steam and dust fizz up. The girls immediately jump up and half scream but one look from Butch silences them.

BUTCH: What is this?

Butch and the girls laugh quietly, the girls trying to suppress their giggles. Butch finally gets out of the Cadillac and struggles to put the top up before the sprinkler drenches the car and contents.

Sandy quickly gets out of the car, locates a wooden apple box, and covers the sprinkler so the car doesn't get wet anymore. Butch looks relieved.

Sound of the police car and the Mercury starting up and driving slowly off. Butch and the girls look very relieved, smiling and waving their arms in victory but still remaining very quiet.

Butch, Sandy, and Sue get back into the Cadillac.

Butch leans across the front seat, opens the glove compartment, and takes out a fistful of American candy bars and chewing gum.

BUTCH: Say, maybe you girls would like a little something sweet while we wait here for things to cool off a little.

Butch turns around to face the girls, all smiles now, and holds out the candy. Each girl, in turn, deliberates and eventually selects one or two items.

SANDY: (*Unwrapping a chocolate bar*) So, how long are we gonna sit here?

LIZZIE: Who cares? This is fun.

THELMA: Are you cracked? I've never been so scared.

LIZZIE: Ya. I know. Me either.

SUE: I've never even seen half this candy before.

BUTCH: Help yourselves.

SANDY: Oh brother.

BUTCH: Anybody wanna smoke?

Butch sighs a deep sigh, turns to the front, slouches down in his seat and automatically digs out a cigarette and without looking back offers the packet to the girls in the back seat. The girls look at each other in surprise.

BUTCH: What am I saying. You girls are too young (*He puts his cigarettes away*).

LIZZIE: Can I have one?

SUE: (*Whispering to Lizzie*) Can I have a drag?

SANDY: (*Whispering*) You guys shouldn't smoke his cigarettes. He's crazy.

LIZZIE: Why not? I need one. I'm a wreck.

SUE: Ya, me too.

Butch quickly takes out the cigarettes and turns around to the girls. Lizzie and Sue take a cigarette each. Butch lights up the car lighter and looks at the girls intently as they light their cigarettes from the lighter. Sue coughs just a little. The girls try to act very cool.

Butch watches them.

BUTCH: You girls ever smoked before?

Pause.

SUE: Let's go for a swim and cool off.

CUT TO:

59. Ext. Secluded Beach — Day.

The girls huddle together and strip down to their bathing suits which they are wearing under their clothes.

BUTCH: I don't have a bathing suit. I'll have to go skinny dipping.

The girls giggle nervously. Butch strips off his T-shirt. The girls stare at him in fascination. He takes of his shoes and socks and smiles at them.

BUTCH: Last one in's a rotten tomato.

The girls and Butch all charge into the still blue lake. They splash and cavort. Thelma's falsies float out of the top of her bathing suit and she nearly dies of embarrassment and laughter. They play catch with the falsies and quite innocently Butch touches Lizzie on her breast. There is another moment of frozen terror and embarrassment. Butch swims way out from the girls and then starts to wave his blue jeans in the air above him.

BUTCH: Hey, this is fun. You guys ought to try it.

Silently, the girls quickly get out of the lake and huddle together on the beach.

SANDY: What if he gets an uncontrollable urge.

THELMA: Ya. And we get in trouble.

Butch keeps his body low in the water and comes toward the girls.

BUTCH: Come on, don't you girls want to have some fun?

LIZZIE: (*Happily*) Ya.

Sandy grabs Lizzie.

SANDY: Lizzie! Don't you dare.

BUTCH: I'm coming to get you.

The girls look terrified and delighted. Suddenly Butch stands up. He has his blue jeans on again. Everyone laughs with relief.

BUTCH: I think we'll be safe now. Let's go.

60. Ext. Country Trail up a Claybank — Day.

Butch and the girls are walking single file back up a trail to the orchard.

BUTCH: So who do you think is going to get to the moon first? Us or the Russians?

THELMA: What do you mean 'us'?

BUTCH: Us. The States.

THELMA: Oh.

CUT TO:

61. Exterior. Orchard — Day.

Sandy is posing Lizzie next to Butch; Sue and Thelma on either side are taking their snaps.

SANDY: Say cheese.

BUTCH: Say sex.

The girls shriek a little, then try to beat up on Butch.

    BUTCH: Take it easy, you'll mess my hair.

The girls take this as a challenge and try to muss his hair. Sandy takes snaps.

CUT TO:

62. Ext. Highway — Long Shot — Day.

The red Cadillac with the top down turns slowly off the orchard road onto the highway.

Music, "The Happy Organ," plays.

The front left headlight of the Cadillac is broken.

    BUTCH: How old are you, Lizzie?

    LIZZIE: Thirteen.

    BUTCH: Same age as Jerry Lee Lewis's wife. He married his cousin, you know.

    LIZZIE: Ya, we read it in the papers.

    BUTCH: Sandy, that'd be like you and me getting married (*He laughs*).

The police car whizzes away very fast.

    BUTCH: Look at him go.

    SUE: Good thing about your dad, eh Sandy?

    SANDY: Ya. Happens all the time.

CUT TO:

63. Ext. Cadillac on the Highway — Day.

Butch has been looking at Lizzie in the rear view mirror. As he drives along they catch each other's eyes in the mirror.

    BUTCH: Hey, Lizzie, why don't you take off your glasses? Let me see what you look like without your glasses.

The girls nudge each other and stifle their giggles as Lizzie takes off her white glasses. Without her glasses she is rendered blind but rather attractive. Butch nods his approval.

BUTCH: Hey, you're kinda cute. If you leave your glasses off you can sit in the front here with me if you want.

LIZZIE: Sure.

The girls can barely hide their giggles as Lizzie fumbles around trying to find her purse to put her glasses away. She grabs at a large, white plastic purse.

SUE: Lizzie, that's my purse. Yours is over there.

LIZZIE: (*Whispering*) Where, where? Help me, I'm blind. Where?

SUE: (*Giggling*) Right here. Here, I'll do it.

Sue carefully takes Lizzie's glasses and puts them into the purse.

BUTCH: You can just climb over the seat. Or maybe you want me to stop the car?

LIZZIE: Oh no, I'll just climb over.

Feeling her way, Lizzie climbs into the front seat of the Cadillac. She settles in and turns around to stare vacantly back at the girls. Sandy, Sue, and Thelma are giggling uncontrollably now.

LIZZIE: Gee, I've never seen such a beautiful car. Butch, it's the ginchiest.

BUTCH: Thanks, Lizzie, glad you like it.

LIZZIE: I've never gone so fast in all my life.

BUTCH: Ya?

LIZZIE: Ya. I thought we were gonna die but you know it was sort of fun. (*She turns to the girls in the back seat*) Wasn't it?

THELMA: I was sure we were gonna die.

SANDY: I don't know why boys have to drive so fast.

BUTCH: 'Cause it's fun, that's why.

SUE: Ya. Sorta scarey fun. My mom would kill me if she knew we went that fast.

SANDY: Ya. I thought we were gonna die and I was never gonna live to be a teenager.

CUT TO:

LONG SHOT *of the Cadillac on the desert highway.*

SANDY'S VOICE: Hey Butch, can I sit in the front seat, too?

BUTCH'S VOICE: Maybe later, on the Ranch Road going home.

We see Butch gesture Lizzie to take over the wheel while he lights up another smoke. Lizzie slides over close to Butch and takes the wheel but, because she is more or less completely blind, just as Butch gets the lighter hot, Lizzie nearly drives them over a clay bank. Butch drops the cigarette lighter and grabs the wheel and directs the car back onto the highway.

He is then jumping around to retrieve the hot cigarette lighter. Soon Butch is in control again but Lizzie stays sitting close to him and he casually rests his right arm on the back of the front seat, so that his hand falls on Lizzie's shoulder. Lizzie looks vacantly out in front of her.

The girls in the back notice all this with great amusement and begin to wave like royalty to the passing scenery. The girls then sit up on the back seat and wave and giggle and jump around.

The radio is playing "Whole Lot of Shakin' Goin' On" (Jerry Lee Lewis).

DISSOLVE TO:

64. Ext. Peach Concession Stand — Late Afternoon.

Butch and the girls are hanging around eating hamburgers.

BUTCH: Sandy, I gotta get you home. If that cop catches us, I'm in trouble.

> **SANDY:** We're both in trouble already.
>
> **BUTCH:** Why?
>
> **SANDY:** I was supposed to be back for tea.
>
> **BUTCH:** Jeez. Get in the car. We're going.

Sandy says goodbye to her girlfriends. Butch takes Lizzie to the back of the Big Peach. Thelma, Sandy, and Sue peek. They watch.

65. Ext. Peach Concession — Back — Late Afternoon.

Butch leads Lizzie to the back of the Big Peach and, after glancing over his shoulder, he gives Lizzie a quick kiss on the lips against his better judgment. Lizzie freezes. At that moment Lenny, Shirley, Rosie, and Mucker walk by. Lenny and Shirley stop holding hands, Shirley looks very annoyed.

> **LENNY:** Kinda young isn't she Butch?

Butch spins around with a look of regret.

> **SHIRLEY:** Rosie, Let's go to the washroom.
>
> **ROSIE:** We just came . . . oh, oh okay.

Shirley and Rosie exit in a huff. Lenny notices this. Butch tries to steer Lizzie away.

> **LENNY:** Butch. We haven't finished that race. I was just warming up.

CUT TO:

66. Ext. Peach Concession — Front — Late Afternoon.

Sandy is sitting in the front seat. Butch hands Lizzie to Sue and quickly gets into the driver's seat. Sandy cheerfully waves goodbye to Thelma, Sue, and Lizzie who watch and wave as Butch drives out too fast and looking annoyed.

67. Int. Ranch House Living Room — Early Evening.

Sandy and Butch are seated on the old couch. The Major is pacing and Kitty stands with her hands on her hips, staring at Sandy.

MAJOR: Alright. That's enough for now. Go to your room Sandra. You are to stay there until breakfast time and you will not go to the Parade. You have behaved in an irresponsible manner and must bear the consequences.

SANDY: But Dad, I just forgot.

KITTY: That is no excuse, now get to your room.

Sandy gets up dramatically, she turns to Butch.

SANDY: Sorry about the trouble, Butch, but I had a fabulous time. Thanks.

KITTY: Sandra!

Sandy turns and exits the room.

SANDY'S VOICE: No one ever listens to my side of the story. I just forgot. I'm sorry.

MAJOR: And I want your car keys young man. You'll get them back tomorrow.

Butch stands up in front of the Major.

BUTCH: But it's my car.

MAJOR: It's your mother's car.

BUTCH: She gave it to me.

MAJOR: You stole it.

The Major and Butch stare at each other.

MAJOR: Look, Butch, I know things aren't happy at home. I phoned your mother yesterday. She told me what happened and that you took her car against her wishes. She says you stole it. Now it's family so I wouldn't go that far. But still, they are your parents and they have asked me to keep an eye on you until they arrive tomorrow.

Butch turns his back on the Major. The Major holds out his hand.

MAJOR: Butch, I don't like to have to do this.

Butch spins around.

68. Ext. Ranch Driveway — Early Evening.

Butch sits in his car. The Major stands next to him surveying the view to the north.

MAJOR: I remember your father fighting with his father when he was your age.

BUTCH: Ya? So what?

MAJOR: Now Butch. These things are only natural. They've been going on for centuries. You mustn't let it ruin your life. *(Pause)* You must grow to the challenge and meet it. Not run away from it.

BUTCH: Some runaway. I can't even run away from them.

MAJOR: They are very concerned. We are all concerned. That's why we are here. To help you. It's because we love you that we must take these measures which you seem to find so objectionable. Now come on back into the house and I'll let you have a beer. Then I must attend to the evening chores.

CUT TO:

BUTCH: You mean my folks are coming up here? And I'm gonna have to go home?

KITTY: Sandra, to your room.

MAJOR: I'm afraid so, son.

Butch fishes the car keys out of his pocket and throws them across the room.

BUTCH: Here's her god damn car keys. They're probably more worried about that stupid car than they are about me.

Butch grabs his jacket and storms out of the room and we hear the screen door slam.

Sandy slips unnoticed just outside the room. The Major follows Butch.

MAJOR: I'll try talking to him.

The Major follows Butch. Kitty picks up the car keys off the floor and sits on the edge of a chair, then jumps up.

KITTY: I'll be late for rehearsal.

Kitty absentmindedly puts the car keys in the silver and enamel Chinese box on the mantle. Sandy sees this.

CUT TO:

69. Ext. Ranch Driveway — Evening.

Once again it is an idyllic, hot, summer evening.

Butch is sitting in the back seat of the Cadillac, smoking. Sandy sneaks up to him. He looks very surprised but remains quiet. Sandy hands him the car keys. Without a word, Butch leaps into the driver's seat, puts the car in neutral, and gets ready to back it out of the driveway. He gestures to Sandy to push. She gestures that she would rather steer, not push. Finally, Butch opens his door very carefully and pushes and steers. Sandy pushes from the front of the car.

The car coasts away from the house and disappears around the corner.

CUT TO:

70. Ext. Bandshell — Early Evening.

It is the Teen Town Dominion Day Dance. The small band shell is situated in a large lawn, shaded by huge willow trees. There are some balloons and crepe paper streamers on the bandshell and in the trees. Three teenage girls stand around a small ticket table. A group of six teenage girls cluster around a park bench and a group of ten teenage boys hang around a bench on the opposite side. Two groups of two girls go to the washroom. There is a local four piece band setting up on stage, some band groupies linger about on stage and the dance M.C. is bustling about on stage.

We TRACK IN *behind Butch and Sandy as they walk into the scene and sit down on a park bench closest to the road. Butch looks at Sandy, she smiles, and Butch turns away in disgust. Butch and Sandy look very glum.*

Shirley, dressed in a red party dress, comes up from behind them.

SHIRLEY: Hello Butch, still babysitting?

Butch jumps to his feet and spins around to face Shirley.

BUTCH: Ah Shirley! Please let me explain.

SHIRLEY: This better be good.

BUTCH: Can we go for a ride and talk?

Shirley stands still, cool, and non-committal.

BUTCH: Listen that little girl means nothing to me.

SHIRLEY: So why were you kissing her?

BUTCH: I was just trying to be polite. It didn't mean anything.

SHIRLEY: And what about me?

BUTCH: (*Coming to her side*) You look so beautiful.

SHIRLEY: (*Moving away*) Quit trying to change the subject.

BUTCH: Hey Shirley, you know I'm crazy about you. As soon as I saw you in the orchard I was crazy about you.

Suddenly Butch remembers Sandy who is watching the scene with interest. He glances over his shoulder at Sandy, who grins at them.

SANDY: Nice dress Shirley. Was that the one in Dean's Tots n' Teens?

SHIRLEY: Ya.

BUTCH: Look, ah, let's cut out somewhere so we can talk.

Butch starts to steer Shirley toward the Caddy parked on the street.

SHIRLEY: Well, okay. But I have to come right back.

BUTCH: Of course.

Butch and Shirley walk off.

SANDY: Hey, where are you guys going?

Butch and Shirley look at each other and shrug. Shirley walks back to Sandy.

SHIRLEY: Ah. Do me a favor. If Lenny comes don't tell him you saw me.

SANDY: Why not?

SHIRLEY: (*Looking exasperated*) Please, I'll give you some of my Little Richard records if you just shut up.

SANDY: Wow. Okay.

Shirley starts to walk away.

SANDY: When can I get the records?

Shirley calls back.

SHIRLEY: I don't know. Next time I see you.

SANDY: Okay.

Looking very dejected Sandy watches as Shirley and Butch get into the Caddy and drive away.

71. Ext. Caddy on the Road — Late Evening.

Shirley is looking out at the scenery and sitting close to her door. Butch looks over to her in a worried way.

BUTCH: I don't know why I kissed her. I don't even like her.

SHIRLEY: Maybe you think that just cause you're up here from California on holidays that you can do whatever you felt like.

72. Ext. Munson's Mountain — Night.

The Cadillac is parked at a scenic lookout point. There are other cars with couples necking in the dark. Butch and Shirley are in the front seat.

BUTCH: I wish I could stay here. It's so nice up here.

SHIRLEY: Well, then why don't you get a job and stay?

BUTCH: Na. Can't. My folks want me to go to university. I gotta go back tomorrow.

SHIRLEY: I wish you didn't have to leave.

Shirley looks at Butch.

CUT TO:

73. Ext. Band Shell — Ladies Washroom — Night.

There is a line up to get into the washroom at the back of the band shell. Sandy is standing with Lizzie.

SANDY: What did it feel like when he kissed you?

LIZZIE: Good. Haven't you ever kissed a guy before?

SANDY: Just Allan Watts at that dumb Christmas party. But that doesn't count.

LIZZIE: I hope I don't have to see Butch again. I'm so embarrassed 'cause I don't think I kissed him right. I don't think he liked the way I kissed or something. I don't know. I just wish I could act normal with him but I just can't.

CUT TO:

74. Ext. Munson's Mountain — Night.

We see the Cadillac alongside various other cars. Butch and Shirley are snuggled together on the driver's side.

SHIRLEY: We used to live in Toronto.

BUTCH: Ya? Where's that?

SHIRLEY: Near Detroit.

BUTCH: Snow all year round, huh?

SHIRLEY: No. The summers are real hot.

BUTCH: You're the first girl I've, that I uh . . .

SHIRLEY: Yes?

They kiss again and then look away, embarrassed.

BUTCH: You're the first girl I've ever met from Toronto.

CUT TO:

75. Ext. Band Shell — Night.

Sandy and Lizzie are sitting on a park bench. Lenny, Mucker and Rosie, Dever and Marie walk past them. Sandy looks nervous. Then Lenny recognizes her and comes back to her.

LENNY: Hi, kid. What are you doing here?

SANDY: Nothing.

LENNY: Seen Shirley yet?

SANDY: Nope.

LENNY: Must be still babysitting.

SANDY: Ya. Guess so.

DANCE M.C.: Welcome to the Teen Town Dominion Day Dance. Alright, everybody. We want to see everybody out on the dance floor for a spot dance. Winner gets a case of Coke. Come on let's rip it up.

Mucker and Rosie come back and hang around with Lenny.

LENNY: A case of Coke!

Sandy jumps up in front of Lenny.

SANDY: Shirley taught me how to jive.

LENNY: You jive?

SANDY: I love to jive.

LENNY: Well hell, let's go.

Lenny leads Sandy out onto the dance floor. The band plays "Ready,

Ready, Ready" (Little Richard). Lenny tries out a few fast moves. Sandy keeps up and they start to really fly around.

CUT TO:

76. Ext. Munson's Mountain — Night.

BUTCH: Aw, come on.

SHIRLEY: No. Don't do that. I don't go all the way.

BUTCH: Shirley, Shirley, Shirley. I would never force you to do anything like that.

There is a long silence as Butch and Shirley embrace.

BUTCH: You mean you and Lenny never . . .

Shirley sits up straight and slides over to her side of the seat.

SHIRLEY: We are saving it till we get married.

Butch straightens up and looks out at the stars.

BUTCH: Is that all anyone thinks about? Getting married? Doesn't anybody just want to have fun anymore?

Shirley slides over and nibbles Butch on the ear. Butch remains aloof.

SHIRLEY: No. Anyways, we aren't engaged or anything.

BUTCH: I have a girl back home.

SHIRLEY: So what. I have Lenny.

BUTCH: You are a terrible tease. Don't stop. Ever.

Finally, Butch can resist no longer, there is another embrace.

SHIRLEY: We have to go.

BUTCH: Not yet. It's early.

Butch and Shirley gaze at each other, Butch touches her face with his fingers, Shirley kisses his fingers, he kisses her neck.

CUT TO:

77. Int. Band Shell — Ladies Washroom — Night.

The washroom is small and very grungy. Tall blonde twins are applying make-up in the mirror. Sandy and Lizzie are waiting their turn to go in front of the small mirror, a ton of make-up in hand.

SANDY: This is so much fun. I'm never going home. Did you see Barry Bent? He is so adorable. And Carol's dress?

LIZZIE: Ya. Wish Butch would come back. Wish I could see.

The blonde twins finally finish freshening up. They look at Lizzie and Sandy with disgust and exit. Lizzie and Sandy immediately put on a ton of gaudy make-up. Lizzie puts on her glasses in order to see what she's doing. Mary and Sophie, two attractive, dark Mediterranean girls, about fifteen, come into the washroom.

SOPHIE: Where did that cute American guy go?

MARY: I think he left with Shirley Darling.

SOPHIE: Oh, oh.

And then Rosie comes into the washroom looking for Sandy.

ROSIE: Sandy, the Major's in town and he's looking for you.

Sandy blanches. She starts to take off all the make-up she'd just put on.

CUT TO:

78. Ext. Lakeshore Drive — Night.

Shirley is sitting next to the passenger's door in Butch's Cadillac. Butch is in the driver's seat.

BUTCH: You don't have to go just yet. I'll bet he hasn't even got there yet.

SHIRLEY: He gets real jealous.

Butch opens his door and gets out of the car and walks around to Shirley's door.

BUTCH: Come on. We'll just go for a little walk. Then we'll go back to the dance.

SHIRLEY: I wish you didn't have to go.

BUTCH: Ya. Me too. We could have been a real team.

Butch and Shirley stroll off down the beach.

CUT TO:

79. Ext. Big Beach — Night.

Mr. Dow, a short man in a greasy apron, and Lulu, his wife, an eccentric, frazzled looking woman, in her mid thirties, are trying to clean up and cook hamburgers at the same time.

The Major is leaning against the counter, surveying the scene with a worried look.

MAJOR: Kids today try a man's patience. This dreadful music all the time.

MR. DOW: Oh, I'm sure she's a good girl, Major.

MAJOR: She'd better be.

MR. DOW: Well, maybe she's in the parking lot (*He gestures*).

MAJOR: (*The Major looks very concerned*) Oh my God.

LULU: Wall, if you don't stop yakin we'll never get to dance.

80. Ext. Band Shell — Ladies Washroom — Night.

The washroom door opens. Rosie sticks her head out. Sandy and Lizzie are right behind her. They all walk out and nod in agreement.

CUT TO:

81. Ext. Band Shell — Night.

The Major is chatting with Gladys, a middle-aged, cheerful looking woman, who is a chaperone.

    MAJOR: A lovely night for a dance.

    GLADYS: We're going to have fireworks later.

    MAJOR: But she's still much too young.

    GLADYS: Oh, Major. I remember when you were younger.

    MAJOR: (*With a smile*) Do you?

The Major and Gladys stroll around the edges of the dance. As soon as they are a safe distance away, Sandy, Lizzie, and Rosie sneak by in the background, toward the parking lot.

CUT TO:

82. Ext. Lakeshore — Night.

Butch and Shirley are strolling along the lakeshore. They pass Dever and Marie, but do not notice them. The dance music can be heard in the distance.

83. Ext. Parking Lot Along the Lake — Night.

Lenny, Mucker, Dever, and Marie are walking along the row of parked cars. Groups of teenagers are hanging around various cars.

    FIRST BOY: Hey, Lenny. Looking for your girl?

    LENNY: Maybe.

    FIRST BOY: Ya well, if you are, I think I saw her strolling along the beach with that American guy.

    LENNY: (*Furious*) Butch.

    SECOND BOY: Ya, strolling soon to be rolling, from the looks of it.

LENNY: Very funny.

Lenny walks up to the second boy and nods. He walks off toward the lake. Mucker hurries to catch up to him. Dever and Marie shrug shoulders and follow suit. The boys by the car follow Dever.

CUT TO:

84. Ext. Band Shell Dance — Night.

The band is playing a romantic, slow tune like "Will You Still Love Me Tomorrow."

The Major is dancing with Gladys.

    GLADYS: Nearly time for the fireworks.

    MAJOR: Yes, and I must locate Sandra.

They spin around a little more, then walk off the dance floor.

CUT TO:

85. Ext. Parking Lot Along the Lake — Night.

Sandy, Lizzie (wearing her glasses finally), and Rosie are sneaking among the row of parked cars. They see the Major approaching and gasp in terror.

    ROSIE: You guys hide. I'll distract him.

Lizzie and Sandy duck out of sight.

CUT TO:

86. Ext. Beach — Night.

Lenny and Mucker, Dever and Marie, and a gang of kids are marching along the beach looking like an angry posse.

CUT TO:

87. Ext. Parking Lot Along the Lake — Night.

The parking lot is nearly deserted now.

Dance music continues in the back ground. The Major is striding along when Rosie steps casually out.

>   **ROSIE:** Oh! Major Wilcox. What a surprise! Are you looking for the fireworks?
>
>   **MAJOR:** No. I am looking for Sandra. I don't suppose you've seen her, have you?
>
>   **ROSIE:** Ah. I think I saw her . . . over there.

Rosie points toward the dance. The Major follows her direction with his eyes, then turns back to look at Rosie.

>   **MAJOR:** Are you quite sure? I just came from there.
>
>   **ROSIE:** Uh ya. She was in the Ladies Room.
>
>   **MAJOR:** Oh. Well, if you see her again, please tell her she's got a lot of explaining to do.

The Major walks off toward the dance.

CUT TO:

88. Ext. Parking Lot — Night.

Sandy and Lizzie are crouching behind a car. The Major walks right past them. Sandy looks terrified.

>   **LIZZIE:** Gee. This is getting exciting.

CUT TO:

89. Ext. Beach — Night.

Butch and Shirley are sitting on the beach. Shirley has his jacket draped over her shoulders.

>   **SHIRLEY:** We better get back, Butch. If Lenny . . .

Shirley, then Butch, stand up and straighten themselves out.

SHIRLEY: . . . ever sees me with you . . .

They turn to walk back. They see a gang approaching them.

SHIRLEY: Oh, my God.

CUT TO:

90. Ext. Ladies Washroom — Back of the Bandshell — Night.

The tall twins tumble out of the washroom. They shake their heads and walk off. Then the Major comes out of the washroom looking very annoyed.

CUT TO:

91. Ext. Beach — Night.

Butch and Shirley are now face to face with Lenny and the gang.

SHIRLEY: Lenny, we just went for a walk.

LENNY: Take that slimey jacket off, Shirl.

BUTCH: Hey, wait a minute. Where I come from, you don't talk to chicks like that.

LENNY: Ya? Is that so? So why don't you just go back where you came from, you no good troublemaker. Sticking your nose in other people's business.

MUCKER: Ya creep. Let's drop an atom bomb on him.

LENNY: Shirley . . .

Butch puts an arm around Shirley. Lenny comes closer to them. Mucker is right behind Lenny.

SHIRLEY: Don't fight. Please don't fight.

LENNY: You stay out of this.

BUTCH: Leave her alone.

LENNY: No. You leave her alone.

SHIRLEY: Lenny, please, this is so embarrassing.

LENNY: Ya? What about your reputation Shirley? And mine too. Just cause this guy comes along in some big fancy car.

SHIRLEY: That's not it at all.

LENNY: Probably his mommy's car anyway. Is that heap of metal mommy's car Butchie boy?

BUTCH: Who the hell are you anyway, the King of Canada?

LENNY: Don't get smart with me.

SHIRLEY: Butch, let's get out of here.

BUTCH: It's okay, it's okay.

Feeling embarrassed and very unhappy, Shirley runs off but no one seems to take much notice.

BUTCH: You wanna fight, I'll fight. But just one at a time.

Butch and Lenny start to circle around each other. The crowd forms a circle around them, taunting them with "Get him. Come on, show him."

LENNY: Guys like you make me sick. Lazy creep. Trying to steal my Shirl.

BUTCH: You can't steal something if it's free.

Lenny finally slugs Butch right in the solar plexus; Butch folds in half but he manages to grab onto Lenny and hold on. They sway together, Butch slugs Lenny in the head, Lenny tries to trip Butch. They break free of each other and circle one another again. Lenny has some blood dripping out of the side of his mouth.

In the hush, the Major appears, not really understanding what he has walked into.

MAJOR: Ah, Butch. There you are.

Butch and Lenny look at the Major in horror. The circle immediately starts to dissipate.

MAJOR: And Lenny. I hope you'll be up bright and early for the parade tomorrow?

LENNY: Yes, sir. I was just heading home now, sir.

MAJOR: Glad to hear it. Butch, get back to the ranch. Immediately.

CUT TO:

92. Ext. Parking Lot — Night.

The Major appears, holding Butch's arm and pushing him along. They stop next to Butch's car.

MAJOR: I've asked Phil McCloud to make sure you don't leave town until your parents arrive, so don't try any more stupid stunts tonight. You've done quite enough damage already.

The Major releases Butch's arm. Butch quickly slips into the driver's seat. The Major strides off.

MAJOR: Now. To find my wretched daughter.

CUT TO:

93. Ext. Town Street — Night.

Butch is cruising along in his Cadillac, trying to get Spokane on the radio. Sandy pops up in the back seat and sits there for awhile.

SANDY: Can I ride in the front seat now?

Butch, caught totally by surprise, jumps at the sound of her voice.

BUTCH: Where did you come from?

Sandy scrambles over into the front seat. Butch shakes his head and laughs a little.

BUTCH: Boy, are you gonna get it.

SANDY: I know. Let's run away.

BUTCH: You? And Me?

SANDY: I'm serious.

BUTCH: (*Considers. Shakes his head. Looks at her*) Got any money?

SANDY: No. Don't you?

BUTCH: (*Looking very disappointed and frustrated*) No.

SANDY: (*She looks up at the starry, starry sky*) Do you ever wonder about the stars?

BUTCH: Ya. As often as I can.

SANDY: Well, do you think heaven is inside the universe, or just outside the universe?

BUTCH: Well, myself, I don't think it's anywhere. No one can prove to me that there is a heaven. As far as I can figure it out, when you're dead it's just like you're asleep but you don't dream and you never wake up. Nothing happens. That's it. Poof. Nothing.

SANDY: Maybe, but I think people's spirits leave their bodies and float around the universe. In fact, I think it's getting a little crowded and I wonder if the universe can sort of expand to take in everybody.

BUTCH: I wanna be cremated.

SANDY: Really? So do I.

BUTCH: I couldn't stand the idea of being in some box, buried under all that dirt. Gives me the creeps just thinking about it.

SANDY: But you said nothing ever happens to you after you're dead. So what do you care?

BUTCH: I don't know. It just gives me the creeps. That I do know.

SANDY: Drive. Let's just keep driving.

BUTCH: I'm almost out of gas.

SANDY: Oh brother.

They sit in silence for a time.

SANDY: Let's go back to the Ranch. I've got a little money and Johnny and Danny will give me some more if I ask them.

BUTCH: Ya. I'm tired anyways (*Starting up the car*).

CUT TO:

94. Ext. Ranch Road — Night.

The still summer night air is broken by the sound of an approaching car, radio blaring. We first see the headlights shine on the pine trees and power lines as the car comes around the corner. The dark shape of the Cadillac comes into view. Only one headlight works. The car speeds around the corner, then slowly coasts to a stop. Car radio continues.

BUTCH: Out of gas. I'll push it. You'll have to steer it.

Butch gets out of the car and starts pushing it to the side of the road. Sandy steers it.

BUTCH: Don't crash it again.

SANDY: I won't.

Butch jumps in and puts the brakes on. There is a long pause.

BUTCH: Let's start walking.

SANDY: Okay.

Sandy and Butch get out of the car. Butch gets his transistor. There is a short silence as Butch and Sandy walk along, now rather close to each other.

BUTCH: I hate walking, it takes so long to get anywhere.

95. Ext. Ranch Road — Night.

Sandy stops and listens.

SANDY: It's Dad in the car.

The trees and power lines light up as the car headlights hit them.

SANDY: Jump.

Sandy disappears over the side of a cliff. Butch dives off after her. The car drives by and disappears down the road.

96. Ext. Ranch Road — Night.

Sandy walks through a gate. After Sandy has latched the gate shut, she hesitates and starts to cry. Butch walks on, notices that she has stopped, and turns around to look at her.

BUTCH: Don't tell me you're crying again.

Sandy can only nod her head and sob all the more. Butch walks back to her and stands close to her awkwardly, running his fingers through his hair.

BUTCH: What's the matter now?

Sandy shrugs her shoulders and starts to walk slowly. Butch follows.

BUTCH: You scared of your dad?

SANDY: Ya. A little. But it's more than that. It's so hard to say it. You'll think I'm crazy. Promise me that you won't laugh at me if I tell you.

BUTCH: Promise. What is it?

SANDY: Well, it's just that we've had so much . . . fun, and now . . . it's all . . . over.

BUTCH: Hey relax kid. You're just starting out. There'll be lots of fun for you. Being a teenager is the best time of your life. Look at me.

SANDY: (*Laughs*) Ya, sure. "Look at you." Out of gas, walking on a dirt road with an ugly twelve-year-old.

BUTCH: Hey. Who says you're ugly?

SANDY: You. You creep.

BUTCH: Ya well, you're not beautiful.

Sandy pretends to lunge at Butch and strikes him with her fists. Butch tries to fend her off.

SANDY: You say that one more time and I'll kill you.

BUTCH: No, no, don't, don't. I never fight chicks. Don't make me do something I'll regret. Okay, okay. You're not ugly.

Sandy immediately stops wrestling with Butch, stands back, and smiles at him.

SANDY: Oh Butch, gee, that's sweet of you. Do you really mean it?

SANDY: Well, it's pretty dark out tonight.

Butch starts to run down the road, Sandy runs after him, Butch gestures surrender.

BUTCH: Just kidding. Just joking. Honest.

CUT TO:

Butch tries to cheer up his twelve-year-old cousin. "Being a teenager is the best time of your life. Look at me."

97. Ext. Ranch Driveway — Night.

Sandy and Butch are standing in the driveway of the Ranch house. They are shoving/holding each other and looking toward the kitchen door.

BUTCH: Well kid, here's looking at you.

Butch shoves Sandy forward.

SANDY: Ya? You go first.

Sandy comes back to Butch and shoves him forward. This tug of war continues.

BUTCH: Uh hu. You go first. He's your father.

SANDY: You're the boy.

BUTCH: You're the daughter.

SANDY: Ya, but you're still the boy.

BUTCH: Ya, well, you're the girl.

SANDY: You're older.

Sandy and Butch pause, they look at each other, then Butch slowly touches Sandy's cheek and gently tilts her chin up toward him. He grins and shakes his head, then bends down to give her a kiss on the lips. Sandy is frozen solid. After a moment, Butch let's her go.

BUTCH: Where did you learn to kiss like that?

Sandy looks at the ground.

SANDY: Okay, now you go in first.

As they giggle and tug at one another a blinding light goes on over the kitchen door. Butch and Sandy let go of each other and fall silent.

BUTCH: (*Very quietly*) Let's go together.

SANDY: (*Very quietly*) Good idea.

Together they walk into the blinding light.

MAJOR'S VOICE: Get to your room young lady. THIS INSTANT. And Butch, give me your car keys right now. You will not be going to the parade tomorrow.

Sound of a couple of door slams, then all is peaceful. A garden sprinkler and a distant night bird can be heard.

SANDY'S VOICE: Come on Dad. I'm sorry. I have to see the parade. Please.

98. *Int. Sandy's Bedroom — Night.*

By the light of the flashlight, Sandy is packing a suitcase. She carefully sorts through her clothes, her ornaments, deciding to pack some, leave others behind. Of course she packs her diary and a favorite Barbara Anne Scott doll.

99. Ext. Ranch Driveway — Day.

Butch is examining the damage done to his front headlight. Sandy dashes out and quickly throws her suitcase in the back, under the seat.

BUTCH: Hey now, wait just a minute.

Kitty comes outside and glares at Sandy.

KITTY: Get back inside. You have work to do.

Sandy looks at Butch. Butch shrugs and bends down over his car. Kitty turns to go into the house.

SANDY: I'll wait for you at the Ranch gate.

BUTCH: But . . .

KITTY: Come along Sandra.

SANDY: I'm coming. I'm coming.

BUTCH: *(Quietly to Sandy)* You're crazy. You're gonna get into trouble.

Sandy, walking past Butch on her way into the house, turns and shakes her head.

100. Int. Sandy's Bedroom — Day.

Sandy is collecting money from Johnny. Eddie yells at the door.

SANDY: Get lost creep.

Sandy slams the bedroom door on Eddie.

SANDY: Okay, you're sure that's all you can lend me?

Johnny nods.

JOHNNY: I got $5.00 from Danny.

SANDY: Okay, thanks. I'll pay you both back when I get a job. Johnny you can have Bimbo the budgie and let Danny have my records, and don't give anything to Eddie, well maybe . . .

Sound of Kitty's footsteps. The kids stop talking.

KITTY'S VOICE: Sandra, you can come out now. I'll need some help with tea. Your father should be back any moment.

Sandy silently swears her brother to secrecy and they leave.

Suddenly they hear Kitty walking down the hallway quickly.

KITTY'S VOICE: Al and Dolly have just arrived. Sandra . . .

Kitty pops her head in Sandy's room.

KITTY: Sandra, you can come out now. I'll need some help with tea. Your father should be back from the Parade any moment now.

SANDY: Oh no.

101. Ext. Ranch Driveway — Day.

Wheeling Johnny in front of her, Sandy goes outside. Next to Butch's red Cadillac is a big, white hardtop Cadillac. Car Radio plays "Canadian Sunset" (Mantovani).

Butch stops singing and doesn't turn around. Al, a very large man with white hair done in a crew cut, an enormous cigar in his mouth, plaid shirt, green slacks, white buck shoes, and a flashy Navaho belt buckle, gets out from the driver's side. His wife, Dolly, a frizzy red head with a purple scarf on her hair, lots of rhinestone jewelry, a purple western-cut outfit, and plastic high-heeled shoes, gets out of the passenger's side and stumbles on the gravel.

DOLLY: Butch baby, you never should have taken mommy's car. I was so worried.

There is a heavy silence.

AL: Oh yes, and the girl, Mary Kay, she's alright. She was just a little late. Nothing to worry about.

DOLLY: So you see, everything's okay and you can come back home with us now.

AL: That's right son, we're here to bring you home.

BUTCH: (*Staring straight ahead*) What if I don't wanna come. Maybe I like it up here or something.

DOLLY: (*Laughing*) Don't be ridiculous Butch. You don't have to marry her anymore. You can come home where you belong.

AL: Besides, John has too much to worry about already.

DOLLY: And Mary Kay keeps phoning, wondering when you're coming home.

AL: Never mind that now, Dolly. (*Going to Butch*) We've got our boy back safe and sound, eh?

DOLLY: (*Coming to Butch*) Why never mind that now? After we've had to come all this way, over that dreadful road.

Kitty, followed by Pixie and Ruth, come out from the house.

DOLLY: Hell, that isn't even a road, it's a goat trail.

Butch has been fiddling with the radio in his car. Sandy is leaning on the passenger's door watching the whole scene very intently. Dolly and Al are now standing next to Butch.

DOLLY: Oh, Kitty. Hi, how are you? We just arrived. Hello, Butch. Aren't you even going to say hello to your mother and father who have driven all this way?

Butch sighs. Al walks over to Kitty. Dolly looks at Butch, shrugs her shoulders, and turns to Kitty with a smile.

AL: Kitty, good to see you. What's it been? Ten years?

KITTY: (*Smiling and shaking Al's hand*) About that. Ten years, I suppose.

AL: I hope our boy hasn't been too much trouble for you.

KITTY: Not at all. Not at all. It was nothing really. It's just unfortunate that things didn't work out a little better.

DOLLY: Kitty, do you drive on that awful road?

KITTY: Nearly every day.

DOLLY: Oh my goodness. I don't know how you do it. I was simply terrified. I mean what if you meet another car or something? It's so skinny.

KITTY: You just pull over and let it go by.

DOLLY: Do you hear that? Glory sakes, Kitty, you're a much braver girl than I'd ever be.

AL: Dolly, why don't you just . . . (*Gestures her to be quiet*).

DOLLY: Al, you know I don't like it when you talk to me like that. Especially in front of other people.

AL: Dolly, this is family.

DOLLY: But . . .

KITTY: Why don't we all have a nice cup of tea. It's a long drive and you must be ready for some tea.

They all start to walk toward the house. Kitty holds the door open. First Pixie and Ruth, then Dolly go through.

DOLLY: Tea? Don't they have any coffee?

AL: Dolly!

DOLLY: Don't mind me, anyone.

Al turns to Butch and Sandy.

AL: Coming in, Butch-boy?

BUTCH: Na, I'll wait out here.

AL: Suit yourself. (*To Kitty, indicating Sandy*) Is that your oldest girl, Kitty?

KITTY: Yes, Sandra.

AL: (*Looking at her appreciatively*) What is she, about fifteen now?

KITTY: She isn't even a teenager yet, Allan.

AL: Oh. You don't say (*He looks at her again*).

Al goes to hold the door open for Kitty. Kitty insists on holding the door open for Al. There is a tiny scuffle; in the end Kitty holds the door open for Al.

AL'S VOICE: Kit. You know, you really ought to sell this place you got here and move to the States. You're wasting your time up here. Why there's so much money down there for a guy like John. You really ought to consider it. I'm serious. Ask Dolly.

CUT TO:

102. Ext. Ranch House Patio — Afternoon.

The ranch house patio is situated near a cliff overlooking the south end of Lake Okanagan. The view of the valley is magnificent. The patio itself is a concrete slab with flowers blooming around it. Al is seated in a folding lawn chair which, when he leans forward, begins to fold up on him so that he appears to be leaning forward all the time. He is so intent on the conversation, however, that he doesn't really seem to notice the discomfort. Ruth and Pixie, Dan and Eddy, Sandy and Johnny do notice and try to hide their uncontrollable giggles. Butch is noticeably absent.

MAJOR: (*Still in his Army uniform*) Sit down, please (*Indicates a folding aluminum lawn chair*).

AL: Thanks John. What a view, what a view. Dolly, can you see this view?

DOLLY: Do you get much snow?

KITTY: Only when it's cold. Tea, Dolly?

DOLLY: Oh, yes that'll be fine.

Al tries to light his cigar but his fancy lighter is out of fluid. Dan is on him with a box of wooden matches; he lights one but Al starts talking and Dan burns his finger waiting. It never does get lit.

AL: What's a place like this worth anyway John?

MAJOR: Depends who's buying.

AL: Okay, so say it's a guy like me who's buying. What's it worth?

MAJOR: You always need a price tag on things (*He laughs good naturedly*).

KITTY: Sandra, pass the cake around dear.

SANDY: (*Grabbing the cake and offering it quickly to Dolly*) Some cake Aunt Dolly?

DOLLY: Oh heck, what's a diet if you can't eat? (*Smiles at Sandy*) Thank you sweetie. How old are you? You're Ruth?

SANDY: No. (*Pointing to Ruth*) She's Ruth. I'm Sandy and I'm thirteen.

KITTY: Oh Sandra. You are twelve.

DOLLY: Um. I was eighteen when I married Al.

AL: Great spot for a resort. John you ever thought about turning this place into a swanky resort?

MAJOR: (*Shaking his head*) Takes a lot of capital. Pretty risky business.

AL: Aw John. I know a lot of guys who'd come up here, away from it all, if it was fixed up a bit.

SANDY: Really? They'd come up here?

Kitty takes a deep breath.

DOLLY: We have to go soon Al. I don't want to be on that road in the dark.

Sandy quickly exits the scene.

CUT TO:

103. Int. Sandy's Bedroom — Day.

Sandy takes a last look at her room, kisses the budgie goodbye, places an envelope under her pillow, and leaves.

104. Ext. Ranch Road — Day.

Sandy, in peddle pushers and a top, with a big plastic white purse on her shoulder, walks up the Ranch Road. She keeps glancing over her shoulder and appears to be talking to herself.

105. Ext. Ranch Driveway — Day.

Al and Dolly are jockeying Butch back and forth between the two big Caddys. The Major and Kitty stand side by side; the kids say their goodbyes to Butch.

MAJOR: Butch, there will always be a bed for you here son. Differences aside, you're still family.

BUTCH: Thank you sir.

Butch and the Major share a warm look of recognition.

MAJOR: Just please try and stay out of trouble.

KITTY: Good bye Butch.

Butch hands his transistor to Kitty.

MAJOR: Could you please make sure Sandy gets this?

KITTY: She is too young but yes I'll give it to her. Now, be sensible.

Butch continues to be jostled by his parents.

CUT TO:

106. Ext. Ranch Gate — Late Afternoon.

Sandy is sitting at the side of the road. She looks hot and tired and very worried. Her purse is on the ground beside her. She grabs her purse and goes through it, puts it down, and lays down to look at the sky.

DISSOLVE TO:

107. Ext. Ranch Gate — Evening.

Sandy's purse is perched on a fence and she is taking target practice with some pine cones. Suddenly she stops and listens. Sound of distant car. Sandy grabs her purse and poses by the latch of the closed gate. We see the red Cadillac lumber into view. Sandy looks very excited; she can hardly stop wiggling. But her face falls very quickly. As the Cadillac reaches the gate we see Al is driving. Butch is nowhere to be seen.

AL: Mind opening the gate, Ruthie?

SANDY: (*Slowly opening the gate*) Sandy. I'm Sandy. Where's Butch.

AL: Oh, he'll be along. (*He drives past Sandy*) Nice seeing you again, Ruthie. Come down and see us some time.

Once past the gate, Al steps on it, leaving a cloud of dust in his wake. Sandy looks first one way then the other, then she starts to run after the red Cadillac, leaving the gate open.

SANDY: But my stuff. All my stuff is . . .

Realizing the futility, she kicks up the dust and flails her arms, looking very alone and unhappy. Once again she listens, once again we hear the sound of a distant car. So she dusts herself off, puts on a confident smile, and runs back to pose by the open gate. The white Cadillac lumbers into view. Once again Sandy's smile falls as the white Cadillac, driven by Dolly, barely slows down as it passes Sandy and the gate. Butch turns around, with a grin on his face, and shrugs his shoulders and shakes his head to Sandy. The car disappears in a moment behind a wall of dust. Sandy stands immobilized, her purse slips off her shoulder, and she automatically picks it up.

108. Ext. Ranch Road — Evening.

Sandy is in the foreground, sobbing.

SANDY'S VOICE: I don't recall ever seeing my American cousin again. Or my diary and stuff and my favorite Barbara Anne Scott doll. Oh, we still got their wonderful shiny Christmas cards, even after Allan and Dolly got divorced and Dad sold the Ranch.

Somehow my dreams about a Prince Charming coming to rescue me were never the same again.

109. Ext. Ranch Road — Sunset.

Sandy is walking down the Ranch Road looking very dejected and unhappy.

SANDY'S VOICE: I never gave up planning my escape, though.

Sound of car. Kitty drives up in the family station wagon. When she sees Sandy, she stops the car.

KITTY: Sandra, there you are. Where have you been?

SANDY: Who cares?

KITTY: Um, well, never mind. Did you see Butch leave?

SANDY: (*Angrily*) Yes, I saw Butch leave.

KITTY: Oh Sandra, as you get older you'll see, boys are like buses, if you miss one, there'll be another one along before you know it.

SANDY: I doubt it.

KITTY: Butch left this for you.

Kitty hands Sandy Butch's small transistor. Sandy's eyes light up and she smiles.

KITTY: Well, I have to go into town for the dress rehearsal, would you like to come?

SANDY: Is Barry Bent going to be there?

KITTY: Yes.

SANDY: Okay, sure.

Cheerfully Sandy walks around to the passenger side; flipping through the dial of the transistor radio she picks up "Bluebird on My Windowsill" (Wilf Carter) and gets in the station wagon. She dangles the transistor out the window.

110. Ext. Ranch Road — Sunset.

The station wagon drives off into the sunset, dust trailing behind and settling once again on the windy dirt road bordered with orchards and pine trees.

SANDY'S VOICE: Funny, I was in such a hurry to get off the Ranch and then after we sold it, I missed it more than I ever would have dreamt possible.

My mom was right about the boys, though.

FADE TO BLACK.

JESUS DE MONTREAL

BY DENYS ARCAND
Translated by Matt Cohen

Three or four years ago I auditioned a young bearded comedian who had been smooth-shaven when I met him a few months before. "I'm sorry about the beard," he told me, "but now I am Jesus." Every evening, for the tourists, he acted out "The Way of the Cross" on Mount Royal, the mountain that dominates Montreal.

You never know exactly where the idea for a film originates, but this strange situation began to haunt me. How could this young actor say "He who earns his living will lose his life" in the evening, and then the next morning present himself at an audition for an erotic film or a beer commercial. *Jésus de Montréal* was born from this contradiction, juxtaposing themes from the Passion according to Saint Mark, my childhood memories of being a choirboy in a far off village that had been Catholic for centuries, and my daily experience as a film-maker in a large cosmopolitan city.

I will always be nostalgic for the time in my life when religion provided a soothing response to the most insoluble problems, even considering the demagogy and obscurantism that were part of these false solutions. Even today I can't help being moved when I hear "Where your treasure lies also lies your heart" or "What merit is there in loving those who love you?" Through the dense fog that separates us from the past, comes the echo of a deeply disturbing voice.

I wanted to make a film full of discontinuities, going from wild comedy to the most absurd drama; in the image of the world around us it was to be fragmented, contradictory, banal. A little like in the supermarkets where in ten meters of displays you can find Dostoevsky's novels, eau de cologne, the Bible, porno videos, the complete works of Shakespeare, pictures of the earth taken from the moon, astrological predictions, and posters of actors or Jesus, while the loudspeakers and video screens emit their endless stream of Pergolese, rock and roll, and Bulgar choirs.

Denys Arcand

JESUS DE MONTREAL

Peace be with men of good will who cry alone in the night.
— *Charles Bukowski*

1. *A Theater Stage. The Auditorium. The Entrance. Evening.*

On the cover of an old book bound in worn black leather, written in gold letters that are now a bit smudged: "The Holy Gospels."
A hand opens the book. From it he takes a thick wad of banknotes. Two characters are visible. Smerdiakov, sitting at a table, the banknotes in his hand. Standing in front of him is Ivan Karamazov, who is taking his fur coat from a chair and preparing to go out. They are in a modest room, lit by a few candles; the window panes are covered with ice and the whistling of the wind can be heard.

SMERDIAKOV: (*Holding out the tickets*) Take them. They're yours.

IVAN: You're the one who killed him.

SMERDIAKOV: You are the one who killed him.

IVAN: I was at Tchermachnia. Everyone knows it.

SMERDIAKOV: I am the one who struck the blow, but you are the assassin. Remember what you used to say! The idea of God must be destroyed in men's minds. Only then will each man know he is mortal, without any hope of resurrection, and only then will each man resign himself to death, proudly and calmly. Then man will cease complaining that life is short, and will love his fellow with a disinterested brotherly love. Passion will bring only brief moments of joy, but the very conscience of their brevity will reinforce their intensity just as formerly it was weakened by the hopes of eternal love, love beyond death. Do you remember?

IVAN: Of course . . . of course . . .

SMERDIAKOV: Did you think I was deaf? When you said that because of the inveterate stupidity of the human race this dream would undoubtedly still be unrealized in a thousand years. But that meanwhile every individual conscious of the truth was permitted to lead his life as he pleased. I believed you! I did!

IVAN: I never told you to kill my father.

SMERDIAKOV: You always wanted him dead but you were too much of a coward to act.

Ivan puts on his coat and puts the banknotes in a pocket.

IVAN: I will bring them to the tribunal tomorrow.

Ivan goes towards the door.

SMERDIAKOV: Ivan Fiodorovitch!

IVAN: What?

SMERDIAKOV: Goodbye.

IVAN: See you tomorrow.

Ivan leaves. Smerdiakov turns towards the camera and stares at the lens. He is crying.

SMERDIAKOV: Hell is the pain of no longer being able to love. Once, in the infinity of time and space, a spiritual being appeared on the earth and was able to say: "I am and I love." Once only was he permitted a moment of living and active love. It was for this that earthly mortal life was given to him. I have pushed away this invaluable gift. I have neither appreciated it nor been capable of love. I considered it with irony. I have been unaware of it when I should have prostrated myself and kissed the ground. I have disdained the love of those who loved around me, when I should have loved everyone and everything without ever letting go. (*Kneeling, still crying and moaning, he opens a trunk and takes out a rope.*) Oh woe on suicides! Woe on those who destroy themselves! No one could be more miserable than them. (*He rises, moves towards the center of* *the room*) In cursing God and life they curse themselves. They can never be satisfied and they deny their own salvation. (*Climbing onto a stool he attaches the rope to a beam and passes it around his neck*) They curse God, Who is calling them, and wish He would obliterate Himself, Himself and all of His creation . . . They crave death and oblivion.

With his feet Smerdiakov pushes away the chair. It falls over. His body falls into the emptiness. The lights go out. Suddenly shouts are heard: Bravo! Bravo! and applause from a wildly enthusiastic audience. The spectators are giving a standing ovation. Among them can be seen: France Garibaldi, who is wiping his eyes with a handkerchief; Romeo Miroir; Regine Malouin. Pascal Berger, the one who played Smerdiakov, takes his bows with the other actors. He seems exhausted and he hardly smiles. THE CAMERA GOES BACK AND FORTH *between the spectators who are applauding and the actors who continue to bow. Denise Quintal and Richard Cardinal are also on their feet. They clap, but discreetly.*

QUINTAL: I want his head.

CARDINAL: His head?

QUINTAL: For my campaign for "The Wild Man."

CARDINAL: He doesn't want to do commercials. He told me so.

QUINTAL: I've heard that before.

In the theater lobby, there is the usual opening night hubbub. Miroir and Malouin hasten towards the door of Pascal Berger's dressing room. Garibaldi, sighing and with handkerchief in hand, follows them.

GARIBALDI: My God!

Miroir and Malouin push away the people surrounding Berger.

MALOUIN: It is beautiful. It's rich. It's powerful. It is so powerful.

MIROIR: I'll tell you right away: I love it. I really love it. This is a show that cannot miss.

MALOUIN: You absolutely have to appear on my program. I have to tell you, this show is a *must*.

GARIBALDI: (*Interposing herself*). Ah you. Yes you. You made me cry from the beginning to the end.

MIROIR: (*With a condescending laugh*) That's no criterion: she cries all the time.

GARIBALDI: But that's not true. In fact . . . In fact it means a lot. You are the greatest actor of your generation! That's what I think!

During this reply THE CAMERA *shows us Daniel, standing, who watches this scene from a distance.*

MIROIR: An awesome actor.

Berger sees Daniel and smiles at him.

BERGER: Excuse me, but there is a good actor.

He runs towards Daniel and embraces him. They are obviously happy to see each other.

BERGER: Greetings.

DANIEL: Greetings.

BERGER: Long time no see.

DANIEL: Long time.

Denise Quintal, followed by Richard Cardinal, tries to slide between them.

QUINTAL: Excuse me. Pardon. I'll see you soon (*She continues on through Daniel and Berger*).

THE CAMERA *moves back to the group of critics.*

GARIBALDI: Are you going to eat somewhere?

MIROIR: Yes. But not at l'Express.

MALOUIN: Witloof?

Miroir and Garibaldi look unenthusiastic. Berger has his hand on Daniel's shoulder.

BERGER: And what are you going to do now?

DANIEL: Jesus. I came to get inspiration.

BERGER: Jesus?

DANIEL: (*Smiling*) Jesus!

2. Sanctuary. Interior. Day.

In the rood-loft of the Sanctuary, a conductor directs a small baroque music ensemble: an organist, a soprano and a contralto. They are rehearsing Pergolese's "Stabat Mater." The musicians are young and wearing jeans and shirts or T-shirts. Initial credits superimposed. HIGH-ANGLE SHOT *of Daniel as he appears. As he comes up the aisle, the music continues.* LOW-ANGLE SHOT *of the roof-loft. Daniel has his face raised towards the music and stops as someone comes up behind him.*

    LECLERC: Good morning, Mr. Coulombe.

Daniel turns around to face Father Raymond Leclerc. He is wearing a grey suit with a Roman collar. He has a golden cross on the lapel of his jacket.

    DANIEL: Good morning, Father.

    LECLERC: Come with me, I'm going to show it to you.

They walk down the center aisle of the Sanctuary.

    LECLERC: It's a show that I first put on thirty-five years ago and has been re-done here every summer. But the last few years it hasn't worked very well. The text is a bit old-fashioned. It would all need to be brought up to date.

Daniel agrees silently.

3. Leclerc's Apartment. Interior. Day.

A scene from "The Way of the Cross" is showing on a television screen. The parts are being played by four young actors wearing white tunics. Their acting is exaggerated and theatrical. Sitting in an armchair near a window from which the tops of the next-door buildings can be seen, Daniel takes notes while watching the video recording.

    ACTOR II: "First station: Jesus is condemned to death."

    ACTOR I: "The righteous man must die."

    ACTRESS: "Why?"

    ACTOR II: "Because he is righteous and we are not."

ACTRESS: "He will bear the responsibility for all our murders."

ACTOR II: "All our sins."

CONSTANCE: "All our adulteries!"

Actor I is carrying a large wooden cross.

ACTRESS: "See the man who is bent under the weight of our sins!"

CONSTANCE: "They have chosen the heaviest wood."

ACTRESS: "They have chosen the hardest wood."

ACTOR II: "Our sins are what make his cross so heavy!"

ALL: "Our sins!"

CONSTANCE: "Poor innocent lamb, are you being crushed by my pride?"

CLOSE-UP of Constance.

DANIEL: That's Constance Lazure.

The image of Constance's face stays fixed on the screen.

LECLERC: (Putting down the channel changer next to the television) Do you know her?

DANIEL: She was in her last year at the conservatory the year that I started.

LECLERC: Good! I don't want to impose anyone on you, but it would be fine with me if you want to hire her again. She is an exceptionally sensitive girl.

DANIEL: Right. I remember.

4. Bonneau Hostel. (Room B) Interior. Day.

In a cafeteria, Constance is behind a table serving meals to a line-up of winos of all ages. Daniel is among them. When Constance holds out his plate, her face is at first closed, then lights up. They smile at each other.

CONSTANCE: What are you doing here?

DANIEL: I came here to find you.

SHIFT *to them sitting opposite each other at a long table.*

CONSTANCE: I still prefer serving meals here. At least it does some good. How long have you been gone?

DANIEL: I didn't count.

CONSTANCE: You can't know how bad things have gotten. Everything.

DANIEL: Would you come and work with me?

CONSTANCE: (*She laughs*) And where are you living these days?

DANIEL: Here and there.

CONSTANCE: You could come to my place. There's room.

DANIEL: Okay. That's good. We need to find two guys and a girl.

CONSTANCE: (*She considers*) Okay.

5. Post-Synchronization Studio. Interior. Day.

In a darkened studio the actresses Celebrity and Famous are seated at a table in front of microphones. Martin is sitting behind them. He is reading a newspaper, drinking coffee, and eating a doughnut. The two actresses have a few moments to themselves while the machines rewind.

FAMOUS: It's like A Midsummer's Night Dream. It's worthless.

CELEBRITY: Oh, I know.

FAMOUS: These actors, listen, you can't understand a word of what they're saying. They have no diction.

CELEBRITY: That's the way it always is these days.

Constance and Daniel come into the studio and silently watch the session. The images projected on the screen are reflected on them, and from time to time the CAMERA MOVES *to them during the dialogue.*

FAMOUS: But after all, diction used to be the very basis of the profession.

CELEBRITY: What do you want, nowadays they improvise.

PRODUCER: (*Voice off*) Okay. Stand by.

CELEBRITY: "Oh Cristelle! Oh! Oh! You're so sweet!"

FAMOUS: "Oh! Your tongue! Your tongue!"

CELEBRITY: "Like that! Like that! Oh, that's good!"

FAMOUS: "Oh!"

Celebrity signals Martin, who puts down his donut and leans towards Celebrity's microphone.

MARTIN: "Oh! Having fun without me?"

CELEBRITY: "Oh Johnny! I didn't know you were here. This is my husband."

FAMOUS: "Hmm. Not bad."

CELEBRITY: "He's better than that. Take your clothes off, my sweet."

Martin plays with his clothes. Constance opens her eyes with surprise, then turns her head. Daniel seems amused.

CELEBRITY: "What do you think of him?"

FAMOUS: "Hmm. What equipment. I'd like to have a taste of that."

MARTIN: "Don't hold back, Madame."

FAMOUS: "Hum! Hum!

CELEBRITY: "Leave a little for me, Cristelle."

MARTIN: "I've got enough for two, ladies. I have enough for two."

CELEBRITY: "Hum! Hum!"

FAMOUS: "Hum! Hum!"

MARTIN: "Oh . . . Look, this is my friend, my friend Burt who is here! Come in a little, Burt, come in and take a look."

A silence.

MARTIN: We have to stop here and wait until the other one comes.

FAMOUS: That's the way it is now: no more professionalism.

CELEBRITY: With Duvivier I was always there an hour before the start of filming.

FAMOUS: That, my dear, was another time and another country.

We see the producer and the sound engineer behind the console.

PRODUCER: We can't wait. Martin, can you do both voices?

MARTIN: I'll be glad to try but I can't guarantee anything.

PRODUCER: Okay. Stand by.

FAMOUS: "Oh, Johnny. Ah, yes Johnny, that's good. That's good!"

MARTIN: "You too, sweetie, oh, you too, you're good to take."

CELEBRITY: "Oh, Burt! You're so hard!"

Martin jumps over to Celebrity's microphone and speaks in a nasal voice.

MARTIN: "You like that, eh, you bitch? Say that you like it!"

CELEBRITY: "Oh yes, Burt, I like it, oh, I adore it!"

Martin runs over to the microphone of Famous and talks in a deep voice.

MARTIN: "Tell him that you like it! Go ahead, say it!"

FAMOUS: "Oh yes, Johnny, oh yes, Johnny!"

MARTIN: *(Deep voice)* "Oh . . . oh . . . Take that! Take that! Take that!"

FAMOUS: "Yes, yes . . ."

MARTIN: (*He goes to the other microphone. Nasal voice*) "All right, you too, take that!"

CELEBRITY: "Fuck me, fuck me, Burt!"

FAMOUS: "Yes, yes, fuck me, Johnny!"

MARTIN: (*Deep voice*) "Oh yes, oh yes, oh I'm fucking you, oh I'm fucking you!"

MARTIN: (*High voice*) "Oh! Oh!"

ALL TOGETHER: "Ah! Oh! Ah! Yes! Yes!"

MARTIN: Shit, shit, shit! I got the wrong microphone there, the . . . the voice.

PRODUCER: (*Voice off*) It's not serious, no one will be able to tell the difference.

CELEBRITY: You were fantastic!

FAMOUS: (*Both pat him on the back enthusiastically*) You were fantastic!

6. Stairway of the Post-Synchronization Studio. Interior. Day.

Martin, Daniel, and Constance are coming down the stairs. There are color posters on the wall.

MARTIN: So, uh, when would you want to start?

DANIEL: Now.

MARTIN: (*He hesitates momentarily and looks at both of them*) Okay. Let's go.

CONSTANCE: All right, but you have to finish . . .

MARTIN: They'll work things out.

They leave the building.

7. Constance's Loft. Interior. Day.

Daniel and Martin go up the stairway leading to the loft. They meet Constance in front of a door.

    CONSTANCE: She has a boy the same age, so . . . we take turns.

The door opens, the neighbor appears and Rosalie throws herself into her mother's arms.

    NEIGHBOR: (*Ironically*) Finally! My God, we were worried!

    CONSTANCE: Thank you.

    NEIGHBOR: You're welcome.

She closes the door. Constance goes towards the door of her loft, with Rosalie in her arms.

    CONSTANCE: (*To Rosalie*) Who would these two gentleman be? You don't know them, right?

Rosalie looks at Daniel and Martin. Martin gives her an enormous wink. Rosalie smiles and blinks her eyes.

8. University Esplanade. Exterior. Day.

Daniel is walking along the esplanade in front of the university with a grey-haired theologian who is wearing a suit and carrying a leather briefcase.

    THEOLOGIAN: You have to understand that the faculty of theology here is entirely financed by the archdiocese. It's not like in Germany or Holland. We aren't free to say whatever we want. In any case, not publicly.

    DANIEL: To say what, for example?

    THEOLOGIAN: There are many recent archaeological discoveries, especially since Israel annexed its new territories. And then there is the computer analysis of texts, which is fabulous. There are also new translations of the Talmud . . . We are beginning to understand what it was.

They approach some parked cars.

DANIEL: Jesus?

THEOLOGIAN: Yes. I made copies of some texts for you.

He takes several sheets from his briefcase and gives them to Daniel.

DANIEL: Thank you.

THEOLOGIAN: (*Turning his head, embarrassed*) Never mention my name, please. You could make serious problems for me. You are an actor, you can say anything.

Daniel looks at him for a long time without responding.

9. Bibliotheque Nationale. Interior. Day.

Drawings of the positions of the crucified in a book. In a modern encyclopedia of archaeology, drawings of the Jerusalem crucifixion. We are in the Bibliotheque Nationale, the mezzanine floor. A serious-looking librarian is solemnly pushing a cart filled with books to the table where Daniel is working, a fat pencil in his mouth. The librarian, a woman, leans towards him and puts some books on his table.

AURORE: (*Whispering*) Are you looking for Jesus?

DANIEL: Uh . . . yes.

AURORE: He is the one who will find you.

DANIEL: Oh yes?

AURORE: May peace be with you.

She moves away. Her manner is holy and mysterious. She turns back towards him. Daniel looks at her for a few moments, then gets back to work.

7. Way of the Cross on the Mountain. Exterior. Day.

LOW-ANGLE SHOT *of the stone statue of Christ, his hands bound, immense, in front of a wall of the Sanctuary. This is the first station of the Way of the Cross. Daniel climbs the steps slowly, looks at the statue, leans against it, considers it.*

10. Constance's Loft. Interior. Day.

Daniel goes in. No one is there. He puts the key down on a counter, his bag on a table, takes off his jacket and, putting it down, knocks some things onto the floor where they roll. He goes to the bookcase and takes a book. Constance comes out of her room on the mezzanine level. She sees Daniel and smiles.

CONSTANCE: Are you already here? . . . Good.

Daniel mimes a question: should I slip out?

CONSTANCE: No. (*She smiles, opens the door to her room slightly*) Good. Listen. Come out, we're not playing a scene from Feydeau.

Father Leclerc comes out of the room, ill at ease. He puts on his jacket. The cross is still in his lapel.

LECLERC: Hello.

DANIEL: Hello.

CONSTANCE: All right. I'm heating up the coffee.

LECLERC: No. I have to . . .

CONSTANCE: Hey. It's too late to save yourself after. Coffee.

In the corner of the kitchen Constance pours coffee into the cups, turns around smiling. Father Leclerc walks slowly in front of the big windows of the loft, his head bowed.

LECLERC: (*He stops*) I'm not a very good priest . . . after all, as you can see. I used to try, but . . . (*He starts walking again*) I come from a very poor and very religious family. I was crazy about theater. At the time it seemed like it might be a solution . . . As it turned out I've done a lot of traveling. I've seen the great productions. Alec Guiness in Richard III, the first act, with his knife . . . (*He acts it out, makes the motion of thrusting in a knife*) "Now that the winter of our discontent is made glorious summer by this sun of York." Ah . . . Gerard Philippe in Lorenzaccio . . . Ah!

Leaning against a wall, Daniel listens to him. Constance brings the tray to the table where Leclerc is now sitting. Daniel goes to sit on the ledge of one of the big windows.

CONSTANCE: And after the play, he would go to see the prostitutes. The black women of Harlem.

She gives a cup to Daniel.

LECLERC: Well, at that time it was rather difficult, for a priest . . .

CONSTANCE: (*She sits down opposite Leclerc*) It's not so much easier now, I should tell you. Unless you have the courage to let go.

LECLERC: I've already explained!

DANIEL: What? What have you already explained?

LECLERC: If I sent my letter of resignation to Rome now, I would have the right to receive a pair of pants, a shirt, a nylon jacket, and fifty dollars in cash. That's all. Bye bye.

CONSTANCE: You could move in here.

LECLERC: I think I'm a little old for sleeping on the floor in a sleeping bag.

CONSTANCE: You could sleep in my bed. (*Silence*) Of course, it probably wouldn't be as comfortable as your beautiful apartment, with nuns to make you breakfast, and everything.

DANIEL: The breakfasts aren't bad here.

LECLERC: I know, I know.

He gets up, walks towards the door while putting on his tie. Constance goes with him. They embrace discreetly.

CONSTANCE: Goodbye.

LECLERC: See you soon.

Leclerc leaves. Constance returns to Daniel. She laughs lightly, sits down beside him.

DANIEL: So?

Daniel takes her by the neck, she leans her head on his knees, he kisses her hair.

DANIEL: Oh Constance!

CONSTANCE: Oh well, it makes him so happy and it doesn't really hurt me.

Daniel kisses her again, and grips her shoulder.

12. Ile Notre Dame. Exterior. Day.

Water and greenery in the distance. Martin is taking Daniel and Constance up a stairway which leads to a mixing studio.

MARTIN: There's a studio up there.

13. Mixing Studio. Interior. Day.

In a large dark room, in the foreground, a technician sits behind an enormous console pushing buttons. In the background René is standing before a lectern illuminated by a weak lamp. The credits reel for a film comes to an end on a screen right at the back of the room. Facing it, René reads.

RENE: "It is impossible to speak of the creation of the world or the beginning of the universe."

THE CAMERA MOVES BACK *to the screen. The whole surface lights up with the image.*

RENE: "The human spirit cannot conceive the time before the starting point, that instant fifteen million years ago when all known matter was condensed into an almost infinitesimal diameter at a virtually inconceivable temperature."

A luminous dot seems to detach itself from the horizon and comes to René where it explodes.

RENE: "The Big Bang. An explosion of unimaginable force. A million years later the heat was just beginning to disperse . . ."

A door opens behind the screen. Martin, Daniel, and Constance come in. They are a bit lost. They whisper.

CONSTANCE: We can't come in this way.

MARTIN: Yes, we can.

CONSTANCE: We're behind the screen.

DANIEL: Shh!

RETURN TO FULL-SCREEN COSMIC IMAGES. WE ENTER INTO THE FILM WHICH RENE IS NARRATING.

RENE: "In the cosmic fluid masses of matter will condense due to the effect of gravitation. Stars are born and die. Our sun is one of them."

Daniel, Constance, and Martin are standing in front of the image. They see the film backwards. Seen from behind, near the immense screen, they seem lost in space. THE CAMERA GOES BACK AND FORTH *from behind the screen to in front of it, and thus the image alternates between the wrong and the right side.*

RENE: "We live on a tiny planet, in orbit around an unexceptional star, at the edge of an ordinary galaxy, one among billions of other galaxies. We do not know if they are many planetary systems in the universe. If most stars have some planets, it is probable that there are millions of other life forms, analogous to our own. On the other hand, if planetary systems are the result of some very exceptional processes during the formation of stars, we might be alone in the world. We may never have answers to these questions: the universe is expanding and distances more and more difficult to cross. Our cosmic horizon is 15 billion light years away, the age of our universe. We will never see beyond that limit. It is not inconceivable that there are other universes beyond our own, but we will never be able to see them. In five billion years our sun will have used up its nuclear fuel. Our planet will return to the galactic gas from which it was made. But we will have long since gone. The world began without man and will finish without him. In a thousand billion years, when the sky is feebly lit by a few slowly dying old stars, the length of life as we know it will have been just a brief moment, one during which we existed, and with the disappearance of the last being on earth the universe will not even have felt the passing of a furtive shadow."

RETURN TO A BLACK SCREEN AND RENE'S FACE. *He turns out the lamp and goes towards the console. He speaks to the astrophysicist, who is now seen to the right of the console.*

    RENE: Did you write that?

    ASTROPHYSICIST: No. That was a collage, a simplification.

    RENE: There are a lot of questions without answers.

    ASTROPHYSICIST: Yes. And what's there is only true for now. In five years things could be totally different.

Martin's head appears beside the screen.

    MARTIN: René! Excuse me. (*He talks lowly, gesturing with his hands*) Can you come?

René leaves the astrophysicist.

14. Mixing Studio Building. Ile Notre-Dame.

From an outside corridor, VIEW *of the city: trees, blue sky, river, sky-scraper.*

    RENE: But what is the script?

    DANIEL: We're going to write it.

    RENE: (*Mistrustful*) A collective script?

    DANIEL: You don't have to work on it.

René goes ahead of the others, who stop. He turns to face them. Behind him, Montreal seen from the Ile Notre Dame.

    RENE: I like being able to read the text before deciding. That's why I don't work very much.

A pause. The other three are surprised.

    RENE: I think you might be better off looking for someone else. Sorry.

He moves off.

    DANIEL: (*Scratches his head, looks at the others*) All right.

René comes back towards them.

RENE: I know a girl who would probably be interested, but she might not be the type you're looking for.

15. A Public Square with a Fountain. Exterior. Day.

A marble pond surrounded by big buildings. Fountains of water spraying into it. Mireille, scantily dressed in a few diaphanous scraps, advances towards the camera. She walks on the water, ethereal. She comes up to an elegantly dressed man, brushes his cheek with a kiss, then disappears. The man looks into the camera.

ELEGANT MAN: "The unbearable lightness of being!"

He brings a bottle of perfume to his face.

ELEGANT MAN: "Esprit, number seven."

THE CAMERA SHOWS *the team filming this advertisement. Jerzy Strelisky and Denise Quintal are standing near the camera.*

JERZY: Cut.

QUINTAL: No, it's not quite . . . airborne! It has to be airborne.

JERZY: What exactly do you mean airborne, darling. Do you want us to make her fly?

QUINTAL: I don't know. But it has to be like Kundera. That's the concept.

JERZY: Kundera, but Kundera how?

QUINTAL: Light. Extremely light. I can't give you the technical details. My job is to be creative . . .

Jerzy turns back, goes towards the cameraman.

JERZY: Pierre!

The elegant man approaches Quintal.

ELEGANT MAN: Was my part all right?

QUINTAL: It was perfect, my treasure. It's just too bad that we can't film your bum.

She pinches his bum.

ELEGANT MAN: (*Exasperated*) Oh! Denise!

Daniel, Martin, and Constance come up to Mireille, who has put on a dressing gown and is smoking a cigarette near the camera.

16. Jerzy and Mireille's Apartment. Interior. Day.

An extremely modern apartment in a downtown skyscraper. Very white and luminous.

JERZY: (*Wearing an undershirt and suspenders he approaches Mireille, who is wearing panties and a sweater. They are barefoot*) The Way of the Cross? And you're going to play the role of the Virgin Mary? Give me a break! My sweet, there are a hundred and fifty girls graduating from theater school every year.

MIREILLE: I don't see what that has to do with it.

JERZY: You don't? Come here, I'll show you how they relate.

He leads her in front of a big mirror.

JERZY: To succeed in life, my little one, as I've already told you, you have to know exactly what you are. Look. (*He lifts her sweater to reveal her buttocks*) Look. You'd give a hard-on to a paraplegic. Your greatest talent, my little one, is still your ass.

MIREILLE: (*Turning to him and leaning on the mirror*) You've always thought that, haven't you?

She runs from the room, going up a stairway that leads to a loft.

JERZY: But I'm telling you that because I love you! If you do this thing you're going to make a fool of yourself! To hell with it!

He watches her from below. She is putting clothes into a bag.

JERZY: Might I know exactly what you're playing at?

MIREILLE: I'm playing the scene where I leave. Watch carefully, my little one. One take. The first one is the good one.

JERZY: Don't try the independent woman! The talent you need for that, my little bunny, you don't have.

16. Constance's Loft. Interior. Night.

CLOSE-UP *of Rosie sleeping in Daniel's arms.*

DANIEL: For example, at the time of the Roman Empire, when a child came into the world and the father, for one reason or another, wasn't happy about it, he took the baby and put it in the street or the market square.

CONSTANCE: (*Off screen*) And then?

DANIEL: Oh, either the baby died or it was picked up by slave dealers.

Constance is sitting on the floor, Martin is sitting further back in an armchair.

CONSTANCE: How horrible!

DANIEL: It was called "displaying" a child. It happened a lot.

CONSTANCE: But what about the mother?

DANIEL: We don't know about that. I'm beginning to realize that it's almost impossible to understand . . .

The doorbell rings. Daniel turns his head, the door opens, René appears. Constance lets him in. She is astounded to see him.

RENE: Hello.

CONSTANCE: Hello. Come in.

René moves forward.

RENE: Gentlemen, good evening. So, here it is. Do you think it would be possible for Hamlet's monologue to be part of the show?

DANIEL: *(With a laugh)* Hum . . . it wouldn't be easy . . . but it might be possible . . .

RENE: I've always wanted to give it. But since there are now few opportunities for me to . . .

The doorbell rings.

CONSTANCE: *(From her room)* Someone get that.

The door opens. It is Mireille.

MIREILLE: Good evening.

DANIEL: *(Who went to open the door)* Good evening.

MIREILLE: You gave me the address, so . . . Here I am.

DANIEL: Come in.

Mireille comes into the apartment.

18. Pizzeria. Interior. Night.

In a pizzeria, the same evening. An Italian is at the cash register. Behind him an employee works in front of the pizza ovens. Daniel enters.

DANIEL: I'd like five pizzas to take out, please. But I don't have any money.

ITALIAN: No money, no pizzas.

DANIEL: I have hungry friends.

ITALIAN: Don't your friends work?

DANIEL: They work, but they aren't paid very well.

ITALIAN: They'll have to work more.

DANIEL: They'd like to, but there aren't always jobs.

ITALIAN: And what about you? Don't you work?

DANIEL: I've just found something, but I haven't started yet.

ITALIAN: When I came here I washed dishes eighteen hours a day. I never asked anyone for charity.

DANIEL: No one likes to.

ITALIAN: There are lots of hungry people.

DANIEL: Yes.

ITALIAN: I can't feed them all.

DANIEL: No. But you could give five pizzas.

ITALIAN: I *sell* my pizzas. I own a restaurant.

DANIEL: Lucky you.

ITALIAN: I work seven days a week, three hundred and sixty-five days a year. From seven in the morning until midnight. You call that lucky?

DANIEL: Things could be worse.

ITALIAN: If I give food away, I won't be able to live. I won't be able to pay the salaries of the people who work for me. The tax deductions, the unemployment insurance, the disability and accident insurance. They've got me by the throat. I have to pay back the bank.

Daniel looks at him without speaking.

ITALIAN: And I haven't even mentioned the city inspectors. My wife, my children. My mother-in-law. My cousins. They're still arriving!

DANIEL: Let's drop it. Forget it (*He smiles and starts off*).

ITALIAN: Five?

DANIEL: That's right.

ITALIAN: But just this one time, this evening. I don't want to see you here again tomorrow!

DANIEL: No, no.

ITALIAN: And nothing on them. Just tomatoes and cheese.

DANIEL: That's good.

ITALIAN: (*Screaming at his worker*) Five medium! Cheese and tomato!

EMPLOYEE: Five medium, cheese and tomato! Okay.

A silence. The Italian looks at Daniel.

ITALIAN: (*Screaming at his employee*) Mushrooms!

EMPLOYEE: Five medium. Cheese, tomato, and mushrooms! Okay!

ITALIAN: Ah fuck! All dressed!

EMPLOYEE: Five medium, all dressed! Okay!

The Italian, pretending to be angry, hits a key of his cash register. The "No Sale" sign appears.

19. Constance's Loft. Interior. Night.

Daniel, Mireille, René, Martin, and Constance are sitting at the table eating pizza.

RENE: Aren't you worried about performing that?

CONSTANCE: Why?

RENE: It's a tragedy. It's dangerous.

MIREILLE: Ah, the danger of seeming like fools. Yeah, that's what Jerzy told me.

RENE: When you put on a tragedy, bad things often happen.

MIREILLE: Oh, don't say things like that.

DANIEL: Anyway, *que sera, sera*.

MARTIN: Whatever will be, will be.

RENE: The future is not ours to see.

CONSTANCE: Que sera, sera.

MIREILLE: Cha, cha, cha!

Laughs. Daniel tries to uncork a bottle, passes it to Martin.

20. Montreal Seen from the Mountain. Exterior. Dawn.

Sun rising on Montreal, its skyscrapers, the river. SHOTS *of the sky.*

21. Constance's Loft. Interior. Day.

Rosalie, wearing pyjamas, comes out of her room and tiptoes towards Daniel who is sleeping on the floor in his sleeping bag.

ROSALIE: Wake up! Hey, wake up! We're going to play the lion game.

Daniel opens one eye, then growls while holding out his arms to her. The two laugh. Constance is fixing her hair in the bathroom. Mireille comes in, looks at herself in the mirror, and makes a face.

MIREILLE: Oh la la. What a mug. Do you have any make-up?

CONSTANCE: I just have some lipstick.

MIREILLE: Oh no! You don't have any powder or eyeshadow . . .

CONSTANCE: Nothing, I promise you.

MIREILLE: Oh no! I can't go out like this. Have you seen my face? No, I just can't.

CONSTANCE: (*Ironic*) I don't know what you're going to do.

MIREILLE: Don't make jokes. This is serious, I mean it. No, no, I don't want anything to do with that. (*She taps the mirror while turning around*) No, no.

Constance laughs.

The breakfast table. Daniel is sitting down with Rosalie on his knees. Mireille is seated at the end of the table. She is wearing dark glasses and is biting her nails. Constance is busy at the stove.

ROSALIE: (*Voice off*) Why is that lady wearing glasses?

DANIEL: The lady is wearing glasses to hide herself. Because she is very ugly. Look, I'll show you. (*Quickly he pulls the glasses off Mireille's nose. She gives a forced smile followed by a grimace*) She is ugly, isn't she? Blecch (*He hides behind Rosalie*).

ROSALIE: Blecch.

MIREILLE: All right, that's enough (*She puts her glasses back on*).

Constance comes up to the table with a coffeepot and a breadbasket. She sits down.

CONSTANCE: You're starting to have a very bad influence on my daughter. We're going to send you off to work on your Passion.

Rosalie laughs.

22. Way of the Cross on the Mountain. Exterior. Day.

The actors are standing in front of the statue at the first station: "Jesus is condemned to death." Sitting at the bottom of the stone ramp, Daniel is rehearsing them. They have the text in their hands, and which they read while acting out their parts. They are in jeans.

MARTIN: (*With a "theatrical" emphasis*) "How will I tell you this story?"

RENE: (*With the same emphasis*) "The most famous story ever told."

DANIEL: No. A little less . . . A little more "in a modulated tone . . ."

RENE: (*Mocking*) ". . . in the storminess of the Passion." All right. "The most famous story ever told."

CONSTANCE: "The one everybody thinks they know. An eastern story, faraway and mysterious."

MIREILLE: (*Very timid and hesitant*) "The story of the Jewish prophet Yeshou ben Pantera, he whom we all call Jesus."

DANIEL: Speak to me.

MIREILLE: What?

DANIEL: Speak to me.

MIREILLE: But it's difficult to do that way, I . . . I'm not made up, I have no costume, I don't know . . . I'm not used to it. (*Daniel looks at her, smiling. He signals her to begin. She starts again, her eyes closed*) "The story of the Jewish prophet Yeshou ben Pantera, he whom we all call Jesus."

She opens her eyes. Daniel smiles at her.

MIREILLE: "The historians of that period, Tacitus, Suetonus, Pliny, Flavius Joseph, take just a sentence to mention him in passing."

The Passion Play begins. "In the year 33, he appeared before Judea's fifth chief magistrate, the Roman official known as Pontius Pilate."

RENE: "The little we know of him comes from a few testimonies, recorded by disciples a century after his death."

MARTIN: "The disciples are generally liars. They embellish."

MIREILLE: "Where he was born is unknown."

CONSTANCE: "We don't know how old he was when he died. Some said eighty years old, others fifty."

MIREILLE: (*Without reading her script*) "But it is relatively certain that on the 7th of April in the year 30, or the 27th of April in the year 31, or the 3rd of April in the year 33, he appeared before Judea's fifth chief magistrate, the Roman official known as Pontius Pilate."

23. *Way of the Cross on the Mountain. Paths. Pond. Exterior. Night.*

First performance of the "Way of the Cross." It is night. Multicolored reflectors hung from the trees light up the actors who are now made-up and in costume. About fifty onlookers of all ages are watching. In this scene René plays Pontius Pilate, Daniel plays Jesus, Martin plays an important Jewish priest, and Constance and Mireille are Roman soldiers. Constance and Mireille are holding Daniel by the arms and pulling him towards René who is consulting graven stone tablets. He is seated at the foot of the statue of Christ with his hands bound. Daniel is struggling.

RENE: What are you accused of?

DANIEL: You're the one who knows that.

RENE: Do you belong to a sect? Are you another prophet? Is that it?

DANIEL: Are you the one who's saying that or did others tell you?

RENE: (*He gets up and approaches Daniel. We see that the eyes of the statue are covered by a red cloth*) You spoke about a kingdom you wished to establish?

DANIEL: A kingdom not of this world.

RENE: You mean a sort of Elysium? (*He sits down on the stone ramp*) After death? You haven't preached against Caesar to overthrow the Roman Empire?

DANIEL: No.

RENE: So, what is it you tell your disciples?

DANIEL: There is no greater love than this: to give your life for your friends.

RENE: (*Disabused*) Don't you find that a bit of an optimistic doctrine? In Rome you wouldn't have lasted a week (*He crosses the stage and comes up to Martin*) Inoffensive (*He gives him back the tablets*).

MARTIN: This man is threatening the established order.

RENE: I can't condemn every fanatic in the Middle East. Half the population would have to be killed off.

MARTIN: This man has spent his whole life insulting priests.

RENE: Personally, you know, I've always thought a priest must be either an idiot or a profiteer. So . . .

MARTIN: The priests are on Rome's side. There are certain rumors you wouldn't want making the rounds. Tiberius Augustus is a suspicious emperor. We want to help you govern the country smoothly but . . . Sometimes an example is necessary. This man attracts crowds, he has his disciples . . .

RENE: . . . who are unarmed.

MARTIN: He performs miracles. He has even provoked riots at the Temple. Crucify him. (*He starts off, then turns towards René*) Better to sacrifice one man from time to time . . .

René comes back to Daniel.

RENE: I'm unable to understand why your enemies are so determined to destroy you. Your own family has more or less rejected you, you have become an undesirable in Nazareth, here in Jerusalem the entire hierarchy is against you. How have you managed to get all of these people to turn against you at the same time?

DANIEL: They hate me for no reason. Just because I have borne witness to the truth.

RENE: (*Begins to descend towards Daniel*) What is the truth? (*A silence. He sits down on one of the steps*) I'm going to give you over to my soldiers. They are brutes, of course. We don't get the best legionnaires here. You'll be flagelated, then crucified. (CLOSE-UP *of Daniel*) That's going to be very painful. You are not Roman, but try to be courageous. Tell yourself that I may be doing you a favor. (*Getting up again, he continues to descend the steps towards Daniel*) One of our philosophers used to say that because life has so many difficulties, the ability to commit suicide was the best thing man received. In a few hours you are going to cross the Styx, the river of Death, from which no one has ever returned. With the possible exception of Orpheus, long ago. Then you will indeed see whether your kingdom is on the other shore, or if Jupiter Catolin is waiting for you, or Athena, or the God of the Germans or that of the French. The gods are so numerous . . . Perhaps you will find the river has no other side, that it sinks into a black hole. In the end you will have the answer to these questions. Be brave. Take him away.

We see the spectators, whom Bob Chalifoux is guiding with his flashlight.

CHALIFOUX: This way for the second station please. Follow the path. It's quite a bit farther than last year.

The actors change as quickly as they can. Second station: looking out over the lights of the city. Mireille and Constance are dressed as modern archaeologists: khaki shirts, boots, many-pocketed canvas vests from which brushes, pens, etc. are sticking out.

MIREILLE: (*Comes up to a trench dug in the style of archaeological sites. She turns towards the spectators*) "Our knowledge of the life of Jesus is so sparse that some people claim he never existed."

CONSTANCE: (*Joining her*) "The paradox is that Jesus was not a Christian. He was a Jew. He was circumcised and he followed Jewish law."

They go down into the trench. Only their heads and shoulders are visible. The spectators come closer.

MIREILLE: "He was obsessed by the fate of Israel. And like all of us he was convinced that the time he lived in was the most important in all of history."

CONSTANCE: "And that the end of the world was imminent."

In the trench, we see a mosaic on a wall.

CONSTANCE: (*Voice off*) "The oldest mosaics show him as a young beardless man."

Constance brushes the earth wall to show a Byzantine fragment.

CONSTANCE: "Later, Byzantine artists drew him with a beard, because in Byzantium beards were a sign of power."

MIREILLE: (*Voice off, while on camera are seen the faces — serious, emotionally involved — of Father Leclerc, Malouin, Miroir, Quintal, and Berger*) "The Jews reproached the first Christians for following a false prophet who was the fruit of fornication. They called him Jesus, Yeshou ben Pantera, the son of Pantera."

She gets up, comes to the edge of the trench with a wax tablet like the one Pontius Pilate consulted. She dusts it off with her fingers.

CONSTANCE: "There have recently been discovered the orders of a Roman soldier. He was being transferred to Capharneum to the German frontier in the year 6. This soldier was called Pantera."

Meanwhile Mireille has turned on a portable computer which has been placed at the edge of the trench. She pushes various keys. On the screen are seen series of numbers and strange characters. Behind her the lights of the city are still visible.

MIREILLE: "Throughout the Jewish tradition, it is always said of a man that he is his father's son, unless the child is illegitimate. When Jesus came back to his village, those who lived there exclaimed: Isn't he the carpenter, Mary's son?"

Mireille and Constance walk along a path, followed by the spectators. Among them is Bob Chalifoux, the security guard. Mireille and Constance are wearing costumes typical of the era, white and brown tunics, grey or white veils.

CONSTANCE: "We have short memories. We are already

no longer able to imagine how people used to live and think just a century ago."

MIREILLE: "This story is two thousand years old. It takes place at a time when people believed the earth was flat, and that the stars were candles suspended from the vault of the sky."

CONSTANCE: "People believed in evil spirits, in demons, is miracle cures, in the resurrection of the dead. The East swarmed with prophets, charlatans, magicians."

MIREILLE: "Judas of Galilee!"

CONSTANCE: "Theudas!"

MIREILLE: "The great Egyptian!"

CONSTANCE: "Simon the Magician!"

Constance waves her arm to the left. The spectators gasp with surprise at a shower of sparks followed by smoke. Martin, dressed as a magician, appears when the smoke dissipates.

MARTIN: With the powers of my mind I can part the waters of the Jordan!

New burst of sparks and cloud of smoke. More cries from the spectators. Martin disappears. A loud puffing is heard to the right of the spectators. They turn. René appears in the sky. He seems to be flying.

RENE: At my command the walls of Jerusalem will collapse. The powerful spirit controls the laws of nature!

René disappears behind a tree.

MIREILLE: "Jesus also was a magician. People used to say he had spent his childhood in Egypt, the home of magic."

CONSTANCE: "His miracles were probably more popular than his teachings."

We are at the edge of a pond. Daniel is in a small boat with Martin and René. René is holding a fishnet in his hands. Daniel gets out of the boat and walks slowly on the water towards the spectators grouped at the water's edge. Then Martin steps out the boat and sinks straight to the bottom.

MARTIN: Save me, Lord!

Daniel looks at him, smiling. In black sky the moon is full.

DANIEL: Man of little faith.

Daniel walks on water to the shore where he comes to Constance, who turns towards him.

CONSTANCE: Cure me.

Her pupils are white. She is blind. Daniel puts some saliva on his thumbs and rubs her eyelids. Constance opens her eyes. She can see.

CONSTANCE: I see you.

Daniel moves away from Constance. Now he is talking to the onlookers.

DANIEL: Don't torment yourself. No one, by worrying about it, can add a single hour to the length of their life.

He arrives in front of Mireille, who is lying on the ground. She is dead, covered by a shroud.

DANIEL: Thalita Khoum. Rise!

He helps Mireille to get up. She moves, she takes a few steps. A young Haitian woman comes out of the crowd and rushes towards Daniel.

HAITIAN WOMAN: Jesus, I am yours! I belong to you! Forgive me, Jesus, forgive me, I have sinned. Speak to me, Jesus, speak to me, Jesus, my sweet Jesus . . .

Bob Chalifoux rushes up to her. Daniel is astounded.

CHALIFOUX: Madame, please. Don't bother the actors.

HAITIAN WOMAN: Jesus! Forgive me. (*She hangs on to him*) I have sinned! Forgive me.

CHALIFOUX: Control yourself, please. Control yourself!

HAITIAN WOMAN: Jesus, speak to me! Speak to me, Jesus! (*To Chalifoux*) Would you please. (*To Daniel*) Jesus, Jesus!

CHALIFOUX: That's enough of that (*He takes her in his arms and starts to lead her away*).

HAITIAN WOMAN: Jesus, Jesus, I need you, I love you, you are my whole life . . .

Chalifoux overcomes her and finally takes her away. Daniel turns his head towards the next scene. Martin, Constance, and René are sitting around a fire in the sand. Daniel goes towards them, picking up a basket of bread from the ground. He then directs himself towards the spectators.

DANIEL: (*Giving them bread*) Don't worry about what you will eat or how you will be clothed. To each day its own problems suffice. Live in peace with one another. Do not fight back against those who would harm you. Whoever wants to take you to court or have your tunic, give him also your coat. (*Coming up to John Lambert and the Pommerlau twins*) It will be difficult for those who are rich to enter the kingdom of God, for where your treasure lies also lies your heart. (*He offers a piece of bread to Lambert, then moves away*) What merit is there in loving those who love you? Love those who wish you evil.

Daniel is sitting by the fire with Mireille, Constance, René, and Martin. They are eating grilled fish and drinking wine.

DANIEL: When you have guests for dinner, invite the poor, the maimed, the lame, the blind. Verily I tell you this: the prostitutes will be the first to arrive in the Kingdom of God.

MIREILLE: (*Jewels clinking, arms naked, laughing and raising her glass, tipsy*) Yeah!

DANIEL: Judge not and you will not be judged. Forgive. Who are people saying that I am?

RENE: Some say you are John the Baptist come back to life.

CONSTANCE: (*Her hair done up, arms naked, wearing jewels*) Others say you are Elijah.

MIREILLE: Or one of the prophets.

DANIEL: And you, who do you say that I am?

MARTIN: We think you are the Christ, the Messiah.

DANIEL: Never speak of me to anyone. I forbid you to say that I am the Christ. I am the son of man. I cannot tell you by whose authority I do as I do.

He rises. The others watch him. Martin also rises.

MARTIN: Where are you going . . . ?

DANIEL: You will follow me later.

He moves off and, turning his back to the spectators, leans against a tree.

HAITIAN WOMAN: (*Voice off*) Jesus! Save yourself, Jesus!

Two shadows dressed in black take hold of Daniel and lead him away.

HAITIAN: Jesus, save yourself! Save yourself, Jesus!

CHALIFOUX: That's enough, Madame. The show is down there, not here. Good. All right, everyone, next station, over there.

The spectators advance. Among them go Constance and Mireille dressed as previously in tunics and brown or grey veils. Daniel, naked, is tied to a tree, facing it. Martin and René flagelate him. The scene is lit by a red projector.

CONSTANCE: "The purpose of flagelation was to make death come more quickly."

MIREILLE: "Crucifixions were frequent. There were probably some every week in Jerusalem. This one was nothing special. Some sort of quack."

CONSTANCE: "At that time, life was short and brutal."

MIREILLE: "There certainly would have been a small crowd, like there is here this evening. Executions have always been popular."

CONSTANCE: "It's the same as for highway accidents: there are always people who can't resist them."

Constance and Mireille keep walking, preceding the spectators towards the twelfth station. Placed randomly on the ground are about ten posts with wooden stands, ready for those who have been condemned. Here and there braziers light the way.

CONSTANCE: "The practice of crucifixion began six centuries before Christ."

MIREILLE: "This represented a softening of standards: the Assyrians had preferred impalement."

CONSTANCE: "In Babylon, Darius, the King of Persia, crucified three thousand people who were opposed to him."

MIREILLE: "After the siege of the city of Tyre in Lebanon, two thousand soldiers were crucified on the beach."

CONSTANCE: "Eighty years before Jesus, Alexander Janneus, the King of Judea, had eight hundred Pharisees crucified."

MIREILLE: "After the revolt of the slaves led by Spartacus, seven thousand soldiers were crucified along the Appian way between Rome and Capua."

They stop in the midst of the posts. Behind the scene, the lights of the city.

CONSTANCE: "The death posts were permanently positioned in public places."

MIREILLE: "Quintilian recommended the use of busy crossroads. He saw it as an excellent means to encourage the public morality."

CONSTANCE: "The custom was that the condemned man himself carry the crossbar of the cross."

The spectators make way for Daniel, who advances unsteadily. His torso is uncovered, his tunic is fastened at his hips. His face and body are covered with blood. His arms are tied by ropes to a wooden beam. He is followed by René and Martin. They are armed with spears and wear carpenter's belts with hammers and nails. They also have ropes slung over their shoulders. Mireille comes close and offers a goblet to Daniel. He declines . . .

CONSTANCE: "In Palestine the condemned was offered wine mixed with myrrh. It was a drug that lessened the pain."

René and Martin pull off Daniel's tunic and knock him to the ground. They sit astride him and nail his forearms to the beam. Then they stand him up, one of them supports him on his shoulder, then they lift him onto the stand of one of the posts. They nail the crossbar to the post. Then they cross Daniel's legs under him and hammer in a nail through the bones of his heels. The scene is rapid, silent, violent. Daniel is now in the crucifixion position he had seen in books in the Bibliotheque Nationale. In the background, the lights of the city. Hung around his neck a sign: "Jesus, King of the Jews."

CONSTANCE: (*Voice off*) "And after all that, the condemned man awaited his death."

MIREILLE: (*Also offscreen, until Daniel's reply*) "It was very slow in coming."

CONSTANCE: "Most of those who were crucified lived for at least two days."

MIREILLE: "The strongest ones could last for up to a week."

CONSTANCE: "Imagine we are in the Middle East. The heat is stifling."

MIREILLE: "The sun, the flies."

CONSTANCE: "The vultures, the stray dogs, the rats. Death came through exhaustion."

MIREILLE: "By asphyxiation, because of the arms being raised."

DANIEL: Thirsty!

A sponge appears, dripping, at the end of a stick. He tries to drink.

DANIEL: . . . abandoned . . .

His head drops and he faints.

CONSTANCE: "The Romans often left the corpse to decompose on its cross."

MIREILLE: "But the Jews found this practice repugnant."

CONSTANCE: (*With emotion, she turns her head no longer able to bear looking*) "Crucifixion was such a frightening spectacle that the first Christians never portrayed it."

Constance moves off.

MIREILLE: "It was not until five centuries later that artists began to paint Jesus on the cross."

She also moves away, followed by the spectators. René comes up to Daniel and buries a spear in his chest. Daniel twists, then dies.

The actors (except for Daniel) leap down a bank to "the grotto" for the final scene. Daniel, alone on the cross, in the midst of the crucifixion posts. Around him the braziers continue to burn. Behind him, in the distance, the lights of the city glow like fires. Chalifoux, the guard, precedes the spectators to the entrance of "the grotto," where he opens the heavy door.

    CHALIFOUX: Last station. Careful on the stairs, they're quite steep.

The spectators enter one by one. We recognize people from the world of the theater.

    MIROIR: They've used this place so well!

    MALOUIN: I am so moved!

Garibaldi joins Lambert in the line and addresses him sharply.

    GARIBALDI: But apart from the mini-series, do you have any other projects.

    LAMBERT: (*Annoyed*) No, nothing has been signed.

Garibaldi gives a look of shock and surprise.

    CHALIFOUX: (*Voice off*) Keep quiet please, don't hold people up.

Seen in the crowd, as they enter, Quintal and Berger.

    QUINTAL: What's wrong?

    BERGER: Oh, nothing . . .

24. *Room under the Sanctuary. Interior. Night.*

Inside the great vaulted room, lit by torches along the walls, Miroir and Malouin arrive at the bottom of the iron stairway. In front of them are Martin, René, and Constance. They are sitting down and they are wearing long white tunics.

    CONSTANCE: "He had been dead for a long time. Perhaps five or ten years. The disciples had dispersed. Disappointed, bitter and without hope."

RENE: "To die, to sleep — no more. To end
The heart-ache and the thousand natural shocks
That flesh is heir to. 'Tis a consomnation
Devoutly to be wish'd.
(*He stands*)
To die, to sleep ... perchance to dream.
Ay, there's the rub;
For in that sleep of death what dreams may come
When we have shuffled off this mortal coil
Must give us pause. There's the respect
That makes calamity of so long life;
For who would bear the whips and scorns of time,
Th'oppressor's wrong, the proud man's contumely,
The pangs of despised love, the law's delay,
The insolence of office, and the spurns
That patient merit of th' unworthy takes.
Who would these fardels bear,
To grunt and sweat under a weary life,
But that the dread of something after death—
The undiscovered country, from whose bourn
No traveler returns — puzzles the will,
And makes us rather bear those ills we have
Than fly to others we know not of?"

CONSTANCE: "No traveler but one. But Him."

At the back of the room is a huge metal grill. Behind it glares a bluish light. Its doors open and close automatically. Mireille runs through the door to Martin.

MIREILLE: (*Glowing*) I saw him!

MARTIN: (*He gets up*) Who?

MIREILLE: Him!

MARTIN: Let's see!

MIREILLE: I swear it! At first I didn't ... I didn't recognize him, it wasn't exactly him. And then suddenly I felt it was him. It was he who was speaking to me. I felt his presence, he was there.

MARTIN: (*Raising his shoulders and moving back*) Hmm!

MIREILLE: I swear it! I swear it, believe me!

Martin joins Constance and they take a few steps together. They come up ulled down over his eyes.

o seem very sad.

We were talking about a friend whom we ago.

exceptional prophet.

af of bread from a cloth bag. He breaks it, gives each

e hold out their hands. They look at the bread, each

My Lord!

René.

CONSTANCE: It's you. It's you.

MIREILLE: "Little by little, many were convinced he had returned. His body had changed. No one ever recognized him at first, but they all ended up believing he was present in their midst. Aside from Peter and John, they were not the disciples from before, but others: Paul the Pharisee, Barnaby, Etienne, and then some foreigners, Greeks and Romans."

CONSTANCE: (*Walking towards the spectators*) "Their conviction was so profound that they were ready to die for it."

MIREILLE: "In their turn they were crucified. Decapitated, stoned."

CONSTANCE: "They remained unshakeable: Jesus had conquered death and He awaited them in his kingdom."

MIREILLE: "They incarnated hope. The feeling at once the most irrational and the most impossible to destroy. The mystery of hope, which makes life bearable, lost in an enigmatic universe."

The actors move among the spectators to return to the stairway at the entrance.

CONSTANCE: (*To an attentive spectator*) Each person must decide for himself when the moment has arrived and which road leads to salvation. Ask no one other than yourself. You must believe in yourself with humility and courage.

MARTIN: (*To some spectators*) Mend the rifts, cross the barriers which exist between you and others. (*To Leclerc*) Love, fear, beg, walk with them.

He passes Father Leclerc, who turns and follows him with his eyes. René is also walking in the midst of the spectators.

RENE: Basically, our life is very simple. It only becomes an insurmountable obstacle when you think of nothing but yourself. (*He has stopped between Garibaldi and Malouin*) From the moment you no longer think about yourself, and instead ask how you can help others, life becomes perfectly simple.

Constance walks between Cardinal and Miroir, touching Miroir's arm.

CONSTANCE: "Jesus is alive, we have seen him."

The actors (except for Daniel) regroup at the top of the stairs. The light is soft. They address themselves to everyone.

MIREILLE: Love one another!

RENE: Seek salvation in yourselves!

ALL THE ACTORS: May peace be with you and may your spirits be at peace!

The reflectors dim. A moment of darkness. Then Daniel opens the door and comes down the stairs. The light comes in from the outside and surrounds them with a halo. A celestial puff of smoke drifts across the scene. In the midst of the applause and the bravos the actors wave. Gabriel is seen wiping a tear between two rounds of applause. Malouin, Miroir, and Cardinal are all clapping. Leclerc, somber, doesn't move.

25. Way of the Cross on the Mountain. Exterior. Night.

Outside, after the show, the critics rush up to the actors.

GARIBALDI: (*His handkerchief in his hand, his arms extended*) My God! . . .

MALOUIN: It's beautiful. It's rich. It's strong. It's so strong.

MIROIR: (*Taking Daniel's hand in his*) I myself, I'm telling you, I'll tell you right away: I like it . . . a lot. This show is irresistible!

DANIEL: Thank you.

MALOUIN: You absolutely must appear on my show.

GARIBALDI: (*To René and Martin*) Oh, it's b . . . it's . . . it's beautiful, it's beautiful! But where do you two come from? This is the first time I've seen you!

MARTIN: Oh . . . well . . . we've done a lot underground.

GARIBALDI: Oh?

MARTIN: And then . . . a little bit of searching . . .

RENE: That's it. Alternative things.

GARIBALDI: Yes, but now, get out of that. Get out! With your talent! That . . . that is . . .

MARTIN: That's it.

RENE: That's for sure.

LAMBERT: (*To Mireille*) You surprise me, Mireille. You surprise me.

MIREILLE: (*Raising her veil*) You wouldn't have believed it, would you?

LAMBERT: In all honesty, no. It's magnificent. (*He turns towards Constance, goes and embraces her*) Bravo.

CONSTANCE: Thank you. You're really John Lambert, that's who . . . ?

Lambert nods and smiles.

CONSTANCE: It's just that it's strange to see you like this, in person.

LAMBERT: I hope we'll work together some day.

CONSTANCE: Uhh . . . yes, of course.

He moves off. Constance pulls back her veil, smiles, obviously delighted.

GARIBALDI: (*To Daniel*) Oh, oh, you there, you, you made me cry!

MIROIR: Encore!

GARIBALDI: It is so involving. It's . . . You are the best actor of your generation. Yes, I think so!

MALOUIN: (*To Cardinal*) It's wonderful, don't you think so?

CARDINAL: Oh yes. Especially with a subject like that.

ZABOU: It's a beautiful subject, that's what I think.

CARDINAL: Yes, but my dear, we've already seen it before.

ZABOU: It was my first time.

Near the entrance of the grotto. Slightly back.

LAMBERT: I find it fascinating, taking chances like that. Acting out the Passion on the mountain is completely crazy. That's what I want to do, things like that.

DANIEL: I could write in a part for you if you like.

LAMBERT: It's so complicated! I have a contract with American television for at least two more years. I have to be there three days a week. I just bought myself a condo in New York.

DANIEL: Where?

LAMBERT: Chelsea. I paid a fortune for it. And down there, now, I'm making a mini-series . . .

The Pommerleau twins appear.

TWIN: Hey, John, you promised to take us to the Metropolis!

LAMBERT: Walk around here for a bit. Go look at the view of the city, it's beautiful.

TWIN II: We've already seen the city, John.

LAMBERT: I'll be there in two minutes. (*To Daniel*) That's it, a mini-series, international, for three or four television networks. It's about the great Franco-American families. I couldn't turn it down: my divorce isn't settled yet. My wife's lawyer is asking for half of everything I earned during the five years of our marriage . . . Basically, I'd like to work for nothing, with you, here, like this. (*A silence*) We'll have to talk again about all this, right?

DANIEL: Whenever you want, John.

LAMBERT: (*He consults his pocket diary*) I'm in New York next week, then I come back here but I go back to the studio for twelve days. I should have a space after that. I'll phone you and we'll go out to eat, okay?

DANIEL: Okay.

LAMBERT: It seems to me we should have something to say to each other.

Denise Quintal is trying to drag along Pascal Berger.

QUINTAL: Just the same, we could say hello, couldn't we?

BERGER: Oh no, I find that kind of thing boring.

QUINTAL: But you know him, don't you, the guy who produced it? Isn't he one of your friends?

BERGER: (*He shrugs his shoulders*) Yes, yes.

QUINTAL: Listen, it won't be so bad. We could at least act like we're here.

BERGER: No, it's not that. I don't feel like talking, that's all. All right, I'm going to get going.

QUINTAL: I don't know what's wrong with you, honey.

Further off, Ariel, Aurore, and the Esoterics are with René and Martin.

ARIEL: (*With a knowing look reinforced by Aurore, who is watching*) If you are performing on a mountain, it's not by chance.

RENE: Oh no?

ARIEL: It was on a mountain that Moses received the ten commandments. Ten, exactly two tablets, five and five.

AURORE: The bible is a code. You have to pay attention to the numbers.

ARIEL: 666!

MARTIN: (*Having trouble keeping himself from laughing*) What?

ARIEL: They talk about it in Apocalypse. 666.

AURORE: 666. The sign of the beast.

ARIEL: Credit card companies use it more and more often, the code 666.

MARTIN: And so . . .

AURORE: That's what AIDS is. It's manufactured in American laboratories.

RENE: (*Voice off*) Oh great.

AURORE: It's like the formula for Coca Cola Classic. They've added things to it, but what?

Martin and René shake their heads.

AURORE: You have to be aware.

ARIEL: (*Very seriously, looking at the sky*) It snowed on Rome . . .

MARTIN: (*A pause*) Pardon?

ARIEL: (*Emphasising the words, and looking back and forth from René to Martin*) It snowed on Rome.

Martin and René try to control their reaction.

AURORE: The astronauts know it, that the moon is hollow, but they can't talk.

MARTIN: Of course.

René has hidden the bottom of the face with his costume.

AURORE: Jesus is so gentle, so positive.

MARTIN: You've had occasion to meet him, obviously . . .

AURORE: Often.

RENE: Great.

ARIEL: Have you been contacted?

MARTIN: Not personally, no.

26. Basement of the Sanctuary. Interior. Night.

In the big vaulted room, Daniel slowly comes down the stairs. The torches throw a last dying light. Daniel and Leclerc face each other, from a distance.

DANIEL: Did you like it?

LECLERC: Are you completely mad?

DANIEL: What?

LECLERC: Jesus Christ the bastard son of a Roman soldier! The Virgin Mary, a teen-age mother! Are you all sick?

DANIEL: In the Gospels . . .

LECLERC: You can make the Gospels say whatever you like. I know it, through my own experience. There are lots of fascists who take communion every day, communists who recite the Sermon on the Mount. As for myself, I belong to a Catholic order. This sanctuary has an administrative council. High class people. You get the picture.

DANIEL: But it's working! People are coming!

LECLERC: But I don't want it to work. This sanctuary attracts two million visitors a year. We don't need publicity.

DANIEL: But it was you who asked me . . .

LECLERC: (*He comes gradually closer*) Oh! I asked you to freshen up a text that had worked very well for forty years! I didn't ask you for *this*!

DANIEL: And what are you going to do?

LECLERC: (*He moves back*) I have to . . . speak about it to my superiors. I can't take the responsibility myself. That would be . . . that would be too risky.

DANIEL: Speak to them. Then we'll see.

LECLERC: I'm afraid that reaction might not be as enthusiastic as that of your friends.

Daniel goes quickly up the stairs.

27. Terrace of the Chalet on the Mountain. Exterior. Night.

Daniel, Mireille, Martin, and René are walking, their arms around each other's waists. They are all drinking wine from the same bottle. They are a bit drunk, they joke, except for Daniel, who seems worried.

CONSTANCE: (*Turns to face everyone, excited*) So! John Lambert kissed me!

MARTIN: Woo—oo.

CONSTANCE: Yes, right on the cheek!

MARTIN: He's so handsome, that John Lambert, he is handsome, he is handsome.

RENE: His eyes are so blue.

MIREILLE: He told me that I had really surprised him.

CONSTANCE: He told me he could hardly wait for us to work together!

MARTIN: I was told that I had a very physical presence!

MIREILLE: Physical?

MARTIN: Very physical!

RENE: And I absolutely *must* be on television. I was asked by a television hostess who is extremely famous.

MIREILLE: And . . . middle-aged!

RENE: Jea-l-ous!

> **MIREILLE:** (*After taking a swallow of wine from the bottle. To Daniel*) And our little one? What did the ladies say to our little Jesus?
>
> **RENE:** Jesus is looking gloomy.
>
> **MIREILLE:** (*Offering him the bottle*) You're making a little face!
>
> **DANIEL:** I just hope that it's going to last.
>
> **CONSTANCE:** (*Turns his face, takes him by the neck*) Hey fathead! Whether or not it lasts, tonight we're happy and that's something special.
>
> **DANIEL:** All right! All right, all right, all right.
>
> **CONSTANCE:** Right!
>
> **ALL:** Right!

They lean on the stone balustrade and look out at the city. We see images of the city, the night, all luminous and vibrating beneath a full moon which is at the height of the tops of the skyscrapers.

28. Radio Studio. Television Studio. Interior. Day.

France Garibaldi is sitting at a table in front of a microphone. She is wearing earphones. Behind her, through a window which takes up the whole wall, a street filled with heavy automobile traffic. On the table: a big purse, orange peels, bananas. At a signal given to her by someone off-screen, she exhales a cloud of smoke and stubs out her cigarette. RAPID MONTAGE *of views of this studio, as well as the one where Malouin and Miroir work. The latter is in the "cultural programming" style. Their voices mix together.*

> **GARIBALDI:** So the word is out: *the* show of the summer in Montreal is indeed the Passion being played on the mountain. And the young director of the hour is . . . is Daniel Coulombe!
>
> **MIROIR:** Daniel Coulombe is first of all a first-prize prize winner at the conservatory . . .

GARIBALDI: Self-taught, this young man never went to a theater school . . .

MIROIR: . . . One of the most brilliant students in the acting classes . . .

GARIBALDI: . . . My God, who spent his youth traveling all around the world . . .

MIROIR: . . . who has always lived here in Montreal, unnoticed . . .

GARIBALDI: . . . and who only came back a few months ago . . .

MIROIR: . . . in . . . in the "underground". . . (*He puts this word in quotation marks with his fingers*).

GARIBALDI: . . . and to whom this show was assigned almost by chance . . .

MIROIR: . . . who has been working on this Passion for several years . . .

GARIBALDI: . . . and who has shown himself to be *the* new Montreal showbiz personality.

MALOUIN: On our scale of one to ten?

MIROIR: Eight and a half.

GARIBALDI: (*Moved*) It's a show . . .

MIROIR: . . . that questions us profoundly . . .

GARIBALDI: . . . gripping!

MIROIR: . . . never falters!

GARIBALDI: . . . tears in my eyes, from beginning to end . . . It's . . . (*She looks at someone offscreen*) That's all.

MALOUIN: This show is a *must*. I have to say it. (*A pause. She turns towards the right. Then to the camera*) So, after the commercial break we'll be back with Therese Gendron-Frappier who has read the book of the summer for us: the memoirs of Pierre-Elliot Trudeau. Right back. (*She keeps her smile fixed for five seconds, then suddenly stops smiling*) Will that do for now?

29. Constance's Loft. Interior. Day.

At Constance's place, Daniel is taking a bath in the bathroom. His head suddenly emerges from the water. Mireille is beside the bathtub, her arms on the rim.

MIREILLE: Say, are you doing anything special this morning?

DANIEL: No. Why?

MIREILLE: (*Her hands moving in the bath bubbles*) Well, I was wondering if you would do me a favor. I would like you to come with me.

DANIEL: Where?

MIREILLE: I have to do an audition for a commercial.

DANIEL: You're going to keep doing that?

Mireille (Catherine Wilkening) tells Daniel (Lothaire Bluteau) she's going to audition for a commercial. "This is the last time . . . It'll bring in some money. I can't keep living like this."

MIREILLE: Yeah, this is the last time, I promised to go. And then I'm almost certain I'll get the part. (*She has started to soap his chest*) And then it'll bring in some money. I want to rent myself an apartment. I can't keep living like this, sponging off Constance. (*She soaps his back*) Only . . . Jerzy is going to be the producer. He'll be there and I don't want to be alone with him.

DANIEL: What sort of thing is it?

MIREILLE: It's a campaign for a new beer.

DANIEL: Yi! Yi! Yi!

MIREILLE: Exactly.

Constance comes in carrying her daughter.

CONSTANCE: Haven't you two finished playing in my bath? (*To her daughter*) Okay. We're going to the daycare.

Rosalie kisses Mireille.

ROSALIE: Bye!

She also kisses Daniel, who roars like a lion.

30. Theater, Room, Stage. Interior. Day.

In the theater where Berger was acting at the beginning, about twenty young men and women are waiting, seated, standing, scattered about the room. The big windows are filled with light. Jerzy arrives. He speaks to and kisses (or gives a sign or friendship if it's a boy) several of them.

JERZY: Greetings, Monique. You're well? You have news? . . . Ah, the golden voices! (*He is in front of the soprano and contralto who were singing the "Stabat Mater" at the Sanctuary*) Christine! Hi Valerie, have we gargled yet? . . . How's it going, Brian . . . (*He bows to an Asian woman*) . . . Hi, Pete, still working out? . . . Good. . . . Hello Rachel! Oh, oh, mustn't lose your tan, we'll be seeing you in your bikini.

Mireille and Daniel are standing in a corner. Jerzy Strelisky comes to them.

JERZY: I didn't expect to see you here, sweetie pie.

MIREILLE: Oh no? Why?

JERZY: I thought you had renounced worldly things and devoted yourself to your mystical theater. In fact I'm surprised not to see you with a halo.

MIREILLE: Is that right? Does your sister have haloes?

JERZY: (*To Daniel*) Did you also come for the audition? I don't think it's your kind of thing.

DANIEL: No, I just came to keep her company.

JERZY: Oh yes? Do you always travel in pairs, like Jehovah's Witnesses? It's better that way. It's more sensible. (*He turns abruptly towards the other actors and actresses and starts to move among them*) Good. Everybody listen. This is for a new beer called Appalachia. Appalachia is the beer for young people, the beer for people who know. Golden Voices, it will be your turn soon. Bob, we're not in the gym if you don't mind. I repeat: Appalachia is an *in* beer. Okay? I want it with a beat, with energy. The concept is dynamite. It takes place in a theater, it's young people who want to become stars, so make it groovy, funky. We start in ten minutes. Thank you.

31. Inside, On Stage.

The set for Smerdiakov's room is still in place. But the props have been pushed back to leave the dancers room. The contralto in the bikini lip-syncs and dances accompanied by a young male dancer-singer who is bare-chested but has kept on his jeans. Music is heavy rock.

GIRL'S VOICE: "It came to me in a flash
I know what you've got in your stash
So don't be mean
Share your Appalachia with me."

In the first row, in front of the armchairs, is a table behind which are sitting Jerzy Strelisky, Denise Quintal, and the five men from the agency and the brewery. The actors and actresses are scattered in the back rows.

YOUNG MAN'S VOICE: "Oh you want to be proud
Of the beer you drink
So I won't be mean
Have an Appalachia on me."

CHOIR: "We are young and proud
And we love our beer
Nothing holds us back
We drink Appalachia here."

QUICK SHOTS *of the men from the agency and brewery. They are attentive, cynical or amused.* SHOT *of Daniel and Mireille. He is serious, she glances at him.*

GIRL'S VOICE: "Don't wanna hear about bombs
Don't wanna hear about money
Don't wanna hear about tombs
Just talk Appalachia, honey."

YOUNG MAN'S VOICE: "There's nothing you want to know
There's nothing you want to hear
So long as we don't hide
That Appalachia beer."

SHOTS *of soprano singing and dancing, in the wings, wearing a bathing suit.*

CHOIR: "We are young and proud
And we love our beer
Nothing holds us back
We drink Appalachia here."

The music stops.

SOPRANO: (*In a speaking voice*) "Appalachia: the young people's beer!"

JERZY: Thank you very much!

QUINTAL: Next: Mireille Fontaine and Greg Roberts.

Mireille leaves her bench.

QUINTAL: You, young man, have I seen your legs?

SOPRANO: (*Approaching Quintal, she clutches her clothes to her chest*) If you want I could sing myself, I mean with my voice: I studied at the conservatory.

QUINTAL: Young lady, the average beer drinker has an IQ more or less equal to that of a performing dog. (*A man from the brewery nods approvingly behind her*) In fact, ten points less and he would be a geranium. So, we're not going to seduce him with Maria Callas. (*The man from the brewery whispers something in her ear*) In fact, you'd be better off betting on your bikini than on your voice.

Shocked, the contralto moves off quickly, walking in front of the clients who give each other knowing smiles. On the stage, Greg, the young actor, has taken off his jeans to show his legs, while behind him Mireille and the chorister wait.

GREG: Okay?

QUINTAL: (*Sighs*) Okay.

MIREILLE: (*Coming forward*) I'm very sorry, but I don't have a bikini.

QUINTAL: Wasn't it on the call sheet?

MIREILLE: I know, but I forgot.

JERZY: All right, take off your jeans.

MIREILLE: I have to?

QUINTAL: Absolutely, my dear. There's nothing like tailored jeans for hiding those rolls of cellulite.

The men laugh. Mireille undoes her jeans and goes towards backstage. The men look about like voyeurs. The one who is always chewing slows down. Daniel, appalled, looks at Fabienne.

FABIENNE: Relax, Max, it's always like that.

Mireille comes back to the front of the stage, her legs bare.

QUINTAL: The sweat shirt, too.

MIREILLE: I don't have anything underneath.

JERZY: You should have thought of that.

MIREILLE: Don't be an ass, Jerzy. You know how I'm built.

JERZY: That was such a long time ago, sweetie pie. Maybe it would be better if you could refresh my memory.

QUINTAL: It's not Jerzy who is the client, it's them. (*Pointing to the men*) And they would like to see.

Mireille starts to take off her sweatshirt. Daniel comes forward quickly. He stops in front of the table at the bottom of the small stairway leading to the stage.

DANIEL: Mireille, don't do it.

MIREILLE: It's not so serious.

DANIEL: Don't do that, okay?

MIREILLE: I'm used to it.

DANIEL: You're worth more than that.

MIREILLE: What do you know about that?

DANIEL: Come on, we're going.

QUINTAL: Great, you can do the big lovers' quarrel for us another day. We're here to work. (*To Daniel*) So you, you go sit down again at the back. (*To Mireille*) And you, you either show us your boobs or you go home. Okay?

Daniel doesn't move. He becomes livid. His voice is angry.

DANIEL: If you don't mind, I'll do a scene for you?

Quintal, unruffled, looks at him. Very calmly Daniel turns over a table at the foot of the stage, covered with props. Jerzy, dumbfounded, leaps up. Daniel gives the tripod of the video camera a big kick. It lands on the first row of chairs and gives off a shower of sparks.

JERZY: All right! All right! Let's stay cool.

Daniel pulls the camera from the row of chairs and knocks it onto the floor. New shower of sparks. Meanwhile Jerzy leads the men towards the exit.

JERZY: Gentlemen!

Daniel unplugs the wires from a television monitor on another table. He knocks it over. He keeps the wires in his hand. Quintal stands up calmly.

QUINTAL: Little actor's tantrums, I've seen them before.

Daniel hits Quintal in the face with the connecting wires. She falls. He goes towards the back of the room while Mireille, dumbfounded, takes two steps towards him. Jerzy is out in the hall, with the men who are putting on their jackets.

JERZY: He's emotionally disturbed. I've had them sometimes when I'm shooting. Don't worry, he'll calm down.

DANIEL: (*Voice off*) Out!

JERZY: (*Leading the clients*) All right, shall we go?

32. The Theater Door. Exterior. Day.

They rush out from the theater. Daniel chases after them, running and shouting.

    DANIEL: Out!

Jerzy and the men go quickly onto the sidewalk. Daniel, in his turn, appears at the door.

    DANIEL: Dogs!

Mireille joins him, her legs still bare.

    MIREILLE: Oh!

She takes him by the jacket, pushes him against the wall. They look into each other's eyes. Daniel becomes calm.

    MIREILLE: I love you, you crazy nut.

She kisses him on the cheek. For a long time they look at each other, smiling.

33. Way of the Cross on the Mountain. Exterior. Night.

VIEWS *of the Sanctuary, the night. The rock music which accompanied Mireille's kiss continues with these images.*

    DANIEL: (*Voice off*) You were told not to perjure yourself. Now I say to you that you should not swear at all. That you should say yes when you mean yes, no when you mean no. Adding anything more just makes it worthless.

Daniel walks in front of the spectators, dressed in his white tunic.

    DANIEL: Woe betide the legislators because you have given the people burdens they cannot bear while you yourselves don't lift a single finger.

Daniel moves briefly by some husky men wearing coats and ties: Francois Bastien and Marcel Brochu. As soon as Daniel is past, Bastien signals Brochu, who moves off.

    DANIEL: Do not trust priests who enjoy going about in long robes, being greeted in public places, occupying the highest places in the temples and the best seats at banquets, who devour the inheritances of widows and affect long prayers. Their punishment will be more severe.

Daniel stops in front of Father Leclerc, who has a grey-suited priest on either side of him.

DANIEL: He who would stand out among you should be your servant, he who would be first among you should be your slave! (*He turns back to the other spectators*) Don't have yourself called "Rabbi" or "my Reverend Father" or Monsignor" or "Eminence" because you have only one master and He is in heaven while you are all brothers!

Daniel moves off. The two priests cast looks at Father Leclerc, who doesn't move.

MIREILLE: (*Her forehead and ears ornamented with jewels*) "At the end of his life, those who were eager to see him crucified were very numerous and very powerful."

Daniel plays his big scene. "At the end of his life, those who were eager to see him crucified were very numerous and very powerful."

34. At the Twelfth Station.

Daniel is on the cross. Bastien and Brochu are standing at the foot of the cross. Daniel is not moving, he seems dead. Bastien taps him gently on the knee.

    BASTIEN: Daniel Coulombe?

Daniel slowly raises his head, as though he were emerging from a dream.

    BASTIEN: Excuse me, sir. I am Detective Sergeant Francois Bastien, from the Urban Community of Montreal. And this is my partner, Marcel Brochu.

    BROCHU: Good evening.

    DANIEL: Good evening.

    BASTIEN: We're going to ask you to follow us please. But first I'll read you your rights.

He searches in his pockets.

    BASTIEN: Christ, I've forgotten it again. (*To Brochu*) Take it from yours.

Brochu takes a plasticized card from his pocket and reads.

    BROCHU: Daniel Coulombe, you are suspected of . . .

Daniel starts to free himself of the cords holding him to the cross.

    BASTIEN: . . . threats, assault, bodily harm, and . . . vandalism causing about one hundred and ten thousand dollars damage.

Daniel takes off the sign he has on his chest, gives it to Bastien. He frees his right arm.

    BROCHU: (*He reads*) "As soon as you arrive at the place of detention you have the right to avail yourself of the services of a lawyer. You are not obliged to say anything but anything you say can be used in court. You must understand that you have no grounds for hope from any promise of preferential treatment, nor anything to fear from any threat intended to induce you to make a confession or declaration."

Bastien extends his arms to Daniel so he can come down from the cross. Daniel accepts, then leaps to the ground.

BASTIEN: Are you all right?

DANIEL: I'm okay. Do I have time to take off my make-up?

BASTIEN: Of course. But we'll have to follow the regulations.

Bastien nods his head to Brochu, who takes the handcuffs from his belt and uses them to attach Daniel's wrists behind his back.

BROCHU: (*Behind Daniel*) I'd like to take this chance to congratulate you: I like the show very much.

DANIEL: Thank you.

BROCHU: Just the same, it's the kind of thing that makes you think. (*To Bastien*) I would have liked to see how it ended.

DANIEL: You'll come back.

BROCHU: (*Extremely dubious*) Yes . . .

Brochu leads Daniel away. Bastien, who was still holding the sign, hangs it on the cross, then takes out a handkerchief and wipes his hands.

35. Basement of the Sanctuary. Interior. Night.

In the vaulted room, at the top of the stairway, in the bluish light and through the screen of smoke, Mireille, Constance, Martin, and René acknowledge the applause. Now and then one at a time, they turn towards the door. Daniel does not appear.

36. Court. Courtroom. Psychologist's Office. Windowed Corridor. Interior. Day.

Daniel comes into the courtroom, behind a uniformed policeman. He waves to Mireille and Constance, who are sitting beside Cardinal. It is a modern courtroom, quite small. In front, the Judge's platform is raised only a few centimeters; in front of him, two court clerks search through piles of documents. On the left side of the platform, two lawyers for the Crown, a man and a woman. They are very young and they, also, are searching through their documents. On the right side, the defence lawyers take their papers out of their briefcases, consult their schedules, and gossip. The atmosphere is relaxed.

FIRST CLERK: Number 25, Daniel Coulombe.

DANIEL: (*Rising*) That's me.

Richard Cardinal gets up and approaches the platform.

CARDINAL: Your Honour, if you please, I am a lawyer and my name is Richard Cardinal. May I speak with the accused for a moment?

JUDGE: (*Calmly, glancing at his watch*) All right, but be quick. There are sixty cases this morning.

CARDINAL: Oh . . . thank you.

Cardinal approaches Daniel. They whisper.

CARDINAL: It was Mireille who asked me to come. Let me represent you.

DANIEL: It isn't necessary. I thank you.

CARDINAL: The accusations are very serious. You could get an unpleasant surprise.

DANIEL: I don't need anyone.

CARDINAL: Are you sure?

DANIEL: Yes.

CARDINAL: It's dangerous.

Daniel turns his head away. Cardinal moves off.

CARDINAL: Thank you, your Honour.

Cardinal goes back to sit beside Mireille and Constance.

JUDGE: Do you wish to assume your own defence?

DANIEL: Oh, I have no defence.

JUDGE: You know you have a right to legal aid.

DANIEL: You are very kind, but I don't need it. I plead guilty.

A pause. The Judge smiles.

JUDGE: Good. So we'll start by having you see the psychologist. (*To the clerk*) Could you call Madame de Villers, please? (*To Daniel*) All right, you can sit down.

Daniel sits down, looks calmly around the courtroom.

CARDINAL: (*To Mireille and Constance*) This could take quite a while, there's no point staying here. My office isn't far, I'll ask them to keep me advised.

He gets up. Mireille, worried, looks at Constance. They also rise. In the office of the psychologist, where tall buildings can be seen through the big windows, Daniel is sitting down. The psychologist paces while she talks with him.

DE VILLERS: How do you feel about your work?

DANIEL: Good.

DE VILLERS: But what I mean, the fact of being obliged to perform the "The Way of the Cross" on the Mountain — don't you find that a bit ridiculous?

DANIEL: No, it's a good subject. It's not very original, but that . . .

DE VILLERS: (*Sitting down at her desk*) Yes, but . . . in the end, for an actor . . . it's a bit pitiful as a job, don't you think?

DANIEL: For an actor, playing Jesus is anything but pitiful.

DE VILLERS: Just the same, you came first at the conservatory. Wouldn't you like to have a good career? Play in the big theaters?

DANIEL: I was away for a long time, so it's fairly normal to start out again at the bottom of the ladder.

DE VILLERS: Are you outraged by commercials?

DANIEL: (*He thinks*) What made me angry was the way

those people were treating the actors, and especially the actresses. I was with an actress friend I like a lot.

DE VILLERS: Do you often have fits of rage like that?

DANIEL: Never. Rarely. But I find contempt hard to take.

DE VILLERS: (*Rises, comes to lean on her desk in front of him*) Do you . . . do you regret having been born here?

DANIEL: What do you mean?

DE VILLERS: Oh, I don't know, if you had been born in, say, Santa Barbara in California, you could act in Hollywood movies. Or if you had been born in New York, or London . . . even in Stockholm you could have met Ingmar Bergman. But here, there's not much, is there?

DANIEL: Yeah. It's definitely a disadvantage. But all right, there's not much I can do about it. And then, it could have been worse: I could have come into the world in Burkina-Faso.

De Villers bursts out laughing. Return to the courtroom. It feels like the end of the day. Daniel is standing in the box, beside him are others who have been charged. Richard Cardinal is sitting in the courtroom, with Zabou Johnson.

JUDGE: Good. So I presume you do not have the money to replace the electronic equipment you destroyed?

DANIEL: No.

JUDGE: All right. I am going to consider your sentence. Then a date will be established, a date upon which it is absolutely necessary that you return here without fail. But *without fail*.

DANIEL: Without fail.

37. Windowed Corridor near the Top of a Downtown Building. Interior. Day.

Daniel, Zabou, and Cardinal are walking slowly, sometimes stopping by a window from which the city can be seen by the light of a fine summer day.

CARDINAL: No, I am a lawyer, but I think this is the first time in five years that I've set foot in a court.

DANIEL: What do you usually do?

CARDINAL: Almost all my clients, in fact I should say my friends, are in the media, showbusiness, literary circles. So I do contracts, financial planning, investments. In certain cases it could even include career planning.

DANIEL: What is a career plan?

CARDINAL: Oh, that's something I do, let's say, with someone who is still relatively young, but doesn't know exactly how to exploit his talent. So we sit down together and then we try to see exactly what he wants to do; in fact, we try to define his dreams. And next, we figure out the steps to be taken for them to come true.

DANIEL: Does it work?

CARDINAL: (*Pointing at the Hochelaga neighborhood*) I know an actress who was born down there in the workers' district and who lives now in Malibu Beach. (*They have stopped in front of a window and are leaning on the sill*) I could name others who came from Quebec or Saint-Raymond-de-Portneuf and who have houses in Paris or lofts in New York.

A man passes, three piece-suit, grey hair, in a hurry. Cardinal shakes his hand and greets him as though he knows him well. Then Daniel and Cardinal begin walking again.

DANIEL: To get all that, what do you have to do?

CARDINAL: Nothing special. What you like doing.

DANIEL: Even acting "The Way of the Cross" at the Sanctuary?

CARDINAL: Right now Jesus Christ is a very fashionable character. But you would have to be in the studio tomorrow morning to be on the cultural programs this weekend.

DANIEL: Except for one, I don't think I've been invited.

CARDINAL: I could make two or three phone calls if you

like. It's never so complicated: there is more space on the media than there are people with something to say.

DANIEL: I don't have that much to say myself, you know.

CARDINAL: It's not really essential. You are a very good actor.

DANIEL: An actor needs a script.

CARDINAL: We could write you some notes. There's a way of saying insignificant things that is extremely popular. Think of Ronald Reagan. And there are others. In every country, now, actors are all over the place. Television, radio, magazines. Everywhere you look, there is nothing but actors.

ZABOU: There are also actresses. There's Jane Fonda.

CARDINAL: So long as they are pretty. But that should never worry you, sweetheart (*He kisses her hair*).

ZABOU: He's an ass sometimes! (*She frees herself and moves off*).

CARDINAL: (*Sotto voce to Daniel*) Seventeen years old! (*To someone passing by whose hand he shakes, spoken quickly*) I'll call you back. (*To Daniel*) Did you ever think of publishing a book?

DANIEL: Do you mean a novel?

CARDINAL: Yes, or a book of memoirs. Your travels, or your battle against drugs and alcohol. Whatever.

They are stopped at the place where the corridor turns. The city can still be seen stretching out behind them.

DANIEL: I'm not a writer.

CARDINAL: I didn't say *write* a book, I said *publish*. The publishing houses have lots of writers available. Talented and poor.

DANIEL: Obviously.

CARDINAL: Does that shock you?

DANIEL: No.

> **CARDINAL:** (*Leaning towards him, in a confidential tone*) I'm just trying to make you understand that with your talent, this city could be yours, if you want it (*They turn their heads towards the downtown, which is shown through the window*).

38. Glassed-in Restaurant, on the Same Floor. Interior. Day.

Zabou, Daniel, and Cardinal go into the restaurant, Chez Charon, at the end of the corridor. The headwaiter greets them.

> **ZABOU:** (*Shaking his hand*) Hello Julien.
>
> **JULIEN:** Good day Madame, Mister Cardinal . . .
>
> **CARDINAL:** (*Shaking his hand*) Julien . . .
>
> **JULIEN:** (*Inviting them to come in, with a nod to Daniel*) Please . . .

Everyone enters.

> **JULIEN:** We've prepared a table for you, it will be ready in two minutes. Can I offer you an aperitif?
>
> **CARDINAL:** Yes, three Virgin Marys.
>
> **JULIEN:** (*Handing them the menus*) Three Virgin Marys. I suggest the lobsters for lunch.
>
> **CARDINAL:** (*To Daniel*) Yes, have you tried the Iles-de-la-Madeleine lobsters this year?
>
> **DANIEL:** No.
>
> **CARDINAL:** They are sublime. We'll take that.

He takes the menus from Daniel and Zabou.

> **ZABOU:** I don't like lobsters.
>
> **CARDINAL:** Have the Matane shrimps.

Zabou moves away.

> **CARDINAL:** (*To Daniel*) Does it . . . does it make you unhappy to be here?

DANIEL: Here? Why?

CARDINAL: Well, I don't know, eating lobsters while there are other people who are eating hot dogs or who go hungry (*Pointing to the city below them*).

DANIEL: Perhaps if I ate here every day, I . . .

CARDINAL: No, I say that to you because there are always charitable organizations, you know, like OXFAM, UNICEF, Doctors without Frontiers, who are looking for spokespersons. It's of interest because it allows you to do good while assuring yourself of maximum exposure. Or just your head, on vinegar bottles, like Paul Newman. That's a stroke of genius!

DANIEL: I'm no gourmet.

CARDINAL: Neither is Newman, no doubt, but it's too bad — you could have brought out a book of recipes, that's almost always guaranteed to be successful.

39. *The Sanctuary through the Trees. First Station. Exterior. Day.*

Constance, René, Martin, and Mireille are standing in front of Leclerc. They seem skeptical and a bit disoriented. Leclerc is handing out copies of the script of the former Passion.

LECLERC: The authorities from the Sanctuary who have seen the performance are demanding considerable modifications. Be assured that I pleaded your cause as energetically as possible, but without much success. Note that there is no question of censuring you. You could have mounted the same production in a downtown theater and there would have been no problem. But you are here in the private grounds of a Catholic sanctuary, and that imposes certain restrictions. (*He comes down a few steps, leans against the stone rail*) So the compromise I'm proposing to you is that you use the old script that the actors used before. Constance is familiar with it, of course. It's clear that it is a more traditional kind of script. But it will allow you to keep working for the next few weeks, during which the whole situation can be clarified, because you understand that right now, as we're talking, we don't yet know when Daniel will return . . .

In the middle of this speech Daniel has appeared at the bend of a path, walking silently in the grass. Leclerc, whose back is to him, has of course not seen him. As he comes closer Daniel gives a small wave to the actors, whose faces immediately show their happiness to see him.

LECLERC: . . . and even then, that is going to cause some problems. So we'll do a quick reading, please. Just to get the picture. Go ahead, Constance.

CONSTANCE: (*Not very seriously*) "Here is the Son of God torn apart by our pleasures?"

LECLERC: Yes, yes, but just the same, with a bit of expression . . .

CONSTANCE: (*Violently*) "Here is the Son of God torn apart by our pleasures!"

LECLERC: (*Amused reproach*) Constance. Please.

Martin, René, and Mireille keep themselves from laughing.

MIREILLE: Like they do it at the Comedie Francaise, would you like that? After all, I'm here, might as well make take advantage of the opportunity.

She hands her script to René. He and Martin move off, leaving her more room. She goes behind the statue, reappears, her hand on her chest, very theatrical.

MIREILLE: "Our sins crush the trembling Lamb! Is that you, Concupiscence?"

RENE: Or there's "method acting," like they do in New York. (*With tics and hesitations, like Al Pacino*) "We attach him by the hands. We attach him by the feet . . . the feet! Who? . . . Who will attach. . . my fate to the wooden cross of the crucified one? Who? (*Shouting*) Well? Who?"

MARTIN: We could do it for you in Québècois if you'd prefer it. (*He, in turn, hands his script to René and goes behind the statue*) "Jesus Christ, here is the innocent Lamb, for God's sake! Killed by our impure desires! Holy Mary Mother of Christ this is crazy!"

RENE: "For sure, damn it!"

CONSTANCE: "Me, I've had it up to here!"

MIREILLE: "Me too! Shit!"

MARTIN: (*To Leclerc*) You don't like it that way? Too common? Not international enough? Japanese! Kabuki!

Martin and René assume "Japanese" positions: their knees bent, their arms waving, loud cries.

MARTIN: "Ho! Heeeere is the Lamb! Ho! Crucified by our desires! Hey! Hey! Ho! Ha!

Constance and Mireille push their eyes back with their hands and also cry out. Daniel performs hara-kiri behind Leclerc, which attracts his attention. He turns around, without reacting, and looks at Daniel on his knees. Then he climbs the stairs towards the actors.

LECLERC: (*Barely restrained anger*) Very funny, very amusing, you certainly have a lot of talent. (*He takes the scripts from their hands*) I wish you good luck. *Elsewhere.*

He goes into the Sanctuary. Daniel runs up the stairs, goes through the actors, and follows Leclerc into the Sanctuary. The black door slams.

40. Sanctuary. Interior. Day.

Leclerc crosses the nave, walking angrily. Daniel runs to join him.

DANIEL: We were having some fun! Shit! It's not so serious.

Leclerc stops abruptly and turns towards him.

LECLERC: Can you tell me exactly what you came here to do? Martin and René used to work, they had jobs. They've thrown it all over. Mireille, the other young girl, is completely ruined for doing commercials. And I am in an absolutely untenable position vis-à-vis my superiors. Constance doesn't even want to speak to me any more. By what right do you enjoy undermining the lives of those around you?

DANIEL: I didn't force anyone.

LECLERC: Are you completely unconscious? Is that what you're trying to tell me? I don't believe you. You're too smart.

He turns about and leaves quickly. Daniel catches up to him.

DANIEL: What would you like me to do?

Leclerc stops, thinks, takes a few steps.

LECLERC: Have you ever come here on Sundays when it's full? (*The lateral door opens and Constance comes in*) Have you seen the Haitian housekeepers, the Guatemalan refugees, the abandoned old people? (*He shows Daniel some crutches left at the foot of an altar*) Here you have a gathering of universal misery. These miserable people don't want to be informed of the latest archaeological discoveries in the Middle East, they want to be told that the Son of God loves them and is waiting for them.

DANIEL: But perhaps that's no reason to sell them a plastic Jesus from Taiwan or bottles of St. Joseph's oil for fifteen dollars each.

LECLERC: The Jesus costs less than a rock star poster, and are you sure the holy oil works less well than coke at twenty-five dollars a gram?

Leclerc walks towards a confessional.

LECLERC: There are many people who can't afford to pay for a Lacanian psychoanalysis.

He opens the confessional door.

LECLERC: So they come here to be told: go in peace, your sins have been forgiven. It does them good. A little. There is at least that. Here is where people touch bottom: loneliness, disease, madness. When you have just found out you have cancer of the intestine or that your child has leukemia, I don't know if you are familiar with our hospitals, but if you're looking for a bit of comfort, you're much better off coming here.

Constance approaches them.

CONSTANCE: Let us do the show one last night.

LECLERC: I can't. It's not up to me.

CONSTANCE: We've worked a lot, you know.

LECLERC: Yes, I do know! When I was your age I tried to stage *The Life of Galileo* at the big seminary. Can you imagine the scandal?

DANIEL: They got you in the end.

LECLERC: It's always that way. Institutions live longer than individuals. My father was a textile worker. He was a unionist. He lost his jobs, he was beaten by the police, he was put in prison. Sometimes he managed to obtain an extra dollar a month, a paid holiday, something. He struggled his whole life. Today those same factories belong to the Japanese and the weaving jobs are controlled by computers. Fifteen technicians produce more, and better, that two thousand workers did before. So what use were the sacrifices my father made?

DANIEL: He had faith.

LECLERC: (*He sits on a church bench*) Oh yes? He died poor and completely paranoiac. At the point where I am now, what I think is that the people who are right are those who live happily for as long as possible.

CONSTANCE: So long as they're happy.

DANIEL: (*He paces, enraged*) Well, life can't be just that: to wait for death as comfortably as possible. I am probably naive, but there must be something else. Look, everyone is here now. The spectators will arrive soon. We're going to play it one more time.

LECLERC: I can't give you the authorization.

DANIEL: (*He shouts*) All right. Then say you couldn't find us and that there was a misunderstanding. Figure something out.

Daniel moves off and exits. Constance comes up to Leclerc.

CONSTANCE: Raymond, what are you afraid of?

LECLERC: I'm afraid of being made chaplain of a retirement home in a Winnipeg suburb. I don't want to spend my winters in Winnipeg.

CONSTANCE: *(She ties his hands together with her scarf)* Leave all that behind, then come with us.

LECLERC: All my friends have left. All those who went into the seminary with me. Their new lives are even more miserable than mine. Even a bad priest is still a priest. If I'm no longer that, I'm no longer anything.

CONSTANCE: You'll be like me! Like everyone!

LECLERC: I'm disabled. I left my mother at nineteen to enter the order. I don't know how to live.

CONSTANCE: So learn!

LECLERC: I'm too old.

CONSTANCE: *(She undoes the scarf, gets up)* You weren't too old to make love to me.

She goes off.

LECLERC: If you leave, my life leaves.

CONSTANCE: *(Her voice echoes in the church)* It's you who want me to leave.

She moves away. He stays alone in the center of the church. The big door at the back of the Sanctuary slams behind Constance.

41. Pizzeria. Interior. Day.

The Italian restaurant owner, still just as surly, looks at Daniel.

ITALIAN: *(Sarcastic)* Still *all dressed*. That's the way you like it best.

DANIEL: It's more nourishing.

ITALIAN: There's still five of you? No one's left?

DANIEL: It's the last time I'm going to ask you for this.

ITALIAN: (*Sarcastic*) That's what you told me last time, too. (*Yelling*) Five medium all dressed!

EMPLOYEE: Five medium all dressed! Okay!

DANIEL: One day I'll pay you back.

ITALIAN: Perfect! I'll count on it to pay my taxes next year.

42. On the Mountain. Exterior. Day.

The sun is setting. First we see Bob Chalifoux, in uniform, making his rounds. At the curve of a path he discovers Daniel, René, Martin, Mireille, and Constance sitting on the grass, eating their pizzas and drinking wine. Behind them, the city.

MARTIN: Would you like a slice?

CHALIFOUX: What are you people doing here?

CONSTANCE: Do you want a slice (*She holds a piece of pizza out to him*)?

CHALIFOUX: No, thank you. Didn't they warn you?

DANIEL: About what?

CHALIFOUX: (*Embarrassed, he takes off his hat, scratches his skull*) Didn't Father Leclerc say anything to you?

They all look surprised.

MIREILLE: We didn't see him.

CHALIFOUX: Oh, well . . . that's very strange . . .

MARTIN: Why?

CHALIFOUX: Oh, nothing. Nothing.

He moves off.

CONSTANCE: But we could perform in a park.

MARTIN: We wouldn't be given permission.

MIREILLE: Aren't there any gardens anywhere?

RENE: They're always private. But maybe . . . (*To Daniel*) What do you think?

DANIEL: (*Depressed*) I don't know. We'll see.

A silence. They are all depressed. Mireille looks at them, then:

MIREILLE: So you're not happy? But you're not going to get depressed on us now! Oh! You don't know what all this means to me. When you came to get me I showed my ass to sell detergent or beer. And everyone was convinced, including the guy I was with, that this was the best thing I could do, given the quality of the ass in question. The worst thing is that I also was half convinced. You're the ones who saved me from that. You don't have the right to let me down. Don't you know how I used to be? My idea of paradise was the beach of Bora Bora. I never met any guys who didn't wear Rolex watches or drive BMWS. I didn't know there were still men whose first thought wasn't to jump on me.

MARTIN: That's just the thing I wanted to talk to you about (*Laughs*).

MIREILLE: (*Very moved*) No, but it's true. What we have is very precious, we have to keep going.

CONSTANCE: All right!

ALL: All right!

MIREILLE: (*Smiling*) All right.

43. In the Sanctuary. Interior. End of the Day.

The door opens and Chalifoux appears. The actors, in costume and made up, are walking towards the door. They are carrying the props for the show.

CHALIFOUX: (*Stops them*) Listen, I've just checked with the authorities, "The Way of the Cross" is canceled . . . Indefinitely. You should have been warned, I don't understand, there must have been a mistake.

CONSTANCE: The spectators are already here.

CHALIFOUX: All right, we'll tell them to go home, that's all . . . It's over. You can take off your costumes.

DANIEL: It's out of the question. We were hired to perform, we're going to perform.

CHALIFOUX: Telephone to the Superior. He'll tell you.

DANIEL: I don't know him. I've never seen him.

CHALIFOUX: Well, I work for him.

DANIEL: Me too. If he has something to tell me, let him come and say it to me himself. Let us by.

He pushes Chalifoux aside. The actors go out.

CHALIFOUX: Wait a second.

Martin and René push Chalifoux a bit.

MARTIN: Move over.

CHALIFOUX: You don't have the right to do whatever you want. You're not in your own house here.

The actors have exited. Chalifoux is desolate.

CHALIFOUX: Shit damn.

He turns to the altar, mechanically makes the sign of the cross, then goes into the sacristy.

44. Sanctuary Sacristy. Interior. Day.

Chalifoux closes the door behind him, puts his hat back on, goes up to a telephone, and dials a number.

45. Way of the Cross. Exterior. Night.

Twelfth station. Daniel is on the cross. At first we see the spectators who are attentively following the show. Fabienne is very visible in the first row.

CONSTANCE: (*Voice off*) "And after all that, the condemned man awaited his death. Imagine we are in the

Middle East . . . A stifling heat . . ."

MIREILLE: (*Voice off*) "The sun . . . the flies . . ."

Noise behind the spectators. They protest. A dozen security guards led by Bob Chalifoux appear behind the spectators. They make themselves a path through them, roughly pushing aside Pierre Bouchard and his wife. They put themselves between the players and the audience.

CHALIFOUX: (*Raising and extending his arms in a cross; behind him, Daniel with his arms extended in a cross; even further back, the lights of the city*) Ladies and gentlemen, we are obliged to stop the show for security reasons . . .

MARTIN: (*In a low voice, to Chalifoux*) We have twenty minutes to go, Chalifoux, give us a chance.

A guard pushes Martin back.

CHALIFOUX: I'm going to ask you to stay very calm and to move in this direction.

Bouchard and his wife look at each other. From Mireille, then Fabienne, looks filled with disappointment.

FABIENNE: You can't do that!

MIREILLE: (*Whose head now appears between the wide shoulders of two guards*) Don't pay any attention. We're going to continue the play.

CONSTANCE: Don't leave!

CHALIFOUX: (*Turning towards Constance and Mireille*) Be quiet.

CLAUDINE BOUCHARD: Let them finish.

CHALIFOUX: Listen, lady, I can't give you a reason. You've been told it's for security considerations. We wouldn't do this without good reason.

CLAUDINE BOUCHARD: All right, but we want to know the ending!

CHALIFOUX: But everyone knows the ending: he dies on the cross and afterwards he comes back to life! There you are! There's no mystery about it! You're not too smart, are you.

Mireille tries to push the guards aside in order to rush Chalifoux.

MIREILLE: Cretin!

She runs. Two guards grab her by the arms.

MIREILLE: Let me go! Let me go!

Bouchard calmly takes off his glasses.

CLAUDINE: (*Murmuring*) Pierre, don't be crazy.

Bouchard advances towards the guards. Fabienne decides to follow him, then a few of the spectators. The struggle begins.

CHALIFOUX: (*He tries to push back Bouchard*) Just a second!

WOMEN'S VOICES: All right, stop . . . Careful! Hey! . . .

Among the spectators, the men leave their female companions to join the skirmish, like in a western saloon. Fabienne struggles against a guard whom she is hammering with her fists.

FABIENNE: You can't do that! You don't have the right! They must be allowed to continue!

Scene of a general battle. There are no real blows struck, but a rather comical mix-up. A security guard still holds back Mireille. She struggles like a wildcat. Bouchard approaches them. He goes behind the guard and takes him in a stranglehold. Chalifoux appears behind them and hits Bouchard in the neck with his flashlight. Bouchard lets go, knocked dizzy. He shakes his head, turns around, looks at Chalifoux with that look big men get when they start to become angry. Chalifoux realizes he is going to have major problems. He steps back prudently. The women spectators, like a choir of gossips, yell their recriminations.

CHALIFOUX: That was a warning, that was! Just a warning!

Daniel turns on his cross. He looks frightened. Bouchard throws himself at Chalifoux like an American football player. He leans his shoulder into Chalifoux's belly and pushes with his feet. Daniel sees them coming at a run towards him from behind. He shouts.

DANIEL: Hey! Hey! Hey!

Bouchard and Chalifoux crash into Daniel's cross. The force of the collision takes the post out of the ground. Daniel has no time to leap. He falls head first and lies crushed beneath the cross. The battle stops immediately. There is silence. Mireille and Constance come up to Daniel and kneel.

MIREILLE: Daniel! Daniel!

Constance leaves, running, bumping into Fabienne as she passes her.

FABIENNE: But do something!

46. Telephone Booth on the Mountain. Exterior. Night.

Constance dials 911.

TELEPHONE OPERATOR: Vous avez rejoint le numéro d'urgence de la communauté urbaine de Montréal. Toutes nos lignes sont présentement occupées. You have reached the emergency number of the Montreal Urban Community. All of our lines are busy right now.

Constance taps her foot, despairing.

47. Way of the Cross. Twelfth Station. Exterior. Night.

The ambulance has arrived, its revolving spots lighting up the night. Daniel's head is fixed into position, on the stretcher, between two supports. The ambulance workers slide the stretcher inside the vehicle. Only a few spectators remain. Martin and René are still wearing their costumes. Constance has put her city clothes back on.

CONSTANCE: We'll go to the city hospital, all right, it's close.

FIRST AMBULANCE ATTENDANT: No, we can't. The Emergency is full. They just called us. We have to go down to Saint-Marc. All right?

Constance acquiesces. Mireille comes running up. She is in jeans and has Daniel's clothes with her.

MIREILLE: I brought his things.

She wants to get in.

FIRST AMBULANCE ATTENDANT: No, only one person is allowed to be with him.

MIREILLE: I have no money. I have no car. Shit.

FIRST AMBULANCE ATTENDANT: (*He resigns himself*) Oh, all right. Let's go.

Mireille gets in beside Constance. Martin and René are behind the ambulance, haggard.

MARTIN: Do we have to go with you? Will you phone us?

CONSTANCE: Yes, yes.

The first ambulance attendant gets in, closes the doors.

FIRST AMBULANCE ATTENDANT: Okay, we're off.

The ambulance leaves.

RENE: (*To Martin*) Remember I had a feeling about this? When I said it was dangerous to perform?

48. Saint-Marc Hospital Emergency. Exterior. Night.

The ambulance arrives with its revolving lights and its siren.

49. Emergency Corridor. Interior. Night.

The room is crowded, people are standing, sitting, in ordinary clothes or hospital garments. The ambulance workers enter pushing the stretcher on which Daniel is lying. Mireille and Constance accompany them. They approach the registry desk.

FIRST AMBULANCE ATTENDANT: Hello Claire!

RECEPTIONIST: Wow! Where did you pick that one up?

FIRST AMBULANCE ATTENDANT: He's an actor. That's makeup.

RECEPTIONIST: Oh. Put him on the bench there.

FIRST AMBULANCE ATTENDANT: No, I can't move him, it's his head. It's too dangerous.

RECEPTIONIST: All right, leave your stretcher then.

FIRST AMBULANCE ATTENDANT: Don't you have any blankets? Nothing? He has no clothes on underneath.

RECEPTIONIST: (*Exasperated*) No, I don't have any. I don't have anything anymore.

FIRST AMBULANCE ATTENDANT: (*Discouraged, to the other ambulance attendant*) All right, put it over there, we're going to get him settled.

They go further into the emergency room. Mireille and Constance follow them.

FIRST AMBULANCE ATTENDANT: Okay, that's great. (*To Constance*) We'll leave you the stretcher and the blanket. We can find some more somewhere else.

CONSTANCE: Okay. Thank you.

Mireille looks at Daniel who is unconscious. The ambulance attendants go back to the reception desk. The receptionist stamps and signs a form which she then hands back to them. Constance comes up.

RECEPTIONIST: (*To whom the first ambulance attendant gives back a form*) Perfect.

FIRST AMBULANCE ATTENDANT: (*To Constance*) Good luck.

CONSTANCE: Thank you.

The ambulance attendants move off.

CONSTANCE: (*To the receptionist*) Is there a doctor on his way?

RECEPTIONIST: Does he have his health insurance card?

CONSTANCE: (*Turns her head towards Daniel for a moment*) I don't know.

RECEPTIONIST: Okay, while you're waiting, go to Admissions.

CONSTANCE: Where's that?

RECEPTIONIST: (*With a wave of her pencil, not raising her head*) Second door to the left.

Constance goes off down the corridor, climbing over sick people, and arrives at an office where the noise of a typewriter can be heard.

50. Hospital Admission Office. Interior. Night.

A secretary types a form behind her desk. An old man is sitting in front of her.

SECRETARY: Contagious diseases?

OLD MAN: (*Breathing heavily as he talks*) Don't remember.

SECRETARY: Speak up, sir, I can't hear you.

CONSTANCE: Excuse me, Madame, it's for an emergency.

SECRETARY: Take a number and wait your turn. All these people here are ahead of you. (*She returns to the old man*) Have there been cases of mental illness in your family before?

Constance, frightened, looks about.

OLD MAN: (*Inaudible*) Don't know.

SECRETARY: Speak up, sir, please.

51. Emergency Corridor. Interior. Night.

Constance comes back to where she had left Daniel and Mireille. Daniel is sitting on the stretcher, bare-chested. He has dried blood on his face. Mireille is close to him.

MIREILLE: He's feeling better!

CONSTANCE: Maybe you should stay lying down?

DANIEL: No, I just have a headache. Aren't Martin and René here?

CONSTANCE: They weren't allowed in the ambulance.

52. Desk of the Emergency Receptionist. Interior. Night.

Constance, Daniel, and Mireille go in front of the receptionist, who is seen in CLOSE UP. *For a moment she raises her eyes from her papers.*

    RECEPTIONIST: Are you feeling better?

    CONSTANCE: (*Ironic*) Yes, it's much better.

    RECEPTIONIST: That's perfect.

53. Huge Stairway. Interior. Night.

Constance and Mireille are helping Daniel down a huge stairway. The light is unreal. There is a little smoke in the air. Daniel seems weak, his voice very faint.

    DANIEL: (*To Mireille*) Life is hard to take, isn't it?

Mireille acquiesces silently. She and Constance are affectionate with Daniel and very protective. During the following speeches they continue to walk, stop, start again.

    DANIEL: We don't have happiness. It's because of that. That's the reason . . . The great events, even theater, everything happens because there is no happiness. The sources of life are hidden. I was abandoned by my father . . .

    CONSTANCE: We're here.

    MIREILLE: You're not all alone.

They kiss him.

    DANIEL: (*Looking about*) Big buildings like this, the big projects, they will all be destroyed . . . one day.

54. Metro Station. Interior. Night.

Daniel, Mireille, and Constance are going down a long escalator. He is in front of Mireille and Constance, facing them. They look at each other intensely.

Daniel's face shows great pain. At the bottom of the escalator he almost falls — the women catch him. They come out onto the platform. Daniel walks in front of a big poster and stops: It is the head of Pascal Berger advertising "The Wild Man." Daniel heaves and then brings up in a garbage can. Constance and Mireille surround him but he gets away from them to go towards the passengers. He speaks right to them; they look at him sceptically. Constance and Mireille follow him at a bit of a distance. It is hard for him to talk. He touches the passengers on the shoulder or the hair.

> **DANIEL:** When you see the terrible devastation arrive, if you are in the plains you must flee to the mountains. If you are on your terrace, don't go back into the house to get your things. If you are on the highway, don't go home. (*He talks, more loudly, to the passengers on the other side of the platform*) Pity those who are pregnant then. Pray that it doesn't happen during the winter. (*He comes back to those who are close to him*) If someone says to you: "The Savior is here," don't believe them. What? Don't believe them! False saviors . . . false prophets . . . the heavenly powers . . . shaken . . . neither the day . . . nor the hour . . . How surprised you will be . . . the judgment . . . watch over . . .

Daniel totters, falls down. Constance and Mireille support him.

He has fainted. Mireille sits on her heels and puts Daniel's head on her thighs. Constance goes to get help. The passengers move a bit closer.

A subway car hides the platform from us. Then it departs with its usual noise. Mireille caresses Daniel's face, still on her knees, stretched out on the platform. Behind them the bare brick wall.

Constance comes running back with the same ambulance attendants as in the preceding scenes. They have a new stretcher.

> **FIRST AMBULANCE ATTENDANT:** What happened? Didn't they keep him at Saint-Marc?
>
> **CONSTANCE:** They didn't do anything. I don't want to go back there.
>
> **FIRST AMBULANCE ATTENDANT:** We'll try the Jewish. If they want to take us.

55. Ambulance. Interior. Night.

Daniel is lying on a wooden board laid on the stretcher. His head is attached to the board by adhesive tape. He opens his eyes, tries to talk.

DANIEL: Save yourself. Save yourself.

CONSTANCE: Don't talk. Rest.

DANIEL: When you have some money . . . you should pay the pizzeria. Can you understand me?

CONSTANCE: We'll take care of it.

DANIEL: Can you understand me?

56. Streets of Montreal. Entrance of the Jewish Hospital. Exterior. Night.

The ambulance drives through the crowded streets of Montreal. It goes past an illuminated sign: "Montreal Jewish Hospital."

57. Emergency of the Jewish Hospital. Interior. Night.

The room is very modern, very clean, and deserted. The ambulance attendants enter, pushing Daniel on his stretcher. Mireille and Constance follow. They are welcomed by Sam Rosen with a nurse who immediately begins working. The doctor opens Daniel's mouth, examines him.

ROSEN: What are his vital signs?

FIRST NURSE: Over 9-6. Heartbeat 56.

ROSEN: Okay. His heartbeat is already too low. Bring me the . . . bag.

The nurse passes him a breathing apparatus.

ROSEN: Okay. Let's bring him to square 10. Prepare for intubation.

He puts the breathing apparatus on Daniel's face and activates it, meanwhile pushing the stretcher.

ROSEN: Let's go! Let's move!

They disappear. Mireille and Constance stay alone, worried. A nurse, Shirley, comes close and puts her hands on their shoulders.

SHIRLEY: Why don't you go sit over there, girls? There's some coffee and some cookies. We have to wait now.

CONSTANCE: Thank you.

Mireille and Constance move off.

SHIRLEY: (*To the first ambulance attendant*) I'll be with you in a second.

FIRST AMBULANCE ATTENDANT: (*To Constance, who was going into the corridor and turned back*) Good luck!

CONSTANCE: Thank you for everything!

FIRST AMBULANCE ATTENDANT: Oh, it's our job. We're here to help when we can.

Constance goes away. Rosen appears in the doorway of the nursing station and speaks to the nurse sitting at the desk.

ROSEN: Neurosurgery! X-rays! Anaesthesia! Inhalation therapy! Staff!

The nurse turns immediately and calls through the intercom:

SECOND NURSE: Doctor Klein. Neurosurgery. Doctor Klein. Doctor Gold. Anaesthesia. Doctor Gold. X-rays, inhalation therapy. 2,3 emergency, 2,3, emergency.

58. Emergency Care Room. Interior. Night.

The five needles of an electro-encephalograph trace five straight lines. Daniel's face is partially covered by tubes and electrodes.

59. Emergency Corridor. Interior. Night.

Rosen goes to rejoin Constance and Mireille in a waiting room. They stand up as soon as they see him.

ROSEN: I have to know your relationship with him.

CONSTANCE: He is a friend.

ROSEN: Does he have a family? Do you know?

CONSTANCE: I don't know. I don't think so. He's alone. He is living with us.

MIREILLE: How is he?

ROSEN: We lost him. (*A silence*) You came in half an hour too late. I'm sorry. We put him on life-support system but his brain is gone.

MIREILLE: Can we see him?

ROSEN: Sure.

60. Emergency Care Room. Interior. Night.

Constance and Mireille go into the room. Daniel is laid out on a stretcher, plugged-in, half-covered by a white sheet. Two specialists, a man and a woman, are sitting next to him. All that can be heard is the noise of an artificial respirator. A moment of silence.

ROSEN: (*Whispers*) I'm going to ask you something.

CONSTANCE: (*Without taking her eyes from Daniel*) What?

ROSEN: Give us his body. He's young, he's healthy, and he's got type "O" blood. That's a godsend.

CONSTANCE: It's okay.

ROSEN: You'll have to sign some papers and stuff.

CONSTANCE: Okay.

MIREILLE: (*Crying*) It's like he's sleeping.

ROSEN: Yes, but he can't ever wake up again.

61. Twelfth Station of the Way of the Cross. Exterior. Night.

The crucifixion posts stand, lugubrious, in the wind and the rain.

62. Leclerc's Room. Interior. Night.

The face of Father Leclerc in the light of the storm. He closes a window behind him. The rain runs down the window pane in front of his face.

63. Montreal Street. Exterior. Night.

Constance and Mireille, holding hands, walk under a driving rain. They walk like sleepwalkers.

64. Operating Room of the Jewish Hospital. Interior. Night.

Daniel is stretched out, his arms extended in a cross, on an operating table. We still hear only the noise of the artificial respirator to which he is attached. An orderly sponges his chest with disinfectant. Later his chest is covered with surgical cloths. We hear, mixed together, the beep-beep of machines and the conversation of surgeons at work. Hands are busy. We see an opened chest, a beating heart. A masked surgeon gives the order to unplug Daniel. A hand turns the button of a machine. The extraction of the organs is finished; the heart is placed in a freezer on a bed of ice.

65. Airport. Exterior. Day.

A Cessna is waiting, its motors going. Mark Sutton, who is carrying the icebox, runs towards the airplane, accompanied by an assistant. They are still wearing their surgeon's coats and their masks are hanging from their necks. They climb quickly into the plane and the door is immediately closed behind them.

66. Door of the Jewish Hospital Emergency. Exterior. Day.

A taxi and a panel truck are waiting. Two doctors, also wearing surgeon's clothes, come out carrying a plastic box. They climb into the truck which starts off immediately. A nursing assistant comes out, at a run, carrying a polyurethane box which she gives to a Haitian taxi driver.

NURSING ASSISTANT: University Hospital of Sherbrooke. It's in the university complex.

HAITIAN TAXI DRIVER: Yeah, I know.

NURSING ASSISTANT: They'll be the ones to pay you.

HAITIAN TAXI DRIVER: Okay, that's all right.

67. Cotes-des-Neiges Crematorium. Interior. Day.

A very simple coffin, almost a wooden box, with a bit of tape on which the name "Daniel" is written, goes slowly down into a trap, the doors of which close with a dry and mournful sound. Constance, Mireille, René, and Martin are present at the ceremony. They are crying. Then they move slowly away down the big corridor of the colombarium. France Garibaldi appears.

GARIBALDI: Excuse me. I know it's not the time for it, I have just one small question. It's because they say he traveled a lot. Do you know exactly where he went?

CONSTANCE: *(In a faint voice)* I don't know. He talked to me about the Indies and Nepal.

GARIBALDI: *(Following them into the stairway)* Ah good. Excellent, excellent. It was a spiritual quest, obviously. You'll see, I'm going to do something very . . . very moving.

68. Intensive Care Unit. Interior. Day.

A man about forty years old is lying in intensive care. He is connected to a battery of sophisticated instruments.

SUTTON: (*Voice off*) Mister Rigby?

The patient opens his eyes.

SUTTON: You have a beautiful new thirty-year-old heart. What do you say?

RIGBY: God! I'm so happy.

Constance (Johanne-Marie Tremblay), Martin (Remy Girard), René (Robert Lepage), Mireille (Catherine Wilkening) — afterwards. "Do you know exactly where he went?" "I don't know. He talked to me about the Indies and Nepal."

69. Richard Cardinal's Office. Interior. Day.

We are in front of some large windows. In the distance, water and trees. Constance, Mireille, René, and Martin are seated or leaning against the window ledges. They are sad. Richard Cardinal is presenting them with a proposed deal.

CARDINAL: The idea would be to form a theater company. In his memory. The Daniel-Coulombe Theater. Obviously a legal organization would need to be constituted, with a president and so on. I don't know but, uh . . . Martin, you could perhaps be the first president.

MARTIN: It would be a way to be sure of continuing.

RENE: I would be interested, but on the condition that we stay faithful to the kind of work he wanted to do.

CONSTANCE: Yes, on the condition that it doesn't become a traditional commercial theater.

CARDINAL: But of course that's taken for granted. Personally, I've always been convinced that financial viability doesn't exclude the search for truth. On the contrary.

Mireille gets up quickly.

MIREILLE: Excuse me.

She goes out.

70. Hospital Room. Interior. Day.

The light is very subdued. We see the face of an old lady. Bandages are being taken off her eyes. A nurse is beside the bed.

LADY: (*She sobs*) La lace!

DOCTOR: Vedete la mia mano?

LADY: Si.

DOCTOR: Quante dita?

LADY: Quattro! Due!

DOCTOR: Va bene.

LADY: Thank you, doctor.

71. Mount Royal Esplanade. Exterior. Sunset.

Mireille is walking slowly along the esplanade. She is crying. She stands against the stone balustrade and leans over. VIEW *of downtown illuminated by the fading light.*

72. Metro Station. Interior. Day.

The soprano and the contralto are sitting on the ground in corridor of the subway. In front of them they have a ghetto blaster and a cigar box with change inside. They are singing the last duet of Pergolese's "Stabat Mater." Behind them is the immense poster of "The Wild Man."

> **SOPRANO AND CONTRALTO:** "Quando corpus moreitur, Fac ut animae ne denetur Paradisi gloria. Amen." "When my body dies, don't refuse my body the Glory of Paradise."

HIGH ANGLE SHOT *of the corridor and the bottom of the escalators. From time to time passers-by throw them a few coins.*

Final credits.

NOTES ON CONTRIBUTORS

WILLIAM FRUET

William Fruet was born in Lethbridge, Alberta in 1933. He began his career in photography and directed medical films before attending the University of Southern California Film School. He has worked in the film industry in California and served as editor for Film Arts and the CBC. He has won numerous awards for his work as a screenwriter, director, and producer, including Canadian Film Awards for Best Original Screenplay for *Wedding in White* and *Goin' Down the Road*. He lives in Toronto.

Selected Filmography
FEATURE FILMS

Goin' Down the Road, 1969. Writer. Prizes: Canadian Film Awards for Best Screenplay and Best Picture (1970).

Wedding in White, 1971. Writer, Director. Prizes: Canadian Film Awards for Best Art Direction, Best Supporting Actress, and Best Picture, 1972.

Slipstream, 1972. Writer. Prizes: Canadian Film Award for Best Picture, 1973.

House on the Lake, 1975. Writer, Director. Prizes: Spanish International Horror Festival Awards for Best Screenplay, Best Actress, and Best Picture, 1975.

Search and Destroy, 1978. Director.

Funeral Home, 1979. Director, Producer.

Baker County U.S.A., 1980. Director.

Spasms, 1982. Director.

Bedroom Eyes, 1984. Director.

Killer Party, 1985. Director.

The Blue Monkey, 1987. Director.

TELEVISION DRAMAS & DOCUMENTARIES

Heritage Italy, 1974. Writer, Director. Prizes: Special Award Certificate, International Film and Television Festival, New York.

One of Our Own, 1979. Writer, Director. Prizes: Yorkton Film Festival Award for Best Actor; Blue Ribbon, American Film Festival.

Full Circle Again, 1984. Writer, Director.

The Playground, 1985. Program: The Bradbury Chronicles. Writer, Director.

Brothers by Choice, 1985. Mini-Series. Director.

Chasing Rainbows, 1986. 5 Episodes. Director.

Friday the 13th: The Series, 1987. 4 Episodes. Director.

CLEMENT PERRON

Clément Perron was born in 1929 in Beauce, Quebec. He attended Laval University before studying linguistics and cinema at the Academie de Portiers and Institut de Filmologie, Sorbonne, Paris, from 1955 to 1957. For twenty-eight years he worked with the National Film Board as a screenwriter, director, and producer of French language films and programs. He is a member of SARDEC and president of Cinéscript, Inc. in Dollard-des-Ormeaux, where he now lives and works.

Selected Filmography
FEATURE FILMS

Jour aprés jour, 1963. Writer, Director.

Caroline, 1964. Writer, Director.

Mon oncle Antoine, 1971. Writer. Prizes: Grand Prize, Chicago Film Festival; Winner of 8 Canadian Film Awards.

Partis pour la gloire, 1975. Writer, Director.

Ann McNeil, 1986. Writer.

Le Marchand de jouets, 1989. Writer.

Chroniques des hautes terres, 1991. Writer.

Au Nom du pere et du fils, 1992. Writer, Producer.

René Levesque, 1992. Writer.

JOHN HUNTER

John Hunter was born in Winnipeg in 1941 and raised in all four western provinces. He received a Bachelor of Commerce degree from the University of British Columbia, then worked in advertising and journalism while teaching himself to write for film.

His first dramatic script was produced by the CBC in 1969. Since then he has worked as writer or producer on twelve feature films and has written ten television dramas. He received a Genie Award for Best Original Screenplay for *The Grey Fox*. He lives in Toronto.

Selected Filmography
FEATURE FILMS

The Hard Part Begins, 1973. Writer, Producer.

Snapshots, 1975. Producer.

Blood & Guts, 1977. Co-Writer, Co-Producer.

Fast Company, 1978. Uncredited Rewrite.

Prom Night, 1979. Uncredited Rewrite.

Misdeal, 1980. Co-Writer as "Logan N. Danforth."

The Grey Fox, 1980. Writer. Prizes: Genie Award for Best Original Screenplay, 1983.

Class of '84, 1981. Uncredited Rewrite.

Cross-Country, 1982. Co-Writer as "Logan N. Danforth."

John and the Missus, 1986. Co-Producer.

Bethune, 1988. Uncredited Rewrite.

The Midday Sun, 1988. Co-Producer.

TELEVISION DRAMA

Black Phoenix, 1969. Program: Sunday at Nine (CBC). Co-Writer.

Banana Peel, 1971. Program: Program X (CBC). Writer.

The Kill, 1975. Program: Peep Show (CBC). Writer.

Assault, 1976. Program: Sidestreet (CBC). Writer.

Intimidation, 1976. Program: Sidestreet (CBC). Writer.

Saturday Night Special, 1977. Program: Sidestreet (CBC). Writer.

Episode #4, 1983. Program: Vanderberg (CBC). Writer.

Episode #5, 1983. Program: Vanderberg (CBC). Writer.

The Boy Next Door, 1984. Program: For the Record (CBC). Writer, Director.

Fatal Ambition (ABC), 1992. Writer.

SANDY WILSON

Sandy Wilson was born in Penticton, British Columbia, in 1947 and grew up in the Okanagan Valley. She graduated from St. Ann's Academy in 1965 and Simon Fraser University in 1969. While at Simon Fraser University she "heard there were some cute guys in the film workshop," so she signed up. Since then she has worked as a director, editor, assistant director, writer, and producer on a number of award winning documentaries and independent shorts. She has also edited the book of poetry "Western Windows," worked as a television news editor, usherette, nanny, and cocktail waitress. She teaches scriptwriting and directing workshops at the University of British Columbia. For *My American Cousin*, she received a Genie Award for Best Original Screenplay.

Selected Filmography
FEATURE FILMS

My American Cousin, 1985. Writer, Director, Co-Producer (with Peter O'Brian). Prizes: International Film Critic Award, Toronto Festival of Festivals, 1985; Genie Awards for Best Picture, Best Director, Best Actress, Best Actor, Best Editor, and Best Original Screenplay, 1986.

American Boyfriends, 1989. Writer, Director, Co-Producer (with Robert Lantos).

SHORT FILMS

Garbage, 1969. Writer, Director, Editor, Producer. Prizes: Best Experimental Film, Yorkton Film Festival, 1977.

DOCUMENTARY FILMS

Penticton Profile, 1970. Director, Editor.

He's Not the Walking Kind, 1972. Director. Prizes: Blue Ribbon, New York Film Festival, 1973; Chris Statuette, Columbus Ohio Film Festival, 1973.

Pen Hi Grad, 1974. Director, Editor.

Mount Chopaka Easter Sunday Jackpot Rodeo, 1980. Director, Editor.

Coming Down, 1980. Director, Editor.

Goin' All the Way, 1981. Director, Editor.

TELEVISION DRAMA

Trying Times (PBS)/*Lics from Lotus Land* (CBC), 1986. Episode: "Moving Day." Director.

Momma's Gonna Buy You a Mockingbird (CBC), 1987. Director.

Max Glick (CBC), 1991. Episode: "Queen for a Day." Director.

DENYS ARCAND

Denys Arcand was born in Deschambault, Quebec in 1941. He studied history at the Université de Montréal before joining The National Film Board in 1963, where he worked as a screenwriter and director until the late 1970s. His feature films *Le déclin de l'empire américain (Decline of the American Empire)* and *Jésus de Montréal* have received international critical acclaim.

Selected Filmography
FEATURE FILMS

Seul ou avec d'autres, 1962. Co-Writer, Director.

Champlain, 1963. Writer, Director.

Jusqu'au cou, 1963. Co-Writer.

La Route de l'ouest, 1964. Writer, Director.

Les Montréalistes, 1965. Writer, Director.

Volley-ball, 1966. Editor, Director.

Parcs atlantiques, 1967. Editor, Director.

Entre la mer et l'eau douce, 1967. Writer.

Montréal, un jour d'été, 1967. Editor, Director.

On est au coton, 1970. Editor, Director.

Québec: Duplessis et après..., 1972. Writer, Editor, Director.

La maudite galette, 1972. Director.

Réjeanne Padovani, 1973. Co-Writer, Editor, Director.

La lutte des travailleurs d'hôpitaux, 1976. Director.

Le confort et l'indifférence, 1981. Director.

Empire, Inc., 1983. Director.

Le Crime d'Ovide Plouffe, 1984. Director.

Le déclin de l'empire américan, 1986. Writer, Director.

Jésus de Montréal, 1989. Writer, Director.

DOUGLAS BOWIE

Editor Douglas Bowie fell into a career in screenwriting when he entered a CBC writing contest on a whim while working for an Ottawa advertising agency. He has since written a number of well-received and widely seen film and television dramas including *The Man Who Wanted to Be Happy*, *The Boy in Blue*, the Gemini Award winning *Love and Larceny* and its sequel *Grand Larceny*, *Chasing Rainbows*, and *Obsessed*. He won an ACTRA Award for Best Television Writer for the mini-series *Empire, Inc.*, which has now been broadcast in 68 countries. He has recently turned his hand to playwrighting, and is the author of *The Noble Pursuit*. He lives in Kingston with his wife Joan and daughter Alison.

TOM SHOEBRIDGE

Editor Tom Shoebridge is the founder and executive director of the Summer Institute of Film and Television in Ottawa. For the past twenty years, he has taught communications, film, and screenwriting at Algonquin College. He regularly appears as an animator, guest speaker, and panel member at film events throughout Canada. He lives on a lake near Ottawa with his wife, Gloria.

WAYNE GRADY

Translator Wayne Grady won the Governor General's Award for Translation in English for Antonine Maillet's *On the Eighth Day*. With Matt Cohen he edited *Intimate Strangers: New Stories from Quebec*, published by Penguin. He lives in Kingston, Ontario.

MATT COHEN

Translator Matt Cohen is the author of many acclaimed works of fiction, including *The Sweet Second Summer of Kitty Malone*, *Café le Dog*, *Emotional Arithmetic*, and *Freud: The Paris Notebooks/ Freud à Paris*. With Wayne Grady, he edited *Intimate Strangers: New Stories from Quebec*, published by Penguin. He won the John Glassco Award for Translation in 1991.

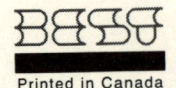
Printed in Canada